EXPLORING MEDIA RESEARCH

'In *Exploring Media Research,* Andy Ruddock provides the theoretical, methodological and ethical tools that enable scholars, students and citizens to dissect the cultural power of media and to apply this understanding to the creation of a more just society. Written in a direct and accessible style, this timely and provocative book firmly establishes Ruddock as one of the premier media scholars of his generation.'

Elizabeth Bird, University of South Florida

'There can be no more pressing topic in current affairs today than the role of the media. From questions of warfare to public health, we get our information as citizens from these massively powerful institutions. But how do we interrogate those very entities whom we trust to interrogate others? Andy Ruddock explains all in a patient but crisp, historically-informed but very contemporary book. We are in his debt.'

Toby Miller, Loughborough University London

'This is a book that is sorely needed: an introduction to media research that is both comprehensive and thorough in its theoretical reach, and absolutely contemporary in its examples, in its applications, and in its conceptualisation of the key targets for media research today.'

Graeme Turner, University of Queensland

ANDY RUDDOCK

EXPLORING MEDIA RESEARCH

THEORIES, PRACTICE, AND PURPOSE

Los Angeles | London | New Delhi
Singapore | Washington DC | Melbourne

Los Angeles | London | New Delhi
Singapore | Washington DC | Melbourne

SAGE Publications Ltd
1 Oliver's Yard
55 City Road
London EC1Y 1SP

SAGE Publications Inc.
2455 Teller Road
Thousand Oaks, California 91320

SAGE Publications India Pvt Ltd
B 1/I 1 Mohan Cooperative Industrial Area
Mathura Road
New Delhi 110 044

SAGE Publications Asia-Pacific Pte Ltd
3 Church Street
#10-04 Samsung Hub
Singapore 049483

Editor: Michael Ainsley
Editorial assistant: John Nightingale
Production editor: Imogen Roome
Copyeditor: Sarah Bury
Proofreader: Leigh C. Timmins
Indexer: Martin Hargreaves
Marketing manager: Lucia Sweet
Cover design: Francis Kenney
Typeset by: C&M Digitals (P) Ltd, Chennai, India
Printed in the UK

Library of Congress Control Number: 2016962396

British Library Cataloguing in Publication data

A catalogue record for this book is available from the British Library

ISBN 978-1-4739-0253-4
ISBN 978-1-4739-0254-1 (pbk)

At SAGE we take sustainability seriously. Most of our products are printed in the UK using FSC papers and boards. When we print overseas we ensure sustainable papers are used as measured by the PREPS grading system. We undertake an annual audit to monitor our sustainability.

Dedicated to Jian, Zhenni & Mum

CONTENTS

ABOUT THE AUTHOR

Andy Ruddock researches, writes and teaches about media audiences, youth and the politics of popular culture and has taught at universities in the USA, the UK, New Zealand and South Korea. He regularly provides expert commentary on media issues, writing frequently for theconversation.edu

Part 1

RESEARCH PRINCIPLES: MOTIVATION, CAUSATION, ETHICS AND GENERALIZABILITY

INTRODUCTION: COMMUNICATING MEDIA RESEARCH

ON MEDIA EDUCATION AND MEDIA RESEARCH

The goal of this book is to make media research 'popular'; not as something that everyone likes, but as an activity that everyone can do. A grandiose objective? Perhaps, except when you consider that most of us have opinions about what media do: they make people want to change their bodies, seek fame and confuse consumption with happiness; they've turned politics into bad reality television; they make journalists chase ratings, not truth. We spend a lot of time chatting about media influence. The outcome is this: we have been talking about media literacy for some time; now it's time to develop media *research literacy*. Today's audiences don't just consume a lot of media content. They also encounter many commentaries about what that content is doing to the world. Evaluating media research is rapidly becoming a precondition for social participation. Media literacy and media research literacy are, in effect, building blocks for *political* literacy. If politics is about explaining why the world is as it is, and imagining how it could be different, then it is hard to separate democracy from the media narratives that make social thought possible. It's difficult, for example, to discuss gun control if you don't know about research on the effects of video gaming. And you can't understand that research without appreciating fundamental issues, like the many pitfalls there are in gathering and evaluating evidence about such influences – if there are any worth discussing.

Knowing *how* media do things – or in fact, don't – has become a basic form of cultural competency. So, too, the ability to communicate complex ideas from media research into the vernacular. The surge in media content about media influence makes the ability to differentiate between reasoned, evidenced-based argument and unsubstantiated commentary an important mechanism in public opinion. This calls for a language that media scholars, media students, media industries and publics can use to speak to each other.

To this end, this book identifies core themes in conceiving and practising media research. Doing this means breaking down a couple of walls: one between theory and method, and the other between teaching and research. Two ideas you should come away with is that it is impossible to do 'theory' and 'method' separately, since (a) you can't theorize media in the absence of evidence about how they work and what they do and (b) you can't deploy research techniques without conceiving why you want to use them in the first place, from a theoretical point of view. In that sense, this book argues that notions of theory and method need to be replaced with a definition of research practice as the ability to deploy conceptually justified techniques for gathering and analysing information. Key, here, is the ability to craft research questions that are equally sensitive to striking a balance between what we want to know with what we can know, given the range of techniques and evidence that we can access.

This brings us to breaking down teaching and research. Reading this book should persuade you that you can't teach or learn about media without doing media research. It's crucial that we all understand this. Contemporary lecture halls are full of international student bodies that bring a diverse range of media experiences into one place. It's foolish not to recognize and capitalize on this. Apart from anything else, we all – teachers and students – live in a world where most other people think that what we do is a bit silly; many people don't take media research that seriously as a scholarly pursuit. It's up to us, then, to get our story straight on why we do what we do. This means using classrooms as places where we converse about the future of media research, informed by structured inquiries into what we know, what we want to know and what we can know. To get that conversation started, this book explains how the work that we all do – professional scholars and students – is shaped by the same concerns and procedures of asking, researching and answering research questions. By mapping the relationship between media studies and other disciplines in the humanities and social sciences, the different ways in which media realities can be conceived and the different techniques we can use to make sense of those realities, *Exploring Media Research* creates a research language that is at once structured, detailed and accessible.

We know this language is needed because of increasing media *attention* to the topic of media *influence* as something that touches everyone, from the most experienced scholar to the everyday media punter. We need to be able to communicate across this spectrum. One way to do this is to break the practice of media research into a series of component parts. This process, briefly, involves scrutinizing issues of causation, the ethical principles of media studies, questions of generalizability, different ways in which media actively make reality, and the various 'entry' points where media researchers – from the most to the least experienced – can observe these processes in action (looking at media people, media markets, media content, media events, media audiences and media regulation). This introduction explains the method of the book.

The project is inspired by what I see as a new public hunger for knowledge about what media do. This appetite is evidenced by the increased attention that journalists and broadcasters pay to media researchers. It's fairly easy to introduce media research into media discourse. A useful trick, in this endeavour, is to understand a formula for connecting public interest with academic insight. But this is more than a gimmick; it also sensitizes us to basic steps in research practice. In the next section, I explain how engaging with the media on matters of media influence offers useful insights into how to go about media research directed at any audience: publics, teachers and professional peers.

TAKING MEDIA RESEARCH TO THE MEDIA

Over the first 15 years of my academic career, I appeared in the media precisely once. I was asked to comment on an apparent wave of 1970s nostalgia that gripped New Zealand in the mid-1990s. Since 2012, I've popped up on television, radio and in the press dozens of times. I've fielded questions about social media, and television interviews about Twitter's impact on the Olympics and War in the Middle East spring to mind. Journalists often ask whether social media are destroying their profession. The allure of fictional serial killers, the part media play in rampage murders, the effects of gaming on gamers, the provenance of celebrity politics and the perennial appeal of boybands are all on my commentary CV. As is Justin Bieber.

I'm sure this 'fame' mostly reflects space-filling needs, but I'm surer still about other things. There are many opportunities to take academic media studies into the public domain. These work best when you have a structured plan for engaging interest, and thinking about how to structure these brief encounters teaches me much about how to go about my day job. The outcome of these reflections has been the development of a model for doing and communicating research, based on an ability to connect often complicated conceptual and methodological issues to media events that become sources of public fascination.

When asked to speak for a few minutes about media events in the public eye, this is my routine. The story usually begins with the premise that media are causing a problem. I generally counter with academic reasons for thinking that this 'problem', if it exists at all, is different in kind from those envisaged in public discussions. Take boybands. Whenever I'm asked about girls who go crazy for One Direction, or whoever it is, the story usually begins from the premise that these fans are funny, stupid, endangered, or most likely all three. I counter that their 'mania' makes perfect sense as an expression of how they understand their place in the world. And importantly, I point out a long history of evidence supporting this argument.

But whatever the topic, the script always goes something like this: I offer that, from a scholarly view, the event in question is really about the many ways that media use has become a central feature of public life. I drop in one, maybe two key thinkers whose work encourages us to look at things in a different way, suggest a different set of questions that we might ask instead, and then I'm done. This, I think, is a practice that structures media research that communicates with public interests, at a time when it's vital for our discipline to do that. Let me give a longer example of how everything works.

CASE STUDY: RAMPAGE KILLINGS AND CHANGING MEDIA LANDSCAPES

I speak or write about media violence a lot. Rampage murders have become a particular topic of interest. I think that's because these outrages visualize the porous line between social life and media with bestial clarity. Opinions flow freely in the aftermath of such murders. Meaningful contributions to public debates on these tragedies demands effectively communicating the many things they mean.

Take the murders of Alison Parker and Adam Ward. Parker and Ward were gunned down while presenting a tourism segment for Virginia's WDBJ7 TV's breakfast show. Shocked studio anchors broadcast on, having seen their own friends butchered. Rampage gun murders are sadly familiar media events, so much so that there's an obscene banality to many of them. But here, a line had been crossed; media workers were targeted so that crimes couldn't be edited according to the usual ethical rules. What did it all mean?

I've written and spoken about many rampage killings. But something here was different. The thirst for media theory was palpable. Appearing on Australia's ABC, I was asked what happens when news is the news. What does it mean to live in a world where the medium that we use to understand reality becomes the reality that we are trying to understand? My interviewer, Beverly McConnell, thought that news felt different now, and a new set of ideas was needed to make sense of it.

My answers reflected the research process that this book will outline. The murders caused reflection on what news is, what it does, and how its changing form affects journalism practice. Here was an event calling for an expanded understanding of what news is. Information, entertainment, yet another form of media violence – whatever one wanted to focus on, news was manifestly part of the world; the presence of news, and an understanding of its genres and functions, had become part of a criminal act. Local live-feed 'soft' news had been targeted to maximize the horrific impact of an abomination. It was impossible to discuss the crime without recourse to conceiving 'cause' and 'effect' in situations where media practices are deeply implicated in making social reality. We could ask whether the event might provoke 'copycat' events, and that's not a silly or unimportant question. Yet at the same time, the level of shock, among journalists and audiences alike, suggested something else. We could look at what this story did to some people, or instead assess why violence is such a familiar form of expression that gets people especially interested in the media's social role. I dropped in the name of a Hungarian scholar called George Gerbner. You'll be reading much more about him. But Gerbner's elegantly simple point – that the causes and consequences of media violence are economic and political in nature – was a quick way to move the discussion from the question of whether the news may inadvertently brutalize its audience to deeper considerations about the basic role of media in social life; the idea, for example, that the only kind of action that counts for anything at all is one that happens in what Nick Couldry (2004) has called the 'media centre'.

THE ANATOMY OF A RESEARCH QUESTION

Let's break that conversation into its component parts. It began with a striking and puzzling event. To do justice to the incident, the first step was to acknowledge that media are reality, in that they orchestrate society. This is a complicated idea that juggles competing claims about causation: What kinds of effects are we interested in, and where should we look for their presence? In Virginia's shadow, there were sound reasons to think that the most traumatized audience comprised journalists, and that might significantly affect how they did their jobs – so questions about whether the story might provoke copycats didn't cover all of the bases. Once you've accepted that single events reflect numerous impact themes, one way to unlock them is to search for a particular author or body of media research that lends a significant or novel insight into some of the forces at play: Gerbner in this case.

That's about as far as things go with writing and talking to the media, but these steps are the foundation for another kind of 'accessible' media research: work that copes with the resource limitations endemic in empirical studies of how media operate in certain settings, by finding ways to test concepts in relation to original case studies. Media encounters have presented me with case studies that test different ideas about media realities. A sense for a good research topic is much like the sense for a good news story; it helps to be able to recognize public events that can be used to introduce media studies perspectives into public discourse. But this isn't just about having an eye for a good topic; it's also recognizing researchable ones. Time and money limit all media researchers. One way to cope is by investigating evidence that is relatively easy to get. Ubiquitous media make evidence just as abundant, as long as we know what to look for, how to look, and how to use observations. This mean being alert to instances of media influence at work, and understanding where our evidence addresses established scholarly concerns. There are several steps to making this happen.

The first is to appreciate media research as a humanities discipline. Why are media things that we care about? How do they touch personal experience? What does it mean to say that media 'do' things in society? Who is research supposed to benefit, and how does this affect research practice? What are the complications in demonstrating media influence at work? How can you address broad trends in media culture by studying specific instances of media in action? These are the background issues at play in any project, and are explained in the first part of the book.

Next, we must appreciate that media make three types of reality: the kind made by media stories, the kind made by media users, and the kind made by the interplay between media and interpersonal communication. These reality effects underscore the complexity of media influence, especially since they coexist. Part 2 explains these ideas.

Having set out how to conceive media influence, Part 3 puts analysis into action, showing how to gather and analyse evidence from seven research settings. We can, I suggest, see media reality processes working by looking at:

- Media people

- Media markets (by which I mean centres of media distribution that forge relationships between different stakeholders in media industries)

- Media content (which isn't just films, TV programmes, games, etc.)

- Media events

- Media data (the evidence that emerges about how culture works, through interactions between media users and Big Data technologies)

- Media regulations

- Media audiences.

The goal is to rearrange the industry/text/audience orthodoxy into something that is perhaps more sensitive to the needs of the resource-challenged researcher.

Part 3 focuses on accessible methods. Specifically, it demonstrates how to address 'big' questions about media influence by choosing 'small', coherent data sets that can be explored through qualitative data assessment (QDA) techniques, using software packages familiar at most universities.

Putting all of this together, *Exploring* demystifies media research. That isn't saying it is easy. It is saying that it is possible to do meaningful media research without access to enormous amounts of time and money. It is possible to do a lot with a little as long as you understand what you want to know, why you want to know it, and what you can say within the context of the evidence and theoretical knowledge that you have at your disposal.

PUTTING THEORY AND RESEARCH TOGETHER: THE RESEARCH CYCLE

The book develops a research cycle for communicating meaningful insights about the social impact of media, with a special focus on connecting observable 'small' case studies to 'big' problems. The cycle assumes that our discipline studies how media industries and practices are implicated in the production of political consciousness, and that the theories and case studies that we deal with in all address these connections, in some way.

The process starts with an appreciation of what media research is for, as a discipline that addresses the political impact of media realities – patterns of thought and perception that can be related to media narratives. When confronted with a media phenomenon – something that seems to have happened in relation to media – out first task is to address what kind of media reality lays before us, and why that reality matters, *vis-à-vis* media and social inclusion. Parts 1 and 2 cover how to achieve this.

Doing media research means, at some point, testing theories in terms of their ability to explain the impact of media for particular people in a particular place and time. Part 3, then, outlines ways to apply conceptual insights into case studies. As already explained, this starts by connecting examples to one of seven 'fields' of case study. However, this leaves the matter of how these 'fields' connect to general concepts. The empirical chapters of Part 3 do this as follows. In each case, general ideas about the political impact of media realities are tied to the particularities of a case study by identifying a 'key paradigm', a specific body of work with ideas and methods allowing us to make sense of data sets. The lesson is that good research is a matter of strategy, being clear about what it is possible to say about media influence by matching appropriate case studies, ideas and methods.

Finally, let's put this academic process together with the method used for talking to the media about media. Faced with any media problem, we can start the conversation by asking why an issue has caught public attention. The next thing we do is connect those concerns to scholarly ideas that help to unlock what the issue is about, in terms of its reality effect. This sets the foundation for original research, finding a subset of the scholarly literature that shows how to demonstrate the 'life' of media theory by applying specific method to a specific case of media culture in action. The trick here is to find an idea that connects to a method that can be applied to an accessible case study. Accessible, here, means a relatively contained instance of media in action that can be studied as a 'whole' (examples in the book include things like live press conferences, critical media reviews, and publicly accessible policy documents covering well-defined areas of media policy over a significant historical period).

The purpose is to develop understanding of media influence by using appropriately chosen theories and methods to provide coherent and plausible accounts of why the 'influence' stories that attract public attention tell us something worth knowing about the relationship between media and society. The idea is not to fix the truth of media influence, but rather to give order to the various and often conflicting ideas about media effects that permeate public talk. This can be done via the following steps.

1. Finding a story about media influence that attracts public attention.

2. Relating that story to a 'reality effect' discussed in academic literature.

3. Finding specific ideas and methods in this literature that fulfil two criteria: first, they promise to add something new to the public debate; second, they can be applied to an accessible case study, that is, one that is comprehensively observable within limited resources.

4. Applying those ideas and methods to a case study.

5. Analysing what we learn about media power in general by looking at this specific instance. This isn't just a matter of finding conclusions, but also of generating new research questions.

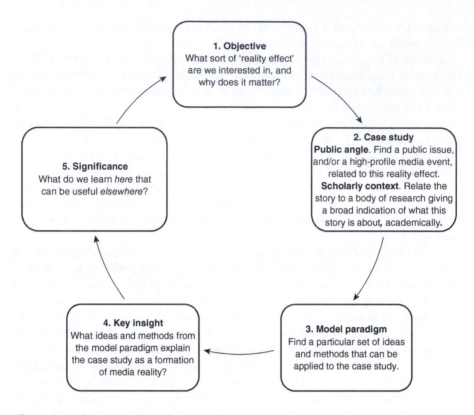

Figure 1 The research cycle

The process can be mapped as shown in Figure 1.

The ultimate goal is to create a framework for talking about media influence that communicates across the boundaries between the media, publics, media scholars and media students. Through this framework, it's possible to assess how thinking about the media follows a similar structure wherever and whoever you are; or at least that trying to make it so makes it easier for everyone to think, discuss and write about the many ways that media shape our world.

The intention of the research cycle is to focus attention on the nature of media research as an interdisciplinary pursuit that combines insights from the humanities and social sciences. The case is made that the future of the discipline – which is of enormous social importance – can be protected by considering what makes it a critical, theoretically informed, evidence-based pursuit addressing core themes in the historical evolution of democracy. Understanding this means overcoming two divides: method/theory and teaching/research. At the end of the book, you should understand that it's possible to teach, learn and do media research at the same time, and that it's feasible to argue that everyone can contribute to knowledge about how media shape society, as long as certain core principles are acknowledged.

1

MAKING MEDIA MATTER

OBJECTIVE: WHY IS MEDIA RESEARCH 'POLITICAL'?

This book explains why the practice of media research is fundamentally grounded in understanding the political purpose of media studies. Why such a grand claim? The reasons are empirical, not ideological. Our social imaginations often draw upon ideas, images and stories that media industries provide. Because of that, like it or not, media industries are *de facto* public resources. As such, it is the responsibility of media studies to scrutinize how those resources serve public interests. That is not the only definition of what media studies is, but it is the one that this book presents.

Of course, it is easier to make grand statements like this than it is to put them into action. So, this chapter establishes a four-stage typology that helps to bring the 'how' and the 'why' of media research together. The argument is not that media studies asks its practitioners to adopt a political perspective; it is that media studies is principally concerned with the operation of power through communication. Sensitivity to this basic principle can be achieved by asking four questions, before embarking on a project. These are:

- Why does a question matter? (Relevance)
- What model of causation does my question assume? (Causation)
- What are its ethics? (Ethics)
- How, if at all, does a particular topic shed light on general dynamics in media cultures? (Generalization)

To explain how this framework structures media research, the rest of this chapter does four things.

- First, it explains why media entertainment is a *de facto* public resource.
- Second, it explores the practical difficulties of coming to terms with the enormous cultural shifts that media industries create.
- Third, it identifies basic understandings that media scholars from a number of different intellectual backgrounds have historically shared regarding the connection between media and society. This consensus is grounded in the concept of culture.
- Fourth, it explains how points one to three lead to the research typology that this book will use.

(Continued)

The end result is to establish an architecture for connecting the practice of media research with the historical development of the discipline's understanding of media power, and methods for understanding how that power works. This framework will then be developed throughout the first section of the book.

WHY MEDIA ENTERTAINMENT IS A SERIOUS BUSINESS

Professor or undergraduate, media scholars are faced with an irritating paradox. When it comes to common sense, everyone accepts that media have powerful social effects. It's strange, then, that many also believe that *studying* this influence is a trivial pursuit. These reservations are often articulated through a clichéd insult: media studies is a 'Mickey Mouse' subject. This wisecrack usually conveys the same combination of criticisms: the discipline is a 'soft option', lacking the intellectual rigour of others. Media studies, so the argument goes, doesn't tell us anything worth knowing, which is why it doesn't get its graduates media jobs.

Yet many media practitioners don't ascribe to these views. If public corporate responsibility statements are to be believed, then media businesses accept that they have an impact on their audience that needs to be taken seriously. It follows that there is a distinct industrial application for media research: holding media industries to account for their commitment to public service, by generating knowledge about *how* media influence works. This involves generating clear principles for how to go about research. Doing this means thinking beyond questions of theory and method towards the purpose of research. To outline this process, let's start with an important and controversial question: How is fictional media entertainment real?

Media businesses are powerful public storytellers whose narratives affect how people live in the world (Gerbner, 1998). They make reality (Katz, 1983). Fact or fiction, media content provides us with ideas that we use in social life. The historian Joanna Bourke (1999) noticed this while studying oral war histories from combat veterans. Looking at soldiers' accounts from the Great War through to Vietnam, she noted a distinct change. Unlike their forebears, Vietnam veterans often deployed Hollywood metaphors. Action hero John Wayne was a common point of reference in these stories, used as an easily accessible analogy to explain what war was like. His movies were 'real' inasmuch as they created a common language that was used to discuss actual events.

Some media researchers think this is a spectacular example of a common media effect. Media fiction sets expectations and guides explanations of the things that happen to us. Let's think this through by considering Van den Bulck and Vandebosch's (2003) research on how the experience of going to prison is affected by film and television.

The study interviewed 33 rookie inmates in a Belgian prison about how expectations of gaol matched the reality of life behind bars. Many confessed that their fears had been coloured by American fictions; they anticipated beatings, rapes, large industrial complexes with no creature comforts, and inedible food. One respondent mentioned his surprise at being offered a colour TV and a nice salad on arrival in his cell.

Van den Bulck and Vandebosch provided an exceptionally clear explanation for how media fiction becomes real, even when audiences know they are watching fantasies. When you're about to encounter something dangerous, it's natural to wonder what it will be like. Prisons are places that most of us only ever visit onscreen, so, on incarceration, one cannot help but use television and film as reference material.

This makes sense, considering the effort that many of its producers put into being authentic. Take, for example, the critically acclaimed HBO prison series, *Oz*. The drama was set in a maximum-security facility where mild-mannered inmates were housed with genuinely evil criminals. One infamous storyline explained how an ex-lawyer imprisoned for vehicular homicide became the target for torture and sexual abuse at the hands of a neo-Nazi gang boss. The villain in this story was so malevolent that it pushed the actor who played him into depression (Smith, 1999). Asked about the extreme, stylized, even ritualized violence that was common in the series, writer and producer Tom Fontana offered the following defence: 'The problem with TV violence, it's a lie, people get shot and don't bleed. They get hit and walk away. If you have to do it, you have to do it as horrifically as it really is' (cited in Smith, 1999, no page).

Launched in the late 1990s, *Oz* was part of HBO's campaign to raise the cultural value placed on television, based on its capacity to articulate 'truth' as opposed to *the* truth. Arts critic Sam Delaney defined *Oz* as part of a stable of HBO titles, alongside *The Sopranos*, *Curb your Enthusiasm*, *Rome* and *Six Feet Under* that 'provided commentaries on some of the biggest social and political themes of our times ... and defined new cultural movements' (Delaney, 2009, no page). Television drama was an art form that, like great literature, provided truthful insights into the human condition.

Oz wanted to say something authentic about prison life in relation to ideas about crime, punishment, justice, good, evil and the consequences of violence. It wanted viewers to think about prison and what prisons are for. And it reached a global audience – unsurprising, since the majority of media prison stories come from America (Van den Bulck and Vandebosche, 2003). In contrast, there aren't many dramas about Belgian prisons. When you put all of these factors together, it isn't foolish at all for Belgian offenders to expect an American experience; imagination wise, they had few alternatives.

Oz was a global hit at about the time that the Belgian research was underway. If we think about the show's producers, on the one hand, and the inmates in the study, on the other, it appears that the realities of global media industries brokered an unspoken reality contract between the two. HBO was committed to producing dramas that reflected ideas about social reality for global audiences. That being so, the prisoner who marvelled at his TV and his salad was not just someone who was especially vulnerable to media persuasion; he was part of a media ecology that has made entertainment a *de facto* pedagogic tool.

The outcomes of this mediated reality are real. Here, the study noted that the disparity between screen and real prison produced genuine tension between the inmate and his guards. The former thought the latter were playing a cruel joke on him by offering him a television. The prison case study captured a crucial point. The complexity of media influence goes beyond concepts of fantasy, persuasion, misrepresentation and trickery. Media content offers designs for living that affect what we expect from life through far more nuanced processes. Fact or fiction, good or bad, media stories end up making ideas that we use in life, and this is why we have to take them seriously.

Many media businesses concur with this point of view. Given that media studies is supposed to be a Mickey Mouse subject, it's interesting that Disney is one of them. There was a time when media studies was a Donald Duck discipline. Or, more exactly, Disney star Donald Duck was used to explain fears about the political power of global entertainment businesses. *How to Read Donald Duck* (Dorfman and Mattelart, 1984) accused Disney comic books of targeting Latin America with stories that celebrated capitalism in an era when the United States foreign policy aggressively stifled socialism in that continent. However you feel about this argument, it's true that the Disney Corporation now accepts, in its mission statement no less, that its fictions have a diversity duty. The company agrees that a global media player has to take an interest in different cultures, and has assumed the responsibility to 'Reflect a diversity of cultures and backgrounds in our entertainment experiences for kids and families' (Walt Disney Corporation, 2014: 30). Disney accepts that its numerous stories about fairytale princesses who battle against evil witches and/or stepmothers in the search for true love do have something to do with the worlds in which its audiences live. So if you hear people earnestly discussing the gender politics of the 2013 megahit *Frozen*, and are tempted to roll your eyes and think 'it's just make believe', remember this: Disney doesn't agree with you.

And it isn't just companies that specialize in family entertainment who think this way. EA Games advocate gaming as a political right. The company actively supports the Video Game Voters' Network, an organization that, according to EA Games, campaigns to have games recognized as an art form that deserves the creative freedoms granted to books, film and music. According to EA Games, gaming is about freedom of expression (EA Games, 2014).

Even pornography gets in on the act. Like or loathe it, many porn users use what they watch when relating to their partners (McKee, 2006a). The people who make it agree, and further concede that their 'fantasies' reflect real gender politics. Shine Louise Houston is the founder of Pink and White Productions, an adult entertainment company specializing in queer content. For Houston (2014, no page), the idea porn transports its user into a private fantasy world couldn't be further from the truth:

> I believe there's a lot of room and need to create adult content that's real, that's respectful and powerful ... I think it's the perfect place to become political. It's a place where money, sex, media, and ethics converge.

So, if you think that the people who entertain us do not believe that their work has an impact on how people understand their world, and how they treat one another, you are wrong. That's one reason why we need media studies.

THE MANY FACES OF MEDIA INFLUENCE

A second reason why we need media studies is that this basic agreement between industries and scholars belies a range of differences over *how* media fictions come to matter, to what effect, and what is to be done to manage a world where media professionals affect audiences' realities, regardless of their intentions. To put this another way, we need media studies because:

- media industries and media scholars agree that public entertainment matters but ...

- questions of *how* it matters, to what effect, and what is to be done to handle this power are complicated and require detailed analysis.

Let's explain this by thinking about the prison study again. On one level, it provides compelling evidence that screen drama works like a map of reality when people find themselves in situations where they have no firsthand experience but plenty of exposure to dramatizations of similar scenarios. But three vital questions remain: What does this mean? How did we get here? And what is the purpose of analysing this situation?

It rather depends on what we see in the evidence. Strangely, from a research perspective this is substantially affected by what we already know. Famed sociologist Howard Becker (2005) wrote that researchers never encounter pure evidence; all we do is see pictures of the social, and what we see in them in turn depends on the 'pictures' that we already have about how society works. What he meant by this is that trained researchers approach problems with ideas and methods that affect what they see before them. Krippendorff (1995) likened the problem to the well-known young/old optical illusion. A picture sits before you. You look at the bottom of the drawing and are told that it is a jaw and a neck; you see a young woman in 19th-century clothing. Then you are asked to look at the very same part of the picture and are told instead that it is a chin, mouth and nose; now you see an older woman in a headscarf. What you see depends on what you are primed to see, and there is more than one truth on display.

So let's apply this to the prison study. The bare fact that screen drama influences the induction of new inmates into prison regimes does not fully explain the significance of this observation. Global film companies might read it as evidence of the need to be more thoughtful about what they do. On the other hand, some media scholars would see signs of the inherent damage done when public storytelling is surrendered to corporate interest. Some would read the study as evidence that healthier public culture needs redesigned media economies. According to some academic views on the 'picture' of global media culture, there is no point imploring HBO to be more inclusive in its storytelling, because HBO is the problem; the company represents the power of a single business to occupy the imagination of millions.

There are also different academic ways of looking at evidence of media in action. In this case, some scholars might argue that the most significant finding of the study was not about prison drama or even prison, but about how television routinely mediates interpersonal relationships. That is, some ways of looking at media influence would see the research as being about how relationships are formed in social spaces through media technologies (e.g. Silverstone, 1994; Moores, 1996; Seiter, 1999). From this way of seeing, the relevant issues on display in the inmate–guard interactions are how rules of conduct between the two are spelled out by using television as a privilege. The provision of the television was a way of communicating to the prisoner that he remained a human being with rights.

Van den Bulck and Vandebosch's study is worth considering at length because it signalled several divisions in media and communication studies research. Controversies over why global media entertainment matters, how its significance can be demonstrated and what should be done with the evidence, *vis-à-vis* addressing the social responsibility of media industries, have shaped media studies; or, if you will, have fixed the viewpoints from which we observe the realities of media influence.

So the people who make different kinds of media entertainment agree that the stories they tell impact public life. What, then, impedes media studies as a recognized academic pursuit? One key problem that we have already explored is the space between academic and industrial understandings of what to do in a world where entertaining fiction is real. There's a huge difference between conceding that a show like *Oz* contributes to public knowledge that a small number of people end up using when they fall foul of the law and expecting its producers to do something about this state of affairs. The lesson of the study is not that people like Fontana should be more careful about the things they write. The problem is much bigger than this; it is discovering how entertainment has become a source of knowledge that is connected to matters of social value. That is why media influence is about more than the intentions of the people who make the entertainment that we consume.

MEDIA INFLUENCE: DEFINING CRITICAL PERSPECTIVES

Media scholars have been arguing this for a long time. In 1941, Paul Lazarsfeld, a seminal figure in the development of mass communications research, wrote of the distinction between 'critical' and 'administrative' research. In a remarkable piece of self-criticism, Lazarsfeld attacked the very academic trend that he was in the process of authoring. Ensconced at Columbia University's Office of Radio Research, Lazarsfeld enjoyed huge funding from media industries and government institutions. He used the cash to refine techniques for examining the effects of media exposure on audiences. But this tied him to 'administrative' problems: specific, business-related inquiries into the success of particular messages in producing desired effects among audiences. Did this public health campaign change behaviours? Did that political advertising campaign affect votes? Such queries masked weightier puzzles. Lazarsfeld believed that mass media had produced a cultural shift every bit as seismic as the Industrial Revolution. During industrialization, European nations had learned through bitter experience that the benefits of technological advancement had to be weighed against the unpredicted inequalities, suffering and injustice that change produced. Lazarsfeld thought there was every reason to see mass media as bringing about equally dramatic changes, and feared that communications researchers were not looking at how media changed the social DNA, a mistake that was all too easy to make when businesses were willing to pay vast sums to pursue more superficial queries.

Acknowledging his part in bringing about this state of affairs, Lazarsfeld underlined the need for 'critical' research. While he and his colleagues were tied up with making media messages more efficient, a more pressing matter was the need to generate ways of studying the general effects of a 'promotional' culture. Lazarsfeld believed that centralized, standardized media production affected the fundamental production of social values. Although he spent most of his time looking for places where deliberate efforts to make audiences think and do specific things succeeded or failed, he was of the mind that far more significant media impacts were to be found in the habits and attitudes that audiences adopted in relation to media in general, and that this sort of influence transcended the intentions of any person or organization. Hence:

> The idea of *critical research* is posed against the practice of administrative research, requiring that, prior and in addition to whatever special purpose is to be served, the general role of our media of communication in the present social system should be studied. (Lazarsfeld, 1941, 9)

As the book progresses, you will see how contemporary Lazarsfeld's words remain. The move from mass to digital media appears to have sent another ripple through society, and academics still worry that their practices struggle to account for what has happened. This indicates a certain circularity in debates about media influence that is worth contemplating.

The 1983 'Ferment in the Field' edition of the *Journal of Communication*, which invited academics to reflect on the purpose of media research in the late 20th century, was a landmark moment in this regard. The project was inspired by the ongoing fear that media research practices were becoming alienated from their purpose. Experientially, it was clear that mass media had ushered in a new way of living, based on a capacity to develop knowledge, feelings and relationships with a world beyond direct personal experience (Garnham, 1983). Faced with making sense of such profound shifts, media scholars had dissected the task into bundles, characterized by specific sets of theories and methods. Some looked at how messages could change behaviours, examining things like the success of wartime propaganda or political advertising. Others investigated how media systems integrated people into social life. These approaches (behaviourism and structural functionalism) operated from the political assumption that privately owned western media industries could benefit democracy. More holistic, cultural ways of understanding why media mattered struggled to be heard against these longer standing, better funded, and more institutionalized perspectives (Carey, 1983). Of course, Lazarsfeld had already said this, but the problem was that in the years since, the grip of administrative questions that centred on business and state interests had only grown stronger (Ewen, 1983; Garnham, 1983; Smythe and Van Dinh, 1983).

Suppose we relate this problem back to the reality effect of *Oz*. What did the 'Ferment in the Field' debate say about the difficulty of understanding how the show became 'real', and what its 'reality' said about the politics of entertainment? Many of the contributors indicated that the hardening of administrative perspectives had discouraged analysis of relationships between commercial media businesses and other sectors of society. Little attention had been paid to the important matter of how the organization of creative activity within particular industries affected the expression of ideas. We can see the problems this causes in looking at how Tom Fontana was asked to justify the use of violence in the show as a personal artistic choice that reflected his own perspectives. This ignored how violence was a narrative tool encouraged by commercial pressures and industrial conventions that were much bigger than *Oz*, HBO and even television.

For many of the contributors to 'Ferment in the Field', the solution to Lazarsfeld's Paradox – that the better funded and technically adept media research became, the less it said about the deep impact of media on civilization – was to refocus on the concept of culture. Carey (1983, 313) defined the starting point for a cultural approach to media like so:

> The mass media are but one important site of study. They, in turn, must be considered in their relationship to everything else. As that is a tall order, the more modest task is to formulate a vocabulary through which it is possible *in principle* to think of the mass media in relation to everything else.

Carey wanted to restore 'criticality' to the heart of media research by connecting the particular issue of media influence to the more general matter of social communication, consensus and conflict. He reminded us that media research is not really about media; it is, as Nicholas Garnham (1983) commented in the same volume, about how human beings comprehend the material conditions of their own existence, which involves not only an understanding of what the social world is like, but also an appreciation of *how* it became so. Media were a productive social force that made reality (Gerbner, 1983). The most pressing issue to be understood – as Lazarsfeld highlighted and others reiterated 40 years later – was how media refereed conflicts between competing views of what should be done to move societies forward. This meant looking at how the particular arrangements of media industries conditioned foundational assumptions about what democracy was, and how people could participate in it. Where an administrative question might ask how a particular political speech encouraged audiences to support a particular policy, a critical perspective would look instead at how the speaker and the issue became a person and topic that audiences care about in the first place, thanks to the particular organization of media industries.

Let's pause to recap. We are in a period when it's important to reconceive the practice of media research, because it seems that media play an increasingly influential role in daily social life. But if we look at the history of the subject, then we quickly see that this state of affairs has been a constant feature of cultural life ever since media research began. In terms of other constants, media researchers have spent decades discussing the purpose of their discipline, and they agree that the most important question before them is how media make reality *possible*. This question is fundamentally *cultural*. It asks how media industries become ingredients in complicated social ecologies that depend, in good measure, on the generation of meaning. Media research essentially looks at how media industries orchestrate the construction, communication, popularization and contestation of perceived and experienced realities.

To get a better handle on what this means, it is important to start thinking about research in terms of *principles* rather than *topics*. The argument coming from Lazarsfeld and the 'Ferment in the Field' contributors was that they shared the same basic 'problem', regardless of the empirical direction that they pursued. What I mean by this is that although the contributors to this discussion were best known for studying apparently disparate things, such as voting and consumer behaviours, television violence, the cultural history of media technologies, the ideological function of popular culture and political economy, they shared an interest in how symbolic resources organized life by telling stories about how society should be managed.

Consequently, discerning common themes that unite apparently different examples of media influence in action is the hallmark of politically informed research. Let's return to crime and punishment to clarify the point.

CASE STUDY: COMPLEX MEDIA EFFECTS IN ACTION: FRAMING CRIME AND PUNISHMENT

Media matter politically because the ability to define a problem through them goes a long way to determining what will be done about it. In the second decade of the 21st century, British comedian Russell Brand seemed to understand this, given the effort he put into passionately campaigning for a reassessment of UK drug laws. Brand, known for his wit, looks, voracious sexual appetite and his drug addiction, had risen to global fame. Open about his opiate obsession, Brand advocated the decriminalization of drugs. He gave evidence on the matter to a Parliamentary Select Committee and made a documentary on the subject for the BBC.

There is so much more to this story than the question of how Brand's campaign affected public opinion on drug policy in the UK. Culturally speaking, before we ask whether Brand significantly increased support for decriminalization, it is far more important to consider how he got to speak in the first place, and how he attracted an audience. Confronted by Brand on BBC's discussion show *Newsnight*, journalist Peter Hitchen asked why the BBC had spent taxpayers' money on a documentary made by someone with no professional drugs expertise, and whose position relied on jokes instead of evidence-based argument. These were good questions, but they implied many more about historical changes in entertainment. Brand was not the first comedian to branch into political commentary. In the US, John Stewart and Bill Maher were already staples of the political communication circuit. So, before anyone worried about the wisdom of Brand's argument, one wondered if his activism capitalized on the global politicization of comedy. And, working in the other direction, what did this have to do with the rise of news as a form of entertainment? Hitchen's complaints were a little ironic, given he made them on a hard news show known for entertaining arguments where respected politicians were routinely humiliated by aggressive interviewers (Higgins, 2010). Moreover, the blending of information and entertainment was, according to some views, the signature of European public service broadcasting (Bourdon, 2000). Summarizing all of this, the critical questions about the episode are less about the effect it did or did not have on public attitudes to drug policy, or whether or not audiences should take Russell Brand seriously, and much more about how certain sorts of figures claim authority on public matters through changing arrangements of media expression.

Understanding what the event was about meant asking how media draw attention to people and events through a particular set of institutional arrangements –in this case, the BBC's obligation to public service in a shifting commercial and regulatory environment that asked it to be popular as well as informative. Clearly, Russell Brand meant to use his leverage as an international celebrity to change opinions on drugs, but, from an academic perspective, the matter of how a comedian gets to even try to become a legitimate political voice is more interesting – and harder to explain. The puzzle concerns how authority is claimed, won, contested and defended. So there are two levels of reality in play. The first is the reality media create around drugs, and the second is concerned with how that, or any reality for that matter, is possible in the first place.

Such queries are similar in structure to those applied to the earlier *Oz* example. Ostensibly, the cases seem different: one is about commercial, global drama and expectations about incarceration; the other, public service documentaries and attitudes on legal reform. But both demonstrate how the fundamental reality effect of media takes on different organizational guises. In one it comes through the marketing of quality drama that people are willing to pay for, and in the other it is how publicly subsidized media organizations legitimate their traditional position in public culture by engaging with emergent trends, such as the rise of celebrity culture. But both topics address how public debate is shaped by media infrastructure. And it is the ability to see relations between disparate examples, in terms of what they say about the role of media in making reality, that defines the critical, political perspective on media influence.

CONCLUSION: FOUR ASPECTS OF A RESEARCH QUESTION: EXPERIENCE, CAUSATION, ETHICS AND GENERALIZABILITY

Before embarking on media research, it is worth heeding a few basic ideas. Everyone agrees that media create reality, but not everyone means the same thing by this, and there are different motives for studying this reality function. To think past this challenge, it helps to note that critical perspectives advocating a cultural approach to media research have been around for a long time, and they persist because old arguments inform new challenges. Consequently, putting these lessons into practice is largely about keeping focus on the larger motivation and purpose for research.

The case has been made that it is useful to note how diverse research topics actually work through an identifiable working process. And this is what brings us to the four-part typology, mentioned in the introduction. Mindfulness about the political purpose of media research helps us to figure out more focused procedural questions of method. In this book, the rest of Part 1 explains four steps to achieving this goal. The first is to ask yourself why you are interested in a topic. Chapter 2 explains how developing a personal investment in a research question – being very clear on why you care about a topic – is a useful and widely deployed device. Personal experiences have directed the careers of many significant media scholars, indicating that one's place in culture can be a valuable resource for articulating why media research matters. Chapter 3 explains how engaging with the concept of causation – broadly the processes through which media influence is conceived as working – helps maintain the holistic, cultural approach to media studies that has historically been advocated as 'best practice' in the discipline. Chapter 4 uses debates around ethics to consider *who* media research is for. Socially responsible research on the relations between media and power must consider how research itself becomes part of that dynamic. In order to do this, we consider how ethical principles in dealing with research subjects reflect more important imperatives about ensuring the visibility of diverse publics in the studies that we do. Closing the section, Chapter 5 uses recent high-profile debates on the effects of video gaming to explain the importance of considering arguments and evidence from different research traditions when assessing media influence. It is quite clear from the history of the discipline that scholars have traditionally acknowledged the need to respect alternative ways of defining and approaching research problems, both conceptually and methodologically. As the video gaming case study indicates, however, this is a principle that can be hard to put into practice. Looking at recent controversies in this area is a useful way to show how the four principles of good research can be used to make sense of a topic that is apparently marked by sharp scholarly disagreements, with a view to finding common ground by focusing on culture.

CHAPTER SUMMARY

- Media scholars and media industries agree that media content plays a significant role in developing social values. This is why media studies is essentially political in nature.

- Media narratives are public resources. Media research is therefore charged with assessing how these public resources are used to allow as many people as possible to take part in the cultural construction of reality.

- Historically, there have been many different ways of conceiving and examining media power, but most scholars agree that the most important question facing us is how the general presence of media in the middle of public life exercises a long-term influence over fundamental values about how societies are, and how they should be managed.

- Good media research keeps a close eye on this 'bottom line'. As Nicholas Garnham (1983, 314) said: 'Whether we are found worthy of the social responsibility now thrust upon us will depend upon the cogency of the questions we pose and the answers we provide.'

2

MAKING MEDIA MATTER TO YOU

OBJECTIVE: USING EXPERIENCE TO FORMULATE RESEARCH QUESTIONS

The first step in media research, then, is to be able to identify how a particular topic is relevant to social life. This is what a 'cultural' approach means. Another way of putting this is to say that good research has a clear sense of why it matters to the lives of real people; it connects with *experience*. One way to achieve this goal is to start research with personal experience. Although this seems to fly in the face of conventional notions of objective research, closer analysis reveals that experience frequently plays a significant role in academic careers.

Consequently, this chapter considers the role that personal experience plays in good media research. It does this by explaining how people with little professional experience with media theory and methods can still make significant contributions to our knowledge of how media shape the world. At the end of the chapter, it will become clear that the position of the first-year student and the seasoned academic are very similar. Certainly the hallmarks of good research are the same, for both figures. Further, it will become clear that the value of media studies, for all concerned, lies in understanding the how media research and learning interface – how both 'do' media research.

To make this argument, this chapter:

- Selects a well-known topic about media impact (cyber bullying) and explains why this subject represents a familiar type of media 'problem'.
- Explains why academics who study this topic want to know more about how it is experienced.
- Locates this discussion within broader debates about media education, as they focus on connections between experience and learning.
- Casts these issues as research matters, by showing the role that experience played in developing the cultural studies approach to media.
- Ends by exploring strategies that everyone can use to put their experiences into their studies.

(Continued)

To bring these subjects to life, the chapter centres on a fictionalized, but entirely plausible scenario. Suppose you are a first-year international student enrolled in a media studies class at an English-speaking university. Is it fair to expect you to say something interesting about a topic that is perplexing experts around the world? And is your situation significant within the global development of media studies? The answer to both of these questions is yes. What this means is that good media research begins by reflecting on who you are, where you are, and being able to explain why media matter in the world in which you live.

CASE STUDY: CYBER BULLYING AND MEDIA EDUCATION

> You teach media because you wish to bring the experience of pupils into the classroom, to validate that experience, and to encourage students to reflect upon it. My own objectives were to liberate pupils from the expertise of the teacher, and to challenge the dominant hierarchical transmission of knowledge which takes place in most classrooms. In media studies information is transmitted laterally, to both students and teachers alike. (Masterman, 2010, 11)

Len Masterman is a leading expert on media education. Among many achievements, Masterman played a role in writing UNESCO's 1982 Grunwald Declaration. This was an important document in the history of media studies because it connected the topic to human rights and inclusive democracy (Masterman, 1985). Above, Masterman captures an important principle, that media education and media research are connected activities. What Masterman is saying here is that students should not expect to simply absorb the content of media research as it is transmitted to them through lecturers. They should expect to enter a dynamic relationship in which knowledge is created. This happens through the exchange of not only 'information', but also ideas and experiences.

For this reason, media classrooms are places where everyone is learning and researching through experience. They are places where everyone contributes to the discipline by developing techniques for *generating* knowledge about how media work within different instances of social life. This is an engaged process that does far more than tell learners things that they do not know.

David Buckingham (2006) puts it like this. Social and media inequality are real and connected. Links are found by listening to the experiences of marginalized people. The purpose is to develop a popular pedagogy. This 'begins from ... people's existing knowledge of the media, rather than from the instructional imperatives of the teacher' wherein 'media education is not seen as some form of protection, but as a form of preparation' (2006, 13).

Decent media education welcomes students as people who already know things (Buckingham and Bragg, 2004; Gauntlett, 2011). The criticism has been made that early media studies viewed media as threats. This was true in a couple of senses. From a mass communication view, the dominant concern was that media could change thoughts and actions. From a cultural studies position, the fear was more that popular culture carried subtle political messages that maintained the balance of power. In either case, the pleasure of popular culture was something to be 'unlearned'. This was seen as having a negative effect on media education (Buckingham, 2006; Sefton-Greene, 2006).

The essential challenge behind this debate is to contextualize media's undoubted political and cultural power in meaningful stories about what using media feels like for those living in a particular historical moment. One reason is that often media power only succeeds or fails in user experiences. Digital culture makes this all the truer. This change amplifies the need to resist the focus on effects and the 'technophobia' that characterized many concerns about media influence (Sefton-Green, 2006, 282). Yet it is also true that the obvious learning potential of newer media devices were easily co-opted for commercial purposes (Sefton-Greene, 2006). Ironically, these antithetical convictions agree that pleasure and formal media education need to be integrated.

This is because the apparent plenitude of digital ecologies sustains familiar political questions. Young people actively negotiate evolving environments with guile, but as Sefton-Greene points out, they are 'actors in a field'. Their options are not endless, especially since their 'actions' are the subject of significant commercial interest. For this reason, the question of 'how new forms of information poverty shape social exclusion and alienation' (Sefton-Greene, 2006, 297) remains a concern, even for those who believe the issue of media influence cannot be reduced to the simple question of what media do to people. This is all the more so since the massive popularization of media has created the business-friendly impression that media have incubated a creative class with inchoate abilities that can be easily converted into positive futures (Buckingham, 2013).

It's one thing to read this idea, and quite another to put it into practice. Media students face a daunting task: saying something meaningful about complicated cultural phenomena, in the face of limited time, resources (books, access to specialized, individualized training) and scholarly experience. Take cyber safety as an example. It is a bewildering new threat that perplexes experienced academics and policy makers alike, so what is the neophyte media student supposed to add to understanding? New media problems like cyber bullying have rapidly become the topic of considerable social and academic concern. There is enormous pressure to define and quantify the nature and extent of the potential risk that the online world poses, and people are especially worried about the damage that young people might already be suffering. This demands an expensive, highly polished and organized approach, something along the lines of the 'EU

Kids Online' project. This endeavour has funded comparative studies of online risks across 25 European countries. One of its defining features is a capacity for sophisticated quantitative analysis, enabling scholars to study the relationships between a number of media and social variables that may affect the harm that does – or does not – befall users when they socialize online (Livingstone, 2013; Livingstone and Helsper, 2013).

Given the gravity of the issue, is it reasonable to expect an undergraduate to say anything that might change the perspective of the person who is teaching him or her on the topic? Just to complicate things a bit more, suppose that undergraduate is an international student, someone who is not just trying to come to terms with a new subject, but also a new language. Let's make things even trickier. Suppose that international student is from Bhutan, a nation that did not have even national television until 1999. Most students can at least draw on an historical reservoir of experience when thinking about media. What if you didn't even have that? Could anyone still expect you to teach the teacher?

The answer is yes. Experience has been an important consideration in the development of media studies and an ongoing debate about what – and who – media education is for. Bringing infrequently heard perspectives 'to voice' through the practice of media education has been a key consideration in debates around media literacy (Kellner and Share, 2005). Moreover, placing these 'voices' at the centre of investigations over why media matter in the world has been a key research strategy. Some of the best media research has come from people who have been driven by the marginalization of their experiences.

So, figures such as our notional Bhutanese student are very important in media research. If you were s/he, the unique aspects of your country's media experience – the fact that it doesn't really have much at all – could be a research strength. The very fact that Bhutan is *not* like the EU would lend a perspective that could feed back, in a significant way, to the framing of media studies, as long as 'experience' is processed through an organized scholarly framework. This chapter will establish that architecture.

Concerns over cyber safety reflect many anxieties about media and society that have been around for a long time. The first step towards integrating research and experience is to relate it to academic study issues that people care about. Cyber safety hits a nerve because it upsets the natural order of things. We cherish childhood and adolescence as sacrosanct periods during which young people can experiment with identities in safety (Livingstone, 2013). News stories connecting social media, bullying and suicide are upsetting since they dramatize a broken social contract between adults and minors. Commercial media platforms allow round-the-clock taunting, and there's little that businesses, governments or parents can do about it. Clearly, then, this particular 'media effect' is about the very basis of social order and human relationships. Heavy stuff indeed.

Interestingly, experienced and novice media researchers alike approach this difficult subject in the same way. Whoever you are, a useful way to address a very real social problem is to recognize that cyber bullying is a 'typical' media subject – a topic of intense anxiety that most of us recognize. It is also a 'good' research matter, in so far as it inherits a series of debates about what media studies is for, and the role that students play not only in learning but in developing media research. This becomes clear when reviewing key works on the development of media education and critical media education, which both place an onus on the research importance of experience.

To put this argument together, let's consider how cyber bullying is being experienced as a rapidly emerging social risk that represents not just a media problem, but also an entire cultural shift.

EXPERIENCES OF CYBER BULLYING

You can be forgiven for thinking that cyber bullying is an unstoppable force that perplexes governments, businesses and families. Worse still, developing nations appear particularly vulnerable to the chaos that social media seem to inflict, on the young in particular. What is anyone to say about such a bewildering problem?

These perceptions were tragically animated by the suicide of English teenager Hannah Smith in 2013. In the days after her body was discovered, Smith's father attributed his daughter's suicide to online harassment on youth forum ask.fm (Sky News, 2013). Joanne, Hannah's sister, claimed that her sibling had become 'addicted' to the Latvian-based site, which encourages users to 'crowd source' information (BBC News, 2013). Cruelly, other users taunted her to take her own life.

The story was as convoluted as it was upsetting. Ask.fm instigated a review of its safety procedures and introduced new features, such as panic buttons and resources for worried parents (Jones, 2013). But the company also claimed that Smith had sent most of the messages to herself (Silverman, 2013). David, her exhausted father, conceded the defence, but countered that this was probably a strategy his daughter had used in a final, desperate attempt to end bullying that happened everywhere in her life – at school, over the phone and online (2013). Mr Smith felt that ask.fm's actions were motivated by simple public relations concerns (2013). He also felt betrayed by the law, which he condemned as being out of sync with changing media practices. He blamed British Prime Minister David Cameron for this. In response, Mr Cameron suggested that consumers boycott sites with risky operating protocols (Sky News, 2013).

Eventually, an understandably frustrated David Smith complained that it shouldn't be his job to direct action on the ethical responsibilities of well-funded media companies. Academics agree. Critics have observed that the practical burden of daily media regulation falls on the shoulders of individuals who have been forsaken by state machinery that cannot keep pace with media businesses (Frau-Meigs, 2008). In this case, all involved recognized that the new world of online social life had opened a Pandora's box of trouble, and no one was entirely sure of what to do about it.

Cyber bullying and social change: The case of Bhutan

Unfortunately, this is one of those heart-wrenching cases where evidence and emotion do not synchronize. It is impossible for parents not to worry about stories like these, but available evidence has not found persuasive causal links between using social media and teen suicide (Patchin and Hinduja, 2012). But this does not mean that public disquiet about teens online is groundless. To make the research and popular concerns fit, we need to consider how the horrible things that happen to a few people might be extreme variants of more widely experienced media trends. In other words, what might the terrible fate of Hannah Smith say about things that are happening to other people whom we never hear about because they are never harmed in a spectacular way?

To ponder this, let's go to a completely different place. Let's travel to rural Bhutan. According to the publisher Lonely Planet, Bhutan isn't remotely like anywhere else in the world. The well-known guide promises a Himalayan paradise where everything is different. It's eco-friendly, cigarettes are an illegal drug, and the giant penises you see on walls aren't graffiti painted by lewd vandals – they're good luck signs.

But things are changing, and media seem to have something to do with that. In 2014, the BBC reported that social media were 'waking up' Bhutan. The rapid advances of Facebook and the like were creating new outlets where young Bhutanese could explore sex, fashion and political reform (BBC News, 2014). Apparently, Bhutan was becoming just like everywhere else, thanks to social media.

In fact, local journalists were already writing about the coming changes. They had become an ongoing theme in Kuensel Online, Bhutan's only English language news resource. In 2010 the site introduced the world to Passang, a 27-year-old mule expert who made his living as a tour guide (Kuensel Online, 2010). According to the story, this free-spirited young man was an evocative icon of a disappearing world.

The worlds of Passang and Hannah could hardly seem more different. Passang spent most of his time with his mules, and that's the way he liked it. The highlight of his year was an annual herding exercise to a remote part of the Himalayas in the summer months, when he and his best friend would get about as far away from the rest of the world as it's possible to be. He'd experienced plenty of sadness, his only memory of his father being a picture of a man holding a bottle of beer, a constant reminder of the booze that orphaned him. The idea that his biggest problem might be bullying from online strangers appeared preposterous. If Passang wanted the world to leave him alone, all he had to do was saddle up and go.

But the globe was closing in. Passang sported a David Beckham haircut – even Bhutanese horsemen aren't immune from celebrity culture. Passang knew that his future was tied to Bhutan's burgeoning tourist trade, an industry inevitably dependent on the promotion of the little known nation through media. And his girlfriend, whom he wanted to marry, was trained to use a computer (Kuensel Online, 2010).

Kuensel Online has published many stories, suggesting that the days when people like Passang can simply opt out of media culture are numbered. Bhutan is going online, like it or not. So there was an air of inevitability when the news site began running stories about young people being exposed to online abuse. In 2013, it reported that two Bhutanese teenage girls posted photographs of themselves on Facebook. In them, the girls fashioned their traditional dresses into miniskirts, and were subjected to offensive comments (Dorji, 2013c).

The incident echoed the Smith case. Bhutan's Infocom and Media Authority recognized that here was a portent, but, much like David Cameron, observed that there wasn't much that the state could do about it (Dorji, 2013c). In Bhutan, cyber safety was just one of the many social challenges, including child protection laws, schooling and the like. Practically speaking, then, the best defence was parental vigilance (Dorji, 2013c).

From this perspective, the social media whirlwind threatened to vacuum Bhutan into an unappetising global media melange. People like Passang can do little other than watch the approaching storm, and perhaps the only rescue is to learn from the developed world that has seen this all before. Passang should listen, because one day he won't be able to ride away from it all.

However, it is not possible to project the outcomes of European research onto Bhutan's digital future, because that future is already being developed in a unique way. The co-existence of radical social and media change has prompted rapid and deep introspection on what media change represents, at a profound, cultural level. Bhutan's Centre for Media and Democracy looked beyond cyber safety alone in connecting the Facebook incident with the commercialization of culture. If young people were being sexualized, this was mostly the outcome of the search for new consumer markets (Dorji, 2013b). So, unlike many parts of the world, the issue of cyber safety was tied to the rhythms of media for profit long before it became a substantial issue for people like Passang.

Also, the first documented incident of cyber bullying *per se* in Bhutan happened to adults. An anonymous Facebook user accused two Bhutanese media figures of insulting the nation's king. Despite their protestations of innocence, the duo was subjected to threats of violence and even death (Dorji, 2013a). Again, the state claimed it could do little to help. Here, the exact impact of digital turbulence was unique to a nation that treats its royalty with a deference that has long since evaporated in other monarchies.

So Bhutan is also a unique place where familiar concerns about cyber safety are folded, in quite self-conscious ways, into discussions about a much bigger matrix of change – political, economic, social and cultural. Democratic possibilities take on a peculiar flavour in one of the world's few remaining monarchies, which to all intents and purposes had no electronic media culture until the 21st century. Change plays out in a context where it feels different from those who encounter it. Passang is interesting because he isn't like many people; he is being propelled from a nomadic pastoral existence into the cut and thrust of media-borne global commerce. People in Europe have had 200 years to acclimatize. What is this like? Passang is one of the few people who can tell us, and letting him explain and analyse his experiences is a core project in studies of cyber safety and media education. According to the Bhutan Centre for Media and Democracy, developing the media literacy of Passang, and others like him, is vital to a nation with a large youth population who are key to political and national development (Bhutan Centre for Media and Democracy, no date). So it is not such a stretch of the imagination to think that he might appear in a media classroom with a story to tell.

Placing unique stories in a global context

People like Passang aren't just data; they are catalysts of media futures, and their perceptions are significant to research conversations on what those futures hold. These general commitments are pivotal to understanding cyber safety and the general principles of media research. Looking at sophisticated studies of the topic, three things are clear:

- Cyber safety is a weighty global issue, characterized by certain common trends

- Data suggest that parts of the world that do not have a tradition of media education might be especially vulnerable

- However, research on this topic is in its infancy. What this means is that listening to the experience of media users is an important part of defining what cyber risk is.

Consequently, the cyber bullying topic reflects fundamental principles in media research as the latest variant on an old conundrum – how do media exert an independent effect over society? Some evidence indicates, for example, that cyber bullying is taking something that has been around for a long time – bullying – and turning it into a new, pernicious force. On the other hand, researchers are aware that the evidence that this is happening should not detract from the equally important work of conceiving other ways that online life might be shaping the worlds of media users in league with other factors. This conceptual work is where the user experience 'speaks', because experienced scholars know that cyber bullying is not a phenomenon that can be described with data alone, however elaborate and well-funded that data gathering and analysis might be.

There are certainly reasons for thinking that there is cause for alarm, regardless of how users may feel about the benefits of living online. Research on the numbers of young people who experience online bullying has produced wildly diverging estimates – anywhere from 5% to 74% (Patchin and Hinduja, 2012). But even the lower estimates make it a significant danger. To compare, consider that in 2009 the World Health Organization called for a ban on alcohol advertising because drinking then accounted for 3.7% of global mortality. Small percentage effects can be devastating.

Another troubling possibility is that online communication aggravates risks already in the world. A major survey of the phenomenon across 25 European countries (Görzig and Ólafsson, 2012) found that cyber bullies are a distinct breed; they spend more time online, are more willing to take more online risks (disclosing personal information, arranging to meet people in the physical world), and are more at home building online identities. Cyber bullying is more prevalent among late teens who are confident online, and girls are significantly more likely to do it than are boys. As Görzig and Ólafsson point out, this raises the possibility that the temptation to become a cyber bully increases with age and self-perceived digital literacy, especially for girls. So, cyber bullying is an index of independent media effects because it is different from traditional bullying. Bullying depends on physical presence, physical power and identity, whereas cyber bullying needs anonymity and the absence of physical space (Erdur-Baker, 2009).

Ominously, Russian research indicates that countries that are relatively new to the online world – like Bhutan – might find it especially difficult to handle cyber bullying. One survey found that Russian children are twice as likely to admit to cyber bullying as are their peers in other European nations, are twice as likely to report being upset by material they have seen online, and have fewer resources to draw on when trying to figure out these problems (Soldatova and Zotova, 2013).

As in Bhutan, Russian researchers have quickly realized that it is important to consider the wider implications of cyber bullying. The challenge that Russia faces, which contrasts with its European neighbours, is that most of the adult population is going online at the same time as the children that they care for. One of the stranger outcomes of this situation is that cyber bullied young Russians are more likely to return to the 'scene of the crime' – online social networks – to seek advice on how to handle their troubles. To Soldatova and Zotova (2013), this is a sign of a potential unseen hazard of cyber bullying, that it enhances social exclusion by making people wary of using what have already become important social living resources.

Surely, such a new and complicated case demands elaborate, sophisticated and expensive research. The advantage of the EU online project is that it allows comparative analysis of multiple variables that might direct the risks of online media (Livingstone and Helsper, 2013). Görzig and Ólafsson's survey is a case in point. It interviewed over 25,000 people aged 9–16 across 25 European nations, reflecting the Herculean nature of evidence-based policy work (Görzig and Ólafsson, 2012; see also Livingstone and Helsper, 2013). The scale of the cyber safety risk needs to be defined and measured. It is a highly professional venture to be left to those well versed in the literature, theories and methods of media research.

Understanding cyber risk: The significance of experience

That said, this is just one approach to a multidimensional problem, where understanding the experience of cyber risk from the perspective of those who encounter it plays an important definitional role. According to Sonia Livingstone, whose skill in combining different media research traditions in policy debates is globally applauded, the main challenge to cyber safety research is that we don't know what we don't know. Knowledge is geographically biased towards the USA, and is gathered by researchers shackled by ethical problems in asking kids delicate questions. Listening to how people understand online experiences in their own words is a key research strategy solution to these challenges.

Evocatively, Livingstone describes the problem by comparing the 'risks' of crossing the road versus the 'risks' of going online. Kids 'have' to do both things. Just as kids must cross the road to get to school, it's also true that they have to use online resources, one way or another, once they get there. But the nature of the risks involved is something else. Road safety research questions are straightforward: What are the chances of being hit by a vehicle when crossing the road, and how badly hurt are you likely to be if this happens? This is something we can figure out. We know how many kids get run over every year, and we know how badly they are hurt. Furthermore, statistics about traffic density, speeds and weight of vehicles model risk implications of changed road use and traffic management.

Things aren't so straightforward online. There is the impossibility of keeping track of user numbers. Then there's the even bigger challenge of figuring out the harms of exposure to upsetting content. One obstacle here is that although we might be clear on What worries us content wise, the reasons why we worry about exposure can be ambiguous. If an underage person is exposed to pornography, do we worry that this will lead to risky behaviour, upset, pressure over body image, gender bias, or something else altogether? Are our concerns about young people, or about our own capacity to preserve childhood as a time of innocence? Is the issue at hand not so much digital media as the concept of childhood itself (Livingstone, 2013)? The bottom line is the risks of crossing the road are clear and calculable whereas the risks of going online are less so.

Livingstone warned us about the dangers of disarticulating research agendas from user input. As an example, when the EU online project has asked young people about online safety, cyber bullying isn't top of their concerns (Livingstone et al., 2013). Livingstone's observation that young media users should be able to participate in the framing of the issue is borne out by the richness of the data they provide. A major survey where 10,000 European children reported upsetting online experiences (Livingstone et al., 2013) demonstrated significant differences in experienced fear and risk. Younger children were most concerned about 'content rather than contact' (Livingstone et al., 2013, 1), (i.e. the violent and sexually explicit material they encounter online, rather than the messages directed at them personally), and boys tended to be most upset by violent content. The latter blasted a hole in the common-sense notion that boys are naturally attracted to media violence.

The survey is a stark reminder that grave scholarly lessons sometimes come from the mouths of pre-teens. When an 11-year-old girl writes that her biggest online fear is that 'somebody will take a photo of me without my knowledge and load it onto an inappropriate website' (Livingstone et al., 2013, 1), one can only be struck by the fear that image exploitation instils in a kid who should be fretting over multiplication tables. The girl provided a timely reminder that audiences don't necessarily worry about the things that policy makers and academics do.

Ultimately, the EU Kids Online project mapped what we know about cyber safety, outlined different national experiences of the phenomenon, warned that there was much more to know about it than is known, and confirmed the importance of user experience in determining the direction of future research on digital media and social inclusion (Görzig and Ólafsson, 2013; Livingstone et al., 2013). Another way of putting this is to say that as the focus goes global, people like Passang – people who aren't like everybody else – bear their own kind of expertise.

EXPERIENCE, RESEARCH AND ACTION

In a global context, then, Passang matters as a gateway to a rare field of data. He lives among some of the last people in the world who will experience media culture as a new thing. He knows he stands between a world that was that of the nomadic Sherpa – and the world that is coming, via his girlfriend's computer. Other media researchers have used personal circumstances like this to say important things about popular culture. One of the best known examples was the sociologist Stuart Hall. Hall, who died in 2014, co-founded the Centre for Contemporary Cultural Studies (CCCS) at the University of Birmingham in the 1960s. He is widely credited as a founding figure in media studies. Hall thought that exposing pop culture to rigorous academic analysis could pave the way for a more inclusive world. Popular culture, he argued, is where audiences start to think about who they are and who they want to be.

He spoke from experience. Hailing from Jamaica, Hall had been a precocious reader of English literature and Marxist theory, but his intellectual career really began with his sister's mental breakdown, precipitated by a doomed romance that foundered on racial prejudice. To Hall, this was a clear indication of how 'emotions, identifications and feelings' (1978, 468) were produced by structured cultural experiences. His sister's fate was sure proof that there is no distinction between the private and the public, because the choice to ignore conventions bears with it the danger of destruction. The idea that culture matters because it is a 'thing' that can hurt people was an important motivation in determining the direction of Hall's research – and so a young woman's depression over her future had a real effect on the direction of media research.

Despite this tragic experience, Hall believed that academic research on popular culture should be about helping people. He believed that everyone developed inchoate theories about how society worked through their experiences, but the role of media scholars was to provide structures to help people theorize – comment and ask questions about – why things were as they were, and what the state of things meant. Good research provokes a social conversation, and that conversation was not possible without connecting with the public. Inspired by the work of the Italian Marxist Antonio Gramsci, Hall was convinced that media studies only mattered when it could be spoken in the language of everyday people. The idea runs like this: media entertainment contains clues about the ideas, values and conflicts that shape the way that we think about and live in the world. Because of this, talking about media is a useful way to talk about politics. To make this really effective, theories and methods that structure organized media research need to be translatable into terms that non-specialist audiences can understand. For this reason, encounters with the public are important because media research develops in a dialogue between theory, research and experience.

By the 1970s, higher education had become the most accessible, regular source for this conversation. Hall started working on his ideas at Birmingham University's Centre for Critical Cultural Studies in 1964. This small research unit specialized in postgraduate education. In 1979 Hall moved to the Open University, an organization specializing in distance education for non-traditional students. He saw this as a chance to 'do' proper research by learning to communicate in a publicly accessible – and useful – way. The sort, one imagines, that might have helped his sister.

Hall's is not an isolated story. The most stunning example of the intersections between personal experience, research and the practice of media education is provided by the story of Brunel Professor of Media John Tulloch. Tulloch has been a leading media researcher for decades. His international reputation came from an enviable flair for connecting cultural theory, everyday life and popular culture. Among other achievements, he has done this by explaining the political significance of *Dr Who* (Tulloch and Alvarado, 1985; Tulloch, 2000), and the role of daytime soap operas in HIV education (Tulloch, 1999).

From the outset, Tulloch had known the value of staying with the interface between experience and research (Tulloch, 2000). This conviction was savagely confirmed on July 7, 2005. On that date, Tulloch found himself sitting opposite 7/7 bomber Mohammad Sidique Khan on London's underground. Khan detonated his device less than a metre from the professor, who had just attended a meeting on his plans to establish an MA degree course on the media, risk and terrorism. Tulloch miraculously survived, but as he was carried into the daylight, he was thrust into the spotlight that he had spent so long writing about (Kingston, 2007). His bloody image was splashed across the front pages, without his consent.

Tulloch's recovery was hindered by the unnecessary trauma of being represented as an icon of a vengeance that the real man did not want. Photographs of Tulloch's bandaged face were used by some newspapers to demand military action in the Middle East. Tulloch was in fact vehemently opposed to the Iraq and Afghanistan wars, and nothing about 7/7 changed those convictions. Worse still, transported into a media world, Tulloch was also the victim of the press phone hacking that inspired the Leveson Inquiry into unethical journalism in the UK. As a final bitter irony, in 2012 Tulloch discovered that since he had been born in India to British parents, unbeknown to him he had never actually been a British citizen. The face of the British public wasn't actually British.

Tulloch fought back in a number of ways. There were copious media appearances, a personal memoir (Tulloch, 2006) and, eventually, a scholarly monograph called *Icons of War and Terror* (Tulloch and Blood, 2012). The latter analysed how famous images of terror-induced suffering become 'iconic', that is, how those images come to summarize what traumatic events are about to a world audience.

In his journey, Tulloch drew insightful parallels between common human and formal academic processes where reality is created. A striking element of post-traumatic stress disorder (PTSD) therapy, for Tulloch, was the realization that success depends on a patient's ability to frame and reframe real-world events. Guided by expert psychiatrists, it's the patient who does the creative work that transforms a traumatic event into something one can live with. This can involve therapies that, for example, equip the survivor with strategies for reimagining things that have happened in the past – to literally give them a different meaning. This, among other things, underlines how making and remaking meaning is a matter of survival.

Tulloch saw echoes between this personal experience and professional scholarly debates about how meaning is made. These debates are explained further in the following chapters, but basically media studies acknowledges that there are different ways of developing truth claims about the world. What this means is that the subject does not believe that widely recognized social science conventions are the only means of generating useful knowledge. For Tulloch, becoming a survivor and an icon of public violence gave him a particular insight into how images have a public interest, and telling this story was a matter of public interest.

Tulloch argued, with remarkable grace, that protecting society from terror needed media industries who would give more consideration to him *and his would-be assassin*. The professor and the bomber were both real, multidimensional people whose complexity had been reduced to voiceless stereotypes used to further political agendas that, in the end, made the world a riskier place (Kingston, 2007). A cardinal point in media studies is a lived reality for Tulloch, that media are public resources that deeply affect our quality of life (Tulloch and Blood, 2012). For Tulloch, the arduous survival business has been made more painful still by the systematic misrepresentation of his experiences and thoughts in media. Public media meanings have interfered with making the private ones that he needs to get by. His story is not universal, but it is real; it shows how media had a real impact on a real person in demonstrable ways. And it all makes you wonder how these same processes play out more subtly for the rest of us.

Experience: From the extraordinary to the ordinary

Of course there is a problem here. The lesson of the last section is that good research is a matter of being interesting, persuasive and thought-provoking. Easy enough when you've been at the centre of a global news event that everyone knows about. But how about everyone else? Different as their lives were, Hall, Tulloch and Passang share something – they're exotic. They have had rich experiences that easily translate into key media studies themes. Moreover, at the time of his ordeal, Tulloch was armed with an encyclopaedic knowledge of media research, one that only years of reading can provide. So what about the rest of us?

There's no need to panic, because it is really important to analyse how media shape people and places in ordinary ways that few people notice. Another way of putting this is that the analysis of ordinary media users is crucial. And there are ways of leveraging personal experiences to get this done. At base, Tulloch moved forward in his life and his work by figuring out what his investment in his research was. Why did he care? Why did it matter? This is something that everyone can do. More to the point, not doing this can get in the way of academic progression.

It has sometimes been argued that the barrier between media experience and media education is the perspective that the latter is hostile to the former (Buckingham and Sefton-Greene, 2003). That is, media students are confronted with the argument that the popular culture that they know and like is somehow bad, and has probably harmed them in all kinds of ways. According to this logic, it's no wonder that students switch off.

However, research on cyber bullying does not support the view that the language of media risk is unfamiliar to young people. And Tulloch's story opens a new possibility. Explaining how his research on media and terror has evolved has taken the author to difficult places. This sort of work can involve confronting difficult truths about ourselves and the world. There is reason to believe that confronting the issues behind ordinary media habits can be just as confronting.

Let's get back to cyber risk. The earlier section made the point that there is an important truth about the phenomenon that lies in the stories that its victims tell. There's a visceral power to the accounts of young people who have encountered upsetting content online; it's our job to preserve as much of the poignancy of such accounts as we can. One way of doing this is by encouraging media students to bring them into their work.

Easier said than done, so the research says. In his earlier work on teens and soap operas, Buckingham (1988) made the case that risqué media content, featuring sex and violence, was an important source of pleasure and sociality for young people. Expressing anxiety or discomfort about this sort of content therefore bears social risk. In research on teenage boys who were fans of the movie *Basic Instinct*, a 1989 thriller that became infamous for its explicit sex scenes, Thomas Austin (1999) also found similar discomfort. It was, Austin found, impossible to discuss the film without also reflecting on the general angst of being a teenager. Through all of these cases, we come to realize that it's sometimes difficult to ask searching questions about the media without also asking searching questions about yourself.

Add in the commonly held view that proper research is deeply objective, and you can see why students might distance themselves from the topic. Take, for example, research that I did among a cohort of undergraduates for a class on Youth and Media. The unit featured a number of topics about how media influence young people. These ranged from familiar topics around violence – the role of rap and school shootings in real-world violence, and the position of advertising in binge-drinking cultures – to less familiar questions, such as how using mobile phones involves the user in gender politics. The former topics, especially those on violence, were very much based on unusual events and experiences: school shootings, what it's like to go to war. The latter were based on media experiences and themes that everyone encountered.

When asked which topics they preferred, violence won. Students were least interested in topics that focused on unspectacular things that ordinary young people did in private places (Ruddock, 2015). These results were consistent with the so-called 'third-person effect' of media (Davison, 1983). The third-person effect describes a tendency to think that media only influence others, that many see media effects as things that only happy to gullible or vulnerable groups or individuals. We are willing to concede that younger audiences, for example, are especially susceptible to corruption, but less enthusiastic about the prospect that media shape our own social perceptions. Ultimately, third-person perceptions are an impediment to searching analysis of how media shape societies for everyone.

There's nothing wrong with wanting to know more about what media mean to others. The point is simply that a lot of influential media research has come from people who were motivated by a desire to explain how they, or people they cared about, lived lives that were shaped by historical and political circumstances. It is also to point out that leading figures in the world of media education see this more introspective approach as a hallmark of effective education. Here, the trick is to employ personal investment to drive research that enables you, as Tulloch did, to explain why your personal experiences aren't about you, but about the culture in which you live. This is not about delivering personal opinions and anecdotes; it's about painstaking reading on theories and methods that build the architecture to reflect on the world, with a view to participating in it. This is what 'voicing' means.

CONCLUSION: TURNING EXPERIENCE INTO RESEARCH QUESTIONS

Let's get back to Passang. Suppose that he were to decide that study is his future. Suppose he really takes to it, and decides to travel abroad for his education. Suppose further that it is media education that he seeks. How is he supposed to put the ideas in this chapter into practice?

His education would not be about reading all that he could about media theory, and then shoehorning the Bhutanese situation into a set of ideas that already exist. Instead, he would be better advised to use theory selectively, to discover which ones help him solve his particular media issue. For example, what does it mean to suddenly appear in global media culture from a place lacking the benefit – or hindrance – of media experience that others have? Into the bargain, Passang has a place in a larger intellectual project of collecting media experiences to assess the adequacy of existing media scholarship in preparing us for the media world that is coming into existence.

This advice does not only apply to people at the cusp of seismic media changes. One of the major issues in cyber safety studies is the matter of the scale, size and relevance of these risks. Before getting to the size of the problem, much work needs to be done in defining what the 'problem' is actually about. Part of this is about listening closely to young media users to discover what worries them. Another important consideration is developing a social conversation on where responsibility for the problem – whatever it may be – does and should lie. In either case, the importance of expanding media education as a 'participation sport' is clear.

The chapters that follow will develop architecture for doing media research with little experience and few resources, but for now the take home message is that this is an achievable goal. Media education works best when everybody does it. What this means, for everyone, is making smart decisions about what you know, what you can find out, and being sensitive to the things that you have yet to discover. But perhaps, above all, it means being clear about why you care. Why do media matter to you? How will understanding more about how media work in your life benefit you and your culture? Think about those questions before reading on.

CHAPTER SUMMARY

- Media education breaks down the barrier between teaching and researching.

- The best way to learn about media research is to do it.

- The place to start is by asking why you care about media, and what experiences you have had where you have witnessed media influence in action.

- Literature on media education, and on major media issues such as cyber bullying, supports the idea that student experience is a valuable research resource.

- Some of the best media scholars have used personal experiences to develop significant insights into how media shape society.

- You must decide why you care about media research, and what you know about their social impact, before reading on. This is the first step in developing good research questions.

3

ON CAUSATION: HOW DO MEDIA 'DO' THINGS?

OBJECTIVE: USING TECHNOLOGY TO EXPLAIN THE CULTURAL NATURE OF MEDIA-RELATED HISTORICAL CHANGE

Chapter 2 illustrated key topics in media studies with a case study about people and events. Case studies are a useful way of showing how media matter in real terms, but in order to work they have to be developed with a particular issue in mind: How do media cause things to happen?

This chapter answers this question by modelling media research on history. Media scholars and historians share many assumptions about the nature of social change, and there are reasons for framing media research as a form of historical thinking. First, historians have developed a model of causation that can be applied across the humanities. Second, research on the impact of media technologies began in economic history. Third, some of history's basic issues, and challenges, are about communication.

Fleshing out this idea, the chapter demonstrates the historical dimensions of media research by looking at digital whistleblowing, the practice of exposing high-level corruption through digital media. Studies of this phenomenon are concerned with the same themes that drive historical work on empire and civilization. The history of empires shows how communication and media gradually became involved in the historical analysis of human development and its obverse, the systemic abuse of power. As such, the way that historians have addressed social development by carefully balancing evidence and interpretation transfers to significant issues that media scholars also face in explaining how media matter.

To exemplify, the chapter uses the online whistleblowing site 'Wikileaks' as a case study in the complexities of accounting for causation. The story of the whistleblowing organization demonstrates the difficulty of understanding media-related change while avoiding a cardinal research error – determinism. Historian E. H. Carr defined determinism 'as the belief that everything that happens has a cause or causes, and could not have happened differently, unless something in the cause of causes had

(Continued)

also been different' (1961, 93). Determinism offers misleadingly simple answers to complicated questions, a temptation that was 'a problem not of history, but of all human behaviour' (Carr, 1961, 93). In media studies this is manifested in technological determinism, the argument that new media technologies make the world better by conquering space and time (Williams, 1974). History shows many cases where 'better' technology has not helped society (Innis, 2008; Morozov, 2011). Many questions follow about the forces that let media participate in social change.

Carr's relevance to media research became manifest in 2010, when Wikileaks released classified information on the wars in Iraq and Afghanistan into the public domain, via *The New York Times*, *The Guardian* and *Der Spiegel*. The material had been leaked by a US Army private, Chelsea Manning. Among the revelations lay evidence that the wars were far bloodier and more sinister than the allied forces publicly stated, Iraqi civilians had been killed in enormous numbers, abuse at the hands of American soldiers was rife, and security in Iraq depended on private contractors (Rosner, 2011). All told, the leaked information laid bare the grim realities of neo-imperialism. It also demonstrated where media influence – in this case, the impact of technologies – intersected with the time-honoured hallmarks of history: war and empire.

Intriguingly, the Wikileaks affair coincided with controversy among historians over the role of communication in the study of empire, especially regarding the recording, storage and movement of information. Yet this is more than coincidence, since research on the impact of media technologies started with the history of empires. Therefore, Wikileaks encapsulated general principles in the relationship between technology, social ideas change and conceptions of causation that cross the humanities. To build this argument, this chapter:

- Explains why media scholars saw Wikileaks as a synecdoche for key themes in the question of how media technologies affect society.
- Outlines how the debates and disagreements that emerged over the meaning of Wikileaks can be organized via the principles of historical research, as they have applied to understanding empires.
- Shows how history and media came together in Harold Innis's work on communication and empire, and demonstrates how his method of conceiving the relationship between media and power helps to explain controversies over the significance of Wikileaks.
- Concludes by showing how the principles of historical thinking establish clear guidelines for organizing research questions around media, technology and culture.

History and media studies share interests in the nature of change, stasis and progression in the cultivation of democracy. The task here is not to fix the truth of what media do, but rather to enrich debates about where society is going, where it has come from, and how media practices are involved in the politics of equality.

CASE STUDY: DO MEDIA TECHNOLOGIES CHANGE THE WORLD? WIKILEAKS AND 'WHISTLEBLOWING'

In 2010, the world saw video footage of a real combat mission, in which an American helicopter crew strafed a group of people in a Baghdad street. A total of twelve civilians were killed, including two journalists from the Reuters news agency (Meikle, 2012). The classified footage had been released by an organization called Wikileaks. Wikileaks' most recognizable figure was the charismatic Julian Assange (Cammaerts, 2013). Nominated as *Time* person of the year in 2010, Assange had a flair for showcasing the whistleblowing capacities of digital media (Gellman, 2010). His goals were nothing less than the subversion of US world hegemony and the mainstream news industry that had failed to hold the powerful to account for their actions.

Time applauded Assange's reinvigoration of investigative journalism. In 1971 it had taken journalists and activists two years to publish similar evidence about the Vietnam War. In 2006, Wikileaks boasted that it could achieve the same feat in moments. Their organization of digital tools made whistleblowing easier, safer and more impactful. Activists could share digitally stored classified information in a way that authorities found hard to stop and trace (Gellman, 2010). The fact that the collateral murder footage had been supplied by a lowly US Army private called Chelsea Manning (Hasian, 2012; McNair, 2012) seemed to underline how well Assange had achieved his goals. The video clip, which Wikileaks transformed into a documentary-style piece, titled *Collateral Murder*, became a key symbol of its claims (Meikle, 2012).

All of this happened almost 20 years after the 1991 Gulf War. Back then, researchers had started to debate the relationship between media, knowledge of civilian casualties and public support for foreign military intervention. One study pointed to the American media's propensity to emphasize the scientific precision of contemporary military hardware, implying in the process that the benefits of freedom outweighed the risks of death and injury for ordinary Iraqis. That same study also found that as American audiences watched more TV, so their knowledge of civilian casualties declined and their support for the war grew stronger (Lewis, Morgan and Jhally, 1991). That was why the new video was political dynamite. It confronted western audiences with the harsh fact of civilian suffering. It also seemed to usher in a new media order.

Wikileaks proclaimed a new age of 'transparency' (Heemsbergen, 2013) driven by 'scientific journalism' (Meikle and Young, 2012). Journalists were better placed to watch governments. Audiences were better placed to watch journalists, because news stories could be checked against primary evidence. Media technology appeared to have changed the balance of power and the facts seemed to speak for themselves. A military attack in Iraq had killed non-combatants. We knew about this because (a) such events are now recorded and stored, (b) Julian Assange had helped develop a digital network that made it easier to release such material, and (c) Chelsea Manning had activated that network.

Whistleblowing in imperial history

Wikileaks' innovation seemed remarkable when compared with historians' efforts to uncover the facts behind earlier overseas military actions. At around the same time, and with much less fanfare, historians were helping ordinary Kenyans sue the British government for the abuse they had suffered under the empire. In 1952, Britain had declared a state of emergency in response to the activities of the Mau Mau, an anti-imperialist military organization drawn principally from Kenya's Kikuyu people. During the Emergency, the colonial administration, and many other Kenyans, painted Mau Mau soldiers as savage terrorists, bent on pursuing self-interest (Clough, 1998). Britain responded with a complex penal system that detained tens of thousands of Kikuyu at the very least, most of whom were innocent (Elkins, 2006).

In 1958, 11 of these detainees were beaten to death by guards at the Hola camp. The incident provoked outrage in Parliament. However, 50 years later, some historians asserted that the murders were not an aberration. New evidence was discovered that colonial authorities had knowingly brutalized the Kikuyu, and had then done their best to hide their crimes (Anderson, 2005; Elkins, 2006, 2011). Victims deployed the evidence in court. In 2013 they received an official apology from the UK Government, and $32 million in compensation.

Harvard historian Caroline Elkins (2011) argued that the case resonated in the 21st century because it raised questions about empire, secrecy and the persecution of innocent civilians that were very much on the political agenda of the post-9/11 world. Revision is a core activity of the professional historian, using new evidence to revise what we think we know about the past. Elkins had 'blown the whistle' on the empire. She had discovered that the rhetoric of post-war decolonization did not match its practice, and that the British Government had known this all along. Officially recorded facts about the numbers of Kikuyu imprisoned, and the terrible torture that was inflicted upon them, proved this case beyond reasonable doubt. Wikileaks had made the same case about the Iraq war, except it had been able to make these revelations public about ten times faster. The central academic challenge in history – how to tell an accurate story by collecting evidence – had become intimately connected to the media. A digital culture could simply do things that were beyond the scope of paper.

So it is tempting to think that the Wikileaks/Mau Mau comparison teaches that digital media let Chelsea Manning achieve in a matter of minutes what it took 50 years for professional historians to do – to unravel the case for foreign intervention. It seems hard to believe that the colonial excesses of Kenya could be hidden again in a world where you don't need to be a Harvard historian to figure out the truth.

Not so. The real lesson of the comparison is that such a conclusion represents a rush to judgement that is an error of determinism.

Optimism about transparency soon evaporated. Manning was placed on trial for treason and imprisoned for 35 years in 2013. Although she was granted clemency and released in 2017, Manning was driven to suicide attempts during her confinement. Assange had his own legal entanglements, having been accused of sexual assault in Sweden. Claiming that these charges were made under political duress from the US, Assange sought political asylum in the Ecuadorian Embassy in London. By 2012 the 'face' of Wikileaks was effectively under house arrest, as British police, under orders to apprehend him, surrounded the Embassy. As Manning and Assange sat in their respective prisons, claims that the world of power as we knew it had come to an end seemed a tad hubristic.

Perhaps, then, the benefits of a digital over a paper-based administration had been exaggerated. Media scholars set about the puzzle. Classic works in their discipline indicated why the case for Wikileaks might have been overstated. Audience research tells us that we can never be sure how people will interpret media content, regardless of how obvious its meaning might be (Lewis, 1991; Ruddock, 2001, 2007). With this in mind, there was no way to be sure that when audiences watched *Collateral Murder* they saw an abuse of foreign policy. Consequently, it was not possible to assume that the leaking of the video had changed public opinion. Apart from anything else, it was also a 'fact' that Wikileaks secured its infamy in partnerships with mainstream news outlets (Christensen, 2011; Fuchs, 2011). The matter of how 'new' the organization's actions were was thus open to question.

So the bare facts of the Wikileaks story did not reveal all that was to be said about the political gravitas of digital media. Certainly, the relationships among media technologies, media industries and human equality were on display. But the question of how change could be understood and explained was far more complicated.

UNDERSTANDING TECHNOLOGY, INDUSTRY AND SOCIAL CHANGE USING WIKILEAKS

Wikileaks and change

A bouquet of cyber utopianism wafted around research on Wikileaks and its apparent impact. However, the democratic promise of the event was carefully placed in a discussion that recognized the folly of trying to establish a causal chain between digital media and progress.

McNair (2012, 86) proclaimed that Wikileaks had 'made the management of the political environment much more difficult for those in power'. Digital media forced political leaders and media industries to yield to greater public scrutiny. The fact that scandals could explode at any time, and from any source, created a legitimacy crisis for both governments and journalists, and *Collateral Murder* was an exemplar of the process in action.

But it is possible to say this without implying that digital media change everything. Consider, for example, the following quote:

> The activities of WikiLeaks present the most dramatic example to date of the capacity of digital communication networks to subvert the control of official information once enjoyed by political and other elites, and to shape

the news agenda in ways that have the potential to seriously disrupt the exercise of power. (McNair, 2012, 77)

McNair was not advocating technological determinism here. Wikileaks, in his view, yielded insights into the unique *capacity* of digital media to produce change. The distinction is vital. Rather than stating conclusions, it establishes a research agenda comprising three activities:

- Conceiving change

- Identifying drivers of change

- Examining continuities between 'new' times and what has gone before in terms of the operations of media industries and their relationships with other institutions.

Included in this last pursuit was the possibility that digital whistleblowing represented the *absence* of change in conventions of media power.

On conceiving change, Cammaerts (2013) thought Wikileaks' relationships with mainstream and alternative media made it a key player in crafting 'transparency' as a new professional and political value. Intriguingly, Wikileaks became the symbol of transparency at precisely the point where it stopped simply giving public access to classified materials and started to process information, as evidenced by *Collateral Murder*. Moreover, if Wikileaks sought to make other institutions transparent, it was markedly proprietorial about its own operations. As anonymity is a key protection in whistleblowing, Wikileak's methods for sourcing and processing of information remained secretive. Any exploration of the case, then, had to take account of the fact that 'transparency' was a term that was hard to define in practice.

Transparency was hard to define because it was a value that everyone tried to own. To alternative media organizations, 'transparency' exposed the inherent corruption of bureaucracies. Ironically, governments and politicians also embraced it as a strategy to regain public trust. For news organizations, transparency was a branding exercise directed at maintaining competitive advantages (Cammaerts, 2013). Mohamed Zayani's analysis of Al Jazeera epitomized Cammaerts' argument, showing how transparency fostered mutually beneficial partnerships between media businesses and the state. In 2010, the Qatari broadcaster came into the possession of thousands of secret documents on peace negotiations between Israel and the Palestinian Authority. The material included revelations that the latter had been far more conciliatory to the former's demands in private than their public pronouncements indicated. To avoid accusations of political bias, Al-Jazeera adopted a Wikileaks model in giving their audience direct access to the documents themselves – indicating a spread of the 'scientific journalism' paradigm (Zayani, 2013).

Commercial and political interests significantly affected the adoption of Wikileaks-style transparency. The 'risk' that the station was prepared to take in aligning with the alternative media practices suited its brand image as an Arab news service prepared to take an aggressive line on Arab politics. It also suited a quasi-national mission. As Zayani (2013, 31) put it:

> The prowess of Al Jazeera in a geopolitically tense region has helped give Qatar more political weight in the Middle East and position it as a mediator that is capable of diffusing tension in conflict-ridden countries like Lebanon, Yemen and Sudan – in some instances even outperforming the UN.

It was a mistake, then, to think that digital transparency was inherently anathema to traditional media businesses and government. Indeed, other nations were even more calculated in their cultivation of digital nationalism. Iceland's Modern Media Initiative set out to make the country a 'transparency hub', affording whistleblowers and journalists the safest possible legal environment for the pursuit of transparency (Beyer, 2014). These measures underscored the value of 'transparency' as a flexible political platform (Beyer, 2014).

Such examples explain why Meikle (2012) characterized Wikileaks as a junction rather than a change in media history. Transparency drew sustenance from longstanding challenges of feeding voracious 24-hour news cycles. Moreover, the vast databases upon which transparency relied ironically made conventional journalism's capacity for editing, assessing and narrating facts all the more important. Indeed, the cumbersome editorial style of *Collateral Murder* – an 18-minute video that few audiences would likely watch in its entirety – illustrated the ongoing need to blend 'database' journalism with its ancestors (Meikle, 2012).

Wikileaks and resistance to change

Other scholars concluded that Wikileaks had not really changed the contours of media or neo-imperial power. The digital landscape was still contoured by corporate business interests that continued to shape the deepest forms of media influence. According to Hasian (2012), the weak narrative style in *Collateral Murder*, and the naïve assumption that the pictures spoke for themselves, facilitated a straightforward recovery mission by the US. The Army complicated the truth of the images, with evidence that the dead journalists had violated their own rules of engagement, that the pilots had solid grounds for suspecting the presence of enemy combatants, and that the helicopter was on a rescue mission.

Hasian concluded that *Collateral Murder* represented the *declining* power of whistleblowing. Wikileaks had compared itself to Pentagon papers and Vietnam leaks. But compared to public reaction stories of US Army atrocities in Vietnam, Hasian argued that by the autumn of 2010 the most remarkable thing about *Collateral Murder* was how little effect it had had on public opinion. The digital power of the state had created powerful counter-narratives that 'domesticated' the crisis. Perhaps the Wikileaks style of digital whistleblowing was less radical that its own rhetoric would allow.

Others doubted it was radical at all, and represented *no change* in corporate media practices. Fuchs (2011) saw Wikileaks as an apologist for the most significant abuse of power at work in the world: that wielded by private capital. Where it set out to expose governments, a more conciliatory goal set out to 'civilize' corporations. From a Marxist viewpoint, Fuchs observed that this ignored the inherently exploitative nature of the relations between private wealth and labour. Wikileaks' intentions were naïve at best, disingenuous at worst. They had the net effect of creating the impression that governments are the main opponents to freedom, diverting attention from the position that the underlying dilemma is the deliberately anti-democratic operation of capital. This sat neatly alongside conservative neo-liberal policy – the very policies that created things like deregulated media markets, leading to the very information monopolies that Wikileaks ostensibly set out to challenge (Fuchs, 2013). For that reason, it was not surprising at all that Wikileaks had partnered with established media businesses to make its revelations about Iraq and Afghanistan. At base, they shared the same business philosophy: to get governments out of the way and let markets do their thing. Whatever we might make of this argument, it certainly chimed with one of the main topics of the original leaks, the growing influence of business in all fields of public life (represented by the privatization of defence). It was possible, then, that Wikileaks reinforced established geographies of political power, where the ideal world imagined was one that was driven by businesses and markets.

However, the disagreements over what Wikileaks represented emerged through coherent research principles on the nature of causality. Scholars agreed that Wikileaks was a significant historical moment (Heemsbergen, 2013), but largely because it complicated the idea of transparency. The only thing that was certain was that the event had demonstrated the delicate balance between facts, interpretation and argument. The helicopter attack, and the actions of the many people who recorded and leaked the information about what had happened, were matters of fact. But the significance of this information depended on how it was processed and released. Clearly, the meaning of this evidence was shaped by the people and institutions which made these events facts that the public cared about – their motives, their working conventions, and the relationships they established with other people and organizations. All of these factors were just as important as – if not more so than – the digital technologies that recorded and released news of the killings.

It is crucial to note that these observations represented historical thinking, thus underlining the status of media studies as a humanities discipline that seeks to complicate matters of causation. In fact, the Wikileaks story reflected in critical historical approaches to the analysis of empire. Indeed, one can argue that the academic study of the effects of media technologies began in the effort to understand how empires started, prospered and decayed.

Wikileaks, history and media studies: Understanding change from a humanities perspective

The 'truth' of Wikileaks changed according to the facts one observed. The task before media scholars was not simply to collect evidence, but also to frame it within different perspectives. This is where they stood to learn a thing or two from historians.

For the last 50 years, many historians have been particularly clear that their discipline does not limit itself to determining the facts of the past. For one thing, reconstructing the past is always an interpretative affair, because facts do not speak for themselves and are usually incomplete. Sometimes, as Elkins had discovered, they are deliberately concealed, and this leads to a second important point: history is deeply implicated in political debates about the past, present and future. Here, studies of Empire have been used to consider general methods for combining facts and analysis in explanations for social progress – or, indeed, systemic forces that block this progress. Eventually, the histories of empires have devoted considerable attention to communication. In this way, for all its focus on new technologies and social networks, the Wikileaks episode belonged in the history of Empire, and the procedures through which that story developed.

When E. H. Carr asked *What is History?* in 1961, he intended to map general principles of inquiry that crossed the humanities and social sciences. 'Empire' coloured several aspects of Carr's thinking. Carr asserted that facts are not pure discoveries, but also the product of considered academic labour. This is because events and facts are not the same thing. Facts are phenomena that can be processed into convincing accounts of why things happen. This observation grounded a distinctive understanding of causation. Historians are tasked with making coherence from chaos, of sifting through masses of elliptical information to discern drivers of social and political change. This was the task that led to the error of determinism. Faced with a flood of evidence, some historians were tempted to see their job as being to explain how society had progressed, and they chose their facts accordingly. This was most apparent in British imperial history. Among 19th-century British historians, Carr noted a troubling tendency to treat past events as if they were building blocks in a story of civilization. These historians took the unprecedented prosperity of the Empire as proof that history told how the world became civilized. This was another sort of grand narrative that slid easily into intellectual lethargy. It prevented scholars from reflecting on the significance of documented incidents as events that happened in their own right, and from looking for alternative interpretations of why they should be remembered.

Carr penned these thoughts during the Kenyan state of emergency, just as a long, painstaking revision of what Britain 'knew' about its actions in that conflict got underway. The story of how this revision was achieved graphically illustrated the value of Carr's observations about using evidence to understand causation, and also shows how the issue of how information is recorded, kept and moved became a matter of historical interest.

In the early 1960s, stories of the savage punishments meted out by colonial forces began to emerge (Clough, 1998). So, historians set about discovering the facts of the Emergency; numbers of Mau Mau killed, numbers of so-called 'Loyalists' brutalized by Mau Mau, and the numbers of innocent Kikuyu imprisoned. They also investigated less visible effects, such as the impact of the conflict on fertility rates (Elkins, 2011).

Bare facts were certainly vital. In Carr's day, the Kenyan Emergency was seen as a regrettable vignette in the period of decolonization that nevertheless bequeathed the principles of good governance and democracy to Africa (Clough, 1998). Most historians had reckoned that around 15,000 Kikuyu had been detained during the Emergency. Then, in 2009, a High Court ruling granted Caroline Elkins access to almost 9,000 documents that had been previously hidden in a secret archive at Hanslope Park. The records meticulously recorded increasingly savage 'counter-insurgency' measures, taken against Mau Mau and other anti-British forces in Malaysia, Cyprus and Aden. These included crimes such as roasting a Mau Mau suspect alive. By the time the documents were discovered, it was feared that they were the tip of a bloody iceberg, much of the evidence having been simply destroyed (Cobain, Bowcott and Norton-Taylor, 2012).

Based on these records, Elkins calculated the detention figure at better than 300,000 (2006, 2011). Similarly, civilian casualties had been vastly underestimated. Add into that the thousands of Kenyans who had never been born, because women were deprived of food and their partners, and we are left with an engineered abuse of human rights that places the Emergency alongside other atrocities that have been subjected to judicial review and restorative justice procedures: South Africa, the former Yugoslavia, Rwanda and even the Nuremberg trials of Nazi mass murderers (Elkins, 2011). Elkins' figures put the British Empire in the dock, accused of knowingly committing one of the great human rights abuses of the 20th century.

That said, Elkins was keen to point out that her work followed in the anti-determinist tradition outlined by Carr. Attacked for exaggerating her numbers, Elkins countered that the problems of keeping records in colonial conflicts, combined with official efforts to conceal what records were kept, made purely empirical history impossible. In this, numbers were simply indicators of cultural patterns and relationships. Her point was that the story of Empire was produced by complex, often contradictory systems for managing people and resources, and equally complex systems of recording and storing the details of that management. More importantly still, Elkins discovered that historical revisionism necessitated engaging with the question of how cultures stored and managed the information that was the raw material for the stories they told.

So, there were indeed compelling connections between the Mau Mau and the *Collateral Murder* incidents, in that both were about Empire *and* the politics of information management. Imperial history was, it seemed, a matter of communication. However, this point had been made a long time ago, in the work of Harold Innis.

Historical revisionism and media studies: Harold Innis, media technology and economic history

Innis was ideally suited to revisionist history of empires and communication technology. A Canadian economic historian, Innis had responded to the call of the British Empire by enlisting in the Great War. He joined the artillery and, at the battle of Vimy Ridge, saw firsthand how new communication technologies helped eviscerate people. He entered post-war life, then ill-disposed towards tales of imperial glory and technological utopia (Watson, 2008). His book *Empire and Communication* (Innis, 2007) defined the economic history of the British Empire as the epitome of history's defining question: How did civilization progress? This was because that Empire operated according to the unprecedented integration of business interests, communication and military intervention and, as such, offered considerable lessons for how 20th-century society was likely to progress, given the growth of global businesses and media.

Innis's sophisticated grasp of the relationship between material facts and culture connected causation issues in history and communications studies. Innis argued that empires depended on geographically-based systems of commercial production. Any understanding of Canada's imperial role, for example, had to start with its network of lake, river and sea access that facilitated certain patterns of economic activity. The pursuit of Empire began with communication, defined as the movement of people and goods (Innis, 2007). The goal of this communication was to maximize the economic potential of raw materials, and this in turn led to particular forms of political organization. The former could be described through facts about the production of commodities. The latter could not.

Innis's argument avoided determinism by making the case that the reality of geography was processed by the forces of institutions and culture. Innis explained the connection between physical, media communication and Empire in the following way. The *foundation* of Empire lay in the ability to exploit geographic advantage through the production and movement of commodities. The *durability* of those empires depended on the concomitant technologies for recording and circulating information. However, the essential problem of communication, *vis-à-vis* its relationship to democracy, was that the commodity status of information rendered it a relatively disposable phenomenon. Media communication was an extension of commodity production, which meant that communication was primarily driven by the search for markets – as opposed to any notion of democracy, or public value. So part of the commercial design of media was to make information obsolete as quickly as possible. Hence, the success of newspapers in the 19th and 20th centuries was substantially explained by the development of the paper industry, better transport, faster printing and success in cultivating an appetite for news among new audiences.

Innis's argument changed how one of the earliest forms of journalistic whistleblowing would be understood. The American 'muckraking' tradition of the late 19th and early 20th centuries made its name through a determined effort to expose political corruption in the US's burgeoning industrial cities. Scholars of the form have debated the extent to which the practice was driven by moral or economic motives (Endres, 1978; Reaves, 1984; Thornton, 1995). Innis concluded that the latter was an important consideration. Tales of urban corruption might be good for society's soul, but they were also good for the paper and newspaper industries, whose increased production capacities demanded the quicker turnover of product. One of the driving forces behind journalism was the desire to make information – and the paper it was printed on – obsolete. It was this that encouraged more aggressive forms of journalism that literally 'made' news by looking for scandal that would embarrass the powerful. In other words, investigative journalism was arguably a by-product of private wealth accumulation – as Fuchs (2011) was later to claim regarding Wikileaks.

Understanding empires and their media as phenomena that grew from the production and circulation of commodities led Innis to reject conventional imperial history. His rejection was coterminous with another common-sense view about new media. Innis believed that the development of communication technologies had led to an obsession with 'space' that had created a crisis for western civilizations. Once we consider economic evidence connecting print culture, commodity production and the exploitation of markets, conventional thought on the relation between print and democracy were problematized. Certainly, the growth of printing could be associated with the development of national identities that played key roles in colonial independence movements. However, the development of printing businesses, especially the press, and the constant demand for 'new' information and scandals actually inhibited the capacity for productive critical thought. The speed of news production, especially on conflict and war, stoked appetites for excitement that mitigated careful policy consideration. The migration of reading publics from book to newspaper mirrored the thirst for information turnover that compromised the capacity for critical thinking. The book, in Innis's view, was far better at preserving valuable ideas through time, whereas newspapers depended on making the knowledge obsolete.

This led Innis to perhaps his most startling conclusion. The history of Empire suggested that advances in communication were hostile to civilization. The printing press, the photograph and the radio established new possibilities for exploitation and instability based on media cultures where information and stories were here one minute and gone the next. Democracy and beliefs in freedom of speech were illusions. The ability to deliver information and images about the world as it happened created an impression of 'being informed', emphasizing the moment and the individual. This distracted attention away from how certain groups of people tended to exploit other groups of people. In essence, Innis's study of Empire ended in a dystopian view of media. Considering Nazism's exploitation of radio as a hate medium, he concluded that if there was any 'grand narrative' in the history of communication and civilization, it was that mechanizations and commerce worked together to make it difficult to sustain progress through time (Innis, 2008).

Apocalyptic conclusion as this was, Innis's work complimented Carr's attempt to turn history into a general model for humanities research, and established a tangible connection between this project and media studies. Historical explanation was a matter of thinking about the interactions among the state, culture and technology, and ultimately this became about communication: first, the movement of people and goods, and second, the media that were used to store and transmit information in forms that affected how it was possible to think about reality. Here, the facts of the material world entered into a relationship with the institutions that managed it. Modes of storing, transmitting and processing knowledge actively shaped how reality was understood. It was this *relationship* that determined the progress of civilization as it faced the challenges of time and space. Certainly, changing media technologies had innate qualities, which Innis termed 'biases'. Some media were especially good at preserving records through time, stone tablets being one. Others were better suited to the challenges of space. The telegraph, for example, made it possible to think about the USA as a nation because of its ability to create real-time communication over vast distances. The outcomes of these innate qualities, however, were subject to political intervention, and this is where the 'better technology causes better society' logic broke down (Innis, 2008).

Certainly, Innis's observations helped to explain some of the more puzzling aspects of the Wikileaks story, as well as underlining the purpose of comparing it to Elkin's work on Kenya. The relative lack of public reaction to *Collateral Murder* could be explained by the speed of information turnover, driven by 24-hour news cycles and the capacity of the US state to rapidly build a counter-narrative. From an Innis perspective, this spoke to the space bias of digital media – easy to transmit quickly far and wide, hard to maintain as an authoritative account of what had happened. Perhaps this is why Elkin's work arguably had more of an impact, securing a large compensation payout and an admission from Britain that its authority had been systematically misused. Empire's paper-based records were easy to hide and destroy, but they remained present in a large physical archive, there to be discovered. The idea that they had been kept and hidden for so long indicated their gravity, and they had also been processed through academic and judicial processes (historians and the courts which ruled on the compensation case), not commercial media systems. Hence the biases of time/space and the different modes of processing information partly explained the different outcomes of the stories that were both about violence enacted on occupied peoples.

Innis, economic history and the internet

Innis's pessimism is apparent in contemporary dystopian writing on digital media and democracy. In *The Net Delusion* (2011), Eyvgeny Morozov returned to the importance of thinking about media influence historically, as a means of avoiding the trap of technological determinism. Morozov criticized cyber utopians – people who thought that the ability to access and send huge amounts of information quickly and cheaply could only be a good thing – for linking the present-day uses of new media with their inherent capacities. A glance at history underlined how little present-day features revealed about media futures. Television, for example, was hailed as a democratic boon not only because it could address a mass audience simultaneously and show them a world beyond their experience, but also because its original expense brought people together. In the early days of the medium, the television's status as a luxury item meant that owners would often invite neighbours over to watch. In the 1950s, television was about knowledge and community. The proliferation of entertainment content and multi-screen homes soon antiquated that vision.

Morozov noted that hopes for digital media mirrored similar sentiments about the telegraph, radio and television – all were welcomed as agents of peace and equity, as all held the potential to carry the truth to more people than ever before. And these claims all looked ridiculous today. This was because the impact of technologies could not be divorced from their uses and management. Radio, for example, had been used to inflame and sooth political passions. Morozov pointed out that 'the age of radio was not only the age of Roosevelt and Churchill but also of Hitler, Mussolini and Stalin' (2011, 292).

Like Innis, though, Morozov's cyber scepticism was not a form of negative determinism that replaced the idea that technologies would make the world a better place with the alternative – that they never did. Rather, his argument was that any discussion of media impact had to take into account the full suite of forces that filled the gap between what technologies could be and what they are. It was not that the capacities of technologies were irrelevant or neutral. It was more that it was a mistake to place technology at the centre of human history. The error of technological determinism was historical in two ways. First, it was, implicitly, an historical claim. The idea was that history was driven forward by machines, or at least that there was nothing to be done about this. Second, this was used as an excuse to avoid analysing key moral and political questions. Technologies offer affordances – things that could be used in specific ways given the right circumstances. The task, then, was to examine how media impact became real when those affordances were unpacked by people, institutions, organizations and networks. Morozov ended his book in a remarkably optimistic way: 'That technologies may fail to achieve the objectives their proponents intended should not distract us from analysing the desirability of these agendas' (2011, 297). At any rate, Morozov's updating of Innis's thoughts demonstrated once again the common need in history and media research to develop a cultural understanding of change with a clear sense of engagement with the political nature of both subjects.

CONCLUSION: USING TECHNOLOGY TO DEVELOP AN HISTORICAL AND CULTURAL MODEL OF MEDIA CHANGE

This chapter has shown how to develop a cultural model of causation by framing media studies as a form of historical thinking. Historical thinking has the following characteristics.

First, it appreciates that facts do not speak for themselves. This is because history is about interpretation; questions of why things happen are just as important as what happens. It is also because 'facts' are produced through pro-cesses of labour involving the storing and processing of information via particular sorts of procedures and media. This is why history and media studies are conjoined subjects.

Second, historical thinking appreciates that the world moves forward through the complicated interaction of nature and culture. The basic needs for sustenance and community are structured by physical environments, and the many different ways in which humans transform these environments direct these general needs towards specific interests. This has always been a matter of communication – the movement of goods, people and ideas.

Third, there is a close relationship between economic interests and the com-munication processes through which humans understand their reality. It is not to say that the economy determines how we see the world, but it is to say that there is strong evidence to suggest that stories of abuse, corruption and political intrigue are significantly affected by the simple need for turnover in markets. This is very important when considering the validity of claims that digital media have had a positive effect on global democracy, which cannot be resisted.

Fourth, it is important to remember that scholarship exists within these same parameters. Carr criticized 19th-century British historians for uncritically accepting the common-sense perspective of the day that the Empire had been good for everyone. Early 21st-century research on colonial violence in Kenya proved how wrong this thinking had been. This is relevant to media studies because technologically determinist cyber utopianism exists as the same sort of threat. It is easy to find evidence that social media and the like help oppressed people, but this is not evidence of an inexorable historical progression. Digital media only do things when they are used by groups of people in organized ways, and, just as with the Empire, not everyone shares the benefits of global media. The academic task at hand is to explore the economic, social and cultural forces that turn the potential of media into a lived reality. Ironically, effective media studies begins by placing media to one side. The operating question of the disci-pline is: How are media involved in the cultivation of social equality? This question is political and historical before it is technological.

The Wikileaks case indicates the value of adding a deeper historical angle to the consideration of the affordances of digital media cultures. Its significance is underlined when it is positioned not just as an instance of media impact, but as the successor in a line of thinking on Empire and progress. This is all the more so since it was on the topic of Empire and communication that the discipline received its earliest research lessons on the relationship between material economic facts and cultural activities.

On the other hand, it is also true that communication and media have long been drivers in the development of Empire, and by virtue of that a significant element in the development of social equity. Putting all of this together, media research is about using evidence and theoretical frameworks to explain how technologies, individuals, governments, businesses and other cultural groups interact to produce significant political outcomes. Here, it is important to remember that this is a task that never truly ends. Carr argued that progress is measured not by the ability to get things right, but by the capacity to produce ever more sophisticated explanations for why things happen, which serves as a useful foundation for future research and political discussions about moral values in social life. The moral position of research is pursued further in the next chapter, on ethics.

CHAPTER SUMMARY

- All media research has a model of causation, that is, basic precepts about how media make things happen.

- A cultural approach to media influence demands a multifaceted model, where media are positioned as motivating ingredients in historical developments.

- Supporting this idea, historians have identified communication as an agent of historical change. This is clearly seen in studies of empires.

- Contemporary studies of digital whistleblowing demonstrate how the subjects of media studies and history converge around practices of collecting, storing, communicating and narrating information.

4

PRACTISING ETHICS IN MEDIA RESEARCH

OBJECTIVE: APPRECIATING THE SOCIAL BENEFIT OF RESEARCH

This chapter explores the topic of research ethics, in order to outline how social responsibility operates as a value in media studies. The purpose is to show that good research knows how it benefits society; we can identify this as a third pillar of quality work.

The issue of social responsibility forces us to reflect on *who* media studies is for, and in what follows research ethics and privacy are used to describe how conversations about social responsibility have evolved in the discipline. For many of us, our academic responsibility becomes especially relevant when we study media users. Evidence about how people use media is readily available in public and semi-public spaces. But it isn't always clear whether we can or should use it, due to privacy concerns. Academics disagree over how public things like online comments really are, and this has major effects on ethics procedures. However, this chapter argues that concerns about the privacy of media users risk obscuring other ethical questions. We should be just as concerned with the rights of non-users; people whom we rarely encounter because they have little access to media. The rights of people who aren't in media research are also an important ethical consideration.

These ideas are illustrated in four stages:

- First, the chapter outlines inherent tensions between conventional ethical requirements and the practicalities of studying media culture, through a discussion of challenges in researching 'live' media events.
- Second, it explains how these difficulties have multiplied with the advent of online and mobile media.
- Third, the chapter considers how privacy concerns clash with values of social responsibility, explaining situations where it is defensible to cause discomfort to research participants.

(Continued)

- Finally, using the work of media anthropologist S. Elizabeth Bird, we consider the view that the most compelling ethical requirement of media academics is to consider the rights of 'invisible' people who can't use media.

The outcome is to add content to ethics debates. That is, ethics isn't simply a matter of understanding and following research protocols, but also about taking a critical view on the political purpose of research in the first place.

MEDIA AND ETHICS: KEY TENSIONS BETWEEN RESEARCH ETHICS AND THE PRACTICE OF MEDIA RESEARCH

Ethical procedures ensure that research serves a social purpose without inflicting unnecessary harm. Research is ethical if it respects human rights, produces results that help people, and serves justice (Horner and Minifie, 2011; Markham and Buchanan, 2012). Unfortunately, these criteria sometimes clash.

Media research ethics are complicated by three things. First, universal guidelines are impossible (Couldry, 2013). Second, the ones that we have were developed in experimental science, and frequently do not suit non-experimental settings (Horner and Minifie, 2011; Buchanan, 2012). Third, the advent of online and mobile communication complicates things still further, since it is not clear whether the material we find there are 'texts' written by producers who want to be heard or representations of human subjects who expect privacy even if their thoughts can be seen (Erdos, 2012; Markham and Buchanan, 2012; Neuhaus and Webmoor, 2012). Consequently, media research provides fertile ground for debating the purpose of ethics: Who are they there to protect, and how is this to be achieved?

Privacy is therefore a powerful sensitizing concept in considering media influence. Where privacy is paramount in ethics, the presence of media changes how we define what privacy is in the first place (McRobbie and Garber, 1978; Hine, 2000; Erdos, 2012; Ruddock, 2013a). Our media habits might feel personal, but history demurs. Newspapers and radio brought crowds together (Butsch, 2008). Teens in the 1930s loved film because cinemas were places where they could get together without adult supervision (Jowett, Jarvie and Fuller, 1996). Talk show television works because it allows its fans to feel connected to onscreen audiences (Wood, 2005). Being 'public', it seems, has long been an appealing aspect of media consumption. It is unsurprising, then, that Hine (2000) argued that one of the internet's primary effects has been to cultivate greater consciousness about the social dimensions of using media.

Online and mobile media have made public aspects of media consumption more explicit. This brings many benefits to media researchers. Their goal is to enhance social inclusion by mediating the voices of media users. Compared to a generation ago, it is far easier to hear these voices today. Social media, for instance, is full of public commentary and the sharing of media content. This creates instant databanks of public thought that are right there for us to use.

On the other hand, it isn't entirely clear who these voices belong to, what they represent, or how they can be ethically handled. These data are aggregated by commercial operations for business purposes (Neuhaus and Webmoor, 2012). According to the agreed terms of usage in some of these platforms, social media content is the property of media industries (Meikle and Young, 2012). Then, even though people know on some level that their social media words are more or less public, there is the question of whether they fully understand what this really means (Elms, 2009). And finally, of course, the only people who get to express themselves via social media are the people who have access to it. So the public aspects of media consumption complicate matters of privacy and informed consent. To unpack this, let's think about an example of a research topic that encapsulates crucial dimensions of media influence, and then explore why it is difficult to follow ethical principles in studying it.

CASE STUDY: ETHICAL CHALLENGES IN RESEARCHING LIVE EVENTS

In July 2014, Malaysian Airlines flight MH17 was shot down over Ukraine, killing 300 people. News of the crash broke around 5.30 a.m. Australian time, just as breakfast news programmes got underway. I saw it across a bank of screens in a gym. As is my habit, I was glancing between sets while listening to my own music, when it suddenly became clear that something was terribly wrong. Each set was tuned to a different channel, but suddenly all carried the same images. Flashing subtitles told of a major air disaster. I tuned in to the commentary as the story developed at breakneck pace. Within minutes, newsreaders reported that the aircraft had been downed by a missile, probably fired by pro-Russian Ukrainian rebels.

The scene dramatized complex processes of mediated reality. The story was being assembled live, on air. A security expert on the Australian Broadcasting Corporation warned that it was premature to decide what had happened, a point of view that jarred with reports of social media boasts from Ukrainian rebels claiming responsibility. Tweets preceded official comments from the airline, or from government officials from Malaysia, the Netherlands or Australia, the nations which had lost most citizens in the disaster. The work of news, the processes showing how reality is made by moulding information into narrative, was there for all to see. But how were the gym-goers making sense of it all?

One of the screens remained fixed on celebrity news on the 'E' Channel. I wondered whether anyone was still watching it. Were some of my fellow runners oblivious to what was before their eyes? Was the choice deliberate? What about people who were still listening to music or catching up with emails? Was this because they were too engrossed in their customary morning repertoires to notice ground-breaking events happening elsewhere in the media sphere? Where they deliberately avoiding what looked like yet another distressing story about air travel in an especially anxiety-inducing period on that topic?

Moments like this capture the essence of media influence: 'spontaneous' animations of elaborate media architectures built around social occasions. The MH17 story reflected many ideas. It was an unsettling example of 'live' television in action. According to Bourdon (2000), television is at its most powerful when it gives audiences the impression that they are viewing history, culture and the world in action – 'live', as it were. This credibility in turn depends on the ability to surprise. Usually, television delivers polished and predictable professional content. But, now and again, it is there to witness chaos reign. Audiences love it when a politician is caught in a lie, or provoked into losing their cool by an aggressive journalist, and such incidents become entertaining (Ruddock, 2007). They thrill when performances unravel – a singer falls over on stage, a reality TV star is outed as a fake. But MH17 offered a different perspective on what 'live' can mean to the media's social function, because it dissembled customary media practices among professionals and audiences alike.

Here, 'liveness' connected with media's 'ritual' function (Couldry, 2003). Ritual, and its connection to mediatization, is a complicated idea that will continue to be unpacked through the book. But to begin with, media rituals can be defined as ordinary user habits that secure media industries' authority to define reality (Couldry, 2003). Audiences do not believe everything that media say, but accept that they need media industries to be able to think about the world at all. Trust is cultivated through daily 'consumption rituals', habitual daily practices where media are used in ways to lend life an order of routine and security (Silverstone, 1994; Sumiala, 2012). 'Liveness', or the unexpected, is ironically guaranteed through rituals, since they ensure that social life brings regular exposure to media content.

More recently, these ideas have been developed through the concept of mediatization. Mediatization is an idea that tries to come to terms with the myriad effects of 'omnipresent' media that multiply the places where the boundaries between social and media experience vanish (Hjarvard, 2012). Occasions when we become the audience for mediated disasters in non-media places are a case in point.

The MH17 episode provided an opportunity to observe these processes in action, in real time. Coming to terms with a world-changing disaster while going about familiar 'start of the day' routines exemplified what Hepp (2013) labelled 'indirect mediatization', the phenomenon where we absorb media narratives while doing something else in 'non-media' places. Hepp's example is fast food. To get to a burger, these days you often have to wade first through a tide of commercial blockbuster film tie-ins. Although eating remains the main activity, eating in the company of media symbols changes the feel of the meal. The idea that media alter the meaning of social habits across a range of settings, and that this represents the most pervasive form of media influence, is the essence of what mediatization offers as a new perspective (Hjarvard, 2013).

With MH17, the mediatization panorama linked 'liveness' and rituals to familiar effects topics, such as fear and user strategies for avoiding confronting content. The idea that exposure to stories about real-world risks can provoke disproportionate fear of victimization has been studied for many years (e.g. Gerbner et al., 1979). Current research examines how viewers judge the applicability of onscreen danger to their own situations (e.g. Custers and Van den Bulck, 2013). The differing impacts of intentional and unintentional news exposure have also been interrogated (Van den Bulck, 2006). The latter interest emerges from the analysis of selective viewing, the idea that any concerns about the power of media messages has to be tempered against the control that audiences exercise over what they consume (Van den Bulck, 1995).

All of these issues appeared on a 'mediatized' gym floor. Athlete audiences were confronted with a distressing news story. Yet they also had a range of editing options to manage the situation. Practices of fear and avoidance, previously exercised while 'doing' media in the home, now came into play while 'doing' something else, elsewhere, and this here was an index of how conventional sorts of media effects and practices came to have a public life. So there's little doubt that this was a legitimate research site. The trouble was that researching it there and then would have been unethical.

The practicalities of doing live research ethically

Had I wished to proceed with this study, I would have had to adhere to the Australian National Health and Medical Research Council's *National Statement on Ethical Conduct in Human Research* (NHMRC, 2014). This document established protocols for interacting with people and vetting processes for the project design stage. The determining factor is whether the project has 'merit', which is assessed according to six criteria:

1. Contributing to knowledge and well-being.

2. Using appropriate methods.

3. Is based on questions that have a grounding in established literature.

4. Respects the well-being of participants.

5. Is conducted by people with appropriate experience.

6. Is conducted in appropriate settings.

The proposed MH17 study would have run into trouble on number 4. Respect requires considering 'the privacy, confidentiality and cultural sensitivities of the participants' (NHMRC, 2014, 11). Doing this means considering the possibility that the research might cause 'harm or discomfort or inconvenience', as well as assessing 'the severity of the harm, including its consequences' (NHMRC, 2014, 12). Applying these criteria to this research would have been very difficult. It was reasonable to assume that some of the viewers may have been distressed by what they were seeing – some might even have been worrying about loved ones who were travelling on that day. Or others might simply have objected to being something of a captive audience – rooted to treadmills and bikes, lacking 'opt-out' opportunities. Immediate data collection could have led to an ethics complaint. Since the complaint would have related to universal ethical requirements (NHMRC standards on privacy are very similar to those of the UK's Economic and Social Research Council [ESRC]; see Charlesworth, 2012), then these lessons probably apply to you as well.

Ethics, then, catch media researchers in a paradox. Mediatization creates data everywhere. Faced with challenges of time and money, technology has made media research easier. However, the conditions that have created these opportunities also prevent us from using them. Mediatization research will always be hard to square with conventional ethics, because it does not lend itself to pre-vetting. So, how have media researchers navigated these challenges?

Understanding conventional ethics requirements

The Association of Internet Research (AoIR) has drafted principles for translating conventional ethics to the particularities of media research, alongside leading a debate on the importance of recognizing where these two fields are incommensurate (Markham and Buchanan, 2012). So it is crucial to appreciate the origins of conventional ethics, and how the concerns its procedures envisaged are quite different from the things that media researchers worry about.

Horner and Minifie's (2011) review of the topic underlined that ethics are a subset of the more general commitment to responsible research:

> The commitment and integrity of researchers – and all who participate in the research enterprise – to the norms of science, who by engaging in systematic, responsible practices while proposing, performing, evaluating, and reporting research contribute to an accurate, worthwhile, and enduring scientific record. (2011, 304)

According to this, 'ethics' requires 'responsibility' at every part of the research process, from project design, to the research itself, and to the writing up and revision of results. It is important, then, not to let the notion of responsibility that develops in one part of this research process overshadow the responsibilities implied at other times.

This is worth bearing in mind when we consider the kind of discomfort participants in media research projects are likely to encounter. Most of the time, they fall a long way from the physical and psychological damage that institutionalized research ethics intend to prevent. The move towards universalized standards for responsible research followed the Nuremberg Nazi trials, which revealed details about intentional suffering inflicted upon patients during forced experiments (Markham and Buchanan, 2012). These truly evil practices were uncomfortably relevant to other research endeavours, because non-consensual research was quite common in the United States in the middle of the 20th century. Vulnerable groups – children, the mentally ill and the poor – were exposed to or refused treatment for serious illnesses and diseases, based on the argument that such practices could be justified in the name of medical progress. The most infamous example was the Tuskegee Syphilis study, where, over a 40-year period, African American men were deliberately denied treatment for the syphilis they had contracted so that doctors could observe the natural progression of the disease (Horner and Minifie, 2011; Buchanan, 2012). Many ethics protocols that media researchers must follow were developed to prevent such calculated abuse.

Psychological experimentation that manipulated emotional states could also hurt research participants, and it is in this area that the idea of 'harm' most applies to media research. Horner and Minifie's review cites Stanley Milgram's 1960s obedience experiments as a defining moment. Milgram tested the power of authority through an experiment that involved participants giving electrical shocks to others when ordered to do so. In reality the shocks were not real, and the victims, who could be heard screaming, were in league with the researchers. But the people dishing out the shocks did not know this, and it isn't hard to imagine that the participants might have ended up feeling guilty about their actions. The subtext of the study was that Milgram was searching for the conditions that explained how ordinary people could have become involved in Nazi atrocities (Babbie, 1990). The knowledge that one exhibited traits of fascist war criminals could hardly have sat comfortably on people's shoulders.

Gaming researchers have also done experiments that tried to make gamers feel guilty. Hartmann, Toz and Brandon (2010) designed a study where violence in video games prompted moral introspection. Subjects were asked to play one of two roles in a first person shooter (FPS) game. Some were United Nations (UN) soldiers, rescuing innocent civilians from a death camp run by paramilitaries. Others played guards whose job it was to kill the peacekeepers and keep the hostages. Participants were then surveyed for guilt, to see if killing bad people to free the good was less upsetting than killing heroes and punishing the innocent. The ethics of this project would have considered the benefits of the outcomes set against the possibility that the research could have disturbed participants. So there are times when concepts of harm that drove the post-war codification of ethics do apply to media research.

Considerable controversy has emerged over how far this thinking applies to qualitative studies. Take studies of the things that people say online. Lipinsky (2008) argued that although the translation of online comments into published research could cause embarrassment or distress, this discomfort is unlikely to ever reach a legally actionable level – at least in the USA. Research of online communities involves gathering information from publicly available resources. It involves no form of deception on the behalf of the researcher – the comments are there for all to see – and it is reasonable to expect that people who provide such content know that anyone on the internet can see their words. Much as publications resulting from this study might embarrass, it is reasonable to assume that the research is done in good faith, and preventing publication would act against the public interest by inhibiting academic free speech (Lipinsky, 2008). Convenient as this argument is, it is unlikely to withstand scrutiny under all circumstances. It rests heavily on the notion that online comments exist in public spaces. Media academics accept that this cannot always be assumed. So let us consider the grounds for Lipinsky's position, and how it became complicated in efforts to arrange discipline-appropriate ethical procedures.

Hine (2000) provided a compelling analysis of how the internet emerged as a public space in the late 1990s, in her analysis of online activism around the notorious Louise Woodward case. Woodward was a teenage British Nanny convicted of the involuntary manslaughter of Matthew Eapenn, an infant in her care. Initially convicted of murder, Woodward was released when the trial judge set aside the jury verdict, replaced it with an involuntary manslaughter conviction, and sentenced the teen to time served. In a world first, the verdict was released online.

Hine thought the case was a defining moment in the internet's emergence as a medium of public communication. An emotive story about the death of a child energized an intense public desire for debate, and was the first event of its kind to fuel significant online community commentary. 'Unofficial' newsgroups worked alongside official websites to debate different elements of the case, in discussions that tried to affect public agendas. Here was an early instance of how online audiences produced content that contributed to public narratives through the provision of comments that were meant to be read. These activities consciously competed against the authority of professional journalism. People who offered their thoughts wanted others to talk about them. This is the sort of situation that Lipinsky's argument assumed.

But the Woodward case study did not represent all online actions. After a decade of reconciling different international privacy conventions, the AoIR decided that no one-size-fits-all international standard is ever likely to emerge about the publicness of online comments (Markham and Buchanan, 2012). Lipinsky's argument glossed over the semi-public nature of much online communication. For example, many online communities are openly accessible but also require membership and registration for participation. This creates a 'community' feel where users might assume that their comments are mostly being read by *sympaticos*. Such content might be public, but ethical researchers need to consider whether it feels public to those who post (Erdos, 2009). Consequently, the ethics of accessing data, and the people who produce it, has to be negotiated on a case-by-case basis.

WHO IS MEDIA RESEARCH FOR?

The key to these negotiations is being clear about larger ethical ideals. Being ethical does not mean seeking approval for the arguments that you make. Some kinds of discomfort that research conclusions might cause are defensible.

Suppose someone says something during a study that you have reason to think they would prefer remained secret. But suppose that comment *is* relevant to the public benefit of the work that you are doing. Should you report it? This is the predicament that Barker (1997) faced while researching fans of the sci-fi *Judge Dredd* comics.

Barker asked readers to explain on cassette tape why they liked the character and then send the recordings to him. Listening back, he was disturbed to hear one of his respondents badge himself as a fascist. *Judge Dredd* is a story about a bleak post-nuclear world where 'Judges' are paramilitaries with licences to kill. Most people understand the story as a dystopian one, but 'David' explained to Barker that it represented a future that he hoped for. This was because he was a fascist who thought life would be better if 'deviants' could be exterminated.

David had taken the time to help Barker with his study. He probably did not understand that Barker's purpose was to explain how popular culture is politically significant. The hesitancy on the tape showed he knew that 'fascist' is an offensive label to wear. So what was the researcher to do? Contact David and ask him to explain further? Throw the data away, or use it?

Barker decided to publish his account, because he believed that the 'truth' it revealed counted more than the upset it might cause. 'David', of course, was a pseudonym, and although he would recognize himself in the published work, it was unlikely that anyone else would. More to the point, Barker felt obliged to challenge David's view. There is, he reasoned, a distinction between respecting audiences and being on their side. Popular culture is a 'place' where we encounter and evaluate important ideas about how the world is, and how it should be. Its users must be taken seriously. Taking them seriously involves exploring the logic of their thoughts, treating them as rational (in so far as they are 'reasoned' in some sense), but then also holding people accountable for what they say. To *not* publish the data would have been an ethical failure in terms of Barker's social responsibility. Media narratives establish a way of seeing the world that does not end when the comic book is shut. David's fascist tendencies were articulated through *Dredd*. They were not caused by the stories, and so did not disappear when he was going about the rest of his day. Consequently, the notion that research should benefit society compelled publication. It was ethically important to confront David, and this outweighed the risk of embarrassment (Barker, 1997).

It is thought provoking that audience-centred amnesia about the meaning of mid-20th-century fascism has featured in other discussions on what respecting audiences means. In a study of German heavy metal fans, Roccor (2000) disturbingly discovered that listeners were keen to avoid the clear racism of a song called 'Turks Go Home'. In a rather self-serving explanation, the fans interpreted the song, written at a time of increased hostility being directed against Turkish communities in Germany, as little more than an index of heavy metals' desire to provoke and shock, as if this had nothing to do with previous uses of popular culture to direct hatred towards certain communities. It is one thing to accept their accounts as evidence that racism in media does not always work in the same way, but quite another to accept as a fact that the song did not contribute in any way to the rise of anti-immigrant feeling in Europe at the time. So it is socially responsible to ask whether there is something disingenuous about these views, even if the people who voice them object (Ruddock, 2007).

Responsible research, then, might provoke discomfort. And this is not confined to those relatively rare occasions where audiences more or less knowingly sympathize with fascist and racist sentiments. Shortly, we are going to consider the work of media anthropologist S. Elizabeth Bird. One of Bird's convictions is that media researchers have spent too much time validating the pleasure of popular culture. Bird's concern was that the explanations of how audiences find cultural value slide too easily into apologies that dodge tricky political questions. A telling example is the peculiar phenomenon of Second World War-themed weddings in London. In the very city where thousands were eviscerated by Nazi bombs, it is now possible to wed dressed in Second World War uniforms and walk down the aisle to the sound of air raid sirens. To Bird, this typifies how the endless recycling and reappropriation of narratives about that war have sanitized a near-apocalypse into a nostalgic object. Such practices represented an alarming evacuation of politics – an escape facilitated by the pleasures of popular storytelling. Celebrating or exaggerating the significance of such practices is irresponsible (Bird, 2011).

So someone decides to dress up like a pilot and marry his partner to an air raid soundtrack. Why isn't this just poor taste? Meikle and Young (2012) provide an answer in their reading of social media parodies of the movie *Downfall*. *Downfall* dramatizes Adolf Hitler's final days in his Berlin Bunker. As Meikle and Young describe, a scene in which Hitler launches into an apoplectic rant has become a mainstay of social media humour. Filmed in German with English subtitles, YouTube and Facebook users play on the ability to edit the latter to rewrite the scene. Instead of being about his determination to create the thousand-year Reich, the scene is re-imagined so that Hitler is driven to distraction by the news that Lady Gaga is refusing to take his calls, among many other versions (Meikle and Young, 2012). Meikle and Young point out that whatever the outcomes and intentions of these jokes, the fact that they are shared through Facebook and YouTube means that this popular creativity is the property of commercial media operations. This reality of form is more important than anything the content aspires to mean. But let's take things further. How might the *Downfall* case study explicate Bird's concerns about the Second World War wedding as an index of the ethical problems of media culture, and media research, *vis-à-vis* confronting suffering?

One of my grandfathers fought his way through Italy with the Royal Engineers during the Second World War. He rarely spoke about it. But once he talked bitterly about how the British taunted Hitler during the 1930s – that hysterical little man who looked like Charlie Chaplin. 'He didn't bloody well make me laugh at Monte Casino', expectorated ex-Sapper William Ruddock.

As neo-Fascism becomes a political factor once more in Europe, socially responsible research has an obligation to do more than simply explain the logic of media users who, one way or another, think the Second World War was funny. Here, the discomfort of those who contribute, albeit unwittingly, to the historical amnesia that concerns Bird is not an especially important matter. It is not that they have spurred the new radical right in Europe. But they do not say much about it either. And if popular creativity largely consists of resource-rich people sharing jokes, *that* is an ethical problem that researchers should at least consider when approaching the purpose of their work. Rather than thinking about the rights of social media users to privacy, others prefer to use their work to develop the rights of non-media users to public visibility. In terms of research ethics, this pays more attention to another value: benefice.

FROM VISIBILITY AND PRIVACY TO INVISIBILITY AND JUSTICE

Bird has demonstrated the significance of benefice in the Asaba Memorial Project, a collaboration with historians to memorialize the mass murder of civilians during the Nigerian Civil War of 1967. The purpose of the memorialization was explicitly ethical. The goal was to address human rights today, especially in regard to truth and reconciliation practices, by recovering past wrongs. This goal was addressed through a rather unusual strategy. Conventionally, a media researcher would interview subjects and then arrange the data to tell a particular story, relating to established scholarly themes. The Asaba Project, however, brought the 'raw' data to the world. The project foregrounded the social benefit for participants, letting the world hear facts that had been hidden for a generation in the voices of the people who experienced them. The main aspiration was to raise funds for a permanent memorial to the massacre. These unusual goals epitomized the convergence between research ethics, mediatization of social experience and the purpose of media studies.

The Asaba Project sought to 'memorialize' rather than 'recall' the massacre of the town's Igbo population because it is not possible to remember an event that was never known. Nigerian Federal troops entered the town in October 1967 as part of their war against Biafran secessionists. Within days, up to 1,000 civilians died at their hands. But these deaths went largely unrecorded in the Nigerian media or in histories of that civil war (Bird and Otanelli, 2011). The pain of survivors was compounded by official histories that ignored the murders. As we saw in the previous chapter, truth and reconciliation practices, grounded in historical research, have become an important part of the pursuit of human rights. The online archive of Asaba survivor experiences, in this context, employed widely available media resources to take a proactive, people-centred strategy to achieving justice.

As we have seen, much of the debate about responsible media research is driven by the potential dangers posed by visibility. The idea that we can find out so much about people online raises all kinds of issues about the status of this information as public or private. These questions best suit media users who have the time, money and cultural capital to create accessible public profiles (Bird, 2003). In Asaba, the central challenge was *invisibility*. Ethics in today's media research protects those the world knows a lot about, the relatively wealthy, relatively well-educated media literate. Asaba was different. The main ethical aim was to ensure that the world discovered more about interviewees.

The Project synthesized media research ethics and history, and it was not surprising that they should meet in Nigeria, around events that happened during its Civil War. Bill Norris (2002) discovered the perils of telling the truth about that war as a frontline correspondent for *The Times*. Norris's wartime experiences had demonstrated the impossibility of developing universal methods of good practice in situations where the consequences of 'truth telling' were unpredictable. On arriving in Nigeria, Norris discovered that government forces controlled access to the areas where the fighting was taking place, and were reticent to take reporters to the frontline. Forging an official pass, he tagged along with a platoon of Federal soldiers, and was there to photograph the murder of a suspected Biafran soldier. The picture became international news. It was hugely embarrassing to the British government, who were aiding the Nigerian army. Stung by international criticism, the army court-martialled the soldier and sentenced him to death by firing squad. Norris was also present as the young lieutenant was tied to a post and shot. Norris ruefully reflected on the complexities of ethics in terms of practices, intentions and outcomes.

If it was so hard to tell the truth about one death, then it is easy to understand why a thousand had been hidden. Norris's story also illuminates the ethical dilemma that the Asaba Memorial Project faced. The task was to tell the truth while protecting those who spoke, or at least ensuring that the benefits of the project outweighed its risks. Here, the task is to understand how the situated research practices that are the topic of concrete ethics procedures reflect disciplinary goals as they connect to public well-being.

Bird's participation in the Asaba Project continued a career examining the integration of media narratives and everyday life. The new setting seemed to be at some distance from her previous work on American audiences and entertainment, such as US tabloid newspapers and *Dr Quinn Medicine Woman*. In fact, the archive was a logical progression in the theme of how symbolic inequalities impinge upon popular culture's capacity to deal with truth.

Media anthropology: The ethical purpose of researching the 'media poor'

Bird's signature is advocating for those who have very little influence over the media industries. This focus locates the intersection of the ethics and critical themes in understanding media influence. To restate, the driving ethical problem in media research is that clear principles about consent and justice are difficult to put into practice because media blur distinctions between public and private. Ethics constructs boundaries that do not tally with the thing that we are studying – the social life of media users, technologies and content. Given this problem, it is not surprising that a media anthropologist has taken the lead in connecting ethics to the pivotal issue of how media practices foster public life.

Bird's anthropological projects use micro observations of media users in action to address the dynamics of larger cultural patterns (Bird, 2003).

Anthropology aspires to observe culture in action as naturally as possible. As such, the integration of media and everyday life means that the most valuable of observations are 'opportunistic' (Bird, 2003). Obvious ethical conundrums follow. Most obviously, it is impossible to get informed consent to study spontaneous case studies of media culture in action, such as the MH17 tragedy. Less obviously, one could argue that informed consent is impossible to gather when so few members of the public appreciate the political weight of everyday media habits and the purpose of studying them seriously.

Bird's work on media audiences addresses these dilemmas by prioritizing justice and benefit. There would be no need for media anthropology at all if audiences were entirely aware of the connection between their habits and the machinations of global media industries. Panics about social media and privacy are one example that illustrates they are not. Respect for research participants, then, comes in the form of making a serious commitment to research that works to maximize public benefit. And sometimes this means saying things about audiences that they probably won't like.

Bird explained how this works, and why it is necessary, by elucidating the nature of the audience. Her anthropological approach to media – studying how media culture works by observing and talking to media users as they use media, or getting them to explain the role that media play in their lives in their own terms – was part of a general trend in media research of using qualitative methods to include ordinary people in debates about media power. However, while the focus of ethics often rests on accessing the voices that have interesting things to say about their media experiences, for a long time now Bird has been more concerned with others who do not have a voice.

To make this point, Bird discussed her study of computer use by low-income families in the USA. There, Bird met 'Kevin', an overweight, unhealthy child who spent most of his days wordlessly watching television. The reasons why he did this were perfectly rational. Kevin's mother had a new baby, could not afford childcare, and television kept him quiet and safe. But the truth was that Kevin wasn't well, didn't seem especially happy, and didn't have many friends. None of this was caused by television, but the screen wasn't helping either (Bird, 2003).

Bird's observation carried a larger academic point. Ethical research interested in justice has to pay attention to audiences who are not in a place to participate in creative ways in media cultures. Also, much as it was important to do away with the 'cultural dope' as the default figure in conceiving the audience, that does not mean that public culture is never harmed by media businesses that do rely on fooling many of the people much of the time – or at least playing at the edges of deception.

Her observations on this were based on studies of different sorts of news. An early project had focused on audiences for American supermarket tabloids, 'newspapers' that told obviously fantastic stories about Hitler being found alive and well in the Amazon rainforest, or a secret elixir of youth being discovered in South America. Bird considered it important to understand why such 'news' was popular. Part of the appeal was a relatively knowing rejection of mainstream news that, on the whole, did a shocking job of cultivating interest.

On the other hand, Bird was concerned that, whatever their readers thought, tabloids represented general trends in media industries where the ability to entertain counted more than the capacity for truth. Young research subjects were disturbingly comfortable with the conflation of fact and fiction in reality-based stories. The use of dramatizations had become a common feature of truth-based genres, especially shows about true crime. As time passed, the convention was also adopted by certain news organizations. Bird thought this was problematic in two ways. For one thing, the tabloid study (Bird, 2003) found audience gullibility. A journalist she interviewed told a story about writing a fantastic piece on the discovery of a miraculous youth-restoring drug in Guatemala, only to receive a call from a reader who had flown there and wanted directions to the source. An extreme case, but indicative, Bird thought, of a bigger trend where audiences trust 'fictionalized' news, where re-enactments were becoming an anticipated part of the show.

The danger here, according to Bird, was that this blurring of genres placed news alongside other media genres where coherence and drama became more important than truth. This was hazardous for journalists and audiences alike. For one thing, the proliferation of storytelling devices opened news to new forms of subversion. If the idea that fantastic stories could be accepted as truth by a few readers seemed hardly worth noting, the vulnerability of mainstream news to modern myths was harder to ignore. Bird had studied how the urban legend 'CJ's revenge' had been reported as news by many professional outfits. The bones of the story go like this. A man goes to a bar and meets a woman. They go home and have sex. When he wakes in the morning she is gone, but has left a note saying 'welcome to the world of AIDS'. The story has different versions. Sometimes the bar is a club, sometimes the note is scrawled on a bathroom mirror, but variants of it were all, at some time in the 1990s, reported as facts by news television and radio. No solid evidence of a real CJ was ever found. Intriguingly, earlier times had seen similar stories about beautiful women wantonly spreading infectious diseases like bubonic plague and syphilis (Bird, 2003). The problem for Bird was that if people bought tabloids knowing that they were not going to read the truth, elements of this practice seemed to be spreading to mainstream news. And if audiences liked that, the dilution of truth as a value did not make that alright.

The other problem was that, according to Bird's evidence, participation in these new storytelling cultures was not evenly distributed. The 'Kevins' of the world did not have the interest, the time or the resources to take part, meaning that while the sheer number of stories that the media circulate had increased, the sources for them probably had not. Succinctly, poor people were either invisible or represented on others' terms.

The ethical principle this implanted in Bird's work was a determination to focus on truth and inclusion as research outcomes. This was significant since although the forces of media convergence were multiplying storytelling modes, they were not widening participation in public storytelling. Bird worried that the main ethical flaw in critical media research was about how respondents were selected, not how they were treated once this process was through. If the field as a whole had an ethical commitment to advancing public interest, then it was systematically failing by not researching those who had little to say about their media habits – because these were often marginalized people.

As time and media progressed, this ethical transgression was exacerbated by a growing scholarly interest in the concept of 'produsage', a term referring to 'the creation of shared content [that] takes place in a networked, participatory environment which breaks down the boundaries between producers and consumers and instead enables all participants to be users as well as producers of information and knowledge' (Bruns, 2007, no page). For Bird (2003), these changes enhanced the need for further thought on the political outcomes of concentrated media power. At face value, billions possessed the resources to create and share ideas with a global audience, and they often did this by 'remixing' mainstream media content. The fact of this undoubtedly widespread change encouraged a distinctly unethical shift in media research, if by ethics we mean a commitment to general well-being. When reflecting on the produsage theme during her Nigerian fieldwork, Bird could not help but think about the school children she had seen whose only encounter with social media was seeing their Principal using his computer.

These kids reminded Bird that the benefits of 'produsage' had to be tempered against the reality that the people who most need to speak in the world are often the most silent. Their absence makes the media world resemble a huge pleasure playground where the value of truth is diluted with a taste for popular storytelling. Unusual as it was, the Asaba Project grew from a general reading of 'irresponsible' tendencies in media research. If the ethical dimensions of our research consistently demand attention to the privacy of the people who we can see using the media in sophisticated ways, then this should prompt another ethical dilemma: are we looking at the right research subjects? The question explains why Bird adopted the unusual strategy of creating an archive as a research outcome instead of a research input, a decision based on her belief that she had a responsibility to reset debates on the politics of media use by spending some time simply listening to voices that had yet to be registered therein.

CONCLUSION: ETHICS AND THE SOCIAL VALUE OF RESEARCH

Ultimately, the point is that good research questions have a well-developed sense of social responsibility, and social responsibility means paying attention to matters of visibility and invisibility. The challenge is that the abundance of evidence about media usage, and the perfectly legitimate procedures that we have for treating that data professionally, means we have to work hard to place equal weight on each concern. Happily, there is a wealth of data out there on how people value media. People's reactions to the latest media event, disaster, scandal or pop culture hit are as close as your computer screen. But before you use it, you need to do two things. You need to consider whether the evidence is really public, and whether analysing it puts anyone at risk. But, more importantly, you need to ask what, and who, it represents. Both are premised on a bigger question: How will your research improve academic and public understanding of how media influence works?

At this point, then, we have identified three aspects of a good research question: (1) Why do you care about it? (or why does it matter?); (2) What model of causation does it involve?; (3) How will society benefit from the answers that you might find? The next step is to show how these principles work together in practice. This is examined in the next chapter in relation to research and public debates on the social significance of video gaming.

CHAPTER SUMMARY

- Social responsibility is an important aspect of media research.

- The topic of research ethics, including the issue of respecting the privacy of research subjects, is a useful device for thinking about how research helps society.

- Conventional research ethics regarding privacy and consent are hard to apply to media research because media use, by definition, changes the meaning of privacy and the ownership of publicly visible expression.

- These obstacles are good for us because they cause us to reflect on the purpose of our work in terms of who benefits from its outcomes.

- The issue of privacy can be contrasted with that of visibility. While most ethical concerns are about the privacy of media users, the biggest ethical matter facing media researchers might well be the invisibility of communities who rarely get to be media users – or at least not the ones who tend to appear in scholarly work.

5

WHAT IS 'GENERALIZABILITY' IN MEDIA RESEARCH?

OBJECTIVE: DEFINING 'GENERALIZABILITY' IN A WORLD OF DIVERSE MEDIA INFLUENCES

The fourth step in doing media research is to think about generalizability. Generalizability concerns how a particular project addresses general social roles that media play. In this chapter, debates about the effects of video game violence are used to explain what this means. The question of whether games cause real violence inherits a history of controversies over the associations between media and aggression. To a jaundiced eye, it might appear that after decades of research, we still don't know very much about how one relates to the other. However, one thing that has become clear, especially since the advent of rampage shootings as harrowingly familiar media events that are often connected to gaming, is that whether you believe gaming is malignant or benign, the narrative of gaming effects has become part of the language that we use to make sense of reality. After the 2012 Sandy Hook murders, research on gaming effects were embroiled in discussions on lofty subjects such as the role of the state, the rights of citizens and the social responsibilities of media scholars – issues that are about far more than games. As a generalization, we can say, then, that whether good or bad, games underline the political nature of entertainment media.

Payne and Williams (2005, 296) call this kind of claim a 'moderatum generalization'. In media studies, moderatum generalizations are provisional models of what a particular media influence issue says about the wider social role of the media. Here, the video gaming case study is a 'moderatum generalization' that clarifies why the conceptualization of media influence changes in social circumstances where media are highly integrated within the practice of social life – the condition of 'mediatization', introduced in the previous chapter. The significant point here is that although the topic of gaming effects might not be of interest to all media scholars, the ideas it accesses about media and the construction of political realities most certainly are. If nothing else, it is an issue that demonstrates how generalizability works as a research attribute. Specifically, studies of gaming effects explain how mediatization highlights moderatum generalizations (henceforth generalizations) as a key reference point in all media research.

(Continued)

Gaming debates are important as dramatizations of how mediatization defines generalization as a key research attribute. To make this point, this chapter:

- Explains why rampage shootings and video game violence are conjoined in public discussions on media effects – and how this unhappy marriage graphically represents the complexity of media influence.
- Shows how contemporary quarrels over video game effects reflect deep questions about the essential role of communication in society.
- Develops a definition of mediatization that identifies common ground between these warring positions and a path forward for media research in general.
- Underlines the point that any topic should ask basic questions about the nature of the communication event that is under scrutiny.

CASE STUDY: USING THE TOPICS OF GAMING AND RAMPAGE MURDERS TO OUTLINE GENERAL THEORIES OF MEDIA INFLUENCE

One of the 'tricks of the trade' in media research involves taking a familiar subject – such as the effects of media violence – and demonstrating how the topic triggers multiple issues, beyond those that usually figure in public conversations. For instance, stories on gaming and rampage murders are usually about the power of the former to antagonize a small number of people into committing the latter. However, it's just as plausible to suggest that what is really at stake is the cold recognition that media profoundly affect all of us.

If any subject encapsulates the history of thought on media effects, and the shift towards mediatization, it's the relationship between gaming and mass murder. Fears about the harm caused by video game violence remix old anxieties about the corrupting power of new media. Parents worry about the damage done by games, just as their forebears had fretted about television, comic books and the movies (Ferguson, 2011). But the song does not remain the same. The media violence debate has a new political edge because of the connection between video gaming and an especially confronting crime: the rampage murder. The search for causal relationships between media violence and actual aggression intensified as school shootings became familiar scars on the cultural landscape (Ferguson, 2007; Ferguson and Ivory, 2012; Elson and Ferguson, 2013; Ferguson and Olson, 2014). When 20-year-old Adam Lanza murdered 20 elementary school pupils in Newtown Connecticut in 2012, anguished political soul-searching found $10 million worth of Federal funding for research on media violence, prompted by the killer's enthusiasm for shooting games (Elson and Ferguson, 2013). The trouble is, the social issues around gaming are about far more than the question of what happens when evil, angry or ill people who play games get access to guns.

The impact of gaming violence on people who never hit, punch or stab anyone

Ask feminist games critic Anita Saarkesian. In 'Women as background decoration' (2014), Saarkesian argued that too many games used women as targets of sexualized violence. Sure, male characters died horribly too, but their demise was never tinged with sexual frisson, as was the case in *Hitman: Blood Money*. That incarnation of the popular series was advertised with images of a scantily clad female corpse, and the legend 'beautifully executed'. The main problem with gaming violence, in Saarkesian's view, was that the desire to manufacture a 'mature themes' appeal slipped too easily into misogyny. Commercial interests led to a flood of nasty messages about gender:

> ... the pattern of utilizing women as background decoration works to rein-force the myth that women are naturally fated to be objectified, vulnerable, and perpetually victimized by male violence. These games also tend to frame misogyny and sexual exploitation as an everlasting fact of life, as something inescapable and unchangeable. (Saarkesian, 2014, no page)

Regrettably, Saarkesian quickly discovered the power of that myth. Her planned lecture at Utah State University was derailed when the university received an anonymous threat. A person claiming to be a student declared that if Saarkesian appeared, he would perpetrate a 'Montreal'-like massacre (McDonald, 2014). 'Montreal' referenced the crimes of Marc Lepine, who had taken a group of students at the city's École Polytechnique hostage, released the men and then murdered 14 women in an openly misogynist assault. When Saarkesian can-celled the engagement, it wasn't because of the threat *per se*; it was because Utah's gun laws meant that police and security officers couldn't protect her. In Utah, it is legal to carry a concealed gun anywhere one wishes, so long as one has a permit. Given that she had been threatened with assassination, the critic felt it best not to speak at a venue that was *not allowed* to ban firearms.

Given the cries of censorship that often come from the games industry and its customers, it was ironic that Saarkesian found herself legally silenced, in a roundabout way. Reflecting on this, the critic was clear that the 'problem' in this story was not the individual who may or may not have intended to kill her. The real issue was how this individual stood at the tip of an iceberg of hostility directed at those who spoke out against misogyny in gaming. Saarkesian was not anti-gaming. Her activism came from the observation that women make up a huge percentage of the games market and deserve more diverse experiences when they play. The lessons of Utah were about gender subordination and the partnership between popular culture and society.

> Online harassment, especially gendered online harassment, is an epi-demic. Women are being driven out; they're being driven offline. This isn't just in gaming. This is happening across the board online, especially

with women who participate in or work in male-dominated industries. So the harassment actually has a very real effect on us as a society, in terms of making this space unwelcoming for women. (Goodman, 2014, no page)

Saarkesian's experience put a new spin on an old story. We are used to connecting gaming and brutality, but here the fear was primarily about the cultural aggression that one group directs towards another. This intersection of gaming and mass murder was about how media set the ground for social participation. Here, gaming was about how we live as women and men (see Consalvo, 2003). Consequently, gaming intruded into weighty political areas: gun control, violence against women, freedom of speech. It underlined, then, the point that we research media in order to get to the ideas and values that structure society.

Academic debates about the effects of gaming are dominated by technical, empirical issues. Such discussions are important, as long as we remember they are but one facet of a complicated puzzle. Amid confusion about what gaming 'does', one truth is incontrovertible. The phenomenon is deeply involved in how societies understand rampage murders. *Talk* about games is part of the language that we use to make sense of mass murder. This, in the end, produces a different view of media influence, one that is less about how media change individuals and more about how societies collectively make social reality. Significantly, this was not the first time that a fairly narrow debate about media and social violence had expanded to encompass general issues in understanding the role of communication in social well-being.

Media violence as a symptom of media power

Academic gaming debates are of general interest because they mark the difference between wondering what some media do to some people sometimes and what media in general do to all of us, as social beings, every day. This is the central 'revision' at stake in 'mediatization' as a sensitizing concept. The question of whether media constitute a sufficient independent force that 'changes' people is as old as communication research itself. Pursuing this question attuned pioneers of mid-20th-century persuasion studies to the possibility that there was more to the social significance of media than met the eye, *vis-à-vis* altering audience behaviours. From the beginning, researchers recognized that media were part of complicated social structures, where reality was made through different kinds of communication. This inevitably affected the validity and reliability of social scientific methods.

Carl Hovland (1959) made this point in an early review of the state of play in media research. Hovland had led an enormous project looking at how propaganda films could boost the fighting resolve of US soldiers in the Second World War (Hovland, Lumsdaine and Sheffield, 1949). Hovland and his colleagues did many experiments, exposing troops to messages that deliberately set out to make them want to fight Axis forces. Yet Hovland realized that you could only grasp how media affected audiences by asking fundamental questions about the nature of communication, the differences between types of communication, and the capacity of different methods to capture different kinds of effects.

At that time, media research was dominated by experiments and surveys. The former made people do things in relation to media, where the latter asked people about media habits that were a part of their normal lives. Hovland (1959) noticed that experiments tended to find stronger media effects when it came to media's capacity to change audiences. He thought that this was because experiments and surveys actually examined different things. By and large, experiments exposed test subjects to media content that they had not chosen to see, such as a new propaganda message. Experiments were confronting. In the social world, however, people exercised more choice over what they saw, and these choices were usually of content that reflected their existing values. So, experiments measured the impact of the new and the shocking, whereas surveys assessed the impact of the familiar. Put this way, it is not surprising that surveys were less likely to find change. But the *absence* of change in audience attitudes was not indicative of 'no effect' but of a *different* effect – reinforcement.

Hovland concluded that the lesson here was about being sensitive to multiple forms of media power. The focus of much of his work, persuasion, looked at how media worked against audiences in the sense that it tried to change them. But it could be that the absence of change found in surveys demonstrated varieties of media influence that worked *with* audiences. Let's think about how Hovland's ideas make sense of Anita Saarkesian's reflections on gaming culture. Saarkesian argues that the problem with gaming culture is that it buttresses gender inequality in cultural industries, and in that sense its main effect is to have no effect on the role that media play in naturalizing gender inequalities. The risk, here, is the *absence* of change among a significant number of gamers.

It's easy to apply the thoughts of a social scientist from the 1940s to the experiences of a feminist games critic in the early 21st century, because the debates about research methods are really about the difficulty of making sense of deep-seated cultural trends. With the passing of time, the conversation came to focus on media violence, then gaming. The emergence of school shootings as media events played a significant role in directing these developments (Scharrer, Weidman and Bissell, 2003; Ferguson and Ivory, 2012).

Researchers recognized that although it is sensible to assume that media affect audiences, showing how media do this is quite another thing. Albert Bandura, for example, is a social scientist famed for his 'social learning' theory of violence effects. Bandura is well known for his 'Bobo Doll' experiments, which examined how exposing children to screen images of adults hitting a clown-like punch bag encouraged them to replicate this violent behaviour when placed in a room with the same toys. Bandura knew that such methods inevitably chase shadows, as they try to make sense of complex social situations where media effects are mixed up with all manner of much more powerful influences, poverty and inequality being prime examples (Bandura, 2009).

Gunter (2008) supported this view in his comprehensive critique of why surveys and experiments struggle to show how media and real violence are connected. After half a century, Hovland's observations still applied. The strongest evidence of effects came from experiments using measures of violence that bore little resemblance to the real thing (such as administering fake electric shocks to people who failed a quiz test), and so the relationship between real-world violence and aggression, as it is measured in experiments, remained dubious.

However, all of this meant that media violence had become a key topic in understanding interfaces between social experience, media content and media use. The advent of school shootings as a particular sort of violent crime has represented this notion with tragic clarity. According to Altheide (2009), when Dylan Klebold and Eric Harris murdered 36 of their classmates at Columbine High School in 1999, they set in train a symbolic process that established school shootings as powerful catalysts in the construction and management of politicized fears. Visions of 'juvenile superpredators' (Muschert, 2007) preying on victims, whose deaths are especially distressing because of their innocence and/or virtue (Muschert, 2007), have become powerful ways to articulate what it means to live in an age of global terror, where anyone can be victimized anywhere. Such fears have become handy alibis for new forms of surveillance (Altheide, 2009). Consequently, school shootings have taken the debate about media and the real world into new territory that demonstrates the need to move the media impact debate away from individual effects towards the construction of political realities and the role that these realities play in determining how we access public life. This shift is the core of the mediatization perspective and changes important assumptions about the practice of media research.

The politics of media violence research

The case against effects

Chapter 1 explained how political and historical contexts affect media researchers. This is relevant to gaming research because the direction of that field and its relevance to the rest of the discipline were significantly affected by two events: the Supreme Court of the United States' 2011 decision to strike down a Californian law prohibiting the sale of violent games to minors, and the Sandy Hook murders of 2012.

Incongruously, everything started with famed action hero turned California State Governor Arnold Schwarzenegger. In 2005, the man who had been responsible for producing more than his fair share of media violence signed a law banning the sale of violent games to minors. The gaming industry won an injunction against the statute and the case was brought before the Supreme Court in 2011 (Ferguson, 2013a, 2013b). There, the law was finally struck down. The judges ruled that the social science evidence on the harm caused by gaming did not merit legal restrictions. The decision prompted an energetic and often rancorous debate on what the case said about the science of media effects (Elson and Ferguson, 2013; Bushman and Huesmann, 2014; Bushman and Pollard-Sacks, 2014; Ferguson, 2014).

The political gravity of the decision was felt after the 2012 Sandy Hook murders. The distinction between gaming research and earlier violence studies centred on interactivity of gaming *and* heightened anxieties brought about by infamous US rampage murders, such as Columbine and 2007's Virginia Tech massacre (Ferguson, 2007). The debate became especially heated after Sandy Hook. Some feared the combination of social outrage and increased funding for studies on gaming risks threatened the credibility of social science; it was easy to be overcome by ideological agendas instead of sound methods and evidence (Elson and Ferguson, 2013). These developments illustrated how gaming added political weight to historical critiques on the validity of experiments.

In 2009, the American Academy of Pediatrics (AAP) released an alarming report about the prevalence and dangers of media violence. Its conclusion was that, considering evidence from content analysis, experiments and surveys, violence was so common in the media that it was impossible to avoid, video game violence was especially troubling as a media form that modelled and rewarded violence, and the connection between exposure to screen violence and real-life aggression had been demonstrated so often that there were few real grounds to doubt its harm. Indeed, that harm was equivalent to things like exposure to lead and cigarette smoke – hazardous materials over which there is no debate. A total of 98% of American physicians recognized media as a risk to the children they treated. Given this news from the front line, added to the confusion that parents experienced when trying to deal with voluntary restrictions such as V-chips and ratings systems, the only path forward was to treat media as a health hazard (American Academy of Pediatrics, 2009).

A social scientist called Christopher Ferguson was the most vocal critic of the declaration. Ferguson accused the AAP of exaggerating the evidence of harm to such an extent that they actively encouraged bad research and bad policy. The first bone of contention involved the validity of proxy aggression measures used in experiments. Experimental measures of aggression were quite different from the real-world violence that most concerned the public. Some studies, for example, claim that playing violent games increases aggression based on the observation of experimental subjects given a word completion task. Those who had done so were more likely to complete 'explo_e' as 'explode' rather than as 'explore' than others who had not. Generally, the strongest effects were found in studies that had the least realistic proxy measures (Ferguson, 2013a, 2013b).

Ferguson thought that the validity weaknesses discussed by Hovland and Gunter had become acute in gaming studies thanks to a particular technique: the unstandardized use of so-called 'Competitive Reaction Time Tasks' (Ferguson, 2007; Elson and Ferguson, 2013). 'CRTTs' make experimental subjects play a reaction time game against an opponent, where the victor then punishes the loser. 'Punishment' takes the form of giving a 'fake' electric shock, blasting the opponent with white noise, or preparing a cup of hot sauce for the loser to drink (Elson and Ferguson, 2013). Critics observe that people who want to be violent 'do not chase after their targets with jars of hot sauce or head-phones' (Elson and Ferguson, 2013, 6). It's worth noting that qualitative researchers have discovered instances where music is used aggressively: as an instrument of torture in war (Pieslak, 2009) or to express hostility in domestic disputes (DeNora, 2000). In a way, though, this underlines the point that CRTT methods mix different measures together, so that adding up the results of all such work exaggerates results by putting different behaviours in the same class (Elson and Ferguson, 2013).

Another twist in the validity debate came through doubts about a new method for calculating effects: meta-analysis. Meta-analysis combines results from multi-ple studies to assess the overall 'effects' that a field has discovered. Anderson et al.'s (2010) meta-analysis of 136 experiments claimed to find small but consistent con-tributions of violent gameplay to aggressive behaviour, both in the short and the long term. As such, the authors claimed that the question was no longer whether gaming posed an environmental risk; the issue now was what to do about it.

Others countered that several things affected the validity of the method (Elson and Ferguson, 2013). First, meta-analyses combine results from sur-veys and experiments, and as we know from Hovland, these are different beasts. Second, the practice of meta-analysis ignores the variances at play in the application of violence proxies in experiments. Third, the question of how studies are included in and excluded from meta-analyses compromises the comprehensiveness of the method. As the Anderson et al. (2010) paper claimed to establish the case for viewing media violence as an environmental risk beyond all reasonable doubt, Elson and Ferguson (2013) thought it appropri-ate to question their selection criteria. They accused Anderson et al. of including unpublished studies from themselves and their colleagues, while making little effort to collect similar materials from scholars whose work did not demonstrate significant effects.

Next, there were issues with 'publication bias' (Ferguson, 2007). Evidence of harm became weaker still in light of indications that it is quite hard to publish studies showing no effect. Publication bias is a difficult phenomenon to demon-strate – how are you to know what isn't published? However, there are methods for estimation, such as calculating how many studies discovering the so-called null hypothesis it would take to reduce discovered effects sizes to insignificant levels. Using these measures, Ferguson's analysis of 25 published studies showed the likelihood of publication bias was higher in research claiming to show media harm than it was in published research that showed either no nega-tive or positive outcomes of game playing (Ferguson, 2007).

Most damningly, Ferguson accused 'strong effects' scholars of possessing a fatal lack of curiosity when it comes to exploring alternative explanations for how gaming became a factor in media violence. The 'strong effects' position was wed-ded to a causal model where gaming violence was thought to manufacture aggression through modelling and social learning. The problem here was that no one asked a crucial question: Should research on gaming effects start with the games or look elsewhere? Ferguson (2013a, 2014) expressed the opinion that it made just as much sense to begin with the motivations of the gamer. We can learn more about the social life of gaming by asking how the conditions that drive a person towards gaming influence how gaming is experienced, and what it does in the life of the player (Elson and Ferguson, 2013; Ferguson and Olson, 2013).

Ferguson was not the first to make this point. The observation that effects research fatally downplays the significance of the viewing context was a staple of qualitative studies of media violence (e.g. Barker and Petley, 1997; Hill, 2005). The difference here was that the US Supreme Court now queried whether media violence was bad for viewers, even ruling that the young people had a constitutional right to access it. In the opinion of the majority of the judges, evidence of risk was insufficient to justify abridging First Amendment rights. To Ferguson (2007), this represented a public recognition that 'strong effects' scholars, along with institutions such as the American Psychological Association and American Academy of Pediatrics, had exaggerated the consensus of expert opinion on the topic. Scholars who backed the Californian law, based on the certainty that their position was as solid as it could practically be, ignored dissenting opinions from the FBI and academic peers.

Ferguson concluded that the strong effects position survived because of politics, not best practice. After Sandy Hook, the greatest danger of gaming was that it had become a patsy for the deep social causes of crime. Funding work on the risks of media violence discouraged scholars from asking alternative questions about the motivations that draw people towards this violence, or the appeal that such content has for particular groups of people who have particular problems. Worse still, it diverted funds away from other projects that might make more meaningful incursions against social violence. Unless media scholars confronted the necessity of changing the violence question, the subject itself risked invalidation as a source of knowledge that people could use.

The case for strong influence

Predictably, the strong effects position fought back, led by Brad Bushman. Bushman was a co-author of the controversial 2010 meta-analysis (Anderson et al., 2010). In the very year of the infamous SCOTUS ruling, he had also co-authored an experimental study that claimed to have discovered a causal connection between violent gameplay, desensitization and real aggression (Engelhardt et al., 2011). That study exemplified everything that Ferguson despised. Players were asked to play a violent or non-violent video game. They had their brain waves measured while doing so, and were then given the chance to administer noise blasts to opponents in CRTT tests. Results showed that exposure to video game violence desensitized players to the phenomenon and correlated with increased aggression, as measured via noise blasts. The experiment also claimed to be the first to show that desensitization – the reduced capacity to be shocked or upset by screen violence – led to real-world aggression (Englehardt et al., 2011).

Striking back, Bushman and Pollard-Sacks (2014) accused Ferguson (2013a) of misrepresenting the SCOTUS verdict. The judgment did not indict the effects case. It was a legal decision that played by an entirely different set of evidentiary rules. SCOTUS can only abridge First Amendment rights when the speaker intends to inflict immediate harm. Consequently, it has always been virtually impossible to hold entertainment media to account for social outcomes that might relate to exposure. The judgment, then, did not dismiss evidence about risk (Bushman and Pollard-Sacks, 2014). In fact, Bushman and Huesmann (2014) pointed out that the judge who had authored the verdict conceded that he had not read the strong effects research.

Several methodological defences were also posed. Anderson et al.'s (2010) study *had* tested for publication bias, and found none. There was acceptable consistency between aggression measures used in experimental studies finding large effects. Real variations between the meta-analyses conducted by the 'weak' and 'strong' effects sides came not in the data, but in the interpretation of what the information meant. The former read small effects sizes as indicating the trivial nature of media effects; the other argued that even statistically small effects can have socially devastating consequences and are worth worrying about (Bushman and Huesmann, 2014; Bushman and Pollard-Sacks, 2014). With an eye towards social significance, it was worth noting that in a debate that was indeed political, in outcome if not intent, the 'weak effects' argument certainly favoured powerful entertainment industries that already had the Supreme Court on their side (Bushman and Pollard-Sacks, 2014).

Then came the matter of causality. The strong effects case had been criticized for assuming that media played an independent role in making people violent. This ignored individual social and psychological factors that *led* people to screen violence. Bushman and Huesmann (2014) thought this was a theoretically flawed misreading of the strong effects argument. They accepted, and always had, that context mediated the outcomes of media violence. But Ferguson's argument also, rather curiously, seemed to dismiss the social experience of using media. If we can accept that exposure to rampant crime, domestic violence and the like can shape aggressive tendencies, then why not the media? Given the evidence about the ubiquity of media violence, what sense did it make to dismiss the phenomenon as a source of learning? Especially when surveys of social scientists show that the majority of them agree this to be the case. Bushman and Huesmann argued that the majority of credible social scientists agreed that media violence was a risk, just as all credible climate scientists agree that global warming is real. Certainly many academics disagreed with this point, but few of them, according to Bushman and Huesmann (2014), knew enough about methods to make their accusations stick.

Strong versus weak effects: Agreements, unexplored questions and general lessons for appreciating the nature of media influence

Yet the bitter academic firestorm ignited by rampage murders and SCOTUS was also quite predictable, given the history of the violence in question. In that respect, it is worth considering what happens if we ask a Hovland-like question:

How did it reflect some basic understandings of media power? We can do this by analysing the debate from the 'relevance/causation/ethics' viewpoint.

On relevance, both sides agreed that their work addressed the political management of society, research and media industries. Ferguson (2013a) feared that effects researchers simply had too much reputational capital invested in their case to ever let it go, no matter the evidence. Meanwhile, the Anderson et al. (2010) meta-analysis conceded that very little attention had been paid to the positive influence of gaming, and there were all kinds of reasons for thinking that such effects happened and were worth researching. There *had* been a funding and public interest bias that prioritized risk over benefit (Anderson et al., 2010). Nevertheless, it was naïve to assume that asking questions about the benefits of gaming were any less limiting (Bushman and Huesmann, 2014). Most obviously, it let the gaming industry off the moral hook. As we saw in the Introduction, that industry pays lip service to its social responsibility, so there are certainly reasons to accept this argument. In a roundabout way, then, warring factions agreed that the media violence topic demanded a reboot of basic understandings about the relationships among academia, the state and media businesses, meaning it was also a subject that raised significant questions about how media research mattered to society.

It was also clear that more work was needed on causation. How was it possible to argue that effects were context-dependent, yet stand by experimental evidence suggesting the risk of gaming was there regardless of who played? The answer was that this conclusion was presented as an empirical fact with a social relevance, rather than a social reality. The fact that researchers found the link time and time again (if that is in fact what they did) did not imply clear social implications, such as the need to restrict access. That was a political decision that had to take other kinds of risk (such as the damage to society done when freedom of expression is curtailed) into account (Bushman and Pollard-Sacks, 2014).

However, when exploring other gaming effects, there were other risks involved in using the individual gamer as the basic unit of analysis, as Ferguson (2013a, 2013b) suggested. The idea of starting media research from the motivations that brought individuals to media content had been floated before, and had been criticized as just a different way of lifting research subjects out of society, history and culture (Carey and Kreiling, 1974). The media choices that we make are affected by all manner of things that we do not choose: the way that media industries match content to their perceptions of markets, the time and space we have to use media, and the people with whom we consume, to name but a few. At any rate, the squabbles over gaming activated another argument about the relationship between choice and structure in understanding what drives media use. Here, just as it's important to recognize that no user is entirely 'passive', so too is it vital to acknowledge that they never do as they please either. Also, where Ferguson called for a cultural turn in thinking about media violence, the direction that he advocated did just the opposite – instead of thinking about common ways of thinking and acting, he emphasized the significance of individual choice and circumstance.

Ethically speaking, the clearest evidence that something was missing from both sides of the argument was that neither explained the Anita Saarkesian incident. It's difficult to tell someone who has been threatened with rape and murder because of the things that she has said about video games that gaming isn't connected, somehow, to social aggression. Moreover, in Saarkesian's view, the frequency with which such venom is directed at women who speak out made her story hard to dismiss as an isolated incident – the product of the individual, if you will. The story does not 'prove' the case for strong effects, but it does indicate the need to hold on to the idea of some sort of centralized cultural power that is more than the sum of individual psychologies, motivations and media choices. The Saarkesian incident showed the need to 'revise' the gaming discussion, combining the strongest points from the pro- and anti-effects camps into a broader framework. The concept of mediatization provides a means to achieve this different view.

MEDIATIZATION AND A GENERAL THEORY OF MEDIA EFFECTS

We know that mediatization sets out to be a different way of thinking about media influence. In this last section of this chapter, I am going to explain how a few basic definitions of what mediatization is, what it says about the nature of strong media influence, and the way that it helps organize the confusing argument over gaming all illustrate its value as a 'generalizing' tool.

The first step in this process is to understand how mediatization relates to cultural understandings of media influence. Hepp (2013) argues that mediatization uses Stuart Hall's definition of culture as 'the sum of the different classificatory systems and discursive formations to which our production of everyday meanings relates' (Hall, cited in Hepp, 2013, 5). Culture comprises the symbolic activities that humans collectively use to create meaning and order in the social world. It names, defines, construes, evaluates and makes meaningful connections between people, groups, institutions, events and issues. Media are central resources in meaning-making processes. Media industries organize the production of meaning. A cultural perspective on media assumes that the creation and circulation of meaning is an unequal process; it is easier for some groups to present their interpretations of reality to the public than others. In adopting this position, Hepp reveals that the 'new' concept of mediatization accepts premises that have always grounded British and American cultural approaches to media (e.g. Carey, 1989).

The next step, then, is to understand what mediatization adds to established cultural understandings of media that Hall discussed. The work of Stig Hjarvard (2013) is especially helpful in this regard. For Hjarvard, mediatization expresses the idea that the process of meaning creation is now obliged to work with media industries as a matter of course. From the creation of individual identities, to the interactions of people in small groups, all the way up to the operations of major institutions – political parties, government organizations, businesses, emergency services – more and more social actions are obliged to sync with media industries.

Hjarvard suggested that this signals a change in public life every bit as dramatic as the forces of modernization. The key to his position lies in the distinction between mediatization and mediation. Hjarvard (2013 [in Kindle locations, 560–563]) stated:

> Mediation describes the concrete act of communication by means of a type of media in a specific social context. By contrast, mediatization refers to a more long-term process, whereby social and cultural institutions and modes of interaction are changed as a consequence of the growth of the media's influence.

Hjarvard saw a subtle yet significant shift in media culture that changes the approach to research questions. Society and culture have always been mediated, in the sense that both are built on communication. We are also used to thinking about how particular communication technologies mediate social relationships in particular ways. The telegraph, for example, is credited with making it possible to think about national identity differently, thanks to its capacity for instantaneous communication across great distances (Carey, 1989; Peters, 1999). The telegraph, in this sense, was a vital tool in a project that was already happening. The physical expansion of the United States could be matched with a mental expansion, such that people on the Eastern seaboard connected with things that had previously been out of sight and mind. The telegraph did not create the reality of national identity, although it did much to shape it. This is why it was a mediation. Mediatization requires us to look at the general impact of total media ecologies, above the impact of specific technologies or events, and ask how the media industries play a deeper role in creating social realities, in the first instance.

It is possible to illustrate what this means by looking at the controversy over media and rampage murders. As an example of *mediation*, we can consider Cho Seung Hui's murder of 32 students at America's Virginia Tech University in 2007. Infamously, Cho paused his crime to record a video message explaining his actions, which he then posted to NBC News. This was a 'concrete act of communication by means of a type of media in a specific social context', as Hjarvard put it above. The video diary became another weapon in a horrific crime intended as a violent expression of alienation. Cho's clip was 'concrete' and 'tied to specific context', because it exploited the capacity of cheap mobile media, the growing use of amateur footage in professional news, and the existence of school shootings as established media events that people are grimly familiar with on the nightly news. That is, when Cho recorded the clip, there were a number of reasons why he could be confident that his words would reach a global audience because of how media industries worked. This is not to say that news caused the events at Virginia Tech, but it is to say that the presence of news was a factor in its staging.

Hjarvard's version of mediatization requires us to take another step by considering how the presence of media *in general* affects other social actions *in general* (Hjarvard, 2013). The move he suggests here is qualitative and difficult to grasp, because an incident can represent mediation and mediatization at the same time, depending on what the researcher wants to discuss. Cho can be read from a mediatization view, for example, if we see his actions as reflecting the idea that the growth of social media and practices of using the public to generate professional media content (in everything from game shows to reality TV to the news) have created the general conviction that the eternal need for validation now implies the creation of public media profiles. But if we look again at the preceding controversy over gaming effects, it becomes possible to see how they explain the change that Hjarvard highlighted. The idea of mediatization suggests that existing social processes 'change' when they are obliged to frame themselves in relation to how media industries work.

Concerns about the social basis of crime, violence and the effects of media content therein have been around for centuries. But gaming does seem to have had a particular effect. The actions of SCOTUS and the academics who have participated in high-profile judicial reviews of gaming regulations show how the interests of media businesses (here, the definition of gaming as an expressive art with rights to protection as freedom of speech) play crucial roles in bringing abstract political reasoning to life, such that political narratives live by or in reference to media. The controversy also shows 'mediatization' as an example of how hard it is to think about real violence without considering its media representation. This is an example of what Hjarvard (2013 [in Kindle locations, 366–367]) meant when he also defined mediatization as referring to a situation where:

> These corporations' production and distribution of symbolic products have changed communication flows in society, both between institutions and between institutions and individuals.

The next step is to show how mediatization helps to make general points about the relevance of the topic that all parties find useful. Opposing camps have clashed over the idea that gaming affects all players, regardless of who or where they are. On the strong effects side, the challenge has been to define and demonstrate this general effect, while respecting cultural differences. On the weak effects side, the problem is that although it is easy to gather persuasive evidence to suggest that anything that gaming does depends on who is playing it, the notion that a medium that entrances millions with its tales of good and evil has no power is scarcely credible.

Two kinds of general media power

Mediatization is useful because it describes two kinds of 'centralizing tendencies' that explain both the strong and weak effects positions. The idea that media exert effects that are stronger than individual wills or culture is expressed in 'centripetal' definitions of mediatization. A centripetal force is something that exercises a gravitational pull over other objects. Centripetal media forces oblige people, organizations and institutions to include media logic in their thinking and actions. This idea first emerged in politics, where the need to connect with the public through popular media, often through the entertaining performances of political celebrities, has become an institutionalized aspect of political culture (see Corner and Pels, 2005; Esser, 2011; Stanyer, 2012). When it comes to gaming, we have already seen two examples of centripetal force. Gaming has affected public discussions about social science and freedom of speech. But also recall how the Introduction referenced EA Games' encouragement of gamer organizations that seek to turn their taste for gaming into a political platform. This is 'centripetal' mediatization because here people adopt political identities in relation to media industries. Such identities – real things that encourage people motivated to act – have no existence outside commercial media culture. This supports Bushman and Huesmann's (2014) dismissal of the idea that gaming only does what gamers want it to do – a notion making little theoretical or experiential sense.

Hjarvard's 'centrifugal' understanding of mediatization is more complex. A centrifugal force is something that disperses objects from a centre of energy. So a 'core' drive produces differences. Hjarvard applies this as follows. First, media logic is fluid. Although we all have to deal with the fact that public life depends on media industries, different sectors of that life utilize different sectors of those industries, and thus respond to different logics. Strangely, this is why mediatization is such a force to be reckoned with – it takes on many guises. As Hjarvard puts it, 'media logic does not suggest that there is a universal, linear or single rationality behind all media' (2013 [in Kindle locations, 505–507]). Consequently, a mediatization perspective does not assume that mediatization is always or even mostly a bad thing: 'Whether mediatization has positive or negative consequences cannot be determined in general terms: it is a concrete, analytical question that needs to be addressed in terms of specific contexts' (Hjarvard, 2013 [in Kindle locations, 553–554]).

Applied to gaming, mediatization is a theory of processes, not outcomes. Hjarvard states that 'The point of this model is to underline the fact that the media environment is expanding and developing in different directions, so that one cannot say that the media are moving society in any particular direction' (2013, [in Kindle locations, 556]). In gaming controversies, we see two things: the value of mediatization as a productive way of approaching any question about media influence, and the significance of gaming as a microcosm of conceptual and methodological matters that affect all media research.

The problem that we left the gaming debate with was the inability of effects research to say much about the significance of the Saarkesian incident. Methodological critiques levelled against the strong effects position do not imply that individual psychologies and motivations are the gold standard indices of gaming impact. Such a focus cannot explain gaming as a collective activity that sometimes builds an atmosphere of gender hostility.

An apparent irony of the Saarkesian story is that gaming was also the solution to this problem. Gaming became a focal point for misogyny because it had also been the vehicle that Saarkesian had used to address the politics of gender and the pleasure of popular culture. For good or ill, gaming was a place where social groups claimed their right to a voice. Seen from a mediatization perspective, this is no irony. It simply reflected the co-presence of centripetal and centrifugal forces. Centrifugally, gaming opens itself up as a space for gender dialogue. Centripetally, this happens because gaming is a major cultural pastime that people use to reflect on their identities. This is not about individual decisions. There are risks and opportunities at play, but whichever aspect interests you the most, the research task is to figure out how both are structured by media and culture in the journey from production to reception.

The lesson here is that generalizability in research involves taking a step back from the controversies that define debate on a particular topic and asking what the problem is 'about' in terms of the social role of communication. Disputes about gaming effects are a useful place to demonstrate this because they inherit issues in conceiving and examining media influence that have been around for decades. Heated discussions about gaming effects represent deeper concerns about living in a world where perception leans on media stories. Exploring the mechanics of how social scientists link screen violence to the real deal remains an important task, as long as we remember that this is not the only reason why that violence matters. The mediatization perspective reminds us that media research uses specific topics to reflect on the general social and cultural role of media communication. All theoretical and methodological decisions relate to this goal, and the 'relevance' sequence of a project involves addressing this matter. The emergence of mediatization as a new research paradigm reflects this point.

CONCLUSION

Questions about media violence endure as perennial memos for general questions about conceiving and exploring media impact. Quarrels about what gaming 'does', and what we should do about it, are driven by disagreements over whether we should start by assuming that they are 'good' or 'bad', and the extent to which things that happen in tightly controlled laboratories have anything to do with the outside world. However, the intensification of the argument in reaction to rampage murders indicates something else. The main effect of gaming, and gaming debates, is that they have become part of the repertoire of ideas that we use when trying to make sense of the incomprehensible.

Rampage shootings are upsetting crimes, partly because of what they are and partly because of how they are represented though the media. In recent years, the impact of violent games has become a common feature of discussions on what causes these abominations. It has become increasingly difficult to speak of rampage killings without mentioning gaming. This is a testimony to mediatization in action, a sad exemplar of how hard it is to discuss reality without using media narratives when it comes to the big issues of the day. Consequently, thinking about rampage murders, their media framing, and indeed the framing of media in conversations about what causes them, helps to explain the importance of taking a cultural approach to media, through the mediatization concept.

Mediatization reminds us of the need to constantly revise research questions, with a view to improving a general understanding of the general role that communication plays in society. Sensitivity to this requirement has always been an aspect of empirical media research, and so what we learn is that methodological debates are not just about technique, but also about the conceptual substance of media research; that is, decisions about whether to use this or that method have to be grounded in how the researcher is going to address culture.

Research on video game violence is dominated by quantitative psychological approaches and sophisticated technical debates about methods. The field reflects a long history of concerns about the validity and reliability of experiments in particular, but has amplified these reservations to an unprecedented level of public acrimony. We can say two things about this situation. First, its genesis can be understood by using our relevance/causation/ethics criteria. Second, mediatization frames the gaming violence issue as being about the nature of communication, not violence as such. This underlines a fourth point about a good research question. It is alert to the possibility that the 'issue' at hand might be about many things. This highlights the value of listening to a variety of scholarly voices in order to problematize one's view of why something is important.

CHAPTER SUMMARY

- All media research aspires to generalizability, in the sense that all of our questions are founded on the assumption that social life is governed by communication. *How* it is governed by communication is the basic 'fact' that we seek.

- We can understand this by looking at the gaming violence debate. The concerns we express about the effects of this particular genre reflect the deeper role that media play in producing stories, ideas and even the social groups that structure social reality.

- Mediatization focuses attention on the importance of connecting all research topics to the question of how media make social life possible. This is the essence of 'generalization' in media studies.

Part 2

UNDERSTANDING MEDIA RESEARCH: FRAMING GENERAL QUESTIONS

6

RESEARCHING MEDIA REALITY

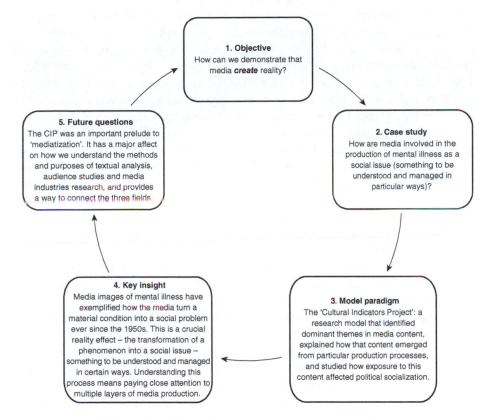

1. Objective
How can we demonstrate that
media *create* reality?

2. Case study
How are media involved in the
production of mental illness as a
social issue (something to be
understood and managed in
particular ways)?

3. Model paradigm
The 'Cultural Indicators Project': a
research model that identified
dominant themes in media content,
explained how that content emerged
from particular production processes,
and studied how exposure to this
content affected political socialization.

4. Key insight
Media images of mental illness have
exemplified how the media turn a
material condition into a social problem
ever since the 1950s. This is a crucial
reality effect – the transformation of a
phenomenon into a social issue –
something to be understood and managed
in certain ways. Understanding this
process means paying close attention to
multiple layers of media production.

5. Future questions
The CIP was an important prelude to
'mediatization'. It has a major affect
on how we understand the methods
and purposes of textual analysis,
audience studies and media
industries research, and provides
a way to connect the three fields.

Figure 2   How media make social reality

OBJECTIVE: DESCRIBING HOW MEDIA REPRESENTATIONS DEFINE SOCIAL PROBLEMS

This chapter explains how media industries make reality by turning real-world phenomena into social problems – things that are understood and managed in particular ways. These are the most significant effects that media scholars from a variety of backgrounds pursue, and constitute one of the foundations of the mediatization concept.

The chapter 'unlocks' this idea by looking at how media industries affect mental illness. Mental illness is a pressing global health problem, and concerns have been raised that media often aggravate things by portraying the mentally ill as dangerous people. Scholars have studied this stigmatization for many years, so it is a rich source of information on *how* media create reality. Here, we will focus on ideas and methods evolving from the Cultural Indicators Project (CIP). The project began in the United States in the 1950s and collected decades of data on how American television represents basic facts of social life. More significantly, it developed innovative methods for associating these representations to the conditions of their production and the political socialization of audiences.

It is always important to explain why a particular model has been selected as a point of research departure. The CIP is a 'good start' for exploring media reality for several reasons. It is one of the most widely cited theories of media influence in the world (Morgan, Shanahan and Signorielli, 2012), although in itself that does not justify the choice. More significantly, the model pioneered methods for showing how the *general* reality effects of media operated through *different* production arrangements. Depictions of mental illness were among the many topics it used to make this point (Gerbner, 1961; Gerbner and Tannenbaum, 1960).

The mental illness case study is methodologically generalizable because it shows how to link social problems to media. The litmus test for any such project is its ability to establish a set of cogent *questions* and methods for making sense of the 'reality' that stands before us. In this case the fact that while some depictions of mental illness might be changing, people worry that most images that audiences see tend to stigmatize those who suffer (Gerbner, 1993; Fischoff, 1996; Wilson et al., 1998; Blood and Holland, 2004; Stuart, 2006; McGinty et al., 2014). Contemplating such questions, the CIP offers an invaluable and unparalleled historical perspective. It explains why imploring media industries to be more thoughtful and accurate could not change depictions of mental illness, and why we should be wary of the capacity of 'key' films or television shows that defy stereotypes to substantially change public perceptions. Studies from the model since the 1950s have discovered that some images become media conventions through production relationships that reflect particular interests. In the process, CIP mental illness studies became exemplars for examining how phenomena are transformed into issues of social concern via media representation. Understanding this affects how we view the purpose and procedures of research in the 'fields' of textual audience and industry research, covered in Part 3. In summary, this chapter:

- Uses the topic of mental illness to explain how media actively create social issues.
- Introduces the concept of 'cultivation' as a useful way to conceive the media's reality effect.

- Demonstrates how the concept of mediatization develops from earlier research on the political effects of popular entertainment.
- Shows how the thinking of 'cultural indicators' explains the structure of research on media texts and organizations.

CASE STUDY: HOW THE MEDIA 'CREATED' MENTAL ILLNESS

Growing interest in mediatization reminds us that, regardless of topic or scholarly perspective, the main task of the media scholar is to show how media play an active role in shaping the world that people experience. Further, it is important to appreciate that the strength of this general effect is secured through the diversity of its forms. Putting this more simply, most of the time critical research on media power *is not* concerned with showing how very powerful people or groups transport their ideas into audiences' heads. That is not to say that there aren't very powerful people and groups who are not good at getting their ideas across to global audiences, and that this state of affairs matters. Clearly there are and it does. But it is to say that there are substantial scholarly reasons for thinking that the most commonplace reality effects are not planned, in the conventional sense of the word.

Media power is hard to analyse because media meanings are made through multiple processes and negotiations that no one completely controls. Media realities are easy to see, on a common-sense level. We can all recognize misrepresentations and untruths, especially when they are about people and things that we know about. The trouble is explaining how these representations come into being. That is the difficult part. Additionally, these abstract observations have to be grounded in real examples, interpreted with coherent ideas and methods selected for sound academic reasons. To this end, the chapter contemplates how mental illness is subject to media reality effects, and how the CIP explains why this happens. This done, it will become clear that the CIP provides a useful framework for explaining how and why media representation is politically real.

Public angle: Media and the production of mental illness as a social problem

In 2013, the World Health Organization (WHO) published the *Mental Health Action Plan 2013–2020*. Its aim was to confront global misunderstanding of a devastating health problem that was being aggravated by war and poverty. The report characterized 'mental illness' as an awkward catch-all phrase for kaleidoscopic conditions 'such as depression, bipolar affective disorder, schizophrenia, anxiety disorders, dementia, substance use disorders, intellectual disabilities, and developmental and behavioural disorders with onset usually occurring in childhood and adolescence, including autism' (World Health Organization, 2013, 6). Knowledge about mental health was virtually zero in parts of the world where such conditions were unrecognized, untreated and unrecorded. Major developmental repercussions followed. Efforts to rebuild after war, for example, were hindered by traumatized populations who needed help.

For WHO, mental health was about civil rights. Poverty was a significant risk factor. The burden of mental illness was, the report warned, disproportionately felt by the poor – those who either were already poor or became so due to their affliction. The stigma of mental illness frequently, in WHO's view, led to double-dose discrimination against minority groups: 'indigenous populations, older people, people experiencing discrimination and human rights violations, lesbian, gay, bisexual, and transgender persons, prisoners, and people exposed to conflict, natural disasters or other humanitarian emergencies' (2013, 7). What WHO was basically saying is this: the main global mental health problem is that most people have the wrong idea about what mental illness is, who suffers from it, and why they develop it.

Media, murder, mental illness: *Bates Motel*

Set against such weighty concerns, it is noteworthy that in 2013 one of the most popular new characters on US television screens was a socially awkward, mentally ill adolescent who murdered his teacher and became a serial killer.

When *Bates Motel* debuted on the A&E cable network, it attracted 3 million viewers and became the organization's biggest ever hit (*Huffington Post*, 2013). It did so with a risky plot that moved back and forward in time, turning one of 20th-century cinema's most terrifying characters into a sweet hero. Bates Motel was the setting for Alfred Hitchcock's 1961 film *Psycho*. The movie centred on Norman Bates, a young man with a severe personality disorder who murdered guests at his hotel while dressed as his own dead mother. *Bates Motel* promised to tell us how Norman became this way. It did so by taking us back to the time when the teenage Bates moved to the hotel with his mother. The twist, however, is that viewers were taken 'back' to the present. Norman was re-imagined as a contemporary high school kid who, for much of the time, was as interested in making friends and making out as the next teen. His pursuit of these normal pleasures, however, was hindered by all manner of problems: the financial pressures of running a poor investment, unrequited love for the girlfriend of the school jock, the murderous underside of a town whose economy relied on drugs, the pressures of dealing with a cooler stepbrother and hiding the murder of a local man who had tried to rape his mother, an unhealthily close relationship with said mother and, beneath all of this, homicidal impulses produced by family trauma.

As the story evolved over its seasons, producers 'explained' Norman by detailing his mental deterioration in relation to a carefully mapped illness. Producer Kerry Ehrin explained:

The interesting thing about the disorder that Norman has, the dissociative identity disorder, is that it's very much activated by stress. It comes out of children who are repeatedly traumatized, either sexually traumatized or live in a very violent environment. They're basically repeatedly scared over and over and over again as children to the extent that they literally retreat into themselves and they pull out a different personality that they can put forward to go deal with whatever is scaring them to death. (Highfill, 2014)

In the context of what research had shown about conventional representations of the mentally ill, a character who was dangerous *and* likeable, vulnerable and understandable was historically significant. *Bates Motel* placed a new spin on two of television's enduring motifs – violence and mental illness. But could one show have a significant impact? What would lead to change, and what are the impediments to making that change lasting?

Scholarly context: Representation and reality

Bates Motel resisted trends in representations of the mentally ill that media scholars had criticized. Content analyses of media representations have found that mentally ill people are usually portrayed as dangerous, violent, unpredictable, lonely and hopeless (Signorielli, 1989; Blood and Holland, 2004; Pirkis et al., 2006; Stuart, 2006; Klin and Lemish, 2008). As an example of how this historical problem has taken a recent turn for the worse in relation to specific kinds of content, some researchers cast rampage murders as media events that reinforce this stigmatization (Höijer and Rasmussen, 2007; Coverdale, Coverdale and Nairn, 2013).

But this is not to say that media *simply* get mental illness wrong over and over again. There are different roads towards stigmatization, and it is important to understand how negative images emerge from different processes (Nawková et al., 2012). As an example, Smardon (2008) observed how recent depictions of mental illness are conflicted between narratives of illness and consumption. Consumer markets for antidepressant drugs require the generation of media narratives that deconstruct the figure of the mental illness sufferer as someone who is lonely, dangerous and generally outside the mainstream. So, if stigmatization still happens, which most researchers still think it does, we do have to account for how this works in different conditions where there are media stories that present mental illnesses as common conditions that strike across social boundaries. Another complicating factor, as Thornton (2010) points out, is that 'positive' messages about the universality of mental illness can have 'negative' effects in that they fail to account for the particular risks faced by marginalized people – an issue that concerns the World Health Organization a great deal. So the contribution of the media to the 'reality' of mental illness, as it is perceived and acted on, is difficult to assess because even if images of stigmatization can be discerned, the issue of why they appear is more difficult to answer.

It is also unhelpful to assume that media always get mental illness wrong, and that commercial entertainment can't play a positive role in reframing its conditions. Along the same lines, research showing overall negative patterns only presents a partial picture (Harper, 2005). Different media genres have different modes of address that establish different relationships with audiences, affecting the extent to which they stigmatize or identify with images of mental illness (Harper, 2005; Caputo and Rouner, 2011). The television show *Monk*, for example, which is about a likeable, skilled detective with obsessive compulsive disorder (OCD), has been credited with closing the social distance between sufferers and non-sufferers among some audiences of the show, and even prompting help-seeking behaviours (Hoffner and Cohen, 2012).

What *is* clear is that mental illness is a real problem whose reality is affected by how it is represented in the media. There are considerable grounds for thinking that sufferers' agony is prolonged by generally negative images that discourage sympathy and help-seeking. That said, these general effects are not the outcome of simple ignorance or wilful neglect. For decades, sociologists have observed that media meanings are made through networks where many people collaborate to produce meanings within the conventions of established genres (e.g. Powdermaker, 1951; Tuchman, 1978; Gitlin, 1987; Eliasoph, 1988). To complicate things further, it can be difficult to distinguish 'positive' from 'negative' images. Although *Monk* has been praised, for instance, critics have questioned the value of a show that presents OCD as an individual rather than a social problem (Johnson, 2008). All that can be said with certainty is that media's production of mental illness as a real problem is ambiguous.

Such complications became especially visible in the wake of the 2012 Newtown murders. In a study entitled 'News media framing of serious mental illness and gun violence in the United States, 1997–2012', McGinty and colleagues (2014) noted the intersecting reality effects of a growing trend where gun rampages were framed as mental health issues. Simply put, press representations of the Virginia Tech, Aurora Colorado, Tucson Arizona and Newtown Connecticut murderers as mentally ill people impeded gun law reform in the US. Most of the nation's 65,000 annual gun deaths attracted little attention, making it easier for pro-gun lobbies to argue that mass murders are not about the prevalence of firearms. To look at how and why this might work, McGinty et al. examined how the US press dealt with mental health issues in its coverage of rampage shootings, from Columbine to Newtown.

They discovered a *specification* of the stigmatization process, relating to narrative form. Significant distinctions were apparent between 'event' and 'theme' stories. Event stories are 'what' reports that describe. These represented the largest proportion of the coverage of all shootings between 1997 and 2012, at 61%. Only 10% of these stories provided facts about mental illnesses. Thematic stories – reports of a 'why' variety – were far more likely to explain mental conditions, but provided a far smaller percentage of the coverage, at 29%. The worry was that this pattern could actively produce two sorts of realities that made the world a more dangerous place for everyone. First, it fostered suspicion of the vast majority of mentally ill people who were no danger to anybody other than themselves. Second, it did nothing to protect the tens of thousands of Americans who were endangered by healthy gun owners (McGinty et al., 2014).

However, McGinty et al. also described a changing culture. Newtown had changed things. The slaughter of very young children led to two weeks of intense media discussion on the need for stricter gun control, something that hadn't happened after Virginia Tech, Aurora or Tucson. All told, then, this was an important study because it revealed three significant principles in researching media realities:

- The need to be sensitive to similarities *and differences* in media representations. Virginia Tech, Aurora *and* Tucson were depicted as being about mental illness, not gun control, but the same was not true for Newtown.

- The need to be sensitive to similarities and differences between genres. Although the 'problem' is that stigmatization has tended to be reproduced across the media landscape, the evidence from this study was that this stigmatization was related to *form* – it is easier to explore the complexities of mental illness in some news genres than it is in others.

- The need to consider how realities are produced through specific kinds of cultural work. Here, what mattered was the distinction between 'breaking news' and feature pieces.

These observations highlighted the importance of being able to frame media power within fluid cultures. If, historically, media have reinforced negative images of the mentally ill, this does not mean that they haven't also changed perceptions for the better in ways that really matter. Stuart (2006) pointed out that media drama has, on occasion, contributed enormously to public understanding of mental illness, while at the same time the majority of stories across all genres have frightened the life out of sufferers with doom-laden fables of social isolation and torture-like treatments. So, the question of how media make the reality of mental illness involves looking at the production of changing realities across changing circumstances, within and without the media.

These are foundational questions in understanding how media create reality. The significance of *Bates Motel* could only be discussed in relation to a deeper question about general media influence. Can one shift established ways of seeing within established media conventions that produce the very impressions that one seeks to change? One way to understand what factors would determine the show's prospects is to consider The Cultural Indicators Project (CIP), a research model that had been analysing media reality effects via images of violence and mental illness for some time.

KEY PARADIGM: THE CULTURAL INDICATORS PROJECT

Introducing George Gerbner

The CIP was developed by a Hungarian-American George Gerbner. Gerbner provides another fascinating example of how valuable it can be to know about the people who do scholarly work in order to really understand what they are trying to say. Towards the end of his life, Gerbner wrote a bitter essay entitled 'If Adolf Hitler ...' (Gerbner, 2001). The essay did two things. First, it summarized Gerbner's view of the essential media problem that America and the rest of the world faced. In it, Gerbner hypothesized that the 21st century's global media and political landscape would have delighted Hitler: the resurrection of Nazism, the massive expansion of surveillance, the eradication of union power and the popular demonization and savage repression of protest. These effects were wrought, Gerbner argued, by the collusion of corporate influence, political conservation and media monopolies. Together, these forces created a frightening neo-fascism. The media contributed to this by building a symbolic environment dominated by aspirational lifestyle images and happy endings that systematically avoided reflection on the social causes of 'unhappy' endings. Groups who were not part of consumer society were either invisible or portrayed as bad. The stigmatization of the mentally ill reflected this wider ideological mission (Gerbner, 2001).

None of this indicates that Gerbner was interested in how popular culture engages audiences with social issues, but there are things you should know about why he felt this way. First, Gerbner had fled Hungary because he was about to be conscripted into his national army, where he would have been forced to fight for fascism. Second, he ended the Second World War with a distinguished record of fighting against Hitler, as an American Special Forces soldier (Lent, 1995; Gerbner, 2001; Morgan, 2012). Third, his views of media power were grounded in detailed analyses of how media stories were put together in particular organizational contexts. His early work on how American television and films told stories about mental illness was a key topic in developing his ideas.

To understand the value of the CIP as a method for conceiving how media make reality, it is important to go back to Gerbner's early work on the role of human communication, the relationship between culture and the individual, and how studies of television portrayals of mental illness stood as an early example of how media industries assumed an independent role in making reality through in-house production purposes. Another value of starting here is that it also shows how the CIP emerged from the same historical interests (in terms of conceiving the relationship between people and culture), as we explored in Chapter 3.

Despite his hard science credentials, Gerbner started academic life as a poet and student of folklore (Morgan, 2012). His background spawned a lifelong interest in creative processes, and early in the CIP he urged media professionals to maximize their creative capacity, given the social responsibility that had been handed to them (Gerbner, 1958b). The CIP was founded on the observation that culture was a reality that people created through symbolic interaction (Gerbner, 1969a). Societies had always socialized by telling stories. The problem in the 20th century was that the diversity of the sources for those stories was shrinking. Where stories had come from schools, churches and parents, by the mid-20th century the ones that most people consumed most of the time came from television. People had always lived in symbolic environments, but never ones so far-reaching and centralized (Gerbner, 1969a, 1994, 1995).

Media professionals had therefore become *de facto* arbiters of political debates. By the late 1950s, Gerbner was already arguing that it had become practically impossible to separate social problems from the media. Indeed, the rise of media industries as central sense-making institutions was *the* defining social problem of the 20th century (Gerbner, 1958, 1998, 2001).

Understanding the political function of entertainment was crucial here. Television, like folk tales, theatre and literature, did most of its teaching through fiction. If news told audiences about how the world was, fiction, according to the CIP, provided explanations for *why* it was that way (Gerbner, 1995). In this regard, television consistently failed to improve the experience and management of mental illness because it preferred stories where mentally ill people were dangerous to others. It was perfectly possible to tell a different tale, that the mentally ill suffered because of social circumstances, lack of understanding and lack of support (Gerbner, 1993). However, the nature of this problem could only be understood by examining the production processes that turned a thing in the world into a thing on the screen.

The Cultural Indicators Project: How media managers affect stories about social problems

The Cultural Indicators Project was an ambitious attempt to map television reality that started in 1967 at the University of Pennsylvania. The Project was established to discover how television depicted the realities of life, and the effects of these depictions on audiences. By 1994, the Project had performed a content analysis of 3,000 programmes and 39,000 characters (Gerbner, 1995), making it one of the world's most detailed records of the recurrent themes that US television showed to its audiences.

The Project was best known for using screen violence to demonstrate the reality effects of media. The CIP spawned cultivation analysis, a project that had a major impact on global media studies by looking at how exposure to screen violence affected the political views of audiences. Beginning in the 1960s, the CIP started to count the acts of violence performed in samples of prime time television. In the 1970s, they also used surveys to look for differences between 'light' and 'heavy' viewers. The method lead to the discovery of the 'mean world syndrome' (Gerbner, Gross, Morgan and Signorielli, 1980). This described a statistical phenomenon whereby across a range of social groups, the more television people watched, the more likely they were to feel the threat of real-life victimization of violent crime, feel suspicious about other people, and support aggressive 'wars' on social problems like violence and drugs over other methods of dealing with the causes of such issues (Gerbner, 1994). The significance of these findings for media studies in general was that they shifted attention away from the particular outcomes of particular sorts of content towards understanding the role that media had adopted in making perceptions of social reality possible in the first place (Gerbner, 1976).

Cultivation analysis was a landmark in understanding media's reality effects for several reasons. Most fundamentally, it outlined a mechanism through which fictional violence had real effects on large numbers of people. Figures showed that the television world was far more violent than the real one, even for viewers living in areas that suffered from high crime rates. Violence pervaded prime time television, and was even more rife in children's programming (Gerbner, 1995). The more people watched, the more they were exposed to media violence. Given this, the combination of content analysis and survey data supported the idea that the main effect of screen violence was to make people passive. Television did not make people violent, it made them fearful, and this fear tended to 'cultivate' conservative views of the world (Gerbner, 1994, 1995).

There was evidence that this 'reality' was loaded in a particular direction. The Cultural Indicators Project did far more than count violent incidents on prime time television. It also categorized victims and villains – who carried out the violence, who was on the receiving end, and who tended to get away with being violent (Gerbner, 1994, 1995). The results of these calculations showed that white, middle-aged, middle-class men had the lowest aggression-to-victimization quotient, whereas those for women, black, Hispanic and Asian characters was far higher. Further content analyses of characters indicated that this victimization coincided with the relative lack of diversity in the roles television offered these groups, leading Gerbner to the conclusion that media violence principally mattered as a dramatization of the social order.

However, this disguised a still darker truth. Gerbner called television 'the cultural arm of the industrial order', (1976, 151), and believed that television violence encapsulated this political function. But if this was so, why did his career flourish in an era when a great deal of funding was directed towards the study of behaviours? The Cultural Indicators Project was boosted by US Federal funding from the National Commission on the Causes and Prevention of Violence (NCCPV). This body, established after the assassinations of the Kennedy brothers and Martin Luther King in the 1960s, commissioned a Media Task Force to examine the role of television in social unrest. Extraordinarily, Gerbner came to the conclusion that this move and the many state inquiries into the effects of violence that followed thereafter amounted to little more than a calculated, diversionary political sideshow. Content analysis showed that television violence was not interested in the causes of violence; it was mainly concerned with ensuring that the bad people who did it for bad reasons got punished. Gerbner thought the same could be said for the state. Screen violence was a means of telling simple stories in which the world was ordered into neat categories where shades of grey did not exist (Gerbner, 1994, 1995).

Gerbner came to believe that US official interests in screen violence were designed to write the same story for political purposes. The tale fostered a worldview where it became more acceptable to be tough on crime and ignore its social consequences. This had real impacts on social and media policy. After decades of being paraded in front of the Senate, Congress and mainstream media, and being asked to answer questions about the behavioural impact of screen violence on individuals, which Gerbner found entirely irrelevant, the eminent scholar could reach only one conclusion: the media violence question provided an expedient way for governments and media industries to avoid their obligations to preserving the integrity of social communication. Media violence was simply a symptom of a more important challenge. Humans have always created reality through the exchange of symbols. For this to work properly, democracies need message systems that deliver diversity. Yet the mass media age had delivered precisely the opposite. Most of the world lives within systems of industrialized storytelling characterized by an ever shrinking range of viewpoints. This could only be solved by a fundamental rearrangement of media industries that ensured greater creativity.

On violence, for example, the problem was not that television modelled aggression, but that it used violence to avoid complicated storytelling that challenged audiences. For centuries, popular fictions had used violence to good effect in order to prompt reflection on the nature of humanity. Now screens were flooded with 'happy violence', with no purpose other than delivering audiences to advertisers in a buying mood. At the same time, the ever present media violence question, and the engagement with industries through debates on voluntary codes of regulation and the development of 'parental lock-out' technologies, created the impression of action while doing nothing about the cause of the problem (Gerbner, 1994).

There was nothing about the success of *Bates Motel* that contradicted this argument. True, the show thrived in the shades of grey that Gerbner accused television of avoiding. Perhaps, one might argue, his views were tied to the broadcast era, and the success of the new show was evidence that market- and technology-driven industries, which furnished international audiences with express content created by niche channels, indeed delivered the diversity that society needed. However, this conclusion underestimates the nuances in Gerbner's work. Gerbner would have said that *Bates Motel* meant little, in itself, set against historical trends in unsympathetic depictions of the mentally ill. The real question, for Gerbner, was how stable patterns of representation solidified themselves in media conventions and public consciousness. What mattered was the big picture – how media treated most of the people most of the time. Gerbner's arguments about violence were that violent images were important because they were the clearest indicator of the media's reality effect, as the dominant theme that reached most audiences. What really interested him was the cultivation of perceptions through repetitive, stable narratives. Gerbner applied the same approach to perceptions of gender (Gerbner, 1958a), education (Gerbner, 1960), heroism (Gerbner, 1969b) and mental illness. In this regard, there was much to be learned about the significance of *Bates Motel* by looking at Gerbner's work on how television 'made' psychological disorders. Gerbner started writing about this in the 1950s, and continued to advise on the topic into the 1990s. He therefore offered valuable insights into where *Bates Motel* came from, where it was likely to 'go' in public consciousness, and what all of this meant for understanding how media make reality.

KEY INSIGHT: MENTAL ILLNESS AND INDUSTRIALIZATION STORYTELLING

Gerbner found that the stigmatization of mentally ill people emerged from the pressures of reconciling conflicting strategic goals that were enforced on media producers. Gerbner was clearly hostile to media industries as political entities, but was markedly more sympathetic to the people who worked in them. One of the reasons for this is that in his early research on television and mental illness he discovered the administrative complications that made it difficult to tell hopeful stories.

Gerbner's approach to popular culture in the 1950s was considerably more optimistic than his later work, and when he turned to stories of mental illness, he spent a lot of time examining the pressures placed on those responsible for holding the attention of large audiences. This period of Gerbner's work was the foundation for the CIP. So it's worth noting that at this time he viewed mass culture with a mixture of wonderment and hope. Where other American scholars in the same period bewailed the absence of creativity in the age of mass-produced stories (e.g. MacDonald, 1953), Gerbner was keen to avoid underestimating the complexity of mass culture. The industrialization of popular culture created a challenging academic puzzle. In post-war societies, it took thousands of people to sell a can of peas, including armies of creatives tasked with convincing audiences that this can was significantly different from that one. If *peas* needed a sophisticated division of labour, then how intricate was the production of mass popular culture? And how important was it to explore these intricacies, given the centrality of popular culture to democracy (Gerbner, 1960)?

Gerbner saw three flaws in popular culture: the concentration of popular culture in corporate hands, the orientation of those corporations to 'careful assessment, cultivation and exploitation of marketable desires', and 'the simultaneous introduction of ideas and products at all levels of society', such that 'the strange becomes familiar' and 'the flow of influence appears lateral, because everyone can be exposed to the same sources' (Gerbner, 1960, 13). Gerbner saw 'instant simultaneous flow' as a problem because, in practice, the consumerist bent of common culture equated the right to access with the right to have fun and be entertained.

The topic of mental illness was one of the first places where Gerbner explained how these abstract political objections related to media representations. The roots of stigmatization lay in the limits on creativity imposed on media producers as they tried to balance the right to be entertained with the right to be informed and, most crucially, the professional obligation to avoid risks. Ultimately, when you put ethical considerations together with commercial ones, media professionals made the reality of mental illness through a series of *ad hoc* professional conventions designed to placate the multiple stakeholders to whom they found themselves accountable. Here, 'keeping the peace' trumped challenging misconceptions.

Gerbner and Tannenbaum (1960) showed this by relating representations of mental illness to codes of conduct that film and television companies were obliged to observe in the 1950s. Through a fascinating combination of content analysis, archive research and interviews with media executives, the authors found that the stigmatization that still concerns media scholars and health practitioners was the outcome of people trying to do the right thing both socially and commercially.

Managing the content of mass culture

The study certainly came up with alarming statistics. Content analysis of all American films released since 1950 which had mentally ill characters showed that only 56% of these characters had jobs, and that even then the leading 'occupation' was professional criminal! However, the more compelling aspect of the research was the explanation of how such clear examples of stigmatization were the ironic outcome of the commitment to commercially viable social responsibility.

Alarming as these figures were, they mattered most as clues to other puzzles. What forces made these patterns, and what did this say about the role of popular entertainment as a new hub of social thought? In search of answers, Gerbner and Tannenbaum set about interviewing staff and examining records from two organizations. One was the Production Code Administration (PCA). This was a branch of the Motion Picture Association of America (MPAA), the industry body charged with enforcing the Hollywood Production Code, which was a set of voluntary standards adopted by the film industry in 1930 to assuage government concerns about the moral content of popular films. The other was 'network censors', who were television executives charged with enforcing the National Association of Broadcasters' production codes about taste and decency. In both cases, Gerbner characterized these people, who were invested with the power to insist on edits or, indeed, prevent the screening of material which they deemed to contravene codes, as key arbiters in the construction of public culture. In the end, the meanings of reality that were written and consumed were highly influenced by these professionals, whose job it was to protect media markets by steering film and television companies through the political dangers of public storytelling. The early days of Hollywood had proved that entertaining images of sex and violence caused enough concern to threaten official legislation. Voluntary codes were a way to avoid this outcome, thereby retaining control in the cultivation of markets. Industry 'censors' – the people at the MPAA and networks who ultimately decided what audiences got to see based on their interpretation of industry codes – were vital 'links' in 'chains' of public communication. However, studying the mechanisms of this power in practice discovered some surprising facts.

One was that morals clauses in the film Production Code aimed at maintaining respect for professionals actually amplified the stigmatization of mental illness. The code insisted that films should retain respect for doctors, lawyers, teachers and the like by refraining from portrayals of such characters negatively. This explained the lack of employment among the mentally ill on the big screen. The morals clauses made risk-averse PCA officials loath to pass such depictions, lest this be read as negativity (Gerbner and Tannenbaum, 1960).

Gerbner and Tannenbaum argued that the administration of television networks made the management of mental illness themes especially challenging. Television censors judged mountains of content, making their decision unavoidably reactive. Network censors were conscious of having a closer relationship with audiences and interest groups than their film colleagues, which made their job even more thankless. Intriguingly, though, Gerbner and Tannenbaum argued that these chaotic conditions gave them even greater reality power.

A key resource in making this argument was the discovery of a 'Mental Afflictions File' at an un-named network. The file contained records of all of the decisions that had been made on television portrayals of mentally ill people since 1948, and had become the key training tool for company censors. It contained a wealth of data on how abstract codes could be negotiated in practice, and this became the authority for company policy. It also, however, demonstrated some of the less obvious variables that affected representations. The file revealed that this company had a sophisticated grasp of real-world mental health issues because one of its early censors had a close interest in Veterans Affairs and was highly sensitive to the concerns of healthcare professionals. The staff member's forensic engagement with depictions of the ill on television was scrupulously recorded in the file, bequeathing a legacy of guidelines to his successors that was far more detailed and nuanced than similar resources held by broadcast competitors.

On the basis of this evidence, Gerbner and Tannenbaum were able to identify a distinct reality effect exercised by privately owned media interests. The internal operations of companies, and the professional socialization of their staff in the ways of corporate media, had a far more powerful role in determining what the public saw than did any form of official censorship or formal industry code. In this case, that seemed to operate in the public interest, but the point was to underline how a commercial system of public storytelling produced a saturated public symbolic environment where relatively few voices were heard, and the channels to public expression – and being heard – were incredibly narrow.

Nevertheless, at that time the research identified significant points of tension in the mass communication process. The biggest was 'possible conflict between the validity of dramatic or documentary presentation and the felt expediency to protect existing markets, tastes and public good-will' (Gerbner and Tannenbaum, 1960, 385). A changing cast of characters smoothed these tensions out. The 'Mental Illness' file of the un-named network showed how different interest groups could affect representations of mental health by establishing relationships not just with writers, but also with network censors. On the other hand, the more pervasive reality across all of the film and television organizations surveyed was that the decisions made by these censors exercised a chilling effect on the creative process, discouraging writers from pursuing stories about mental health in an era where the topic was practically viewed as taboo by risk-sensitive executives. This reinforced Gerbner's view that popular culture was politically important, that the stories it told could have a positive effect on real political issues, but that the daily realities of the mass media discouraged efforts to give novel and challenging treatment to uncomfortable subjects.

SIGNIFICANCE: UNDERSTANDING REPRESENTATION AS A SOCIAL AND INDUSTRIAL PROCESS

When it comes to mental health, the World Health Organization has announced that the most pressing problem the world faces today is ignorance and misunderstanding. Evidence of content analysis since the 1950s has consistently found that the media tend to exacerbate the problem, and the rise of rampage murders as highly visible media events probably makes things worse. Coverage of these crimes seems to say out loud what media have been whispering for decades: the mentally ill are dangerous.

On the other hand, not all media representations are the same. Challenging portrayals that break stereotypes have become international hits, indicating that change is possible. But the issue of how the occasional story can affect general patterns of understanding has long been a matter of controversy.

Taking all of this into account, whatever its producers thought, *Bates Motel* was a 'cultural indicator' of debates on how media became involved in managing mental illness. We can't 'fix' what the show 'did' to audiences' understandings of mental illness. But we can identify the pertinent questions to ask about this by looking at research on the issue. We can note the significance of a show that took a detailed look at a particular condition as it was experienced by a complex but largely sympathetic character. The history of general patterns could hardly have predicted the success of a show whose hero is the sort of character that audiences have been taught to suspect. On the other hand, we can note the unhelpful aspects of a narrative arch that *must* turn the hero into a serial killer, thereby maintaining a historical trend where television has always tended to treat the mentally ill as dangerous. These are both valid interpretations, but it is probably more useful to ask how production conditions at the A&E network supported experimentation, and also wonder whether these conditions represented a larger change in global television culture.

These observations speak to the heart of media realities. They represent the importance of being able to explain change and stability in what media tell us about the world. The task, at that point, is to identify a model that allows us to schematize these reality effects in a coherent conceptual and methodological form. This chapter has done this by telling the 'story' of media and mental illness through the lens of the Cultural Indicators Project.

The CIP teaches us the value of seeing *Bates Motel*, or any media product for that matter, as a clue about how culture works. The task is not to discern its message and decide whether it is 'good' or 'bad' in terms of its portrayal of mental illness. The job instead is to assess what the show 'indicates' about the forces that shape how real-world issues become sources of entertainment. To do this, the researcher must be able to clearly articulate why and how a show matters. The CIP modelled two valuable methods for achieving this. First, it modelled the value of being able to locate particular stories within the dominant patterns of representation that audiences encountered over time. Second, it demonstrated the importance of explaining these patterns through the analysis of production decisions, as they were made through the interactions among writers, producers, administrators, and other social groups who managed to catch the ear of media professionals. The CIP also showed the value of explaining media meanings as the outcomes of delicate negotiations among commercial, professional and social priorities. Gerbner concluded that, at least in his lifetime, evidence indicated that commercial pressures had a chilling effect on public storytelling. The mental health case study was one of the places where he made this general point. The poverty of media stories about mental illness – a media fact that continues to be noted by scholars – reflected a general tendency towards risk aversion and a surprising outcome of self-regulation. Gerbner's work on mental health taught that on-the-hoof management decisions were just as – if not more – important in determining the shape of public culture as was the creativity of writers or the regulatory power of the state. This was an early example of a general research principle that would govern his later research on violence and gender: that media constitute a vital organizational chain in the production of social reality. Things in the world become things in the public mind when media organize interactions between social groups and media professionals, and the main way that media affect reality is by serving as this social hub. As his thinking progressed, Gerbner certainly came to believe that this system favoured homogenized, conservative methods. But this should not distract attention from the imagination behind his methods, and their capacity to discover surprising things about why media stories were told in certain ways. And there is certainly a contemporary value to these ideas. They teach that, when faced with *Bates Motel* – or any apparently ground-breaking phenomena, we should not ask whether it is good or bad, negative or positive, but how it was possible, production wise, and how likely it is that its innovation can be nurtured across media industries.

Whenever faced with a question like 'How do media affect reality?' it is useful to ground answers in a particular point of view, applied to a particular example. The CIP is useful here in several ways. First, it helps to historicize mediatization debates. Gerbner's work showed that social institutions were already adapting to media in the 1950s. Mental health's existence as a public issue was influenced by in-house socialization of media professionals. Gerbner's work taught the importance of being inventive when looking for evidence about how significant junctions in the chain of public communication took public storytelling in particular directions. This was an enormously significant observation because, as we shall see later, it had a major impact on how we understand the significance of media texts and the actions of media audiences. Overall, Gerbner taught us that the ability to explain how media make reality is just as significant as arguing what that reality is.

CHAPTER SUMMARY

- Understanding *how* media create perceptions that affect how societies perceive social issues is a foundational task in media research.

- Media representations of mental illness are a valuable case study that demonstrates why this is an important question. The misunderstanding of mental illness is a major obstacle to social inclusion and economic development. Content analyses suggest that global media tend to stigmatize the mentally ill in the stories that tell. There are grounds, then, to think that media are exacerbating a real medical challenge.

- The Cultural Indicators Project offers a valuable method for articulating and schematizing these concerns. It is unique as an approach that both charted trends in representations of mental illness and explained how those representations evolved in different organizational contexts.

- The CIP was unique in its capacity to say that the 'production' of mental illness as a social issue in media represented the general reality effect of media industries.

- It also demonstrates the historical roots of mediatization and outlines ways to go about studying how the process works – particularly combining textual analysis with organizational research.

- This contributed the methodological innovation of learning to identify 'key informants' in the chain of media communication. These techniques apply to studies of media people and media markets.

7

RESEARCHING MEDIA'S ROLE IN SOCIAL LIFE

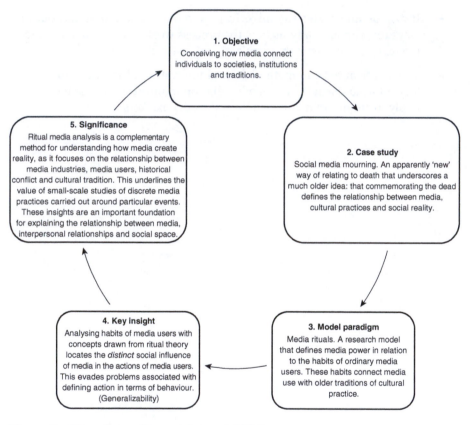

Figure 3 How do media organize social life?

OBJECTIVE: UNDERSTANDING HOW MEDIA USERS MAKE REALITY

This chapter uses media ritual theory to explain how media connect ordinary people to culture and society. This area is explored with reference to the phenomenon of social media mourning (SMM). SMM is a 'media practice'. It is a set of communication behaviours that media users perform. SMM seems to have changed the experience of grief, and this widely shared impression creates an opportunity to define the value of studying how ordinary people use media. Anthropologists have shown that grieving is a cultural ritual that creates the meaning of death. Meanwhile, historians have shown that these rituals have profound political effects. Consequently, SMM specifies what research on media use contributes to anthropological and historical analyses of how people participate in constructing social reality.

There are three steps to understanding the general significance of SMM as an index of media influence, in relation to the ritual concept. The first is to appreciate the cultural role of mourning, the second is to see how the practice became involved in the construction of history, and the third is to understand how media helped transform mourning from a spiritual ritual to an act of cultural history. After providing evidence to show that SMM is an important emerging area of study, the chapter reflects on how death can be conceived as a symbolic reality, by drawing on anthropologist Victor Turner (1978, 1985). Turner explained how death is an event that we use to make sense of the meaning of life. We do this, he observed, through symbolic actions. Turner's work is relevant because it allows us to see SMM in relation to spiritual rituals. Next, we see how the anthropological interest in death rituals assumed an historical and political significance by considering the work of the Great War historian Jay Winter. Winter showed that in the 20th century mourning assumed a political edge. European societies in particular coped with the unimaginable trauma of the Great War through a variety of symbolic commemorations. In combination, these actions became implicated in the evaluation of civilization and modernity (Winter, 2014). Significantly, media quickly assumed an important historical role, as mourning was transformed into a political practice, which expressed far more than personal grief.

By this point, the chapter will have established that mourning is one of the things that people do to understand their place in history. For this reason, mourning is a symbolic action that carries political outcomes. The next step is to show how 'media rituals' play a distinct role in this process. Ritual is a concept that scholars have used to explain how media structure social life through the routines of media users. Ritual theory explains how doing things with media has become a common proxy for other meaningful actions that have been used to 'stake out' the social world and its boundaries. It is also an idea that allows us to trace connections between SMM and the cultural history of mourning. This done, it's possible to see that SMM is a topic of concern because it is a media habit that connects media users to familiar symbolic processes that people have always used to make sense of life.

(Continued)

Popular and academic interest in SMM therefore has a clear genealogy that is worth establishing, because in doing so it also becomes clear how small-scale studies of the things that people do with media in reaction to moments of social transition or crisis reveal much about how media influence society by making tangible connections between cultural traditions – and all of the political conflicts that they imply – and common forms of media practice. Appreciating these connections achieves a number of goals: it improves the ability to explain the effects of media technologies, and it sets the foundation for appreciating the role of media in interpersonal communication and the creation of social spaces.

In summary, this chapter:

- Explains why SMM raises significant questions about the influence of media technologies.
- Situates the significance of SMM within research on media rituals, which analyses how media users make media influence 'real'.
- Describes how a 'ritualistic' approach to media usage provides a compelling way to create associations between individual actions and cultural politics. That is, it allows us to make associations between the ordinary things that people do with media and the political conflicts that define the age.
- Clarifies how insights derived from research on SMM can be applied to establishing meaningful cases in media research.

CASE STUDY: SOCIAL MEDIA MOURNING

Public angle: How social media make grieving more painful

From the point of view of contemporary public opinion and media research alike, it certainly seems that social media has changed the grief experience. In 2012, Newtown primary school teacher Victoria Soto died while shielding her students from a rampage murderer. Three years later, her family tried to trademark her name. As they explained to BBC journalist Rajini Vaidyanathan (2015), the reasons were emotional. The pain of the 26 year-old's death was aggravated by daily abuse from social media users. The family was bombarded with accusations from conspiracy theorists that Victoria was not really dead, or had to fight a flood of bogus Twitter accounts taken out in her name. Fake Facebook sites even established scam appeals. For the Sotos, the monumentally difficult task of accepting Victoria's horrific death was made impossible by the strangers who exploited social media to place malicious narrative spins on her murder.

On one level, the Sotos' story is about the effects of media technologies. Devices and platforms are credited with possessing 'affordances', structures that significantly influence how we use them. Technological affordances partly explain the rapid evolution of SMM etiquette. Marwick and Ellison (2012) suggest that the practice has been directed by four conditions unique to social media: replicability, scalability, persistence and searchability. Online mourning is structured by templates for enduring acts of grieving, performed for global audiences in retrievable form. On the one hand, the idea that social media provide a language to express sorrow to a global audience in a way that can be easily preserved seems like a good thing. But this isn't necessarily so. To understand why, imagine a Facebook memorial site as a grave. You don't need to worry about a memorial site becoming overgrown and forgotten, but online 'vandalism' is a much more pertinent threat.

The scale and persistence of online grieving produces 'context collapse' (Marwick and Ellison, 2012), where funereal etiquette is thrown into chaos as strangers trample on the privacy of the bereaved. In the movie *Wedding Crashers*, comedian Will Ferrell played a characteristically absurd role as a man who gate-crashed funerals in order to meet women. The joke is predicated on a sacrilegious idea: that anyone would intrude on a grieving family to serve their own needs. Yet this is common practice in SMM, and it adds to the work of grief. Anxieties about 'trolling' provoke hyper-vigilance, where great effort is directed to preserving the reputation of the dead people who can no longer defend themselves. We have never liked 'speaking ill of the dead'. But this age-old taboo assumes new significance when it is channelled through global social media. At stake are the tensions between death as a private and public affair. Media added to this tension when newspaper obituaries began sharing news about the dead with a general public. This set in train the mechanics of 'context collapse', where the grief of the bereaved was publicly shared. Facebook mourning ups the ante as these strangers can now form a relationship with the dead, and contribute to their biographization and memorialization (Carroll and Landry, 2010).

Scholarly context: The political impact of mediated grief

The political significance of popular media mourning is especially clear to those who have researched its role in atrocities and disasters. The 'affordances' of online communication assumed a global significance in terms of defining major turning points in international relations and became a significant matter in the wake of the 2001 9/11 attack on New York. Certainly, the case has been powerfully made that 9/11 became an historical landmark through media framing. Kellner (2004) argued that broadcast television evoked emotional responses which energized and legitimated George W. Bush's 'War on Terror'. But there was more than media persuasion at stake here, because the public quickly found ways to participate in the construction of 9/11 as a moment of geo-political change, and mourning via media was part of that process.

According to Kitch (2003), US news magazines, such as *Time* and *Newsweek*, immediately invoked mourning rituals. These rituals conventionally move through three stages: initial shock, a process of events, and a period of acceptance where the bereaved find a way to move forward in life. This third stage was represented by the shift from stories about victims to those about heroes, and others about the resilience of ordinary New Yorkers as the city got back to work. But 9/11 also endures as an historical landmark because media *users* made and preserved the contemporary relevance of the attacks through acts of media mourning. Silverstone (2004) argued that 9/11 was a first as a media event made by the public as media industries stumbled. Kellner and Kitch stressed the authority of media institutions, but Silverstone reminded us that the immediate public experience of 9/11 was largely a confusing one. New Yorkers quickly became more conscious of their 'media practices' – the every-day routines used to make sense of life. Faced with challenges such as the inability of news to give an immediate, authoritative account of what had happened, and overwhelmed telephony networks, the public quickly adapted to combine different kinds of media use to build a narrative for themselves. In this way, 9/11 almost immediately dramatized how people and mobile media played a significant role in defining media events.

So the symbolic mourning practices that Kitch (2003) had noted in main-stream news outlets also featured in public media use, where the mediation of mourning rituals assumed an important role in determining the lessons of 9/11. Silverstone (2004) noted how the dual forces of mainstream and mobile media had in effect produced the ability to blend personal experiences and public history, and this has continued to be a feature of online 9/11 mourning. Memorial websites, for example, often use personal narratives to establish mourners' place in history (Hess, 2007a). Moreover, the blending of mobile and mainstream media in reporting the attacks has become a key feature of official commemoration practices. The Ground Zero Memorial makes exten-sive use of smartphone apps, which let visitors create a personal connection to the scene (Hess, 2007a). 9/11 mourning is a media practice that infuses the attacks with an ongoing political legacy. The event has become a key source of political socialization, where parents commonly teach their children about the world through media-enabled conversations about what happened (Houston, 2013). It is also a source of political conflict, and this can be seen in controver-sies over how it should be commemorated through acts of mourning, including an ever-present media element (Donofrio, 2010; Smith and McDonald, 2010; Hess and Herbig, 2013).

Putting all of this together, SMM is noteworthy as an incarnation of ordi-nary media practices that serve political functions of global importance. People are quite accustomed to using media when processing trauma, and these habits affect how events are recorded as matters of historical signifi-cance. Moreover, these media practices make the associations between people and society very clear. SMM sensitizes the public to their place in history, and this can become a powerful political force. It follows that SMM is a phenome-non that clarifies the distinct contribution that media studies makes to understanding society, culture and history. In what follows, this connection will be made clearer by exploring this historical significance of mourning ritu-als and the way that research on *media* rituals adds a distinct element to understanding the political salience of mourning practices. This is significant as an example of how media make reality by directing how people adapt their engagement with culture to changing symbolic resources.

KEY PARADIGM: MEDIA RITUALS

From rituals to media rituals

The task at hand is to explain how media power works when the 'affordances' of media technologies lend themselves to established cultural practices. Social life needs a structure; that structure depends on the creation and sharing of media through symbols, and media become powerful when they provide a ready-to-hand way of achieving these goals. We have already seen how these ideas apply to the stories that media industries tell, but it is also true that the same monopolization process – where media takes the place of the other meaningful activities – can be seen in everyday media practices. Mourning illustrates this transition. In order to demonstrate this, anthropological work on the symbolic qualities of mourning will be outlined, and then we will see how his ideas explicate the significance of the Sotos' experiences.

Anthropologist Victor Turner's analysis of symbolic mourning rituals is a useful place to begin this discussion. This is because Turner explained how the cultural roles of traditional religious morning rituals had migrated to media use in the late 20th century. In *Image and Pilgrimage in Christian Culture* (1978), Turner defined mourning as something that people do in order to feel connected to transcendent ideas; in this case, the existence of a supreme being. For our purposes, there are two elements of this work worth noting. The first is that contemplating the meaning of life and society through mourning was as much about *doing* as thinking, and meaning could not be separated from action. Second, Turner interpreted mourning as a method of processing historical change. Mourning was symbolic and dramatic because it typically took the form of a three-act play. Each begins with a separation. First, death takes a loved one from the living. A family or community then enters a 'liminal' phase. Here, social values and hierarchies are brought into question. People who troll grieving parents through social media, for example, damage our faith in humanity. Finally, mourning involves acts of aggregation, where symbolic actions reconstruct a new moral order that people can believe in.

Turner let us understand that bereaved people routinely connect with communal values by engaging in symbolic activities that unite meaning and action. He also opened a way for appreciating how ordinary people make significant contributions to the creation of social reality in conceiving rituals as open processes where values can be contested. Turner argued that rituals functioned through dominant symbols that, somewhat ironically, became dominant because they could be interpreted in a number of ways. Driven by this insight, he turned his attention to ritualistic qualities of media events – phenomena that invited people to participate in cultural practices through the sharing of common symbolic resources that could be used to serve different ends (Turner, 1985). As we shall see, this idea became important in later work on *media* rituals, but for now let's just note that Turner acknowledged that traditional cultural practices were being channelled in the direction of media. He believed that ritual practices were largely being transferred from institutions to the leisure sphere, meaning that small-scale, individual leisure practices were likely to become the place where culture 'happened', with media consumption being a case in point (Turner, 1985).

Certainly, the Soto episode can be explained using Turner's concepts. Regrettably, one of the things that made the Sandy Hook massacre a 'dominant' symbol was that it could be used to tell different stories. Trolling kept the Soto family in a liminal stage where the narrative of their daughter was hard to control, and they had to use their own knowledge of media – that is symbolic – processes in order to complete the mourning process. The Soto family's efforts to brand their daughter's name could, according to this logic, be interpreted as a symbolic act of faith in the legal system surrounding media industries.

So, Turner established that mourning was a culturally meaningful act that involved ordinary people in the production of symbols. However, the question of why this mattered politically remains, and this issue can be clarified by returning to the discipline of history. Of particular interest here are researchers who have related the 'transcendent' aspiration of mourning to ideas about nationality and civilization.

Studies in this area go a long way to explaining why SMM excites such interest. If we contextualize the challenge that social media present for mourning as a recovery process, the problem is that social media strip death of its finality. Profiles linger after death. Such anxieties echo previous concerns about the ambiguity of death, and creating the right relationship between the quick and the dead. Nowhere was this more keenly felt as a personal and political reality than in the aftermath of the Great War, when mourning defined the political realities of the 20th century.

From the personal to the political: The Great War: Mourning, modernity and media

German historian Jorn Rüsen (2003) regarded mourning as the key link between historical thinking and ordinary life. It was, quite simply, the place where scholarly debates about the nature of history as a story of human progress took on a public resonance. Mourning means coming to terms with traumatic events that question the very possibility of meaning at all. The Soto tragedy was partly about symbolic representation. The family's pain was exacerbated by disruptions to conventional ways of representing the dear departed. Now, imagine a world where millions of people simultaneously faced the same dilemma. This was the world of 1918. Making sense of the senseless became a major preoccupation for entire societies as industrialized atrocities questioned the very possibility of civilization. According to renowned Great War historian

Jay Winter (2014), mourning defined the 20th century, as everyone set about reconciling catastrophic loss through symbolic rituals. There are three aspects of his work that inform our understanding of SMM. First, Winter explained how mourning become an epoch-defining, political problem. Second, he showed how this 'problem' was addressed through symbolic activity. Third, he outlined how mourning and commemoration became a kind of popular culture, and how media became crucial in this transition. Anthropologically, Winter argued that the Great War cast Europe into a prolonged 'liminal' stage, created by an unprecedented negation of any notion that human life had spiritual meaning. The Great War was a catastrophe whose effects and implications reached from the imperial ambitions of European superpowers all the way down into the guts of the everyday lives of ordinary people. Intriguingly, his explanation of how and why he had reached this conclusion started with a film.

The year 1919 saw the completion of one of the first movies about the Great War, Abel Gance's *J'accuse*. Made in France, production started in 1918. Gance and his assistant, a poet and veteran called Blaise Cendras, recruited scores of convalescing servicemen to work as extras. Most featured in a scene where dead French soldiers returned from the grave. Eerily, by the time of *J'accuse* made it to the screen, many of its actors had been killed (Winter, 2014).

Such a poignant irony underlined the industrialized emotional problems facing combatants at the Armistice. *J'accuse* symbolized the confusion over how to process mass death. Conventional funeral rites were impossible for hundreds of thousands of bereaved families with no bodies to bury, their loved ones having been eviscerated. Others grieved brothers, fathers, husbands and lovers interred in mass graves hundreds of miles away. Such mass emotional agony was a political challenge. Managing dead bodies aggravated class divisions in French society. It was determined that the remains of soldiers who had been buried on the battlefield should rest where they were, rather than being returned to their families. Wealthy families often got around the problem by funding illegal exhumations, then bringing the bodies home (Winter, 2014). So the 'liminal' mourning stage disproportionality affected the working class. The sheer scale of the tragedy, then, made mourning political. Making sense of personal grief and making sense of the nation, and humanity, went hand in hand.

The resulting conflicts played through symbolic practices that quickly became commoditized and, eventually, mediatized. This lets us understand a crucial mechanism that makes media so seductive – the capacity to provide easy solutions to existing 'ritualistic' challenges. The year 1918 was also one of opportunity for the powers that be. In France, the Catholic Church capitalized on the politicization of mourning to counter-attack secularization (Sherman, 1998). By funding 'ossuaries' – memorials containing recovered bones of dead soldiers – building monuments and helping families to track down missing relatives, the church reconnected with its congregation, filling the gap left by state ennui (Sherman, 1998).

Winter (2014) argued that this strategy worked because 19th-century 'popular piety' had already spawned a cultural industry. In a century of war and pestilence that left the French public feeling especially vulnerable, tales of religious visions flourished, and created an eager market for pilgrimages and mass-produced religious icons. Sometimes these phenomena made for practical alliances among church, state and populace. For example, in 1871 citizens of Pontmain reported seeing the Virgin Mary, who promised that the town would be spared from the approaching Prussian army. Everyone wanted to believe the story, and thereafter Pontmain became a nationally treasured pilgrimage site. The myth sparked a cultural industry, built to satisfy public thirst for religious objects and experiences. Pontmain was a prototype for the role that symbols, consumption and media would play in reconstructing post-war society. People knew what to do with new memorials and museums, thanks to established leisure practices that were effectively about tourism and souvenirs.

Winter's thesis, then, was that the Great War stays vivid in popular memory thanks to sophisticated mechanisms of symbolic commemoration that bound individuals and families to nation states and history. Mourning linked religious rituals to mass cultural production. This connection explained why mourning the Great War's dead became the bedrock of popular political thought in the 20th century.

When millennial sensibilities returned to commemorating the Great War in the 1990s, it underlined how the personal desire to 'own' history was supported by a vast technological expansion in the capacity to remember. This trend crossed representational practices from high art to film, television and the online world. When Winter advised on the staging of the Historial de la Grande Guerre at Péronne, the Somme, he was party to the innovative decision to end the Museum tour with an exhibition of a false ear and eye attached to a pair of spectacles. The artefacts were worn by wounded servicemen, and poignantly captured the inadequacy of the post-war care. It was also an editorial decision that ended the story of the war with the suffering of ordinary people, rather than the global political fall-out for nation states (Winter, 2014).

The decision showed the political potency of symbols in leisure spaces. Winter (1999, 17) observed: 'Historical thinking is part of the equipment of citizenship.' This obligation was gaining popular support through a media-driven memory boom. As the centenary of one of the world's great catastrophes approached, and as its last survivors disappeared, it may have seemed natural that the world should take stock of the lessons learned from the Great War. These desires to preserve the experiences of veterans were aided by an improved capacity to preserve and store and reproduce ordinary voices. Media made cultural history – the story of historical landmarks from the point of view of the people who experienced them firsthand – a popular pursuit. But, as in 1918, the boom was also about markets. The rise of popular history reflected 'a hyper-market outlet for the consumption of memory' (cited in Winter, 2001, 59). Understanding the ordinary experience of the war from the soldier's point of view became a way to imagine oneself into history, and all of this was supported by media and leisure industries who allowed the public to immerse themselves in the war.

Winter provided an insightful bridge between Turner's anthropology and media studies because he explained how popular religious rituals were gradually transformed into leisure practices through first, the necessity and second, the popularity of mourning and commemoration. The 'memory boom' was just the sort of 'privatized', 'secular rituals' that Turner had predicted, and Winter's research explained how media worked alongside art, architecture and folk practices in affecting this evolution. The significance of Winter's work is the insight that the development of social media mourning drew energy from existing traditions of popular commemoration.

Death and media rituals

John Durham Peters and 'uncanny' communication

To communications scholars, it is no surprise that mourning captures the emotional appeal of media use. Thomas Edison's memoirs revealed his ambition to record the dead as the final step of his mission to subjugate time and space (Sky News, 2015). According to John Durham Peters (1999), Edison's aspirations epitomized the utopian appeal of electronic media. Peters wrote that 'the new media of the nineteenth century gave new life to the older dream of angelic contact by claiming to burst the bonds of distance and death' (1998 [in Kindle locations, 2648–2649]). Peters' work suggests that the politicized mourning that concerned Winter was built upon ideas and actions that grew around the social impact of the 19th-century revolution in media technologies.

Peters clarified what Winter's research said about the relationship between the physical, symbolic and emotional realities of Great War mourning. *J'accuse* powerfully summarized the defining challenge of the age: how to mourn authentically in the absence of the body. The images of dead people playing dead people painfully reminded audiences of another absence. The pictures were there, but the bodies lay far away. With the benefit of Peters' work, it is easy to see how *J'accuse* was far more than a metaphor; it was a paragon of electronic communication. Such communication was inherently melancholic because it drew attention to the distinction between representation and dialogue. Electronic communication allowed us to 'preserve' and communicate *about* dead people, when we all know that what we really want to do is communicate *with* them. Nineteenth-century hopes that electronic recording could conquer death had brokered a Faustian pact where the power to represent through symbolization had come at the price of the ability to mourn. As Peters put it: 'Photos of departed loved ones, letters that may never arrive, disembodied voices that cannot reply — these and many other facts of everyday life add to the haunting of communication' (1998 [in Kindle locations, 3283–3284]). Recordings and photographs of the departed added zest to an eternal philosophical problem: Do we ever really understand other people, or are we all doomed to live forever in prisons of self-perception? According to Peters, the penetration of daily media consumption into everyday life lent this puzzle unprecedented relevance, and this partly explains how the symbolic practices that evolved to commemorate the Great War had such a profound impact on 20th-century consciousness.

The 'uncanniness' of electronic communication sparked interest in how authenticity applied to media. This was the concern behind Winter's decision to complete the Péronne tour with a prosthetic eye and ear, which itself represents the idea that practical decisions about what to do with symbols bear consequences for the realities that those symbols build. However, what remains to be explained is how these processes came to be appropriated by media industries and media users in the course of ordinary social life. This is where the value of media ritual theory becomes apparent.

James Carey: From religion to media ritual

Media ritual theory establishes the connections between research on media industries and research on media users. This connection is vital to understanding how questions about the political effects of symbolic mourning became associated with the impact of technologies and industries. James Carey, one of the founding figures in this tradition, likened the cultural roles of religious rituals to the outcome of media use within commercial message systems. Carey famously defined communication as 'a symbolic process whereby reality is produced, maintained, repaired and transformed' (1989, 23). Like George Gerbner, Carey's work was premised on the observation that the defining shift in 20th-century public life came when the social role of communication was annexed by *media* communication. That is, also like Gerbner, Carey believed that the role that communication through symbols had always played in creating reality had shifted due to the industrialization of this process. Like Gerbner, Carey believed that industrialized communication narrowed the range of ideas that got to define reality, as this process was tied to corporate interests that severely limited the range of voices that could be expressed. But unlike Gerbner, Carey thought that these values found their ultimate expression in the things that people do with media. Drawing on anthropology, Carey argued that a holistic, convincing account of media power needed to understand culture as a process of human action. 'Meaning', he wrote, 'is not representation but a constituting activity whereby humans interactively endow an elastic though resistant world with enough coherence and order to support their purposes' (1989, 85).

The purpose of this observation was to vary the focus on media influence. Carey thought that the analysis of media use reminded us that media didn't just define meaning, but also determined how meanings were made. Media technologies arranged the parameters of social thought, and many social boundaries were drawn by how people used media.

Popular grieving as a media event

Carey's ideas seemed prophetic the late 20th and early 21st centuries, as the participation of people in the construction of media events became a defining feature of social life. The funeral of Diana, Princess of Wales vividly demonstrated the distinct role of media rituals to established social ones. A solemn occasion, a state funeral, was made to seem more solemn still through public mourning practices that drew intense media attention (Couldry, 2003; Cottle, 2008). The notion of a grieving Britain was certainly conveyed by visions of a million people lining the funeral route, but the idea had already been built by extensive coverage of ordinary people laying flowers at the site of the crash that took Diana's life, or at the gates of Buckingham Palace, and of people signing books of condolence at sites around the country. The powerful impression of a nation in grief was thus built not just by media organizations, but by the symbolic actions of ordinary people (Couldry, 2003).

However, this was not to be taken as a symbol of democratization. Nick Couldry (2003) thought the funeral represented another 'annexation' of culture by media. He developed this thought through the concept of 'media practice'. Echoing Turner, Couldry defined a ritual as an 'action that is associated with transcendent values' (2004, 22). Media practice referred to what 'people [are] doing in relation to media across a range of situations and contexts' (2004, 23). These 'practices' linked the media habits of ordinary people to the professional activities of media organizations. This was not to say that media habits simply reflected strategies of powerful media businesses, but it was to say that social life was frequently carried out in the cognizance that there are significant connections between media technologies, media businesses, and the things that we do, every day, to figure out our place in the grander scheme of things. The decision to, say, lay flowers at Buckingham Palace in the early hours of the morning after Diana's death was more than an expression of grief. It was also an act that inserted an ordinary member of the public into the writing of history. In an event that raised questions about the relevance of the monarchy to the public, and where 'spontaneous' acts of mourning became a familiar feature of the coverage, such actions had a historical gravitas. Some grieved, others simply wanted to be there as history was created, but regardless of their motivations, the way that people acted around the funeral showed how mourning had become synonymous with understanding the reality effect of media (Couldry, 2004).

Couldry's insight bears a striking resemblance to Winter's work. Acts of mourning were one of the first places where the world had felt the political effects of popular culture, as grief was expressed by combining religious rituals with the consumption of mass-produced symbols. It's not that surprising, then, that a state funeral would be one of the first places where the political significance of new media environments, where people *participated* in media events, would be seen.

KEY INSIGHT: PEOPLE CONNECT TO THE SOCIAL THROUGH MEDIA HABITS

So, media users have developed the historical, political significance of mourning practices by playing a vanguard role in the creation of symbolic practices that actively construct the meaning of death. This trajectory explains why Johana Sumiala's *Media and Ritual: Death, Community and Everyday Life* (2012) is a significant work in terms of understanding the connections between media practices and the creation of reality. Sumiala's work demonstrates how Winter's understanding of the associations between mourning, cultural practice and national consciousness can be used to understand how media cultures work. Recall that Winter saw mourning as a political entity whose effects emerged through the interlocking ambitions and actions of individuals, families, the state and other social institutions. In a similar vein, Sumiala showed how mourning national tragedies took on national, regional and political significance through the diverging *actions* of media institutions and media users, where the 'effects' of these actions resulted from the conflicting motivations and logics of each party.

The unique contribution of Sumiala's work to the discussion is that it emphasizes how media habits *constitute* social reality (the key creative notion in Carey's definition of media rituals), by starting research from the things that people do with media, as opposed to defining historical moments, as they are usually understood. What I mean is this. In the anthropological and historical works referenced so far, it can be difficult to see how reality is 'created', given the nature of the events under discussion. Death is a universal reality, and much as we have already seen that the argument that many historical 'facts' are produced by scholars, the Great War slaughter could scarcely be hidden, as were British excesses in Kenya. This perhaps diverts attention from Winter's important argument that symbolic actions play a vital role in subverting what we think we know about historical truths. Hence his bold assertion that a cheap, flimsy, fake eye provides a more telling comment on the war than does any official monument. Taking all of this into account, Sumiala's analysis of how ordinary Finns shaped the nation's political memory exemplified how media users shape history by engaging with media industries.

Sumiala developed Turner's work by explaining how, in times of national crisis, dominant national symbols *become* dominant national symbols through a variety of media practices that emerge to deal with the collapse of social order. Her point was that media rituals endeavour to impose order on a chaotic world. The ritual is literally creating stability, not celebrating or representing it. Yet strangely, this happens because media technologies and industries complicate reality by multiplying the practices that make it.

To appreciate the general significance of the Finnish case study, it's important to remind ourselves that we have mapped a trend where the kind of 'change' produced by media comes in the form of taking established cultural traditions and then leading them in particular directions. Hence, after the Great War, the existence of a consumer market for burgeoning cultural industries laid the ground for the politicization of mass mourning to an unprecedented degree. In a similar vein, Sumiala describes how the combinations of time, geography, the politics of post-war Finnish national identity, the changing role of citizens in media events, *and* the presence of social media enhanced the *constitutive* power of media rituals as things that consolidate particular realities from a range of possible alternatives.

We started the chapter with the sad story of Victoria Soto, and we return again to rampage murders to explain how SMM assumes political dimensions. In 2007 and 2008 Finland suffered two mass murders, in the provincial towns of Jokela and Kauhajoki. Both outrages were committed by young men who had announced their murderous plans via social media before committing their crimes. In a nation that prides itself on a high degree of social trust, and where the design and manufacturing of media technologies has played a key role in building an attractive, modern post-war identity, these crimes struck at the heart of Finnish values.

As we know from the discussion so far, European nations are well versed in reconstructing national identity through mourning, and the Finnish experience showed how media industries and media habits had assumed a primary role in the process. Finnish journalists had a well-established set of procedures to draw upon, in making sense of the horrific. The packaging of highly emotional public performances, witnessed around the death of Princess Diana, had also become part of Nordic cultural repertoires (Pantti, 2005). Sadly, Finnish publics and journalists were used to the site of grief-stricken publics performing *ad-hoc* rituals in front of the media, in the wake of the 2004 Thai tsunami that had claimed 179 lives. Faced with the inexplicable murders of so many young people, journalists used characteristically emotional language and scenes of crying, traumatized citizens to convey the idea that this was far more than a crime.

However, what was different this time was that social media affected the 'liminality' of these events. YouTube in particular had become a new mourning space, where people could post home-made memorial videos – a proxy, perhaps, for laying flowers in public places. But more importantly, it had also become a place where common media habits challenged the authority of established news institutions. The shootings provided evocative examples of the eternal space and time challenge in the history of media technologies. Helsinki-based Finnish journalists were only too aware of the dilemma as they rushed to reach the crime scenes while stories about what had happened were already being circulated through social media. But more than this, the Jokela and Kauhajuki murders also saw the rise of so-called 'hate' communities, who gathered online to express their sympathies with the murderers. The killers themselves established aesthetic conventions for celebrating murder, characterized by 'aggressive music, guns and strong colour contrasts' (Pantti, 2005, 107). These symbolic devices are easy to replicate, and have fuelled the proliferation of online hate communities that are hard to police, and this has had an identifiable influence on creating the reality of mass murder. Sumiala put it like this:

> Through this circulation and remediation of violent material, civic rituals assume meaning in relation to earlier rituals of death. At the same time, these civic rituals that are circulated from one media to another continue to shape interpretations of future events. (2012, 207)

For Sumiala, the proliferation and circulation of symbolic ways to commemorate death solidified how social media had assumed the ultimate ritual function in society. According to Turner, rituals are about making sense of historical disruption with a view to determining the future of society. This was a conflicted process because rituals involved conflict over the meaning of symbols. The use of social media to make sense of mass murder in Nordic regions vividly showed how these ideas applied to public death. The Norwegian Utoya murder of 2011 underlined the sense that such crimes were media events that cast doubt on Scandinavia's reputation as a haven of social justice and respect (Sumiala, 2012). This was not to say that SMM is inherently bad; it is to say that it had affected the terms on which nationality and humanity were understood:

> ... it is conceivable that with the advance of new media technology and social media ... major events and catastrophes generate a new kind of agency that may well foster imagined communities on local, national but also transnational level – at least momentarily. (Sumiala, 2012, 121)

Methodological implications of media rituals: Framing media habits as cultural rituals

Methodologically, media rituals demonstrate the value of beginning research by looking at media users. Methods for doing this will be explained in future chapters, but before doing this it is important to clarify what we are looking for in these 'ordinary' moments. Revising key concepts in mourning rituals helps to do this.

The key task in explaining media use is to explain the cultural logic of a particular act or acts. This is not synonymous with the conscious, individual motivations behind them. The analysis of SMM is particularly useful in making this clear. The problem with trolls and online hate communities is that online anonymity invalidates any ambition to find out why people like abusing others via social media. However, framing SMM as a media practice that inherits the cultural and historical role of rituals helps define a way of getting around this problem. This is mostly a matter of being clear on what evidence of 'ordinary' symbolic behaviours represents.

Let's ground this discussion by returning to the Sotos story. The question at hand is why would it occur to a grieving family to copyright Victoria's name, and how can we explain this by relating the story to the history of mourning? How can we see this as an important incident that was about more than the simple, understandable desire to be left alone? The task here is to provide a plausible argument from what we know about the importance of mourning, and the way that media have influenced this immemorial life ritual.

When you take into account 20th-century conflicts over mourning practices, and the way that media have always complicated the relationship between the living and the dead, the Sotos' actions, and the reasons for talking about them, make perfect sense. The Great War showed how mourning developed through conflicts over the departed as 'property'. The Sotos' efforts to reclaim their daughter from internet conspiracies resembled the efforts of French families to bring their loved ones home so that they could be interred as members of families, not martyrs to a national cause. Both were actions that people took to remove the departed from one symbolic context to another. Both 'acts' were also conducted in cultural settings where a variety of institutions were invested in the politics of mourning. As we have seen, Sandy Hook became a political battleground in the United States, which is unsurprising given that rampage shootings are now often used in conversations about national identity, whether that is the validity of the US Second Amendment or the future of Nordic-style social justice. Finally, both situations were supported by established practices of cultural production. Eventually, Great War mourning drew on the public appetite for pilgrimage and symbolic consumption, which was maintained by media industries through to the end of the 20th century. The memory boom which Winter (2001) noted entrenched the role of media in letting people symbolically own history, and this trend slides neatly into the notion that the memory of a loved one is, among other things, intellectual property. There is much more that could be said about this, but the main point is that the media habits that interest us are the ones that we can invest with a strong cultural history – they are actions that can be persuasively shown to have come from a place that speaks to deep social values.

SIGNIFICANCE: IDENTIFYING MEDIA HABITS THAT MAKE POLITICAL CONSCIOUSNESS

It isn't really surprising that we should give people who abuse others online for the sake of it (Hardaker, 2010) a supernatural name, as the uncanny has long symbolized the promise and perils of media. The meaning of life needs the meaning of death. This meaning is hard to achieve in the absence of an authenticating body or spirit, and since the 19th century electronic media have provided problems and solutions in addressing this question. No surprise either that the topic of SMM captures so many important aspects of how ordinary people make social reality through symbolic actions. In this chapter, we have seen that SMM is a media habit that demonstrates how media research addresses the old humanities conundrum of how the individual connects with cultural history. Anthropologists and historians have long found ways to relate the things that people do in relation to death with the existential and political questions that define the age. These actions are understood in symbolic terms, as things that attach meanings to death that carry with them social consequences. Both fields have acknowledged that the way that media industries facilitated the production, circulation and consumption of symbols had a major influence on the impact of mourning as a reality construct. Taking all of this into account, we can argue that public concern about the dangers of SMM are well supported by understandings of mourning as a thing that people do that has material outcomes for society. This is why the study of ordinary media habits plays a crucial role in explaining media effects.

CHAPTER SUMMARY

- Media matter as phenomena that connect people to society, history and culture. This is the main lesson of an important area of study known as media ritual research.

- Current concerns about the effects of social media mourning reflect the fact that mourning has always been a source of cultural cohesion and political conflict.

- Studying SMM using media ritual theory shows how media practices play a distinct role in shaping how society relates to death. This specifies what media theory contributes to anthropology and history.

- The key methodological insight that results is that the success of small-scale case studies lies in an ability to persuasively relate the actions of media users within historical narratives of cultural practices.

8

RESEARCHING THE SYNTHESIS OF MEDIA AND INTERPERSONAL COMMUNICATION

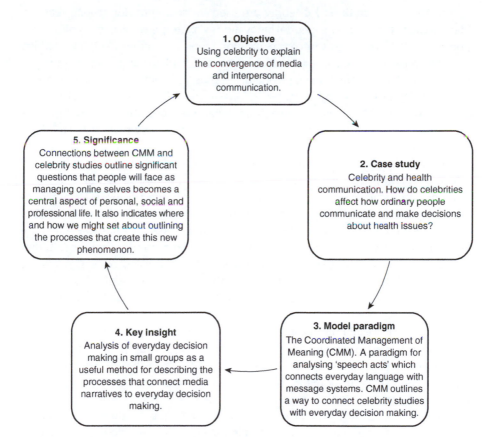

1. Objective
Using celebrity to explain the convergence of media and interpersonal communication.

2. Case study
Celebrity and health communication. How do celebrities affect how ordinary people communicate and make decisions about health issues?

3. Model paradigm
The Coordinated Management of Meaning (CMM). A paradigm for analysing 'speech acts' which connects everyday language with message systems. CMM outlines a way to connect celebrity studies with everyday decision making.

4. Key insight
Analysis of everyday decision making in small groups as a useful method for describing the processes that connect media narratives to everyday decision making.

5. Significance
Connections between CMM and celebrity studies outline significant questions that people will face as managing online selves becomes a central aspect of personal, social and professional life. It also indicates where and how we might set about outlining the processes that create this new phenomenon.

Figure 4   The synthesis of media and interpersonal communication: celebrity

OBJECTIVE: USING CELEBRITY TO DEMONSTRATE THE INTEGRATION OF MEDIA AND INTERPERSONAL COMMUNICATION

The topic of media ritual introduced the valuable idea that media power works *with* people as *they* make reality. Next, we follow this thought to consider how media industries also influence everyday speech. What is at stake here is a 'convergence' between media and interpersonal communication. This intersection is an essential effect that speaks to the core of the mediatization process. The effect of celebrity health choices is used as a case study to explain how the connection works, and why it illuminates a significant, general kind of media influence, where the output of media industries becomes the raw material for social thought and speech.

The topics of health and celebrity are used in illustration for several reasons. Media's capacity to promote medical innovations via interpersonal communication is one of the founding topics in communication studies (Chaffee, 1975). Meanwhile, celebrity gossip is credited with the power to affect what we all expect from life (Turner, 2010). Taking these ideas on board, the chapter begins by making the case of celebrity culture, now a major organizing force in social life (see Turner, 2010; Rojek, 2012; Cashmore, 2014), and connects traditional questions about the diffusion of public information to popular entertainment. There are many reasons for thinking that celebrity stories about health issues affect society because they enter into the conversations we have with family, healthcare professionals and friends. This kind of effect reflects the idea that mediatization concerns the intersection of media and interpersonal communication, a 'convergence' that has figured in efforts to shift ideas about media influence beyond persuasion for some time (Katz and Lazarsfeld, 1955).

We can ground these ideas by considering the career of Angelina Jolie. The celebrity industry has transformed Jolie into a global authority on humanitarian issues. Academic celebrity studies have also anointed Jolie as an icon *par excellence* of celebrity culture. Jolie is a celebrity, and this is why her decision to have her ovaries removed in 2015 drew attention to the synthesis of media content and everyday speech.

This chapter uses Barnett Pearce's 'coordinated management of meaning' (2007) paradigm (CMM) to make sense of this fusion. CMM analyses how people make important decisions through 'speech acts', that is, ways of talking that support particular ways of acting in fateful moments. The model is connected to media studies through the following steps. First, the chapter outlines how Pearce defined speech as a social action. Second, it describes how CMM connected these actions to dominant 'languages' that structure social worlds. Third, it explains how celebrity links media and interpersonal communication, due to evidence indicating that the former is an easily accessible medium for making sense of personal experience.

The interlocking themes of speech, health and celebrity have a general validity because they encapsulate how media narratives affect the management of personal life. To support this argument, the chapter ends by showing how the discussion on their relationship lends useful insights into studies of online identities and well-being.

In summary, this chapter:

- Uses the topic of health communication to explain the relationship between media and interpersonal communication.
- Uses Angelina Jolie as an illustrative case study to explain the reasons for thinking that celebrity culture is one of the narratives that people use when deciding how to manage their lives.
- Uses a leading model of interpersonal communication – CMM – to frame Jolie's actions as the first 'turn' in a public health discussion, and explains the key questions we have to ask in deciding where to look for the effects of the incident. This indicates that media are important due to their capacity to initiate conversations, rather than to the power to make audiences think this or that.
- Demonstrates how these issues reach out to more general questions about the management of online identities, which research suggests is the key point of convergence between media and interpersonal communication.

CASE STUDY: CELEBRITY AND HEALTH COMMUNICATION

Public angle: Angelina Jolie and BRCA-1

In March 2015, Hollywood star Angelina Jolie wrote an op-ed for the *New York Times* explaining her decision to have her ovaries removed (Jolie-Pitt, 2015). Genetic tests found the famous actor, director and activist carried a mutation to the BRCA-1 gene, placing her at extreme risk of breast and ovarian cancer. Having already undergone a double mastectomy in 2013, she decided that further surgery was needed to prolong her life.

Jolie thought her predicament was a matter of public interest, since it was likely to become a common dilemma in the new age of preventative medicine that genetic testing had ushered in. She chose surgery after reviewing her family medical history and treatment options. She invited other women to take charge of their medical futures by seeking information and advice that would enable them to *use* testing, in conversation with their family and health providers.

Jolie's actions activated several media research themes. Across a variety of health issues, scholars have discovered that behaviour change turns on a delicate balance between media messages and interpersonal communication networks (Tulloch, 1999; De Santis, 2004; Kitzinger, 2004; Meyer, 2004). This is all the more the case given the frequency with which people now turn to internet communities to find both information and emotional support when faced with illness (Macias, Stavchansky-Lewis and Smith, 2005). Health information works when people start discussing it. Jolie's invitation to begin a discussion on genetic testing and health choices accessed this idea.

The idea that the main effect of Jolie's action was to start a conversation about gene testing and health management helps make sense of some of the media framing that followed. American news organization CNN featured a story where medical experts discussed what the celebrity's dilemma meant for other women. The clip was then shared on YouTube (CNN, 2015). Looking at the clip, as it was shared via social media, gestures to the idea that although the celebrity's disclosure was historic, the question of why she chose to disclose was quite another matter.

Describing the clip clarifies the advantages of viewing media influence from a CMM viewpoint. It began with Jolie's surgeon speaking about how crucial Jolie's decision was. Anchor Michaela Pereira then explained that Jolie had 'started a conversation' about women's health. Next, medical expert Seema Yasmin observed that although breast cancer is common, the gene mutation that afflicted Jolie is extremely rare. In response, Pereira changed subject to 'The Angelina Effect' on BRCA testing, which a graphic revealed had increased 40% since her 2013 announcement of the mastectomy. CNN's medical correspondent Elizabeth Cohen then noted earlier celebrity influence on testing demand, but cautioned that BRCA testing is only warranted with the co-presence of a family history of breast and ovarian cancer. Yasmin agreed, warning that rushed testing can mean unnecessary treatment. However, Cohen remarked that this was not the case for Jolie, and indeed that some doctors felt Jolie had waited too long to act. Pereira asked how lasting an impact the story was likely to have, given that Jolie had access to all the medical expertise that money could buy. Cohen, however, countered that testing is becoming more affordable, and that in any case the lesson is that everyone can become proactive about their healthcare.

The clip attracted a small number of comments from YouTube subscribers, covering several themes. Some praised Jolie. Others dismissed the move as a cynical PR strategy. Some discussed testing and insurance. Others insulted each other over whether it's worth worrying about endless testing, while others saw this as a perfectly sensible extension of the equally sensible idea that we should take more care of our health.

There isn't much point in asking how 'successful' this clip might have been in persuading audiences to do one thing or another. It offered a series of viewpoints on whether Jolie's story did or did not relate to viewers' lives. And judging from the handful of public responses, there were evidently reasons for leaning either way. However, another reason for looking at the clip is that it introduces another way of thinking about how such stories influence the social world as conversations. We will return to the clip on this point towards the end of the chapter, but before then it is important to explain all the reasons for thinking that Jolie's health and medical travails are something that a lot of people would have ended up discussing in the first place.

Scholarly context: Celebrity and health communication

One thing is for sure: Jolie's predicament reflected a paradigmatic change in the nature of health communication that scholars had already identified. In *Talking about Health: Why Communication Matters* (2009), Roxanne Parrott argued that the BRCA-1 and BRCA-2 checks exemplified communication problems that defined a new age in healthcare. The genetic test promise is compromised by poor interpersonal communication. One key breakdown is between the doctor and patient. The implications of genetic results can be difficult to interpret, especially when over-stretched professionals deliver them. General practitioners can find it hard to keep up with scientific innovations, or to develop the language to translate developments into lay language. Patients find it equally difficult to research and discuss family health histories. Then there are sensitivities around collecting and sharing health information. Quite rationally, some fear that knowing about risks might preclude insurance. Finally, a major shift in public thinking is needed to frame personal medical history as a social commodity. Parrott warned that 'personalized medicine is not personal' (2009, 149). Our decisions affect public resources, so we are obligated, as citizens, to communicate with doctors, members of the family and even institutions to ensure equitable distribution. Testing decisions need to be based not only on public awareness of illnesses and treatments, but also on conversations about how to best manage the scarce resources.

Parrott's analysis indicated the richness of Jolie's story. Her decision to go public with her health problems gives the chance to reflect on how celebrity figures in the coordination of personalized medicine. We can extrapolate general principles about how media narratives permeate everyday thinking and talking from this. The gravity of Parrott's observations, and Jolie's allegory of a new medical age, is underlined by research on the political impact of celebrity culture.

Understanding celebrity: The 'Angelina Effect'

Seasoned readers of media research would have expected a celebrity to iconize the new health consumer. And a betting person may well have laid odds on that celebrity being Angelina Jolie. When scholars set about explaining how celebrity affects public discourse, Jolie is a recurrent prop, and existing scholarship explains why her celebrity persona was especially suited to capturing core characteristics of the medicalized self.

Celebrity exposure is a key catalyst for getting people interested in health. Celebrity stories initiate communication behaviours, like role-playing, that play a part in defining health norms for media users (Hinnant and Hendrickson, 2014). Beck et al. (2014) portrayed celebrity disclosure as a familiar feature of contemporary health communication, and this started when another famous woman chose to disclose her battle with breast cancer. US First Lady Betty Ford took this step in 1974, and her actions encouraged thousands to have their own examinations. Since then, according to the authors, 157 celebrities have sought to change the way that people behave around specific conditions, from drug addiction to Parkinson's disease. There's a message systems angle to this development: social media and 24-hour news cycles make disclosures less 'voluntary' than they once were (Beck et al., 2014). So 'push' and 'pull' factors make celebrity illness a mainstay of health communications, and Jolie's disclosure made sense within this narrative.

Research on celebrity cancer stories has also outlined the intricacies of defining the effects of media on health. Noar et al.'s (2014) meta-analysis of 19 such projects found significant but short-term effects on health behaviours. Nevertheless, this does not dismiss the possibility that the accumulation of such stories over time has long-term consequences for comprehending health. The possibility is worth pursuing since breast cancer has been a major theme in US network news since Ford's 1974 disclosure (Cho, 2006). Niederdeppe's survey research (2008) found an alarming possibility. According to his data, celebrity cancer news encouraged information seeking among better-educated audiences who already had the knowledge and means to take care of themselves. In other words, the success of health information depends on social networks, and well-intentioned awareness efforts can inadvertently aggravate health inequality.

The emergent gist is that celebrity is a topic that elucidates the politics of personal choices. Angelina Jolie has been the quintessential informant in this regard. When scholars have sought to examine the 'celebrity effect' on political behaviour, her name has often been invoked as a test case. For example, she has been used in research on the role that celebrity endorsement plays in voting decisions (O'Regan, 2014). Becker (2012) showed how interest in the political influence of celebrities inherited orthodox questions about the role that persuasive messages could play in getting audiences to become either more or less involved in political issues. She did this through experimental research looking at the differential impact of exposure to celebrity and expert media messages on the topic of humanitarian aid, and the 'stimulus' used in her case was Angelina Jolie. Nickel (2012) was less positive in holding Jolie significantly responsible for creating the sentiment that private charity can solve global injustice. But that doesn't change the fact that when scholars discuss the impact of celebrity on political debate they quite often take Angelina Jolie with them.

When it comes to the politicization of personalized medicine, Jolie's willingness to put her body where her mouth is lends her peerless authenticity. McHugh (2014) attributed Jolie's political capital to her propensity to craft a celebrity narrative in her own blood – from writing Johnny-Lee Miller's name on a shirt in her blood to politicizing her family and her maladies. Jolie's 'story' is about her transition from 'wild child' to mom where 'mother' took on a particular, political meaning in the context of her global humanitarianism. Jolie's public mother persona is so strong that it has been credited with rescuing Brad Pitt from Himbo status, allowing him to pursue an activist career of his own (Fuqua, 2011). Overall, Jolie is *the* exemplar of the do-it-all celebrity mother against which others are judged (Charlesworth, 2014).

Her 'mother' image has become a political force with substantial international clout. As Wheeler (2011) observed, Jolie's humanitarian work is a paragon of the power of celebrity status to change the nature of political communication. Celebrity unites studies of popular culture and public opinion, since the categories of politician and celebrity have become somewhat interchangeable. Certain entertainment genres have become adept at producing stars who carry political gravitas (Street, 2002), and politicians increasingly curry public favour by emphasizing their personal lives, much as celebrities do (Stanyer, 2012). Jolie's career as an ambassador for the United Nations Commission on Human Rights (UNHRC) has played an important role in elaborating this theme. Jolie has been credited with creating a celebrity narrative, combining personal change and managerial experience, to lend the role real authority. This is important as there is evidence that the UN has, since then, deployed celebrity as an integral part of its international strategy (Wheeler, 2011).

The question of how celebrities impact health decisions, then, associates medicine with politics at a time when it is vitally important to appreciate how this connection impacts individual choices. And no one, it seems, explains that better than Angeline Jolie. The most significant work on this topic is Chris Rojek's *Fame Attack: The Inflation of Celebrity and Its Consequences* (2012). In this book, Rojek observed that women celebrities in general, and Angelina Jolie in particular, are recurrent figures in discussions about public health, which reflects the general cultural relevance of celebrity. Famous females make us think about mortality, because they don't last very long. Figures show that celebrities die earlier than ordinary people – especially if they are women. According to some research, in 1974 the average American women died at 75.8, but the average female star only made it to 54 (Fowles, cited in Rojek, 2012).

Celebrity, according to Rojek, seems an inherently dangerous pursuit thanks to a prolific PR industry that produces a deluge of information about the risks that celebrities take with their health. Stories about what celebrities put their bodies through signpost the risk border. Celebrity addicts are common media fodder. Across four seasons, the TV show *Celebrity Rehab* featured the struggles that musicians, actors, singers and reality stars fought against everything from alcohol to prescription drugs and sex. Movie publicity frequently underscores the authenticity of onscreen performances by telling about radical weight gain and weight loss, where performers like Anne Hathaway, Matthew McConaughy, Christian Bale, Jake Gyllenghal and Bradley Cooper lost or gained organ-wrecking amounts of weight. When American documentary maker Morgan Spurlock made *Supersize Me*, using his own liver to demonstrate the alarmingly rapid damage that a fast food diet could do, he set in train something of a genre. Several British television personalities committed to a month of excessive eating and alcohol consumption to show the less than earth-shattering lesson that doing such things is bad for you. As Rojek (2012, 37) put it: 'It is ordinary people who pay their bills on time, never step out of line and make themselves scarce when bold, life-changing challenges come along. … Stars do what the rest of us are too frigid and timid to try.'

Celebrities live as if rules do not apply to them. Because of this, Rojek continued, celebrity dramatizes how to deal with life's challenges. Jolie, in this regard, is one of a handful of elite superstars who take this performance to the level of global sustainability issues. Her name crops up 15 times in Rojek's book. This is because she offers a pliable set of ideas that can be used to take different positions on a variety of global issues in the management of well-being. On a positive note, she stands out from the celebrity pack as a global authority who, despite being the product of a classic celebrity 'formula', is also a leading 'celanthropist' who gets involved in the management of issues, as opposed to those who simply lend their names to publicity or fundraising appeals. Less positively, she also represents the limits of celebrity politics. Rojek portrayed Jolie as an exemplar of an 'Icarus' syndrome, where celebrity hubris – the idea that they can solve complex historical and political problems through sheer will and charisma – is seen as doing more harm than good. On humanitarian aid, Rojek points out that Jolie, Bono, Bob Geldof and Oprah Winfrey have all been accused of actually creating problems. The criticism goes that they operate from a 'one world' point of view that is hopelessly out of touch with reality, and that a lack of cultural knowledge creates all kinds of unimagined outcomes – for example, the idea that African aid ends up fuelling violence and inequality by giving capital to criminal gangs who then have even more power to persecute local populations. Rojek identified Jolie as unique even within this small cadre as one who personalized this criticism through her mother role. The adoption of children from Cambodia, Ethiopia and Vietnam, respectively, has been criticized as a specific instance of fame hubris, where 'the ambition of creating a multicultural mix in one family ... is regarded as the ill-judged expression of star power' (Rojek, 2012, 145).

But for good or ill, it's clear that Jolie is a key player in celebrity culture, and her personal medical history encapsulated the politics and realities of the new era of 'personalized medicine'. For a long time now, scholars have argued that Jolie 'embodies' the 'reality effect' of celebrity. Poignantly, her actions around her BRCA status underlined how true this was in the field of health communication, as her plight, and the media hubbub that surrounded it, heralded key issues that everyone will have to face, and talk about, in a new era of preventative medicine. She also represents a case study that we can use, then, to consider how media communication, in the form of celebrity, might play a role in determining the shape of this future. So there are many reasons for identifying the Jolie disclosure as a significant moment.

The next challenge is to figure out how she percolated into the health decisions that people make. One way to do this is to consider how media communication relates to the study of interpersonal communication, through engaging with the 'coordinated management of meaning' (CMM). Developed by Barnett Pearce (2007), this model provided a framework for analysing the effects of critical speech acts. These are forms of communication where people try to change the world. Pearce's CMM offers a useful perspective on defining what the Jolie disclosure represented, and helps identify the multiplicity of outcomes that it was likely to have engendered. It also offers a medium for appreciating how media influence – in this case the pervasive presence of celebrity culture – affects the 'speech acts' that we use to make decisions in everyday life.

KEY PARADIGM: THE COORDINATED MANAGEMENT OF MEANING: CELEBRITY DISCLOSURE AS SPEECH ACTION

In the previous chapter, we encountered the idea that social reality is literally created in the things that people do with media. Pearce's work applied the same argument to everyday speech:

> The private talk among friends, the patterns of daily talk in families, and the normal patterns of official and unofficial talk in organizations are all important social processes, in which personal identities are forged and people develop and test their ideas about what is real and what is good. (Pearce and Foss, 1990, 10)

In *Making Social Worlds* (2007), Pearce argued that recognizing 'critical speech acts' and understanding how to act constructively in these circumstances are crucial social skills. In what follows, I am going to explain how this perspective is useful for understanding media influence in two ways. First, the CMM view affords a sophisticated and flexible model of media effects. Second, the model provides a typology for identifying how this influence infiltrates exchanges between people. Overall, this improves the ability to explain how people make reality in relation to their media environment.

Pearce's CMM was grounded in a series of assumptions about communication's *constitutive* role. That is, CMM, like ritual theory, understands communication as something that *makes* social phenomena, rather than just labelling things that already exist. Pearce based this idea on two suppositions. The first is that no one is an individual. We cannot conceive ourselves or our environment without communicating with others. Consequently, our sense of self does not exist until we talk to people. This is significant because it directs attention to the idea that identities mutate in relation to how we communicate.

Second, Pearce nuanced the idea that communication forms affect content. Pearce's version of this argument referenced the relationship between speech acts, rather than the affordances of media technologies. What really interested him can be summarized under the concept of 'punctuation'. Communication created meaning, identities and actions through the articulation or 'turns' and 'episodes'. Even the simplest of conversations is characterized by a complex dance where people alternately speak and listen, where each change or point of punctuation can take the conversation in different directions, producing different outcomes. Pearce's model was called the 'coordinated management of meaning' because he emphasized that the outcomes of conversations were as much about the coordination of actions and roles as they were the intention of either speaker.

Let's pause briefly to illustrate how CMM explains the construction of reality through communication. As an opening example, Pearce mentioned a conversation between a motorist and a police dispatcher which achieved national attention in the US because of its tragic outcome. The driver had noticed a mattress that had been discarded in the middle of a busy highway. She then called the local police to warn them of the hazard.

The well-intentioned motorist happened to call a force whose jurisdiction did not cover highway safety, and the dispatcher duly informed the Good Samaritan of this fact. The conversation, which was reported verbatim in the press, witnessed an escalating spiral of mutual frustration, as the driver reiterated the urgency of the situation, while the dispatcher tried to impress upon her that s/he was in no position to dispatch help because she did not have the authority to do so and that the only way to resolve the situation was to call people who did. The frustrated motorist hung up, with the tragically prophetic phrase 'never mind, I'll just let someone get killed' (cited in Pearce, 2007, 2). Moments later, that's exactly what happened. Another car hit the mattress, killing the driver.

The main problem in this conversation, according to Pearce, was a lack of coordination between speaking roles. Looking at the escalating frustration in the conversation, Pearce concluded that the problem was that neither speaker took the opportunity to change their position in the conversation in accordance with what the other person was saying. Both acted quite sensibly – the first as a concerned citizen, the second as a professional who had the obligation to create the rapid understanding that she had no power to dispatch help. Each turn of the conversation provided a chance to be more empathetic by playing a different part – a concerned citizen who understood she was dealing with a complex organization where actions are controlled by chains of command or a public official who understood how this looked like red-tape nonsense. The problem was not about meaning and understanding; it was about the lack of action, and the lack of ability to become another person in response to another.

Now, let's return to the concept of punctuation in order to apply these insights to media communication. Pearce's CMM model hypothesized that conversations were also punctuated by a higher order of frameworks called 'episodes'. The CMM analytical technique involves looking at how each turn in a conversation is affected by what has gone before, such that there is no such thing as a pure statement. In the Californian highway tragedy, the driver's mounting frustration would be incomprehensible in the absence of the dispatcher's repeated insistence that s/he could not help. But each conversation also exists within a larger sequence of other 'episodes' that affect how we act in new encounters. These episodes are organized into hierarchies, and conflicts happen when people apply different ones to the same situation. Actions cannot be coordinated when participants in a conversation don't agree on the episode they are in. We might, for example, investigate how this failed conversation was affected by the driver's previous experiences with law enforcement and the expectations she had before starting the conversation.

Usefully, for our purposes, Pearce explained how episode hierarchies produced conflict in reference to reproductive health. In 2005, US health officials recommended that all girls should be given a new vaccination protecting them from cervical cancer, at the age of 12. The advice was resisted by religious groups, based on the fear that such steps might encourage sexual activity at a young age. Both factions placed the presence of the vaccine in a different episode, one of progress, the other of decline. To the pro-vaccine groups, here was a way to protect women from a rampant, deadly yet easily preventable disease. To religious groups, here was another secular assault that did nothing to attack the root cause of the problem – sex outside marriage. Antagonistic interchanges between groups were communicative actions that were promoted by different ways of punctuating what vaccination was about, within a larger narrative about the direction that society should be going.

The contention that conversations are arranged by higher order 'episodic' structures pinpoints where Pearce's work on interpersonal communication intersects with media influence research. Pearce insisted that CMM provides a productive way to approach global sustainability challenges. His ultimate 'hierarchy' was the 21st-century environmentalist shift, whose defining political challenge is coming to terms with a world where demand exceeds resources. Sustainability was the irreducible ethical reality that humanity faced. In this regard, one of the major challenges that people, organizations and governments alike faced was the difficulty of being able to act differently by stepping outside 'patterns of communication', by which he meant 'clusters of episodes that have a strong family resemblance' (Pearce, 2007, 158). Speech acts existed within larger patterns of communication, which 'once developed, maintain their boundaries and resist change by actively attracting episodes that share their central characteristics and relating those that differ or would change them' (2007, 158). When it comes to global sustainability and health – the question of how the possibilities of genetic testing have to be managed within the realities of limited resources – one of these 'emergent patterns' is the role of celebrity discourse, and the figure of Angelina Jolie, in grounding the meaning of abstract issues.

Pausing again to recap the goal of this chapter, the idea is to use Pearce's CMM to conceive the relationship between media and interpersonal communication as another way of exploring how people make reality by operating in a media environment. Discussing Angelina Jolie's medical disclosures using Pearce's ideas is productive for the following reasons. First, the disclosure was positioned as the kind of 'critical moment' that interested Pearce. It was an invitation to respond to a changing paradigm. Second, Pearce's focus on communication actions, as opposed to meanings, raises interesting options on where to look for the effects of these actions. But third, the sustained attention that has been paid to Jolie as a celebrity shows how media celebrity studies contribute knowledge to how interpersonal communication may be affected by the structure of media industry message systems as powerful 'episode' definers.

KEY INSIGHT: BASING RESEARCH ON KEY *MOMENTS* IN MEDIA COMMUNICATION

Pearce designed CMM as a method for asking productive questions about how communication makes social worlds. He recognized that identifying the episodic structure of conversations was a matter of interpretation. But while he accepted that speech acts were virtually infinite in terms of their origins and outcomes, the reality of cultures, which only exist because some meanings are made more often than others, meant that the same was not true of episodes – most of our interactions are framed within dominant networks of meanings. This is where, by Pearce's own admission, the CMM model reached its limits.

What we have seen, however, is evidence suggesting that the celebrity industry creates episodic structures. The value of seeing the Jolie CNN story from a CMM point of view is that it raises a number of useful questions about how to understand effects. Rather than asking whether this will change opinions, instead we see how the piece is a complicated conversation, full of crucial turns that might have different outcomes, where identifying such turns, and the episodes that might inform them, is a useful place to start asking the questions that will address the role of media in personalized medicine.

Following Pearce's method, the task here is not to figure out what the story meant, but to identify the 'turns' and 'episodes' that might have led it in different directions. For example, one of the first turns – quite literally – is when anchor Pereira follows Yasmin's observation that Jolie's condition is rare by raising the topic of 'the Angelina Effect'. This 'turns' us towards the power of celebrity as opposed to the conditions that warrant BRCA testing. This isn't wrong *per se*, but one can ask how the segment would have been different had another choice been made. We might further ask how this 'turn' placed the story within the 'episode' of Jolie the star, and how this might have activated episodes among audiences that, for example, promoted cynicism about her motivations.

Such queries raise larger issues still. We might ask how the articulation of testing within the celebrity 'episode' shapes what is said about genetic testing – about, for example, whether it is seen as the latest symbol of the gap between celebrity and ordinary lives. But probably the most important question we could ask would have nothing to do with the clip. Instead we might look at how 'effective' it was at starting conversations between mothers and daughters, in families, and with medical professionals, and between medical professionals too. How is the message received and acted upon? What do people understand?

Who do they talk to? And how do those conversations influence what those people end up doing? The CMM viewpoint reminds us that one of the most important influences media have is the instigation of a range of communication behaviours, which underlines the idea that media industries play a fundamentally organizational role in society, which is just as important as looking at their power to make us think this or that.

This approach – identifying critical speech acts where media meanings enter interpersonal relationships – is crucial to understanding media influence, and has been for some time. In later chapters this will become very important in looking at how audiences interact with entertainment, but for now it is also important to explain how a CMM on celebrity and health also frames important technological changes in the relationship between media and the self.

SIGNIFICANCE: IDENTIFYING MEDIA MOMENTS THAT START SOCIAL CONVERSATIONS

In this chapter, the topics of celebrity and health have been used as proxies for a more fundamental issue – the role that media communication plays in the management of social well-being. To underline the significance of this topic in general issues about media influence, this last section considers how celebrity and the management of well-being through communication also ground significant issues concerning the impact of mobile media technologies.

To begin, let's return to the concept of convergence. In the early 21st century, convergence has become a key sensitizing concept that describes how changing technological, economic and cultural conditions cross-pollinate media systems, hence deepening the symbiosis of media and everyday life (Jenkins, 2006; Meikle and Young, 2012). However, it's also worth noting that the term was used in one of the biggest surveys of media use in the mid-20th century: Katz and Lazarsfeld's *Personal Influence* (1955). In this, the authors defined convergence as the intersection between media content and face-to-face talk. They observed that movies, news and advertising were a common topic of discussion among people. People liked talking about the latest films, fashions or political developments because it was a way of winning peer status. It was already, back in the late 1940s, a means of managing impressions and developing a sense of security within one's own group. It was good to know that when people wanted to know who to vote for or what to watch, they valued your opinion. You mattered.

This older version of convergence is reflected in more recent studies on the growing penetration of media technologies into everyday life. Notably, these works suggest that the discourse of celebrity provides a crucial handle on the critical communication acts that people engage in on a regular basis. What this underlines is that the close analysis of interpersonal communication, as advocated by CMM, provides a valuable way to show how media influence becomes real under particular circumstances as people endeavour to look after themselves.

As we have seen, asking about the health impact of Angelina Jolie's management of her health means thinking about the relationship between the international superstar and ordinary people. What, the CNN clip asked, did her public action have to do with the rest of us? According to some work on mobile media, the answer supports CMM because it concerns the analysis of communication action and the articulation of that action to general communication frameworks.

In *Status Update* (2013), Alison Marwick argued that the basic structure of Web 2.0 technologies turns us all into celebrity-like creatures via the decisions that we make in how to communicate the self. Her argument is that these technologies encourage acts of communication that take the form of 'micro celebrity'. Her argument is that the North Californian tech community in the early 2000s was driven by people who became famous within their own communities through the careful construction of online identities: strategic releases of personal information that cultivated public images, based on the assumptions that their identities were of interest to other professionals. These people, although not strictly celebrities, led celebrity-like lifestyles in that they paid careful attention to putting together a public image through the production of their own media content. This, Marwick continued, had pioneered the logic of social media, where all users are encouraged to be similarly vigilant and self-promoting. Technology, then, has brought the concept of celebrity to life as a set of critical communicative acts.

danah boyd concurs in *It's Complicated* (2014), where her research on young social media users connects the popularity of new platforms with an eternal wish to 'be public'. When boyd wrote that 'what teens do online cannot be separated from their broader desires and interests, attitudes and values' (2014 [in Kindle locations, 3278–3279]), she meant that social media make media and interpersonal communication synonymous by satiating an eternal youth desire for publicness, which is vital to well-being. boyd argues that for most of the 20th century media have offered young people a chance to 'be themselves' while being with their peers. That said, this yearning is mediatized by the outsourcing of 'public-ness' to commercial platforms. This 'episode' informs the conversations that teens have about themselves and the world in which they live. The 'persistence, visibility, spreadability, and searchability' (2014 [in Kindle locations, 3303–3304]) characterizing online communication nurtures celebrity-style social lives. Individual acts of communication are informed by close attention to the mechanics of publicness. For example, boyd found that Facebook and Twitter updates differed according to young users' perceptions of the nature of publicness that each brings (the former is like speaking to friends, the latter addresses the world). The main social media effect, boyd concludes, is cultivating the feeling that one is always public, which heightens sensitivity to the critical nature of communication acts. Thus 'as social media becomes increasingly ubiquitous, the physical and digital will be permanently entangled and blurry' (2014 [in Kindle locations, 3432–3433]).

Respected anthropologist Sherry Turkle (2011) characterizes this situation as something of a devil's bargain. The possibilities of online communication carry with them anxieties produced by the new figure of the 'tethered self'. This moniker elegantly captures boyd and Marwick's contentions that the social existence of the individual has been significantly synthesized with the operations of commercial media systems. And, as with all contracts, there is a price to pay. The most compelling evidence for this deal is found in the way that young people juggle their relationships through a series of critical communicative acts that work through complicated networks of media practices that add flexibility and tension to personal relationships. For instance, Turkle discusses Julia, a teenager who uses electronic media to go about the difficult task of repairing a relationship with her estranged father, all under the guise of a much simpler request for permission to go on a school trip. Using email to ask for his signature, so that she might go on an overseas trip, was a gambit towards re-establishing connections. And Julia was clear in the sense that email was the best medium for their relationship, at that point: 'We have to build up. If we talk awhile on the computer, then I can call him and then maybe go and see him' (Turkle, 2011, 44).

Taken together, Marwick, boyd and Turkle's work shows how interpersonal and media communication are conjoined because media technologies and narratives significantly shape how we deal with important social relationships. Mobile media networks attract us by rapidly expanding the breadth and depth of the ones that we can have, and 'always on' identities model themselves on celebrity-like approaches to communication.

These insights bear several implications for researching media audiences and media places, and these will be discussed in later chapters. For now, the point is that the topics of celebrity, health and well-being help us to understand how mediatization integrates media and interpersonal communication. Further, this can be appreciated by looking at media influence from an interpersonal point of view, as represented by CMM. Equally, research on what we might call the celebritization of mobile media users indicates that the maintenance of social relationships through communication often happens in relation to media content and practices. Moreover, the age of personalized medicine is an example of an emergency political reality that makes close attention to this relationship a matter of social urgency.

Health communication scholars have observed that the types of decision that Jolie had to make about managing her public image really aren't so different from the things that ordinary people do. Within grand concerns about the general effects of celebrity, this might seem like an ominous possibility. Rojek (2012) thought the main celebrity 'health' issue was the creation of a new age of narcissism where media relations can usurp social ones. From a CMM perspective, however, the task is to look for how one impacts the other through a close examination of speech acts on interpersonal levels, asking, for example, how the celebritization of health affects relationships of trust between doctors and patients? Whatever the outcome, the question itself underlines the significance of small-scale interactions as being generalizable or mediatized in so far as they can be connected to a bigger media universe. Unlike rituals, where media effects operate through the monopolization of folk traditions, here the question is how the celebrity critical moment cognizably initiates critical interpersonal conversations. This is an *initiating* power, as it is seen in interpersonal communication informed by the media variety. This initiating power is a valuable addendum to the concept of media rituals, and will become especially relevant to the later chapter on media audiences.

CHAPTER SUMMARY

- People make reality when they talk to each other.

- The discipline of speech communication has developed a method for analysing how this works, which is called the 'coordinated management of meaning' (CMM).

- CMM views speech as being guided by hierarchies of meaning.

- The influence of celebrity on the way that audiences understand and discuss health shows how media play a significant role in shaping these hierarchies.

- This is significant given the emerging idea that a celebrity-like attitude towards social media communication is becoming a defining feature of social life.

Part 3

DOING MEDIA RESEARCH: PEOPLE, MARKETS, TEXTS, EVENTS, USERS, AUDIENCES, POLICY

9

RESEARCHING MEDIA PEOPLE: JOURNALISM, ORAL HISTORY AND ARCHIVES

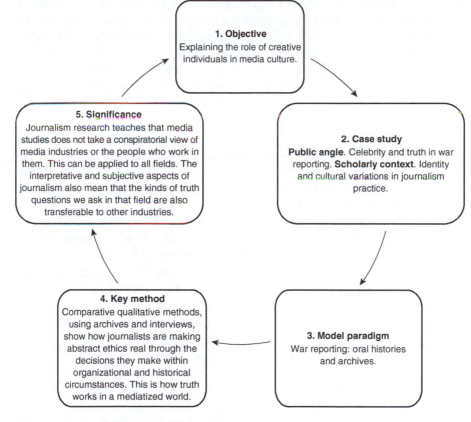

1. Objective
Explaining the role of creative individuals in media culture.

2. Case study
Public angle. Celebrity and truth in war reporting. **Scholarly context**. Identity and cultural variations in journalism practice.

3. Model paradigm
War reporting: oral histories and archives.

4. Key method
Comparative qualitative methods, using archives and interviews, show how journalists are making abstract ethics real through the decisions they make within organizational and historical circumstances. This is how truth works in a mediatized world.

5. Significance
Journalism research teaches that media studies does not take a conspiratorial view of media industries or the people who work in them. This can be applied to all fields. The interpretative and subjective aspects of journalism also mean that the kinds of truth questions we ask in that field are also transferable to other industries.

Figure 5   Researching media people

OBJECTIVE: CONCEIVING THE INFLUENCE OF CREATIVE INDIVIDUALS IN MEDIA CULTURE

This chapter demonstrates how we can explore media power by researching carefully selected media individuals. It explains how talking to people who work in the media helps to place media content in an historical context. This is a valuable way to understand that media studies *does not* subscribe to a conspiratorial view of media power. These ideas are explored in relation to journalism. The benefit of the case study is that it applies the purpose of researching media people, with the goal of dodging conspiracy theories, to the issue of truth: Why is it reasonable, despite all we know about the reality-shaping power of media, to still expect journalists to tell the truth?

Oral history and archival research on war journalism is used as a case study. This research shows how media studies deploys the idea that individuals become important historical figures when they represent the intersection of significant political and cultural trends. Historical studies of war journalism make a riveting case that individuals can affect media industries by creatively managing intense professional and political pressures in the pursuit of truth. By talking to war correspondents and their families, or sifting through archives of their work, researchers have discovered intriguing cases where reporting excellence has rested on personal ingenuity and integrity. Research on how war journalists have laboured under harrowing demands because of who they are vividly shows how talking to the right person, in the right context, yields innovative insights into how individual circumstances affect media realities. These insights have the general benefit of dismissing the misconception that media scholars take a conspiratorial approach to media power, and specify the role that unique stories play in writing general media histories.

It's a popular misperception that media studies is a thinly disguised conspiracy theory. To critics, media studies is a polemical pseudo-academic pursuit, bent on proving that media are inevitably biased towards the whims of media moguls, governments, commercial interests, or perhaps all three. This problem has been a particular feature of journalism studies (e.g. the critique by Windschuttle, 2000). Consequently, studies explaining how journalists retain admirable ethical standards in the face of mortal danger outline several important ideas: that media research does not aspire to prove collusion between media creatives and their employers or political masters, and that individual creativity often flourishes under the direst of circumstances. History shows that when journalists are placed under direct political duress to spin truths, they often end up finding ingenious ways to tell the stories that they want to write. Historical studies of journalism practices, using oral histories and archives, have been instrumental in making this case. In the process, they have shown how evidence from key individuals is valuable to appreciating the unpredictability of media power, where sometimes individual decisions made at key times when the forces of media and historical memory collide can make all the difference.

Four points lead to this conclusion. First, conspiracy theories aren't very good at explaining how news works. Second, looking at British journalism research from the 1970s, 'conspiracies' never prevailed in the minds of journalism scholars. Third, historical examples of war media practices, conducted under repressive political regimes, show journalistic creativity has flourished under the most trying of circumstances. Fourth, recent research on war reporting offers sophisticated insights into how subjectivity operates as a key factor in the production of ethical news. Taken as a whole, war reporting research illustrates how individuals matter in media systems, as key agents who realize creativity and ethics within historical and professional boundaries. Consequently, subjectivity is an important theme in international comparative journalism research. In particular, gender has exerted a positive influence on journalistic ethics. What we learn from this is that by carefully understanding the personal, professional and political contexts in which media individuals do their work, it is possible to appreciate how personal testimonies shed considerable light on how media realities that pass into historical memory were made through design, force, chance and creativity.

In summary, this chapter:

- Examines war journalism as a valuable topic that highlights significant general questions about media representation and truth.
- Explains how critical journalism studies aims to establish productive relationships with media professionals by understanding their lived practices.
- Outlines how identity has a legitimate place in ethical journalistic practices.
- Shows how interview- and archive-based research on properly selected individuals yields general insights into the role of media practice in the creation of media truth and historical consciousness.

CASE STUDY: WAR REPORTING AND WAR CORRESPONDENTS IN 'POST TRUTH' SOCIETY

Public angle: War reporting, ego and truth in competitive news markets

War reporting enjoys particular kudos among journalists. Great combat correspondents are lauded for their robust commitment to truth (Knightley, 1976; Markham, 2011b; Smith and Higgins, 2012). This trend has been amplified by the rise of the celebrity war reporter (Markham, 2012a). When we add in to that the role of the star anchor as a landmark on the digital television landscape (Andrejevic, 2013), it's easy to see why famous American news host Brian Williams' suspension for misreporting his combat experiences in 2015 seemed like a dagger to the heart of his calling.

Williams claimed to have been on a US military helicopter that was hit by a rocket-propelled grenade in Iraq. Under pressure from soldiers who said differently, Williams confessed this never happened (BBC News, 2015). A few months later, the *Los Angeles Times* reported the headaches about the errant anchor's future. There was the commercial value of a show that drew $450 million in annual advertising revenue. Then there was the relationship between NBC and its parent company, ComCast, which was sensitive to consumer opinion. And what about NBC's other journalists? How would colleagues feel about being led by a figure who had been caught out committing a cardinal sin? Complicating things further, if Williams returned, it would usurp Lester Holt, the first African American to anchor a national free-to-air nightly newscast in the US. How would that look (Battaglio, 2015)?

But how was Williams' comeback even imaginable, given the gravity of his actions? Academically, it is not for us to judge on his redemption. Instead, our job is to consider what his lapse said about journalism as a cultural form. What is it about journalism, as a particular way of telling the truth, that might have fostered his actions? What does this say about the reality of journalistic ethics? And, most importantly, what does an examination of critical research on journalism tell us about the purpose and methods of critical media research? Journalism offers a chance to define how media studies actively contributes to the future of media. Journalism research specifies how normative principles emerge from a commitment to understanding journalism ethics as a practice, rather than as a set of abstract principles divorced from what reporters do and, crucially, who they are.

Scholarly context: Comparative ethics

Critical media research is not about debunking the idea that news is about truth. If this were so, then globally noted popular cynicism directed at news media indicates that this job is already done. Wariness about news veracity has been noted in Afghanistan, China, Denmark, Iran, Kenya, Spain, Tanzania, Uganda, the United Kingdom and the United States, to name but a few (Skuse, 2002; Jones, 2004; Sepehri, 2010; Jebril, Albæk and de Vreese, 2013; Shen and Guo, 2013; Xu, 2013; Kalyango, 2014). Some research has found that audiences living in non-democratic countries are less trusting of state-owned media than are their counterparts in the West (Tsfati and Ariely, 2014). Most publics know that news is coloured by state–media relations, commercial interest, journalistic ego, and so forth. After all, you don't have to look hard for the evidence. In the UK, the Levinson Inquiry into press ethics uncovered astonishing tales of hack excesses. The editor of a famed tabloid confessed his shame at forcing young reporters to write a series of anti-Muslim stories (Phillips, 2013). Miladi's (2008) research on North African television viewers in the UK indicated that audiences had figured out institutional racism before the inquiry. The viewers in this study found British media's coverage of 'the war on terror' to be historically inaccurate and culturally insensitive. This was especially problematic for UK citizens, who felt that the lesson being taught was that they were not welcome in their home nation. Here, knowledge did not empower.

This is why critical journalism studies cannot be about identifying the inherent bias of news organizations towards the interests of the powerful. The accumulation of knowledge on the factors that lead news organizations to produce politically loaded visions of reality has *redoubled* faith in the importance of journalism as a medium that does have a unique relationship with truth (Couldry, Madianou and Pinchevski, 2013; Zelizer, 2013). A media studies that helps Miladi's viewers identify what's wrong with the news without offering them a view of how things could be better isn't much use. A media studies that does not connect how things should be with how things are, in terms of the pressures that journalists encounter in doing their jobs, is equally worthless. There is little value in discussing incidents where a respected news anchor has told a story about coming under fire that isn't true, or when we hear that a newspaper editor has deliberately set out to foster anti-Muslim stories, if the conclusion is simply that media are too invested in the interests of economic and political elites to be of any value.

The task, then, is to explain how a subject that does generally assume that media are often compromised by the inequalities of late capital (Andrejevic, 2013) remains sensitive to how truth does and should work in news culture. To begin to explain this, it helps to look at British approaches to news analysis. These approaches devoted considerable attention to developing 'non-conspiratorial' understandings of news analysis that help to explain events across a variety of contexts.

JOURNALISM STUDIES: BEYOND CONSPIRACY THEORY

In the 1970s, British scholars set about studying the role of news in the management of social conflict. In this early period, the Glasgow University Media Group (GUMG) were influential in defining the field of critical journalism studies. *Bad News* (GUMG, 1976) and *More Bad News* (GUMG, 1978) used content analysis to argue that television journalists tended to take a very particular position on the relationship between the economy and social conflict in 1970s Britain. That decade saw numerous clashes between the UK's Conservative party, during its terms of government, and the union movement. Controversy raged over the causes of economic decline. In this struggle, the GUMG argued, television news tended to characterize organized labour as an obstacle to 'modernization'. *More Bad News* boldly stated that the title had been chosen because their evidence showed television journalism frequently misrepresented unions and economic processes. Accusations of conspiracy came to the fore when the group turned its attention to armed conflict. *War and Peace News* (GUMG, 1985) scrutinized UK television's coverage in 1982 of the Falklands War, which was fought between Britain and Argentina. In the course of that research, the authors were denied access to minutes of meetings held by senior BBC news editors. A testy exchange followed between two members of the Group, John Eldridge and Greg Philo, and Alasdair Milne, the then Director-General of the BBC. In correspondence with Milne, Eldridge and Philo argued that the embargo was hardly what the public would expect from a publicly funded institution. Milne retorted that all organizations kept confidential operational records, and he could further defend his decision in his firm belief that the GUMG would have manipulated the evidence to portray his corporation negatively. Both sides, then, accused each other of self-serving misrepresentation (Eldridge, Milne and Philo, 1985).

However, Richard Hoggart's introduction to *Bad News* (GUMG, 1976) made a crucial distinction between critical journalism studies and conspiracy theories. The latter took two forms. 'Low' conspiracy theories looked for moments when powerful figures – presidents, prime ministers or newspaper owners – stopped reporters from telling what they know. 'High' theories, as the name suggests, are more sophisticated arguments that examine how news agendas are shaped by informal relationships, for example, the idea that certain political viewpoints are rarely presented because professional journalists and the political elite share the same upbringing and value system. It's not that these things never happen; it is just that they provide a woefully incomplete model of how most news works most of the time. It may well be true that political ideas emanating from powerful groups shape the realities that journalists show to their audiences, but this idea doesn't adequately explain how journalism works its ways into the bones of society as an authoritative kind of knowledge (Hoggart, 1976).

It was more accurate to see the *Bad News* studies as efforts to understand the alignments of changing news industries and a changing world. The research was prompted by the coexistence of two empirical realities: the economic and political crises of the 1970s and the rapid rise of television news as the most widely accessed and trusted source of information. The intersection of these conditions was an opportunity to examine how a relatively new kind of journalism contributed to public life in a changing social world. While notions of power and influence were crucial to this project, the situation at hand was far more complicated than the question of how television forced a dominant viewpoint on its audience. There were two evidential points that refuted this possibility. The first was survey data showing that although the majority of the British public rated television news far above the press as a source of reliable information, that same public drew significant distinctions between the publicly funded BBC and its commercial rival, Independent Television News. The latter was seen as being less formal, more human interest based and accessible. Audiences, it seemed, appreciated that there were different ways of 'doing' the news.

That said, what was the public putting their trust in? The second evidential motivation for the Group was the absence of systematic research on television news as a cultural form. The medium had usurped radio and newspapers as the popular medium of record in less than 20 years, yet there had been no sustained attempt to examine how professional ethics transferred from the written and spoken word onto the screen. *Bad News* (GUMG, 1976) set out to fill this gap by mapping the distinct features of television news discourse.

The GUMG sailed further from 'high conspiracy' theory because of its interest in change and conflict. It hardly made sense to look for uncomplicated 'dominance' in a society where battling viewpoints were so obvious. National miners' strikes plunged the nation into chaos in 1973 and 1984; rioting broke out in cities across the country in 1981; armed violence escalated in Northern Ireland. And all of the time, television news was becoming more important to how everyone made sense of these struggles, even as the nature of journalism changed through technologies, genres and the growth of the commercial sector in British broadcasting. Given all these facts about how the world was, the GUMG approached news as a 'contested' space where different groups and alliances battled to win the high ground of common sense. The project was not about the identification of dominance, but its choreography.

So the furore over the GUMG's analysis of television war news obscured the fact that their work never assumed a 'conspiracy'. If we set out to show that journalism simply reflects the values of people who already have power, then we cannot explain journalism as a practice. Studies of war reporting show that even when powerful forces directly affect what journalists can say, they still manage to tell the truth by creatively managing their role as small cogs in a bigger media machine. Journalism practice emerges through a wrestling match between professional standards, political, economic and cultural forces and identities. Moreover, recent studies of war reporting illustrate how these insights can be converted into research practices. Specifically, there are compelling ways for researching how the subjectivity of the journalist becomes a key variable in defining good practice, and this is a valuable means for connecting the reality function of the media with common-sense understandings of the role of the individual in media culture.

KEY PARADIGM: HISTORICAL WAR JOURNALISM STUDIES

Revealing the Holocaust: Truth and identity in Soviet war photography

Since research on war reporting examines how journalists work within overt constraints, the topic lends itself to understanding how normative ideals work in highly pressured situations. War correspondents make creative, courageous personal choices even when they are being told what to say. Consider David Shneer's extraordinary study of the Russian Jewish war photographers, and their ground-breaking documentation of the Holocaust. Shneer tells a haunting tale of how journalists told the truth as they saw it while even on the tightest of official reins. Jews, who were savagely discriminated against in the Tsarist and Soviet eras, and who were instructed to record the mass murder of Eastern European Jews as crimes against Soviet citizens, broke the truth of the Holocaust as a Jewish genocide. Researching the life and work of photographers such as

Emmanuel Evzerikhin, Yevgeny Khaldei and Dmitri Baltermants, Shneer discovered a fascinating paradox: forces that restricted Jewish participation in Russian life *and* recruited photojournalism as a propagandistic tool for celebrating Soviet ideology fostered a professional ethic that broke the full horror of genocide to a general audience. This truth emerged thanks to photojournalists who were historically empowered to make decisions that counted.

The photojournalists who accompanied the Red Army's counter-punch from Stalingrad to Berlin knew the official story they were to tell before a single shutter snapped. In 1917, Lenin proclaimed 'that the camera, as much as the gun, was an important weapon the Bolsheviks had at their fingertips to secure the revolution' (Shneer, 2011 [in Kindle location, 232]). Beginning in the 1920s, professional photographers set about defining a 'socialist realism' that canonized workers and deified the Communist leadership. During the Spanish Civil War, professional bodies developed specific techniques for war photography. By the time hostilities broke out with Germany, the Soviet Union was able to call on loyal cadres of photojournalists who understood the political role that they were to play in the Great Patriotic War. Shortages of film and developing chemicals made it doubly important to capture the war as Moscow wanted it to be seen, and failure to deliver saw photographers banished to punishment battalions.

Jewish photographers faced the additional threat of being purged for being Jewish. So how did they come to make up 60% of the Red Army's photojournalism corps, and how did their identity make Soviet photography a pioneering record of the Holocaust? They were there in such numbers because since the late 19th century, photography had been an especially attractive profession for young, creative Jewish men. Subsequently, Jews had played a leading role in defining the Soviet art form. Before the revolution, being a photographer exempted people from Tsarist bans on Jewish people living in St Petersburg, and, as a new profession, photography was not marked by the institutional racism blighting other vocations. This was underlined by the rise of people such as Mikhael Koltsov, who played a leading role in defining Soviet photography in the 1920s and 1930s (Shneer, 2011).

By the time of the Second World War, the evolution of Soviet news photography as a political art, and the integration of photojournalists into the Red Army, placed many young Jewish men in a unique place to tell a vivid visual story about the war. Ironically, the intense political scrutiny directed at the profession in the Soviet Union granted a creative licence that other Allied colleagues did not enjoy. This mattered enormously when it came to revealing the Holocaust. In the face of relentless fighting that took the lives of Soviet millions, photographers were under orders to provide two stories: Red Army heroism and Nazi atrocity. One gave hope, and the other an understanding of just what the people of the Soviet Union were up against. Soviet photographers were encouraged to record the grimmest details of mass murder. But there was one caveat: attacks on Jews in conquered Soviet republics were to be recorded as attacks on Soviet citizens.

Well-versed in the art of visual storytelling, Jewish photographers and their editors found codes to signify to their audiences that the Nazis were targeting Jews in particular. Entering Kerch in 1941, they were the first Allied photojournalists who 'saw with their own eyes the effects of Nazi occupation and the war against European Jewry' (Shneer, 2011 [in Kindle location, 1258]. Just a few weeks earlier the Gestapo herded the city's 7,500 Jews towards a trench and shot them. Mark Redkin took images that spread around the world. By publishing 'Russified' Jewish family names of victims, and making references to 'victims of ethnicity' in covering atrocities in places known to have sizeable Jewish populations, these photographers and their editors left their audience under no illusion that the Nazis were systematically exterminating Jews. Often discovering the gruesome fate of their own families, Jewish photographers who were ostensibly discouraged from covering the targeting of Jews were the first to break the story of the Holocaust (Shneer, 2011).

Shneer's study, based largely on interviews with surviving photographers and their families, developed a nuanced argument about subjectivity and creative choices that transpose onto other work on how journalists make reality in terms of where and who they 'are', professionally, politically and historically. One of the keys to a non-conspiratorial analysis of journalism is to appreciate how structural forces direct professional practice. In this regard it is significant to note how Shneer understood the role of 'Jewishness' as an identity that affected journalism. One of the cardinal precepts in qualitative media research is that we cannot assume that a person possesses a certain worldview that simply reflects their group identity (Morley, 1980). In this regard, it is significant that Shneer rejected the idea that his photographers shared a 'Jewish eye'. Evzerikhin, for instance, was hostile to the idea that Jewishness had anything to do with his work. That said, 'Jewishness' was a factor that made generations of photojournalists who defined Soviet propaganda *and* the conventions of Holocaust photography. Historical circumstances gave their identity a meaning that in turn gave their creativity a certain path. Ultimately, that gave a particular power to the universal 'truth' ethic shared by reporters everywhere.

Persona and gender in turn-of-the-century war reporting

Tim Markham's (2011b) interview research on war correspondents provides a framework for specifying how Shneer's insight – that subjectivity plays a positive role in truth-telling – explains why war reporters are seen as a benchmark for journalism practice. Through interviewing journalists, Markham set out to discover how particular war correspondents seemingly embodied 'good' journalism. The reason for his project was very clearly set out. War reporters enjoy renown as blends of professional excellence, personal integrity, courage and tenacity, representing the best truth-telling tradition under the most trying of circumstances. But what, Markham wondered, had produced this situation? Why was war reporting so prized, and how did celebrated war reporters win acclaim? Subjectivity was a key issue here, as journalists think that elite war reporters possess a natural nose for news that cannot be taught. But, Markham asked, what was it about journalism as an organized creative profession that led most of its practitioners to agree that good journalism relied on personality?

In answering, Markham dissected subjectivity in meticulous, structural terms, drawing on the work of French sociologist Pierre Bourdieu. One of the core strengths of the approach was to be very precise on what it is possible to say about subjectivity as a variable that plays a part in collective cultural practices. To explain journalism as a structured activity – something that works according to commonly understood rules that are codified in training and tradition and are shared through less formal conventions of practice – it is necessary to explain the circumstances that allow great journalists to use their 'gut instincts'. That is, the subjectivity of the journalist becomes a significant factor in shaping news when circumstances allow it to matter. Subjectivity matters in journalism because journalists bear the history of their calling: the evolution of journalism as a practice, the history of organizations and their relationship to other political and economic structures, and the politics of the situations they cover. 'Gut instinct' is a misnomer for a finely honed skill – understanding how the intersection of training, professional persona and context creates the possibility to speak. The trick is to strike a balance between mystifying elite war journalism as the child of personal *je ne sais quoi* and debunking it as accidental heroism. Instead, elite war correspondents are analytically useful objects that condense multiple factors when contemplating what good journalism is (Markham, 2011a, 2011b).

As an example, Markham cited revered BBC journalist John Simpson. In his 40 plus years as a television reporter, Simpson came under fire and was wounded in numerous war zones, winning acclaim in the process for his daring cool-headedness in putting his body on the line in search of truth. Undoubtedly there was something 'about' Simpson that explained his success, but his eminence as a journalistic authority also depended on the presence of conditions beyond his control: a market for war reporting as an especially valued field; professional benchmarks for judging excellence; and a vested interest among Simpson's peers in promoting his personality traits as desirable professional ones. One of Simpson's achievements was to establish that a disdain for authority is a useful 'value' that others can use to leverage their own reporting autonomy.

Ultimately, Markham (2011a) argued that personality is a medium that translates professional ethics into situated common sense. Personality, in the form of the elite reporter's 'nose for news', is an umbrella term for many ideas about how good journalism gets done. Markham lucidly developed a method for recognizing journalism as a privileged reality-making agent in terms of its own cultural practices. Journalistic ethics and creativity are exercised within the subjective experience of objective historical and institutional realities, and it is the analysis of these realities that is our goal. Markham's study was exemplary for delineating a founding principle of contemporary international comparative analysis on journalism practices, which seeks to understand how 'truth' is pursued under different circumstances. On this question, the matter of how gender affects war reporting has emerged as an especially vivid theme. To this end, the topic of war reporting can be used to explore how gendered identities play a role in journalism – how can this 'given' be interpreted within changing ideas about journalistic authority?

KEY METHOD: ARCHIVAL RESEARCH

The interplay of identity and ethics is a major theme in recent research on journalism. Two trends can be noted. First, personal interpretation of general ethical principles is a central research theme in comparative international studies. In this, there has been a marked move to embrace subjectivity and experience as key variables in understanding the realities that journalists make. A useful way to ground all of these ideas is to look at research that assesses gender as a key variable shaping journalism practice.

Second, the changing technological structure of news and the rising profile of disaster reporting have questioned the viability of impartiality. Tsunamis, earthquakes and the like demand appropriate emotional responses (Wahl-Jorgensen and Pantti, 2013). This is all the more so given the role that user-generated content plays in contemporary news telling. The common practice of integrating eyewitness footage in news narratives has made emotional register part of news conventions (Wahl-Jorgensen, 2012, 2013, 2014). However, this underlines a truth that has ever been – the journalists we like the most are the ones who put a little of themselves into their stories. In a study of Pulitzer prize-winning stories from 1995 to 2011, Wahl-Jorgensen (2012) found that critically acclaimed stories drip with subjective language. This, in her view, calls for a major rethink on the way that emotion versus rationality and subjective versus objective are operationalized as opposing values in discussions of journalism ethics.

Evidence suggests that the role of subjectivity in 'good' professional journalism is a theme with considerable international relevance. A survey of 1,800 journalists from 18 countries found universal agreement on the importance of impartial, fact-based reporting, but also disagreements over the role that subjectivity should play, in the form of 'personal evaluation and interpretation' (Hanitzsch et al., 2011, 283). Non-western journalists in the survey were far more likely to promote a situated ethics that granted journalists interpretative licence to construct 'truth' within a reading of political and working realities that affected what could be said. They were significantly less likely than their western colleagues to support universal principles.

Perhaps this is because in recent times non-western journalists have faced the greatest dangers, at least in the field of war reporting. Between 2003 and 2009, 139 journalists were killed covering the Iraq War, of whom 117 were Iraqis (Kim, 2010). The fall of Saddam Hussein opened a flood of opportunities for Iraqi journalists – but not for all the right reasons. Hundreds of new news operations opened, and demand for on-the-ground reporters boomed. However, one of the reasons for this was that reporting the war was incredibly dangerous, and the higher you went, the harder it got – journalists with glamour assignments based in large, urban television organizations were incredibly vulnerable, and Iraqis bore the brunt of the casualties. Iraqi journalists worked under unimaginable anxieties where they felt endangered by every armed group in the struggle, including the police and the US military (Kim, 2010).

Previously, I highlighted Shneer's work on Jewish war photographers as a lucid illustration of the idea that restrictive conditions can work together to produce new truth-telling freedoms. This principle again seemed to be in play in Iraq. Al-Rawi (2010) argued that the post-2003 period saw a raft of new opportunities for Iraqi women journalists in particular. Surveying interviews from these professionals, Al-Rawi discovered that in some respects, post-Saddam Iraq was a meaner place for female journalists. Journalism promised a lucrative career in an economy where 90% of women were unemployed, but it was also especially dangerous in a context where journalists were targeted for being Iraqi and being female. The traditional allure of prize-winning fame was a disincentive in a country where most journalists needed anonymity, and in many respects Iraqi society had become more conservative in its attitude towards female reporters than it had been in the 1970s. Iraqi female journalists lived in perpetual fear, and this clearly, understandably affected how they did their job. But at the same time, their plight did attract attention to the significance of cultivating a new generation of female reporters. Several non-governmental organizations and professional organizations have been established to train and address the particular barriers placed in the path of Iraqi women journalists, all based on the conviction that Iraqi news told from a woman's perspective has a vital role to play in a country whose largest population group is women between the ages of 30 and 49 (Al-Rawi, 2010).

Kate Adie: Using an archive to identify an historically significant journalist

In the United Kingdom, debates about good war reporting have adopted a marked gender tone in the controversies that have swept around famed BBC war correspondent Kate Adie. Adie has become a touchstone for a wide-ranging debate over the role of war reporting within the institution of a public service broadcaster. Adie's existence as a journalistic *cause célèbre*, evidence suggests, has much to do with her gender. Having bequeathed an archive of her work to the University of Sunderland in the UK, Adie is likely to become a key figure in developing an understanding of how late 20th-century war reporting took shape in the UK.

Higgins and Smith (2010) credit Adie as the personification of a particular understanding of the war correspondent as 'witness'. One way or another, Adie's embodiment of this controversial role has objectified a long-running battle over the politics of war reporting in the UK, and her gender has been a factor in explaining how general issues of impartiality and professional practice have taken on a particular shape in the controversies that have helped make her a renowned journalist.

The Adie archive provided a fascinating glimpse of what it was like to be on the 'inside' of the history researched by the Glasgow University Media Group.

War and Peace News (GUMG, 1985) had documented a battle between the BBC and the Conservative government of the 1980s over the duties of a public service broadcaster during war. In particular, the BBC had been accused of failing national interest by being *too* impartial in reporting armed conflict between Britain and her enemies. This criticism fell upon Adie when she reported on the 1986 bombing of Tripoli by US forces from inside Libya. When Adie fielded a report about civilian victims, she triggered a complaint from the Conservative party concerning what they saw as a disproportionate emphasis on non-combatant casualties.

Twenty-five years later, access to Adie's notes on the event showed a careful drafting process, through which she established a position on the bombing that was in keeping with one professionally legitimate form of war reporting: the role of witness. The notes showed the tensions she balanced: knowing her Libyan handlers led her to dead bodies and rubble for propaganda purposes; the rights of the dead and wounded to dignified privacy; questions of decency and taste; and the importance of letting the audience understand what bombing raids do. Kate Adie, the person, mattered because she decided how these conflicting considerations would shape the truth that could be told about Libya. This was in keeping with an embodied understanding of best journalism practice where 'the professional acumen of the journalist underpins the discursive power of war reporting' (Higgins and Smith, 2010, 355).

Adie deserves attention, then, as a key figure who made on-the-spot judgements that affected debates about ethical journalism. Higgins and Smith (2010) noted that Prime Minister Thatcher was cautious about attacking Adie personally because of her public popularity. Her authority was further enhanced by her work during the 1991 Gulf War, and by the mid-1990s she had established herself as a bastion of excellence. But what does this have to do with her gender?

One of the ideas that emerges from research is that although journalists appear as powerful figures in the construction of media realities, they remain vulnerable to subjectively experienced situations that affect the job that they do. Just as Jewish Soviet photojournalists had to negotiate periodic outbursts of anti-Semitic purges, so too evidence suggests that sexism has been a force to be reckoned with in Adie's career. It's possible that her indefatigable nature was fuelled by professional sexist antipathy. Markham (2012a) found a distinct difference in how Adie's personal behaviour was judged by her peers when compared to male colleagues. When late-middle-aged men flirted or became involved with younger women in the course of their duties, this was attributed to a certain roguishness that went with the territory for men who were good at what they did because they weren't too fussy about protocols. Stories about Adie flirting with British soldiers during the Gulf War, when she was in her 40s, however, was met with disdain and also as evidence of a person who would do anything to get a story (Markham, 2014).

The point is not that Adie did her work in a certain way because she was a woman, but the fact that she was a woman did play a part in the truths that she told and the questions about truth that she raised. And this is a tremendously valuable effect that helps to understand journalism as a genre. Additionally, the critical analysis of journalism also sparks productive debates about what we expect from media industries that are tasked with supporting inclusive public cultures. At significant moments in history, individual journalists have made professional choices that sparked soul-searching debates over the purpose of media truth. Adie's decision to report civilian casualties of the Libya bombing questioned the political independence of a state-sponsored news organization. Similarly, Brian Williams' decision to misreport his war experiences encapsulated the fear that we live in a 'post truth' culture (Andrejevic, 2013), in which the quality of public discourse is eroded by a media environment where the entertainment quality and political utility of a story outweighs its veracity. In either case, understanding the subjectivity of journalists as a condensation of identity, professional training and historical circumstance becomes an effective means of explaining how ethics applies in a world where political truths are constructed, and where understanding this process is an integral part of debates about inclusivity in mediatized societies.

SIGNIFICANCE: BEYOND CONSPIRACY: UNDERSTANDING MEDIA CREATIVES AS PEOPLE WHO NEGOTIATE ORGANIZATIONAL, HISTORICAL AND POLITICAL PRESSURE

Conceptually, research on those who work in media industries underlines significant qualifications concerning the propositions that reality is something that culture makes, and that media industries have colonized many aspects of this process. A few points need to be noted here. First, this is a disinterested ontological assumption. What we are saying is that media studies seeks out those occasions where the distinct structure of media industries and media practices has empirically verifiable reality effects, and this does not assume that those effects always work in one direction. The proposition that particular forces structure media representations does not imply the presence of a global conspiracy to maintain the power of people who already have it. Second, the contention that reality can be cast in different ways does not imply that any old reality will do, and that there is no basis upon which media representations can be criticized – or praised – in relation to things that happen in the world.

Another theme so far has been the idea that it helps to relate challenges in accounting for media influence to general issues in the humanities. Drawing from history, I have argued that many media problems access debates on the nature of causation and the role of the individual in society that have been developed elsewhere – in history, for example. With regard to the latter, general debates about media influence often boil down to the actions of individuals who seem to hold a particular sway over the public imagination, whether they intend to or not. Angelina Jolie is an example of this.

Consequently, war reporting is a topic that usefully summarizes the purpose of critical media research by showing how this research continues in a long humanities tradition of analysing the nature of causation and the role of the individual therein. Taking this focus also helps outline a productive relationship between media academics and media industries that is not shaped by a *de facto* hostility. Media scholars do not assume that media industries, and the people who work for them, are bent on maintaining social inequalities, and recent research on war reporting helps make this point. Today, journalism is generally understood as a crucial job. This is why it is vital to understand how journalists are trained, how they embody and deploy ethical values, and how a range of cultural and global factors coalesce around celebrity journalists whose identities become embroiled in the truths that they offer. The idea here is not to debunk the notion of truth, but to understand how it is shaped by professional practice. That is, a productive discussion on journalistic ethics can only happen in the presence of an understanding of how journalism works, and in particular how universal ethical principles vary according to the systems in which they are articulated. The decisions that journalists make about how their training and principles apply to the stories that lay before their eyes is part of the analysis. There are sound reasons for basing research on global ethics on the things that individuals and groups do in different circumstances. It's a basic ontological assumption that journalists mediate between general professional values and local conditions, be they historical, political, commercial, technological or, most likely, a volatile mixture of all four. At any rate, the study of what journalists *actually* do within the affordances of their place remains central to any realistic discussion on what they *should* do, ethically speaking (Dickinson, Matthews and Saltzis, 2013).

And this insight has relevance across all forms of media research. The purpose of paying attention the media reality effects is *not* to paint truth as relative. It *is* to draw attention to the democratic consequences of living in societies where the truths that count are the ones that get to be written, shared and popularized. This is why the Williams story was so important. In an age where the entertainment value of news has become an important power ingredient in a global media market, it reminded us that conventional ethical principles still apply. It is interesting that, in his defence, Williams invoked his family's military history as he fought for his career. Looking at historical and global comparative journalist research, it's clear that identity and personality have always mediated professional ethics. However, the case studies reported here – on Holocaust photojournalism, women reporters in Iraq, and the life and times of Kate Adie – suggest that ethical journalists put themselves into their work in reflective ways, and carefully consider the political consequences of the work that they do. Seen this way, the purpose of pointing to the constructed nature of media reality is to focus on the embodied processes that put ethical principles into practice. Equally, talking to media professionals about their experiences of these processes in action is a useful antidote to any reflex to view media power as a *fait accompli*.

CHAPTER SUMMARY

- Being critical about the media does not mean assuming that media industries are the centres of conspiracies to mislead the public.

- Research on war reporting shows how subjectivity plays a productive role in developing situated ethical standards, matching 'truth' with the realities of professional practices.

- This allows us to see how normative questions (about what media should do in democracies) connect with professional practices (committing to understanding how media industries work in practice).

- This understanding provides a constructive platform for media academics to engage with media industries, across a variety of genres.

- These points have been made through compelling stories of how journalists face real pressures, made through historical practices such as oral history and archive research.

10

RESEARCHING MEDIA MARKETS: A CULTURAL INDUSTRIES VIEW ON PORNOGRAPHY

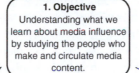

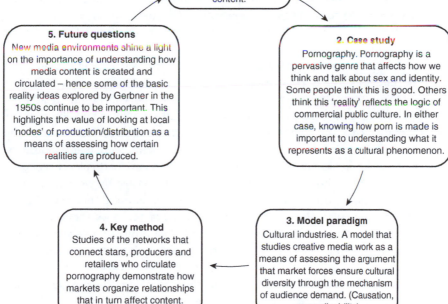

1. Objective
Understanding what we learn about media influence by studying the people who make and circulate media content.

5. Future questions
New media environments shine a light on the importance of understanding how media content is created and circulated – hence some of the basic reality ideas explored by Gerbner in the 1950s continue to be important. This highlights the value of looking at local 'nodes' of production/distribution as a means of assessing how certain realities are produced.

2. Case study
Pornography. Pornography is a pervasive genre that affects how we think and talk about sex and identity. Some people think this is good. Others think this 'reality' reflects the logic of commercial public culture. In either case, knowing how porn is made is important to understanding what it represents as a cultural phenomenon.

4. Key method
Studies of the networks that connect stars, producers and retailers who circulate pornography demonstrate how markets organize relationships that in turn affect content.

3. Model paradigm
Cultural industries. A model that studies creative media work as a means of assessing the argument that market forces ensure cultural diversity through the mechanism of audience demand. (Causation, generalizability)

Figure 6   Researching media markets

OBJECTIVE: UNDERSTANDING HOW MARKETS AFFECT CREATIVITY, CONTENT AND INCLUSION

This chapter explains how to research the operation and impacts of media markets. It does so by applying concepts from cultural industries research to pornography. There are two goals here. The first is to show how a cultural industries perspective, especially in its framing of creative labour, adds sophistication to the debates on pornography and harm. The second is to describe how 'small' markets – ones that are relatively accessible – give vital clues about the political dynamics of larger operations.

The chapter begins by outlining the significance of porn to media studies. Whether they see porn as good, bad or indifferent, opposing factions agree that the genre has become a fixture in how we talk and think sexual identity. The availability of porn means most of us have to deal with it. By virtue of its sheer ubiquity, pornography has become a vehicle for discussions about commercial media and social inclusion. Some credit commercial porn with diversifying public representations of sexuality (McKee, 2012; McNair, 2014). Others think it has created a world where ordinary people work hard to make their sex lives look like porn and feel disappointed when they fail (Paasonen, 2010). Either way, pornography is a subject where the production and distribution of media content has been explicitly connected to its outcomes.

Competing claims about pornography's significance can be assessed by looking at the people who make and sell it. In recent years, innovative research on the places where pornography is made, sold and shared has underlined the value of cultural industries research. Cultural industries research examines how cultural activities – expressing ideas through telling stories – fare under market conditions. In this, conceiving 'art' as 'work' has been a useful method for understanding the creative potential and limitations of contemporary media. This addresses the most basic media reality effect: the extent to which democracy can be imagined within particular arrangements of media industries.

Research on pornography shows how this approach solves a particular challenge in debates on the genre and its effects. Studies on the relationship between porn retailing and porn content transcend the urge to judge – an impulse that does little to advance debates on what the presence and popularity of porn says about the health of gender relations. Research on how porn producers, performers, purveyors and public relate to each other through small media markets – focusing on community-based networks of production and retail distribution – successfully locate the porn problem within political effects of market-driven media systems. Where the previous chapter outlined what we can learn from individuals, this chapter centres on how to observe relationships between people as they are arranged in identifiable markets.

In summary, this chapter:

- Explains why pornography is an important media genre.
- Outlines key concepts in cultural industries research.
- Explains how situated research on making and selling pornography elucidates the relationship between grounded, particular accounts of media production and global questions about political economy.

CASE STUDY: PORNOGRAPHY

Public angle: Pornography as sexual assault

In 2015, porn actor Stoya claimed to have been raped by fellow performer James Deen. Following the tweeted charge, others alleged that Deen had assaulted them too on film sets. The story made international front pages. Commercial judgements were quickly made. Deen, a bona fide celebrity who had been credited with normalizing porn, was quickly dropped by a number of companies (Carroll, 2015). Meanwhile, the idea that female performers were sex workers who needed better workplace protection became a matter of public interest.

The story had considerable ramifications for the way we see porn content. A few years ago, I was asked to give a professional opinion on the suitability of a porn film for public distribution. It featured a scene in which a female performer engaged in what to me looked like a violent sexual act. Certainly, tears, snot and drool streamed from her eyes, nose and mouth as the camera rolled. I remember thinking that if I could ask the actor if she had fun in that scene, and if she said yes, I wouldn't believe her. So there wouldn't be much point in asking in the first place. On the other hand, it would have been a stupid question. Porn actors aren't playing. Don't take my word for it, ask Asa Akira.

Akira possesses a lucrative contract with elite porn company, Wicked Pictures. Like Deen, she's enjoyed mainstream film success. According to her autobiography (2014), Akira did not run to porn from a lack of options. Privately educated, she needed cash to open a yoga studio. She started porn for the money, and never left. She likes the lifestyle and yes, the sex, too much.

You'd expect a porn star to say that. After all, she profits from the impression that she's in it for the sex. Her autobiography is part of the act, alongside appearances at fan conventions and, of course, on the screen. Which makes it all the more interesting that Akira's book doesn't argue that porn is nothing but fun. It is work. Sex work. Work that she likes, even finds addictive, but work. And like everybody else, she has bad days.

Akira describes one of them in her introduction. Early in her career she combined porn with escorting, and accompanied a friend to a job with a wealthy client. The session involved far less strenuous work for much more money than she would find on a film set. But there were potential risks: rape, assault, murder, enough to warrant a can of mace. Entering the client's apartment, Akira feared she needed the weapon. In the living room, on a large-screen TV, one of her own films was playing. She was then instructed to play an encore. The scene was discomforting enough to encourage Akira to keep the mace within arm's reach. She didn't enjoy the image of her own face – unflattering, she thought. Worse still, she was nonplussed at the realization that people really do act out porn fantasies, even down to repeating 'cheesy' lines.

Akira's anecdote outlines the alienation that can happen through the work that makes media realities. It's a vivid tale of how media and mediatized culture make social situations that you really can touch. The integration of media and work (porn and escorting) lets the consumer live fantasy – providing he can pay. But for Akira, this had the distinctly odd effect of denying the materiality of her own body. The client was having real sex with her, but, mentally speaking, he was more engaged with the image on the screen. Sure, they were fornicating, but he would never know her, and she would never really know him.

Akira presented this story as a bad day at work. The strategic risks she takes with her body as a porn performer left her unsure about the relationship she had with her fans, or indeed what her work 'meant' in the world of hum-drum sexuality. If we think of culture as something that brings us together when it's good, then here was an instance where her creative labour had the opposite effect. This sort of 'alienation', where work somehow diminishes the quality of human relationships, is a key consideration in studies of media work, conducted from a cultural industries point of view (Hesmondhalgh and Baker, 2013).

All in all, it's clear how wrong I was in thinking that there isn't much point in talking to porn performers, because all you will hear are predictable defences made by people who have to justify what they do for money. There are good reasons why we need to know more about its stars. Porn users tell us their pleasure depends on how scenes are made; many don't want to watch material where people are being coerced into sex (McKee, 2006a; 2006b). Second, a focus on porn work offers a crucial addendum to understanding its nature as a cultural product. Porn may or may not be art, or free speech, but the people who make it have the same rights to respect and safety as anyone else. For example, the problem with the clip I had seen was not just about the willingness of the participant, but the obligation of the producers to inform and protect subcon-tractors from disease. If we accept that porn is commercial labour just like any other entertainment genre, then its performers have the right to workplaces that maintain healthy and equitable social relationships. In the end, it is the bal-ance between commercial media markets and healthy, non-exploitative, non-alienated human relationships that is at the core of a cultural industries approach to pornography. As we shall see, these studies of the porn industry have put the core conceptual principles of the cultural industries approach to work to good effect.

Scholarly context: What is pornography, and what does it do?

There are two very basic reasons why pornography is a significant issue in media research, and why a cultural industries perspective has an important role to play in making sense of the battles that rage over what porn says about con-temporary society. We must study porn because societies worry about it. European evidence shows that young internet users fear exposure to porn (Livingstone et al., 2013). Moreover, new methods of production and distribu-tion present new risks. Most tellingly, the ease with which anyone can become a producer and distributor of pornography is a factor to be reckoned with in teen social life. 'Sexting', for example, puts teens at risk of unwittingly doing porn, not just seeing it, and they have to bear the legal consequences (Albury and Crawford, 2012; Hasinoff, 2013; Tungate, 2013). Porn is at the cusp of changing techno-cultural conditions of production, distribution and consumption. These changes have experiential outcomes, such as minors who find themselves on the end of child pornography charges over images sent from one phone to another (Paasonen, 2010).

According to Coleman and Held (2014), pornography is an index of mediatization in action. In a mediatized world, the old adage 'if you don't like it, switch it off' clearly doesn't work, and the visibility of pornography underlines this point. Never has pornography been so accessible and shareable, and never has culture been so 'porned', they argue. In porned cultures, pornography speaks to fundamental issues around sexual identity, the politics of markets and human rights. Coleman and Held do not use 'porned culture' as a pejorative term; the moniker simply acknowledges pornography as a source of images and ideas about social justice. This is why porn is a legitimate object of study that is not radically different from other areas of media research (Coleman and Held, 2014).

The significance of pornography: From effects to industries

That said, it is important to distinguish between the significance and the demonstrated influence of pornography. Research on what porn 'does' to society resembles the violence issue, that is, there are studies showing that porn hurts its audience and others that point to the conceptual and methodological weaknesses of that evidence. As with violence, meta-analyses of experimental studies on the effects of exposure to porn claim to show reliable and valid connections between exposure and sexual aggression (Malamuth and Hald, 2003). Survey research from young patients at sexual health clinics in Europe indicates that porn use contributes to disease by creating the impression that unsafe sexual practices – like anal sex without a condom – are normal (Rogala and Tyden, 2003). Following the normalization theme, Asian survey studies claim to have discovered evidence of desensitization. Here, ease of access to pornography means that the more young people consume, the more they are likely to see porn use as perfectly normal (Lo, Wei and Wu, 2010). This is troubling for some, because content analysis of popular porn movies shows a preponderance of sexual practices that seem demeaning to women (e.g. slapping) and certainly carry health risks for performers (such as anal to mouth ejaculation) (Bridges et al., 2010).

Of course there are many researchers who argue that porn use *is* perfectly normal, and that the demonization of its users is politically unhelpful (Smith, Barker and Atwood, 2015). This gestures towards the major, and really quite obvious, reservations about the case for porn damage. But as with violence, it's important to note that effects researchers don't argue that the case against porn is clear, or that the use of pornography is not consistent with healthy sexual attitudes and behaviours. As with violence, they acknowledge the limitations of trying to assess porn with experiments and surveys. They concede that there are circumstances where exposure to pornography coincides with positive outcomes. In Scandinavia, for example, researchers have a positive correlation between porn consumption, healthy sexual attitudes and low levels of sexual assault (Hald and Malamuth, 2008; McNair, 2014). When it comes to damage, then, the question is not whether porn is inherently harmful for all users, but rather it is about understanding the circumstances under which it can harm or help the well-being of some (Hald and Malamuth, 2008).

Wright's review of the literature on children and pornography provides a useful summary of the state of the field (Wright, 2014). Data from many parts of the world show that large numbers of young people are exposed to online porn. Content analysis on topics such as the use of condoms, the status of men versus women, and the prevalence of slapping and choking, usually done by men to women, suggests that if porn offers lessons, then the outcomes aren't healthy ones. It's reasonable to assume, then, that most parents wouldn't want their kids to learn from porn. On the other hand, ethical issues around researching kids and porn means that, as with violence, there's a whole bunch of things that we don't know. In particular, more work is needed on the circumstances and processes through which exposure does affect attitude. Included here is the importance of paying attention to where porn use correlates with progressive social attitudes. For example, in his other surveys, Wright has found that porn users tend to be more supportive of same-sex marriage among American males (Wright and Randall, 2014; Wright, Tokunaga and Bae, 2014).

We also need to be mindful that fears about porn aren't necessarily about porn itself. There's a plausible argument that the porn problem is about location. For many, the problem of porn lies not in its content, but in its availability (Reading, 2005). On this, mainstream media are culpable due to the publicity created by TV reality shows and documentaries that 'go behind the scenes' of the industry (Attwood, 2014). Taking this into account, it's worth asking whether the issue that concerns us is porn or the ubiquity of sexually explicit material across many genres, including advertising (Bartlett and Elms, 2011).

For others, the effects debate is a ruse. According to Jensen (1997), controversies about effects data are one of several academic 'dodges' that buffer pornography as a lucrative global exploitation industry. Arguing about the challenges of defining pornography, the extent to which the industry deserves protection on the grounds of free speech and methodological qualms all distract attention from a simple truth: material that is mostly sold to men for their pleasure frequently features women who are abused, either verbally or physically. For Jensen, alongside Gail Dines (2010), porn is a kind of hate speech. They feel that there is sufficient evidence from media research and content analysis to support the idea that porn routinely depicts women as second-class sexual citizens whose main role is to please men. This is not a matter of free speech – such debasing commercial exploitation is not worthy of such lofty ideals. Nor does the inability to conclusively demonstrate the causative link between exposure and anti-social outcomes dismiss the case for harm.

Following Gerbner, there are just as many reasons to ask a new set of questions, such as how the prevalence of porn narratives are used in everyday life as the scripts where we learn the lines to act out our own sexual scenarios (Jensen, 1998; Dines, 2010).

Understanding pornography as a complex cultural product

Set against the positon outlined by Jensen and Dines, other scholars have stressed the importance of recognizing pornography as a complicated cultural practice where the key to addressing its role in society lies in appreciating its existence as a media practice, just like any other kind of commercial entertainment (McKee, 2012). This perspective runs the gamut from those who dismiss the political case against porn as empirically flawed, to others who argue that commercial pornography is positively good for society. But again, the evaluation of these positions comes back to the need for a greater understanding of how the porn industry works.

Ronald Weitzer (2015) takes Jensen and Dines to task on a number of issues. Succinctly, the charge that pornography in general depicts unequal and abusive gender relations is shaky at best, given the way that both authors cherry pick the evidence, ignore the flourishing of porn niches that are not directed at a heterosexual audience, pay little attention to the sense that audiences make of pornography in its various flavours, and, perhaps most tellingly, conflate porn acting with all kinds of sex work on the basis of anecdotal evidence drawn from a tiny sliver of the 2,000 or so women who make their living from porn in the US alone.

McNair (2014) explains that to make these points is not to defend porn as such. It is simply to draw attention to the distinctions between evidence, political argument and moral judgement. Low rates of sexual assault in the countries with liberal pornography laws illustrate to him that the case for a causal connection between pornography is weak, and fits equally well with the argument that the availability of porn goes alongside more open attitudes towards sexuality that are good for society. Authors have every right to argue that porn is exploitative, as long as they recognize that this is a political argument based on a moral judgement that can be countered with confounding evidence concerning how pornography is made and used.

An Australian scholar called Alan McKee has produced a sizeable body of work arguing that porn is healthy, and that this underlines the social benefits of commercial porn. A demand-driven industry, porn caters for popular cultural tastes, and this has led to a far more open sexual public sphere, where a broad range of sexual identities enjoy unprecedented visibility (McKee, 2012). In his work, McKee has generally argued that any discussion on the role of porn in society has to be based on audience perceptions (e.g. McKee, 2006a; 2006b). Australian users found no pleasure in watching coerced sex, and porn was mostly a device for couples to enhance their sex life. It was not, in other words, an exercise in self-interest. McKee further pointed out that the sort of porn that worries critics the most – such as the scene that I described at the start of the chapter – isn't what most people consume (McKee, 2006). Judging porn by looking at a handful of titles is a bit like judging all films on the basis of having watched *Snakes on a Plane*.

A further flaw, in McKee's view (2012), is the failure to understand porn as entertainment. The kind of porn that most people like is ribald, self-reflexive and accedes to popular taste – and this is what all decent popular culture has always done. Subsequently, porn is far more diverse and non-judgemental on sexuality than mainstream television and film. Porn is no less than popular culture at its best and a beacon in debates about the cultural value of commercial culture. If ever there was a case study on the benefits of running public cultural interest through the market, it is pornography (McKee, 2012).

It's here that the debate about effects connects with the analysis of media industries. The idea that porn is a paragon of popular entertainment is a claim about the organization of culture itself. There is more at stake here than what audiences think about porn. First, from porn users themselves, we have heard that pleasure depends on knowing that the industry works ethically. Second, in invoking the benefits of the market, McKee opened the debate to the analysis of how those markets – including production and distribution – actually function. Commercial forces might prevent people like me from foisting my elitist views about media industries upon the public. But it's naïve to assume that judgements – moral, aesthetic and economic – aren't in the DNA of commercial media industries and play no role in structuring markets and affecting what the public get. From a cultural industries vantage point, there are many reasons to think that organizational barriers prevent ethical, diverse porn, and these profoundly shape what porn means as a symbol of commercial public culture. Moreover, in looking at how research on porn producers, performers and retailers connect with ideas from the cultural industries model, we can learn a great deal about how media industries set the stage for public thought on issues that matter to us intimately, as individuals.

KEY PARADIGM: CULTURAL INDUSTRIES, MARKETS AND CULTURE

Art, culture, media and markets

In *Beyond Consumer Capitalism* (2013), Justin Lewis argued that commercial media damage global sustainability by telling stories that constantly equate happiness with consumption. Lewis defined this as a catastrophic failure of imagination produced by media industries whose organizational logic strangles creativity. His argument was relevant to pornography, since it challenged McKee's assertion that the wheels of commerce would support diverse representations of sexuality. Lewis and McKee shared the perception that the organization of markets and creative work was fundamental to media diversity.

They differed, however, in their view of how well commercial interest in itself could sustain inclusivity. As a result, understanding Lewis's argument is a useful tool when assessing McKee's claims on the benefits of the porn industry.

The root of Lewis's thinking can be traced back to his 1990 book, *Art, Culture and Enterprise*. Here, Lewis explored how questions of popularity and value could be pursued by looking at the way that culture was organized, especially in its distribution. Since current porn debates centre on the intersection of what people like and what is good for society, it's worth looking at where these ideas originated and how they developed in media research.

Lewis criticized arts policy that accepted the distinction between high art and popular culture, and the related belief that art and popular culture should be managed in different ways. What was needed was a new approach to arts policy that strategically funded popular media activities that people understood and enjoyed. This was the logic of the *cultural industries* strategy launched by the Greater London Council (for whom Lewis had worked). Instead of giving money to, say, tours of the Royal Shakespeare Company, the idea was that it would be better to fund things like local video production courses, where people could work with the things that they liked. Such strategies empowered audiences by presenting culture as something that is done, not just consumed.

Lewis's focus on culture as participation led to an interest in how organization and distribution fostered inclusion and sustainability. He identified three barriers that most ordinary people encountered when they tried to participate in culture. Most obvious was a class-biased system of aesthetic judgement that was entirely arbitrary – the line between art and junk lies where a small number of accredited people put it. But more practically, this was compounded by difficulties of accessing cultural places. Lewis argued that people were hardly likely to be lured from the comfort of their own homes to battle the hazards of public transport if the reward was grimy community centres or middle-class theatres thoroughly coded with the conventions of the high arts that few understood.

A new generation of entertainment complexes that served as a hub for a variety of activities, including concerts, nightclubs, films, art exhibitions and workshops, all catered for by vibrant bars and restaurants, showed the path forward. Engagement with the politics of popular culture required engagement with the work of cultural management. Art wasn't just about art anymore; it was about the entire organization of leisure, and the work that went into it. This idea – that the organization of cultural work, in all its guises, is a vital precondition for the democratic inclusiveness of popular culture – is an essential insight of the cultural industries position, and one that helps clarify why a new generation of work on the production of porn is so important.

For Lewis, then, the phrase 'cultural industries' was useful as a means of including popular media in national conversations about art, culture and public participation and social value. Cultural industries policy and research involved looking at how macro-economic changes, and the political thought that accompanied it, could be managed through detailed engagement with the operation of local markets. Lewis accepted that commercial media culture had a social role to play; he just didn't think that this function had to be left to the vicissitudes of the market, since local British experience showed how targeted public subsidies worked well. The lesson was that a vibrant public culture was one that knew when and where to pick its battles with global mass markets, finding inventive ways to create 'shelters' for artists and audiences alike. Ultimately, pockets of the porn industry operate according to this logic. In this sense, they exemplify how his ideas have developed in cultural industries work since the late 1980s.

Cultural industries and the concept of work

Lewis's ideas echoed through the development of 'cultural industries' as an academic field. The term itself needs unpacking. 'Cultural' is selected to preserve the idea of 'culture', especially the idea that expressive arts are valuable as a form of social critique (Hesmondhalgh, 2004; Oakley and O'Connor, 2015). Symbolic expression allows us to contemplate the common-sense values that structure societies. As Lewis made clear, popular culture can do the same thing.

'Industries' is trickier. We've accepted that media products are valuable, expressive artefacts, but at the same time they are produced through standardized commercial processes. This is important since media products are 'semi-public' (Hesmondhalgh, 2004). Films, songs, television shows are media for social thought (and as an example, you can think about the way that politicians sometimes try to communicate with the electorate through the selection of popular songs as campaign themes), but there are significant barriers to creativity imposed by the requirements to save costs by standardizing production and preserve market share by avoiding risk (Hesmondhalgh, 2004). Creative expression relies on risk-averse systems of production (Hesmondhalgh 2004, 2009). For this reason, better understanding about how cultural work is performed is important when evaluating the social benefit of for-profit media. If we want to 'normalize' porn by looking at it as commercial entertainment, then its role as a cultural industry has to be taken seriously and subjected to the same analysis as is devoted to the rest of public culture. In this regard, the plural 'industries' is used in preference to 'industry' to acknowledge that different media operations in different parts of the world deal with these same tensions in different ways. Comparative analysis of these differences helps determine where a mixture of commercial and non-commercial approaches brings about the best results for 'creatives' and the audiences they serve (Hesmondhalgh, 2004). The object is to produce 'a politics of cultural production informed by social theory and empirical work' (Hesmondhalgh, 2009, 246).

The marriage of theory and research has been put into action in studies of creative labour. Hesmondhalgh and Baker (2013) outlined how studying workers in film, television and the music industries is a valuable way of connecting abstract political reasoning to the material practice of culture. In particular, they argued that the 'problem' of alienation through work addresses the gap between how cultural industries do work and how we would like them to work. Simply put, comparative analysis of creative work helps to identify the limits of expression created by the particular organization of cultural labour.

A labour approach solves the judgement challenges involved in discussing expressive culture. It is difficult to distinguish good and bad art, but far easier to discuss the positive and negative experiences of the work that people do to produce it. Defining creativity as work connects symbolic expression to debates about social and self-realization. At base, cultural policy is premised on the position that society works best when as many people as possible become what they want to be, and that the ability to say what you want to say is connected to this goal. At various times, scholars of varying political persuasions have argued that work is something that gets in the way of fulfilment. Karl Marx thought that labour under capitalism robs the worker of identity by denying the full value of his or her work and the time to be other things. That is, you work to make profit for the owners of the means of production, and in this sense your labour keeps you where you are, and don't become the person that you wish to be (Hesmondhalgh and Baker, 2013).

Hesmondhalgh and Baker pointed out that this idea didn't just belong to socialism. Interestingly, American sociologist Robert Blauner broadly accepted the value of American capitalist democracy, but agreed that bad work was a barrier to self-realization. Rather than the inherent inequalities of the market, Blauner blamed bureaucracy for robbing most workers of the sense that they control what they do. Generally speaking, from his perspective 'good' work happens when workers control how they meet their goals (Hesmondhalgh and Baker, 2013).

So regardless of whether one believes that the state should play an active role in funding and regulating public culture, or that such matters are better left to markets, 'good' or 'bad' art is connected to conditions of production. Hesmondhalgh and Baker concluded that when it comes to media work, everyone agrees that the best stuff comes from people who have the time, space and resources to produce and distribute things that they are proud of. So, comparative labour analysis across media industries helps identify the general attributes of good work. For example, there are reasons for thinking that creative workers across media industries are being subjected to unprecedented conditions of exploitation. Media work sounds glamorous, but in reality many media industries feature long hours, low pay and highly bureaucratized working conditions where the chances to do work of which they are proud, and for which they can be properly rewarded, can be few and far between.

Pornography belongs in this comparative approach; or, at least, a cultural industries method allows us to say what's 'wrong' with porn in terms of the labour that it demands. Overall, cultural industries research suggests that political conversations about how inclusive public cultures should be must start with the popular culture that people enjoy and then look at how that culture encourages participation and diversity under local conditions of production and distribution. Often, these matters can be condensed to studies of creative work and the factors that distinguish the 'good' from the 'bad'. In studies of the porn industries, these criteria have been applied most effectively to produce a far more nuanced position on the social meaning of porn than has often been the case in the effects debate.

KEY METHOD: FIELD RESEARCH

Linking production and consumption: Alternative retailing and creativity in the porn industry

Porn scholars also distinguish 'good' from 'bad' porn according to conditions of production and distribution. Instead of concerning themselves with the matter of whether porn is harmful, benign or beneficial *per se*, these scholars explore the conditions under which diverse, non-exploitative production can happen, alert to the fact that mass markets present a formidable hurdle to such aspirations. There are producers and performers who are interested in producing porn that has a public value, but the struggles they face in realizing their ambitions are a stark warning against blanket optimism. These works on pornography have a general relevance across cultural industries research because they provide vivid stories of extreme conditions where social well-being is intimately tied to the role of commerce in determining the kinds of media content that is produced and shared. Methodologically, scholars who observe porn professionals as they work within market relations have also demonstrated innovative methods for scrutinizing circuits of cultural production through people who work at key nodes in those arrangements. In sum, studies of sex industry retailing capture the 'why' and the 'how' of cultural industries research.

Looking at this literature, it's clear that positive aspects of pornography can be appreciated without seeing the market as a simple boon to sexual equality. In fact, for alternative communities, the market is a problem that has to be solved through inventive, community-based initiatives. Ethical porn happens when producers find shelter from unbridled market economic imperatives (Mondin, 2014). Ethical porn is easily defined: performers only have sex with people they want to, and perform the sex acts that they like (Mondin, 2014; Trouble, 2014). But getting it made and seen is another thing.

Working, talking and learning in retail spaces

This is why some of the most compelling work on pornography comes from researchers who examine sites of porn distribution as places where the industry's potential and pitfalls are realized in the organization of markets. One fascinating element of pornography is that performers, producers and scholars share common interests. The views of feminist academics have captured the attention of renowned actors, like industry stalwart Nina Hartley and Courtney Trouble, so much so that Trouble's writing features in scholarly publications (Trouble, 2014). As Lynn Comella points out, this novel situation has been brought about through events like Adult Video Conventions and boutique retailing operations, such as the feminist sex toy retailer 'Babeland' (Comella, 2011, 2014). Indeed, Comella's Babeland study encapsulates a history of conceptual thought on media message systems and power. Earlier in the book, we mentioned George Gerbner's discovery that corner shops affected the confession magazine industry of the 1950s (Gerbner, 1958a). Recall the disjuncture between cover and content that reflected the place of magazines in a 'happy' retail space. In effect, cultural industries research has outlined similar associations of media industries operations and localized leisure spaces (recall Lewis's observation that successful arts policy has to combine media tastes with accessible urban night-time economies). Comella's Babeland study not only followed this tradition, but also underlined how vividly sex retailing practices capture how hard it is to realize the political potential of popular culture.

Babeland encouraged ethical porn by connecting non-traditional producers with non-traditional audiences. This arrangement was brought about by the combination of a feminist company ethic with local communities and markets that made ethics commercially viable. In the introduction to this book, we heard from Shine Louise Houston, a feminist pornographer who accepted the 'reality effect' of her own work. Tristan Taurmino is another producer who operates in this space. Taurmino cut her creative teeth working on the floor of a Babeland store. The experience provided a wealth of information on what women of different sexualities wanted from porn. That's not coincidental, given the way that the store set out to become a hub for alternative sexualities in a particular community setting, and one which only engaged with pornography under strict conditions (Comella, 2014).

Comella also worked in a Babeland store to access the company, its customers and a national 'sex positive' distribution network for commodities aimed mostly at women, lesbian and transgendered consumers. The history of the store, and its relation to similar ventures, showed that pornography is educational within ventures that actively set out to *create* ethical markets. Babeland drew its influence from San Francisco's 'Good Vibrations' store, which was founded with the aim of creating a comfortable, female-friendly retail space where women could discover and discuss products that supported their sexual identities in a non-threatening space. Notably, the store did not carry pornographic materials until their customers indicated that they would be interested in such fare – as long as it was made with a female audience in mind. This created an opportunity where producers such as Candida Royale, a former performer who had advocated for more female-friendly productions, discovered that they could demonstrate the market for a new kind of porn through alternative retail outlets that made it easier to find the audience. Shops like Babeland, therefore, were vital 'feedback loops' where producers and consumers could communicate with each other.

Thus Babeland became a 'lab' where pornographers could experiment with educational porn. Although the stores do carry titles from major companies, 'superstars' like Akira share shelf space with titles that explore a diverse range of sexual practices and identities. Through conversations with customers, Taormino came to the conclusion that many women wanted educational erotica. She has put this information to work in a 'canonical' approach to porn, where good, ethical porn respects rights of choice, diversity and social responsibility. Good porn, in this sense, does feature people doing things that they are comfortable doing with people they are comfortable having sex with, and accepts that education and entertainment go hand in hand. This approach is possible because of a retailing network with a company policy of providing service to niche markets. Bottom line: the Babeland case study showed how the work of production and distribution connect to shape media content. Babeland made 'good work' possible for those who made and sold porn. Both were able to do things that were profitable and helpful to those whose sexual identities are usually ignored. In terms of alienation, Babeland let everyone enjoy rich, mutually beneficial relationships with the self and other people (Comella, 2011, 2014).

When porn is bad: A labour perspective

You can't say the same things for all of the places where producers, distributors and consumers meet. Comella has also written about the research value of events such as the annual Adult Entertainment Expo (AEE) in Las Vegas. At this convention, fans, consumers and anyone who's interested can access stars, producers and industry insiders from all niches of the genre to gather firsthand knowledge about how the industry works. The event offers a cornucopia of insights into why people like porn, and why they make it. They also offer places where one can ask performers about their working conditions. Sometimes the answers are forthright. Sometimes they are less so.

An encounter with Asa Akira and fellow porn superstar/mainstream actor James Deen left Comella less than convinced on the veracity of the information to be gleaned from these settings about what porn work is like. Q & A sessions where fans get to quiz porn stars are a familiar feature of the AEE. Most of the queries are the clichés one might expect. Do female stars really enjoy what they do? Do they have organisms? Are there pressures to work without condoms? The answers given to these questions were either the ones you would expect (pleasure, yes, orgasms, yes) or evasive (Condoms? No comment).

The point is that these events are, in part, about preserving the space between performers and their audiences, betraying a lack of interest in the personalities or needs of either party. That's not all that goes on at all of these conventions, but it does characterize the marketing of mass-produced fare. At any rate, what we see is how the comparative analysis of different retailing spaces where the entire market can be seen at work plays out the ambiguities that characterize the porn industry, and indeed the cultural industries as a whole. This is why porn provides a vivid instance of cultural industries research in action, showing what we can learn from the people who make cultural products, especially when they connect with markets and people.

Elsewhere, interviews with stars whose careers enjoy the space created by alternative ethical production and retail practices show that they remain vulnerable to an exploitation that, in their words, remains inherent in mainstream porn. Stars like African American 'BBW' (Big Beautiful Women) performer Betty Blac still have to work in an industry where, in the grand scheme of things, they remain at the 'bottom of the pile' when it comes to defining their working conditions. 'Bad work', where they have to engage with less pleasant acts for less money than is paid to white, smaller women, is *de rigeur* in an industry where work still means turnover, most of the time. That is, in Hesmondhalgh and Baker's (2013) terms, they are still alienated by frequent occasions where they do work that offers little pride. There can scarcely be a more graphic example than Blac's account of working for 'a company who will regularly find women who are down on their luck, and especially young, pregnant black women who are beautiful, and offer them $1000 to do four shoots' (cited in Miller-Young, 2015, 348). The common theme here is that the question of ethical porn often comes down to highly localized production settings where the varying technical and market conditions make for both good and bad work, depending on how the connections are made. The prospects of ethical porn are constantly challenged in an industry with significant financial problems (Comella, 2011). Where in the 1980s porn was the proverbial licence to print money, the era of internet free sharing makes it harder to hold on to principles – hence the rise of the openly exploitative practices Blac describes (Miller-Young, 2015).

Ultimately, a 'labour' approach invigorates porn debates by shifting the focus from good and bad content and effects towards the consideration of the conditions that allow for ethical production and distribution – or good work. It also helps researchers identify key places where they will find key informants who will explain how these labour effects come into being in real contexts. This is in keeping with the cultural industries position that there is an inherent tension in public culture, based on the reliance that culture has on industries that are not, and cannot be, held strictly accountable for public well-being. Here, the extent to which porn is an entertainment genre that provides a public service to diverse audiences who want to be responsible citizens (McKee, 2012) depends not on 'the market' – the stark global choice between commercial operations and state-funded media – but on markets.

Henderson (2008) elegantly locates the politics of the situation in the call for a 'slow love' movement. The main problem of pornography, for Henderson, is that the acceleration of its output and availability is assumed to in turn accelerate its negative effects. The best way forward is to stop and slow down. Stopping means forensically asking whether, and if so why, sex work and pornography are more dangerous and demeaning than other low-paid, demeaning occupations. Slowing down means adopting a 'place based curiosity about alternative sexual cultures and a critique that resists the language of negative sexual acceleration' (Henderson, 2008, 223). Like the 'slow food' movement, this means looking at 'networks of producers, distributors and consumers who know each other and negotiate, in some contexts, in terms intended to protect an environmental and social future' (2008, 223).

Once we do this, for example, we can explain in abstract terms why Asa Akira had a bad day at work. Everything was too quick. This was not good work because the alienation she encountered was in many respects the product of a large and disconnected market – a place where she was confronted with a performance made with other occasions in mind (she had not imagined that she would end up being her own audience) and where the confronting scene was brought about by a sex industry market where the circulation of texts combined with the circulation of the bodies they feature – for those who can pay. The questions of the motivations of the consumer remained a mystery because the encounter was orchestrated by a mass 'quick' market. The benefit of a cultural industries approach, which is based on an interest in work and markets, is that it establishes material judging criteria that evade the criticisms that have been made against politically motivated anti-porn studies. That is, a cultural industries approach to pornography shifts the terms of the harm debate away from behaviours towards relationships, where criticism is founded on material iniquities of labour relations and a comparative approach to eminently researchable small markets that valuably demonstrate how hard some communities have to fight to express their sexual identities. This observation places a question mark against the proposition that vibrant commercial operations foster innovation.

SIGNIFICANCE: OBSERVING LABOUR AND CONSUMPTION IN SMALL MARKETS OFFERS USEFUL INSIGHTS ABOUT POWER IN GLOBAL MEDIA INDUSTRIES

This chapter has shown how debates about the quality and influence of popular culture can be usefully grounded in studying media work. In illustration, it has shown how controversies surrounding pornography reflect general concerns about the costs and benefits of commercial culture. This connection relates risk to social inclusion and sexual identity. Defining porn as work develops an empirical basis on which to judge the genre not in terms of its effects, but in terms of the ethics of its production, and the proximity its various markets foster among producers, retailers and consumers. This creates a framework for hearing perspectives from a diverse range of interest groups in the porn debate. Methodologically, it demonstrates the power of small-scale community research, based on an ability to identify meaningful networks of distribution, that allows interactive communication between producers and consumers via retailers. Consequently, a work perspective allows us to see that the pornography debate can be usefully connected to bigger issues around the politics of cultural production and public participation.

The other goal this achieves is moving the focus of production studies away from conspiratorial visions of nefarious media industries towards a more nuanced model that situates politics in the ambiguities and tensions of commercial public culture. The pornography industry vividly illustrates the complex relations among profit, technology and creativity. It is also an instructive case study of how media industries integrate with other sectors, such as the retailing and leisure spheres. Given this complexity, close examination of the pornography industry's operations shows how the question of the 'damage' it does cannot be reduced to the question of what its 'symbol creators' set out to achieve, even if there is evidence that their actions have significant impacts on the sexual socialization of its audience. Pornography is not simply another case study of mediatization in action, but is especially useful in clarifying what we can learn about media influence by looking at the production and distribution of media content and the others who drive various components of the media machine. The growing interest in porn labour studies is explained by its connection to core themes in the management of public culture, observed from a cultural industries standpoint.

CHAPTER SUMMARY

- Defining pornography as work establishes valuable criteria for evaluating the genre.

- Talking about good and bad work evades some of the pitfalls involved in discussing good and bad content. It allows judgements that are based on evidence from performers.

- The work focus emerges from the cultural industries paradigm. This paradigm is useful because it shows how some of the concerns in earlier media research, about the role that cultural intermediaries play in media culture, still apply to contemporary media systems.

- The cultural industries paradigm connects questions of culture and politics to the organization of markets through message systems.

- Research on porn stars, porn directors and porn distributors demonstrates how retail and leisure sites provide meaningful places where global media industries can be observed working in tangible ways in local, and observable, settings.

- These techniques can be applied to any situations where people participate in the construction of identity through the operation of consumer markets.

11

RESEARCHING MEDIA CONTENT: GAMES, TEXTS AND DISCOURSE

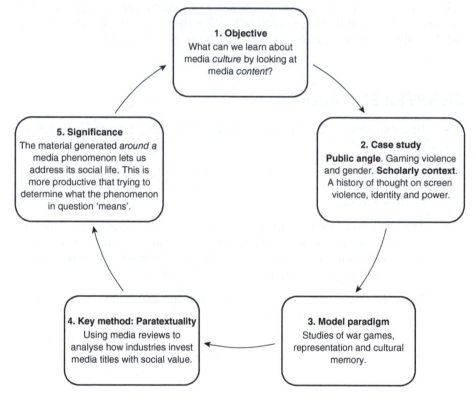

Figure 7   Researching media content

OBJECTIVE: USING AN EXPANDED NOTION OF 'CONTENT' TO ADDRESS THE SOCIAL LIFE OF MEDIA PHENOMENA

This chapter returns to the topic of video game violence to explain the value of studying media content. Gaming content comes in many forms – reviews, advertising, websites, modifications, walk-throughs, cheats and online communities (Crawford, 2012). In combination, these phenomena offer novel insights into the organization of media industries, the life-worlds of media users and the relationship between entertainment, politics and historical consciousness. Gaming research combines various methods of content research to direct conventional concerns about media, violence and sexism into compelling discussions on the political nature of media culture. Intriguingly, these innovations underline the continuing relevance of 20th-century debates on television content. Gaming content, in all its forms, addresses questions about the politics of representation that have been in play for some time. Gaming studies also demonstrate accessible ways to analyse media culture through a comparative approach to media content. As such, looking at how gaming researchers have dealt with the issue of violent gaming content teaches general lessons about how we can use media content to leverage significant insights into the mechanics of media culture.

The chapter begins by asking why representations of violence and gender concern games critics, showing how these reservations echo earlier themes in television studies. Included here are foundational methodological issues on the relative merits of quantitative and qualitative methods. Paying special attention to the journal *Games and Culture*, I show how both methods have been used to explain the significance of gaming as a cultural and political activity. The territory and tactics shared by television and gaming studies show how important discussions about violent screen content have been in defining the politics of popular culture.

Core themes in gaming studies also show how the idea that violence has political effects has never been more important, given fears that war games influence attitudes to global conflict. Addressing these fears, the chapter concludes by using media content – in this case critical gaming reviews – to connect gaming, historical consciousness and political thought. Earlier, we saw Jay Winter characterize Great War mourning as the ritual that sutured politics, culture and media in the 20th century. Following this theme, the chapter outlines a method for demonstrating how the critical reception of the Great War game *Valiant Hearts* located gaming as an activity that creates affective historical identities. As such, this places gaming content at the centre of debates on the relationship between media and culture. It also demonstrates the value of content research in organizing a structured conversation about how media affect social sensibilities.

In summary, this chapter:

- Demonstrates how to use quantitative and qualitative approaches to media content analysis to gain insight into how media shape social sensibilities.

(Continued)

- Outlines a method for connecting the topic of media violence to the issue of how media generate social discourse.
- Explains how gaming content can be seen as a practice that contributes to the development of historical consciousness.

CASE STUDY: VIDEO GAMING: OLD PROBLEMS, NEW PROBLEMS

Public angle: Gaming and sexism

In 2015 Anita Saarkesian's *Feminist Frequency* website posted results of a content analysis of games showcased at the 2015 Electronic Entertainment Expo (E3) in Los Angeles. The study coded and quantified representations of gender and violence across 76 titles. Male protagonists outnumbered female counterparts by more than three to one, and non-violent games represented slightly less than 25% of the fare on show (Petit, 2015). Difficulties of defining and counting gender and violence were acknowledged, and the rise in games allowing payers to pick avatar genders was lauded. Even so, the gender violence baseline of the global industry, as it was presented by that industry, did little to confront sexism. From the perspective of media studies history, it's interesting that *Feminist Frequency* made a point with a method that replicated Gerbner's research on television. According to *Feminist Frequency*, technology hadn't done much to alter how gender looked on screen.

The question of whether you can say much worth knowing about what gaming means by counting violence and gender is controversial. Brendon Keogh (2012), for example, provided a detailed walk through *Spec Ops: The Line* to show that the violence in that title was different from the fare that players usually encounter. *Spec Ops* forces gamers to think about combat ethics. So the violence in this game might look familiar graphics wise, but its meaning was anything but.

Others observe that gaming culture is driven by out-of-context images. Public advertising confronts non-gamers with gaming violence (Stermer and Burkley, 2012, 525–526). Counting is a good way to explain why this is an issue. Scharrer (2004) looked at over a thousand ads from popular games magazines, finding violence in over half, an average of 2.5 weapons per advertisement and a male to female ration of two to one.

Quantitative content analysis seems all the more valid, given how it chimes with popular experience. The UK's Advertising Standards Authority has received complaints from people who have unwillingly encountered violent content in public places, like shopping centres (Advertising Standards Authority, 2010), or trailers included in software for other games (Advertising Standards Authority, 2014). People encounter decontextualized violence as they are going about daily business, and so we can argue that methods that account for decontextualized patterns make sense.

So, discussions about gaming content sometimes centre on the relative strengths of quantitative versus qualitative methods. Sometimes the case can be made that the most important aspect of a game might be how its manifest content relates to common patterns that cross genres. *Feminist Frequency* asserted that the problem with gaming is that these patterns send the message that gaming is about violence and masculinity. This is a problem not because it means gaming is bad, but because the industry seems unwilling to let it be good, to let gaming fulfil its potential value as a medium that can serve diverse creative desires. On the other hand, sometimes content can only be understood within the ecology of *a* game, implying a careful analysis of particular titles on their own terms. Both arguments have merit, but one interesting aspect of the discussion is that it reflects similar methodological controversies that occurred in television research. Looking at these earlier debates gives a better understanding of how gaming studies has reinvigorated content research as a mixed method strategy for turning violence debates away from the behaviours towards the political significance of media industries.

Scholarly context: Establishing the prevalence of gendered screen violence

Gaming and television content both caught academic attention for the same reasons. Like the former, television's technological, economic, institutional and aesthetic qualities were credited with unprecedented storytelling power (Gerbner, 1958b; Fiske and Hartley, 1978; Fiske, 1987; Newcomb, 1987; VandeBerg and Wenner, 1991). Scholars agreed that television irresistibly dramatized social values and conflicts. How to make sense of this content, and its political fallout, was another matter. On the broadest level, this project was divided between quantitative and qualitative methods – the coding of manifest aspects of a text versus the analysis of ideology (Gitlin, 1978; Kellner, 1987), genre (Feuer, 1992), discourse (Deming and Jenkins, 1991) or semiotics (Fiske, 1987). But beneath methodological differences, scholars agreed that analysing content was a useful strategy for raising questions about how media arbitrated in struggles over class, race, gender and sexuality. Whatever the method, critics agreed that popular entertainment conveyed serious ideas about how the world worked.

Violence played a major role in quarrels over the best way to make sense of television's social weight. George Gerbner's violence profiles are, as has been mentioned, one of the most famous examples of content analysis that the discipline has seen. Gerbner became an influential proponent of quantitative content analysis, particularly when it came to counting violence and gender roles. His approach, then, very much foreshadowed *Feminist Frequency*'s strategy. So it's worth looking at how he developed his methods.

Gerbner used content criticism, in his view to spark debate on how media content seduced publics into the values of consumer society. This ambition led him to favour quantitative content analysis: counting the most recurrent symbols on television as evidence of its politics. Gerbner believed the political effects of commercial media were rapid, deep, insidious, and demanded methods for elucidating connections between corporate interest and popular entertainment in the least contentious terms. In this regard, numerically coding content provided relatively non-contestable evidence about how the media fed audiences politically loaded representations of the 'facts of life'. A notable early example was a review of almost 1,000 Hollywood films featuring unionized labour, where 80% depicted trade organizations negatively (Gerbner, 1958b). So *Feminist Frequency*'s activism echoed Gerbner's earlier thoughts on the ideological significance of representation of gender and violence. Consequently, it's worth dwelling on how Gerbner defined media content as cultural artefact. Gerbner thought films and TV shows were embossed with the values of consumer societies, and it was important to develop methods that could reveal this ultimate 'meaning' of drama, comedy, advertising and news:

> The social determinants of cultural industry thus find their way into the consequential meaning of the material. They are expressed not so much in conventional forms and 'messages' as through patterns of selection, omission, juxtaposition, through just the way things are 'looked at.' (Gerbner, 1958b, 90)

Gerbner's position drew criticism from others who believed that qualitative approaches to content, sensitive to the differences between representations of the 'same thing', were most appropriate to understanding television. Violence was again used as a medium to make the point. Horace Newcomb explained the cultural shift from cinema to television in relation to another 'shooter' – the cowboy. Newcomb compared the movies of John Ford with *Rawhide*, the television drama that gave Clint Eastwood his break. Where cowboy films focused on the individual who did little other than fight for self-preservation, lost in the expanse of the West, *Rawhide* was about friendship and family. According to Newcomb, the narrative change accommodated smaller screens and production sets. Television's physical constrictions favoured plots about intimate groups of people. So sure, there had always been screen cowboys doing screen violence, but in *Rawhide*, the meaning of violence, when it happened, was different. This aesthetic was one reason why television became the fulcrum for conversations about cultural life. The bias towards intimacy and relationships made it the perfect vehicle for discourse on the meaning of everything – even in shows that were ostensibly about shooting.

In 1978, Newcomb offered a 'humanistic' critique of Gerbner's cultural indicators project. Newcomb's main criticism was that Gerbner focused too much on television as a message system and too little as an art form. That is, Gerbner's work on violence had gone too far in portraying television as a simple conduit for the reproduction of power – especially male power through acts of violence – and paid too little attention to the role that different kinds of content, or different interpretations of the same content, could lead to alternative social ends.

Gerbner and Gross (1979) retorted that analysing recurrent patterns across television genres was an attempt to match textual analysis with the rhythms of viewing. Viewers watched by the hour, not by the show. Most of the time, most of the people watch television regardless of what is on. The basic background details of television – people, settings, places and events – are worth noting because these are the building blocks of the connection between television and society. For example, a legal drama may be dismissed as outlandish, but basic perceptions of how courts work might remain. The idea was to identify the most unambiguously recognized features of television content in order to make a few simple points.

Newcomb conceded the point, agreeing that representation and power are empirical affairs. For example, the feeling that television tends to treat women as inferior to men is strengthened by the quantitative observation that most of the women on television drama at the time were either married or engaged and were of child-bearing age, whereas men were more likely to be unmarried and older. So wherever else the conversation went, the idea that critique is aided by the simple ability to deliver relatively uncontroversial facts about media content was conceded. In this, the basis for a mixed method approach, sensitive to the needs of alternative research questions, was established.

At this point, it's possible to make a connection between scholarly conversations over how to conceive and demonstrate the significance of television content, and gaming. Television was a novel, pervasive and immersive storytelling form that dramatized social relationships. Violence, as a common feature of this content, was a valuable topic to consider this new power. There was, however, disagreement over whether such functions were best understood by enumerating generic acts and contexts of violence versus paying particular attention to the structures of particular shows (like *Rawhide*). When it comes to gaming, however, the benefits of combining both approaches in a strategic fashion become clearer. Like television scholars, games researchers use violence to explain how games function as cultural artefacts – not simply cheap thrills that glamorize violence for no particular reason. Unlike television scholars, the different ecology of gaming cultures makes it easier to see the case for a mixed method approach.

Gaming studies

The conversation so far has led to this point: media content is a 'cultural indicator' (Gerbner, 1969a) of the processes that make entertainment socially significant. Video gaming studies continue a tradition of investigating how content 'indicates' how gaming works as a set of symbolic activities that create realities. Garry Crawford's *Video Gamers* (2012) characterized gaming as a cultural practice located at the interface between the general pleasure of play, representation and sociality. Within this framework, content is relevant for three reasons. First, social play creates content in 'websites, mods and hacks, private servers, game guides, walkthroughs and FAQs, fan fiction and forms of fan art' (Crawford, 2012, 66). Second, 'there will always be a set of non-negotiable rules inherent in the video game's program' (2012, 70). Third, it is easy to overstate the interactive, creative aspects of gameplay. In fact, according to Crawford, 'what seems strangely under-represented in video game studies is the use, or debates concerning the relevance of, other forms of content analysis, discourse analysis and semiotics' (2012, 89).

Gaming reinvigorates content research because it is a social, rule-based activity that leaves all manner of textual evidence. This is probably why quantitative content analysis and textual analysis are prominent in the journal *Gaming Culture*. This journal has historical interest as it is attempting the same kind of shift that television scholars agitated for in the late 1970s, replacing the idea that a medium is a black box that does things to audiences with a more sophisticated understanding of gaming as an anchor that grounds its users within certain perspectives on how the world works.

In an early editorial for the journal *Games and Culture*, Shaw (2010) observed that gaming researchers have to assert the value of gaming as a mode of cultural participation by confronting popular anxieties about violent and sexist content. In fact, the journal has validated some of these fears. Titles have been criticized for their representations of race and sexuality (e.g. DeVane and Squire, 2008; Brock, 2011). The international hit *World of Warcraft* was accused of racial essentialism, since it features characters whose abilities are determined by their race (Monson, 2012). Conflict and strategy games have been chastized for circulating western-centric versions of global history (Carvalho, 2015). But *Games and Culture* innovatively used content research to *query* the association between gameplay and damage. Since media violence has played a major role in *blinkering* public discussions about media influence, it's enormously significant that analysis of war games and first-person shooters has led the line in exploring how media are involved in the evolution of historical and political consciousness. This trend places gaming in a firm academic trajectory on the role of media research in understanding culture.

KEY PARADIGM: WAR GAMES AND MEMORY

Studies of war and violence-focused titles in *Games and Culture* have vividly sharpened the argument that screen violence is a political issue. War games are obvious places where, we might assume, ideologically tinged versions of historically significant moments are paraded before the public. There, different interests battle over the causes and rationales for past and future conflicts. War games are tapestries of history, memory, empire and communication.

Historically-based first-person shooters are an obvious example. Hong (2015) argued that such games are exercises in pleasurable nostalgia. Second

World War games, he continued, let players enjoy 'good' violence, put to use on the side of the righteous in a clear battle between good and evil. As such, gaming has become one of the 'mourning rituals' that proliferated in the face of wartime slaughter. This is a problem since it involves a highly selective kind of remembering that erases more contentious views of what we should remember about the 'Good War', and why we should keep that conflict in mind.

Celebrating the defeat of Fascism hardly seems controversial, but the *manner* in which such games encourage ethical pleasure is less straightforward. Kingsepp (2007) explained through examining techniques for dealing with dead bodies, typical in historical war first-person shooters like *Medal of Honour*. The franchise's launch coincided with awakened public interest in the Second World War, symbolized by the release of Steven Spielberg's epic *Saving Private Ryan* and television blockbuster *Band of Brothers*, both concerning the American experience of D-Day. *Saving Private Ryan*'s opening sequence was so bloodily realistic that it disturbed many veterans (Halton, 1998). The evisceration of soldier's bodies was the signature that distinguished this representation of the Normandy landings from what had gone before, in celluloid. With the benefit of Jay Winter's work in mind, we see again the relationship between bodies and historical memories. Against this knowledge, Kingsepp remarked that in most Second World War first-person shooters bodies simply vanish. As we know, disappearing bodies were a profound source of trauma during the Great War. In games, they are an absolution. You don't have to look at the dead face of the person you shot, and thus there are no moral questions to ask about what you do. The troubling possibility that this raises is that gaming becomes another place where mediated memorializing creates a comforting distance between the present and the past, such that the relevance of those past events is lost.

Hess's work on *Medal of Honour: Rising Sun* (2007b), set in the Second World War, critiqued the idea that the title could offer a novel insight into what the Second World War was like for the people who fought it. Notably, Hess found a way to describe how the game's story, its gameplay options and the extra learning materials that were embedded within it worked to create on overall experience where gamers learned from violence. *Rising Sun* invites the player to occupy the body of a young marine who is caught up in the Japanese attack on Pearl Harbor. The player has to escape a sinking troop carrier, and is thereafter immersed in a range of missions where he battles Japanese enemies in the search for a lost brother. At the completion of each level, the player is rewarded with a clip of a veteran of the Pacific theatre recounting his experiences. These clips often focus on weaponry, adding an authentic feel to some of the gameplay – it's especially engrossing to use rifles that veterans pinpoint as having been pivotal to the war. Hess argued that the interface between story gameplay and pedagogic extras produced a 'smooth', morally comforting experience where the authenticity of detail – as far as weapons and veteran stories went – legitimated the entire experience. The trouble was that some historical facts were buried with the bodies. The Second World War didn't end with the rescue of a long-lost brother and the vanquishing of an evil soldier. It ended with the atomic bomb. Hence, in the end 'the memory of World War II ... is tainted with a selective retelling of the events that not only glamorizes the war, but constructs an Orientalist image of the Japanese Empire' (Hess, 2007b, 339).

But why should games service historical memory? One reason is that these games were certainly part of a rebirth of interest and a thirst for more authentic narratives about that conflict that crossed the screen of many genres. But perhaps more interesting is the relevance of past to present, for the kinds of questions that had been asked about historical first-person shooter games were soon applied to combat titles focusing on present and future wars. And again, these works have indicated the ongoing value of research methods using quantitative and qualitative approaches.

The power of numbers

One of the main questions that can be directed at any study of any particular title is: Why has *this* game experience been selected? It is fairly easy to pick a game that illustrates whatever point you want to make about gaming, so it's doubly important to start any study with a clear explanation of why one is talking about *this* instead of *that*. *Games and Culture* provided a superb example of how quantitative content analysis can irresistibly achieve this goal with the elegant simplicity of figures. The concern around war games with regard to the political present is that when gaming experiences like those offered in *Medal of Honor* are updated to contemporary conflicts, in games like *Call of Duty* and *Ghost Recon* they serve as the vanguard for a militarized society (Allen, 2011; Schulzke, 2013).

Hitchens, Patrickson and Young's 'Reality and terror: the first-person shooter in current-day settings' (2014) punched through conspiratorial takes on the relationship between the games industry and the military by asking a quantitative question. The project merits close attention for its copious lessons on the purposes, promises and pitfalls of content analysis. Like Lasswell (1971) on Great War propaganda, the authors observed that fears about the ideological effects of first-person war shooters were usually based on the observation of a few titles, leaving the question of how typical the narratives of some games were across the genre. To create more order to the picture, the study looked at 160 titles. Fears of militarization run like this: there are close parallels between some first-person shooter games and army simulators used to train recruits. In some examples, cooperation has occurred between army simulators and games designers, and veterans have been used as advisors in certain special operations games. This prompts fears that the games industry prepares players for future wars by identifying enemies and rehearsing scenarios that future soldiers are likely to encounter. But how well grounded are these fears when we look at the prediction conditions and content of a wide range of titles? Hitchens and colleagues researched this puzzle by examining who players typically shot at in first-person shooter games.

Importantly, the researchers warned that it's hard to answer these questions, given the nature of the form. Gerbner and his colleagues could easily watch hours of television and count acts of violence, but gameplay requires more time and the number of acts of violence depends on how many the player puts in. Hitchins et al. (2014) coped with this question by drawing data from other sources – online reviews, screenshots, gaming magazines and gaming communities. This done, enemies were tabulated across titles, encapsulating the period from 1993 to 2009. The proportion of titles using clearly labelled terrorists as the enemy actually dropped between 2005 and 2009 (from 42% to 27%). If there is still an ideological war on terror, then since 2005 game developers have been less enthusiastic about fighting it. The point is that if there is a fear of a consistent collusion between the gaming industry and the Pentagon regarding the prosecution of the War against Terror, the numbers do not support such an argument, and this represents an important context for the deeper consideration of particular titles.

The crucial thing is that where for a number of years quantitative and qualitative content research were seen to be in opposition, studies of gaming and militarization show how they complement one another. The broad picture that Hitchens et al. (2014) painted helped to specify why certain franchises are worth so much attention. Research on *America's Army*, for instance, can be justified because it is representative of the kind of extreme threat that Hitchens et al. address. One issue with the quantitative study is that it did not control for the success of the title – in other words, a hugely successful title that does demonize non-western terrorists might have more impact than dozens of others that do not. Given this, there are solid reasons for thinking that detailed analysis of the content that surrounds a specific title can be insightful, as long as one is clear on *why* that title has been chosen. *Games and Culture*'s publications on *America's Army* give an insight into how this can be done.

You don't need to be a media expert to figure out why *America's Army* piqued academic interests. Here was a free first-person shooter (FPS) made in conjunction with the US Army which aspired to encourage young gamers to consider military service (Allen, 2011; Schulzke, 2013). This also rendered it an ideal case study for deconstructing conspiratorial takes on gaming. Schulzke (2013) pointed out that the idea that *America's Army* represented an explicit attempt by the Army to militarize society made no sense, given the fact that it was soldiers who would pay the price – literally, in blood – for such an effect. If there is one organization that does not want to live in a gung-ho world where the public demand boots on the ground against all enemies, real and imagined, it is the Army. Moreover, one of the major appeals of gaming is the way that it gives recruits and soldiers a chance to practise how to behave ethically in combat situations. All in all, *America's Army* was the hub of a network where the military, gaming industries and leisure sport industries found common strategic grounds for cooperating to reach the public at the same time and place, albeit for different but complementary reasons. Given the sophistication of these operations, and the way that they combine different ambitions, it's not surprising that it's hard to find the bottom line on what gaming does, because there isn't one.

Except in one regard. It is gaming content that holds this loose network of interested parties together. *America's Army* success significantly depended on its use of a revamped unreal game engine, which gave a radically improved gaming experience. The game was attractive to the industry as a way of popularizing an innovation in an established, well-known FPS genre – in this case, the unreal game engine was updated to give a dramatically better visual experience (Allen, 2011). Games are popularized when their content serves diverse interests in pleasure and politics. Gaming content 'works' by offering attractive solutions to established social objectives. This is why gaming eventually became involved in the formation of cultural memory about the Great War.

KEY METHOD: DISCOURSE ANALYSIS OF PARATEXTS

The last part of this chapter uses content research to show how gamers construct the value of gaming as a learning experience in regard to one of the defining historical preoccupations of the last century – making sense of the Great War. The topic is the game *Valiant Hearts*. *Valiant Hearts* was about four characters caught up in the tragedy of 1914–1918 France. Like *Medal of Honour: Rising Sun*, it interspersed problem-solving episodes completed in the pursuit of dastardly enemies with snippets of historical details about the conflict. Unlike the Second World War game, *Valiant Hearts* players spent most of their time dodging violence or dealing with its aftermath – as in the real event, bodies did not disappear. The story was told from multiple perspectives: Allied, German, male and female. Reviews of the game quite clearly positioned *Valiant Hearts* as a title that showed how war game violence could be used in creative ways to inspire introspection, in this case showing how gaming contributed to the many acts of public commemoration instigated to mark the centenary of the outbreak of the Great War.

Coding content

Valiant Hearts is a useful case study because it demonstrates strategies for identifying *why* and *how* a media phenomenon comes to matter, by combining quantitative and qualitative approaches to media content, thus securing the argument that gaming studies have a general relevance as a topic where the benefits of mixed methods approaches become evident. As we have already seen, there are a couple of problems in accounting for media influence relating to the choice of case study and the selection of data used to make sense of them. The selection of a particular title has to be justified – we can't just pluck examples from thousands of alternatives without a reason for doing so. In this case, *Valiant Hearts* merits attention because experienced critics identified it as a departure in gaming conventions. Apart from anything else, it differed from the conventions criticized by *Feminist Frequency* in featuring a woman lead character and using violence sparingly. But how to justify this claim?

The task is to present a coherent reason for arguing that this game reflected matters of importance when it comes to the politics of popular culture. You can't do that by picking evidence that fits this argument; you need a coherent data set. This is where gaming reviews become useful. We cannot say what *Valiant Hearts* meant to the millions who played it. For some, it may have been a poignant introduction to the Great War; for others, just another game. But what we can ask is whether *Valiant Hearts* was coherently *presented* to the public as a game of creative and didactic value. This can be done by collecting reviews that were collated for gaming site *Metacritic*. This is a meaningful data set as it constitutes a resource that was presented to a gaming community as a comprehensive account of what to expect from this game.

The next step is to make sense of this evidence set as a *discourse* about this game, and gaming in general. In textual research, the word 'discourse' combines the concepts of speech and action. A discourse is a way of talking about something that frames that 'thing' with a view to encouraging a particular outcome (Fiske, 1993). In this case, the idea is to establish whether the *Valiant Hearts* reviews encouraged gamers to see it as a title that carried a particular currency, as a symbol of the cultural value of gaming. The idea of discourse can be used to justify the choice of reviews as a particular type of gaming content, and the choice of this particular set of reviews from this particular location. Reviews are, by definition, 'texts' that set out to establish the value of cultural products, and this collection of reviews was collated with the intention of summarizing the gist of expert reactions to this game.

Having established the validity of the data, the next step is to specify how to do discourse analysis, and also to consider its potential as a basis for multi-method strategies. Discourse analysis is, at base, a qualitative, interpretative approach that sets out to discern patterns of meaning in communicative artefacts (media content, everyday speech, institutional documents, policy documents, and so forth). These meanings are related to particular social experiences and ways of looking at the world (Fiske, 1993; Tonkiss, 1998). The analytic task is to connect content and discourse to show, in material terms, that the pattern discerned in the data reflects a set of ideas that operate elsewhere in culture. In this case, the job is to show that critical reviews are related to discourses about the cultural value of gaming, which in turn relate to positions on the political significance of media.

One way to do this is by using theoretically sensitive coding criteria as a basis for a 'grounded' approach. We know that gaming is surrounded by different discourses – patterns of talk that frame it as a threat, fantasy, art, expression, propaganda, critique, communal activity. At the same time, it's important to stay alert to the fact that the things we research are always about more than we imagine at the start of a project; otherwise, there wouldn't be much point to studying anything. This is where the grounded approach comes in. A grounded approach refers to the practice of starting research from a data set, searching for themes that emerge from that data, rather than a pre-existing coding scheme (Schatzman and Strauss, 1973). What this means in practice is that a discourse analysis of media content requires reading that content time and time again in order to identify the presence of core themes, the emergence of new ones, then refining categories to significant patterns (Tonkiss, 1998; Gray, 2001; Stokes, 2013).

A useful way to do this is by loading data into analytic software. In this case, the reviews were loaded into a package called NVivo. This software allows you to record and store coding processes as you develop them. The other benefit of this software is that it allows you to record not only the presence but the recurrence of themes, thus addressing the relationship between quantitative and qualitative methods.

Taking all of this together, we can provide the following justification for applying qualitative and quantitative content techniques to critical reviews of *Valiant Hearts*. Set against decades of debate over the significance of violent media content, there are many reasons to identify the critical reaction to *Valiant Hearts* as a significant moment. For decades, scholars have used media violence to illustrate the political impact of popular culture. Gaming studies elaborate the theme, classing violence as a creative resource that allows audiences to reflect on profound moral subjects. This is all the more so since gaming culture works through the production of content from media users and media professionals alike. Reviews, for example, can be seen as efforts to intercede in debates about games, risk, creativity and participation, encouraging gamers and society to reflect on the creative and didactic potential of gaming. Taken together, there are reasons to think that the critical reception of *Valiant Hearts* was a place where discourses designed to locate gaming as a culturally valuable activity gained traction by linking it to one of the defining cultural practices in human history, the commemoration of the Great War.

Procedure

At base, discussions about quantitative and qualitative methods are about the best way to demonstrate how a particular event encapsulates the role that media play in constituting social realities. Such decisions are strategic – they depend on the kind of questions one asks – and involve balancing occurrence and recurrence. We are looking to explain how particular things happen, but sometimes we also need to explain how similar things happen time and time again. Additionally, research always involves taking a 'slice' of reality. We inevitably try to say general things about how media work by looking at particular incidents, selected from a range of possible alternatives. The analysis of a particular set of media content has to be justified both in terms of selection and analysis. As with all projects, the job is to persuade readers that the sample and data analysis have not been gerrymandered to support a pre-selected argument.

The reasons why reviews of *Valiant Hearts* have been selected to represent discussions about why gaming matters has already been explained, but what about the data themselves? In practice, grounded discourse analysis means looking for two things: places in the data that speak to key ideas in games studies, as identified by literature reviews, and also patterns that emerge from the data – ideas that seem to crop up time and time again that fall beyond the initial research questions. As most researchers realize, this 'method' is a rather 'messy' business that involves reading and coding data over and over again, developing and then redefining categories in an effort to generate meaningful patterns of response.

For the *Valiant Hearts* reviews, the procedure worked like this. Reviews are a kind of media content that frame gaming as a significant and rich art form and cultural experience. Looking at *Games and Culture*, we know this positioning depends on the interplay of several themes – the creative, participatory and pedagogic potential of the form – balanced against the inherent political compromises of production – aesthetic, technical and industrial limitations. Additionally, in this case, there was the question of how these general interests in the political potential of gaming were channelled into the particular theme of the appropriate place for the commemoration of a century of mourning.

So I approached the data looking for the following themes:

- Cultural politics: 'uncreative' violence, genre innovation, gender, identification.

- Gaming content: aesthetics, technology, gameplay experience, narrative.

- The cultural politics of the Great War: memorialization, the topic of bodies, learning.

Coding was designed to identify how far the ideas that motivated games researchers reflected things that gamers read about when they were deciding whether a title was worth playing.

Coding reviews for these elements in NVivo achieved a couple of goals. Very often you read published studies that mention 'analysing' qualitative data sets, like web posting or transcripts, and then presenting direct quotes from that data without explaining how the researcher made the decision about what to report, in a systematic way. This is what leads to the suspicion that qualitative research is susceptible to researchers who only report what they want readers to see. By systematically analysing data sets for key indicators, it is at least possible to specify how that step is made. It gives you a better grounding for arguing that the quote selected is representative of a wider class of response in the data set, and identifies particular elements of that data set that are worth special attention since they are especially 'rich' (in this case, the coding reveals that some reviews consider a wider range of themes than others), and also lets you quantify the relative presence of themes. In this case, the method's quantitative aspects allowed commentary on how far the reviews approached *Valiant Hearts* as a pleasurable gaming experience versus how much they stressed its qualities as a *meaningful* one. That said, as the coding progressed, the key theme that emerged from the data, which hadn't been predicted by the coding scheme, was that *Valiant Hearts* was an emotional experience – something that moved the reviewers before it 'did' anything else.

Results

The coding exercise created a quantitative pattern that structured a more interpretative exploration of what and how *Valiant Hearts* touched gamers. Quantitatively, each theme was coded according to the number of reviews that referenced it and the number of times that each was mentioned. This identified a hierarchy of themes that offered useful insights into the nature of the experience that reviewers saw in the game. The notion that *Valiant Hearts* counted most as an emotional experience presented a novel vantage on the *historical* debate on violence and understanding content. Coding produced the following table, combining number of sources and references.

Table 1   The appeal of *Valiant Hearts*

Theme	# Sources	# References	Impact score
Emotional experience	18	27	45
Gameplay	15	27	42
Learning	13	18	31
Aesthetics	12	13	25
Genre innovation	10	14	24
Technology	8	10	18
Boring violence	7	8	15
Identification	5	5	10
Commemoration	4	4	8
Narrative	4	4	8
Bodies	4	4	8
Sharing	1	1	2
Killing	1	1	2
Gender	1	1	2

It is important to note that these patterns become the basis for an argument; they do not simply measure content in a scientific way that produces irrefutable truths. One observation is that the coding scheme could be reordered to produce different results. For example, many references to innovation in *Valiant Hearts* included comments about violence, so if we combine them with others on how the game dealt with bodies and killing, then violence emerges as a far more prominent theme. But what they do achieve is creating a systematic logic on which to base an argument. This reflected the value of content research as a means of arranging a structured conversation about what media do.

That said, the purpose of the research was to assess how the game's unique take on media violence afforded reflection on the idea that this kind of content affects social sensibility. In this respect, the fact that reviewers placed so much emphasis on how *Valiant Hearts* made them feel is worth stressing because it confronted one of the most commonly assumed effects of screen slaughter – desensitization. Reviewers liked the game because it sensitized players to the real events that inspired shooting and war games. For some reviewers, the most remarkable thing about the game was that it was profoundly moving. The number of such respondents suggest that understanding the game as an emotional experience is a gateway to considering how it worked this way, and to what effect. This is the point where qualitative insights come in. Looking at places in the reviews where emotion was coded, we find the following comment:

> By the end of *Valiant Hearts* I felt … emotionally drained, affected by some remarkably simple stories that are told masterfully. … So confident is Ubisoft Montpellier in its animation and UbiArt framework … that there's not a word of spoken dialogue between characters. The animation and events going on around them is more than enough to make us as players connect with their plight. (Matt S., 2014)

This quote supports the idea that emotional impact emerged from deft aesthetics. Emotionality became a 'hub' of reviewing discourses that generated into other issues. Here, for example, it becomes the place from which the writer considered how technological and narrative devices produced an affective outcome that signalled *Valiant Heart*'s distinctive nature. The other thing to note is that the coding scheme justifies how to focus on this quote as opposed to its alternatives. It represents a place where emotionality is connected to other key themes – it isn't just randomly plucked from the ether. Looking at other qualitative and quantitative coding results, this appeared as a common pattern.

Overall, the numbers told this story: *Valiant Hearts* was an emotional experience that revealed much about how skilled gaming design could revamp familiar war game conventions to alter understanding about the creative possibilities of that genre. The game deserved attention as a testament to the cultural value of gaming. *Valiant Hearts* participated in the commemoration of an historical landmark. Because of this, it was a best practice exemplar that confronted popular biases about the inherent anti-social nature of the form. As a result, it indicated how games can instigate empathy-led curiosity. Qualitatively speaking, again, the numbers outline a pattern that can be demonstrated by quotes by reviewers who put these ideas together. For example, the notion that this was emotional because it used violence in a different way was represented here:

> In video games about war, we typically assume the roles of gun-toting soldiers who singlehandedly save the day. … Through phenomenal visuals and audio, *Valiant Hearts: The Great War* highlights the horrors faced by normal people in extraordinary circumstances. (Jobe, 2014)

And that its pleasures were afforded by gameplay that dealt with the consequences of violence were represented here:

> On a gameplay level, there's nothing here that you won't have done a thousand times before. But the context provided by the narrative and atmosphere takes these run-of-the-mill mechanics and turns them into something much, much more powerful … sometimes it means using a pile of your fallen comrades corpses for cover from enemy fire. (Codd, 2014)

And that the game deftly enhanced its emotional draw with the inclusion of narrative-relevant learning opportunities was represented here:

> The game's narrative is based on letters ... that soldiers wrote to their loved ones back home during the actual war. ... There is something profoundly sad about playing a game that is a visual representation of a letter. (Matt S., 2014)

Emotion therefore worked as a hub for an 'input–output' model of influence. It was the product of an innovative gameplay engine, which was put to work with novel aesthetics and fact-based storytelling, that produced the 'output' of a game with significant 'learning' appeal in terms of encouraging thought about the greatest violence-driven catastrophe in human history.

In combination, this analysis of the reviews suggests that they focused on general themes on the value of gaming to provide a grounded explanation of how screen violence could be about edification as well as entertainment. The idea that you can learn about the Great War from a game might seem strange, silly, offensive or plain out of step with the realities of entertainment. But the idea that you can learn to *care* about it is less so, at least from the perspective of writers keen to promote the integrity of gaming as a participatory experience. If nothing else, looking at *Valiant Hearts*' content shows how gaming fits in the history of a century that has been mostly concerned, according to historians, with figuring out what violence means.

SIGNIFICANCE: 'TEXTUAL ANALYSIS' ADDRESSES THE SOCIAL LIFE OF MEDIA PHENOMENA, NOT THE MEANING OF A TEXT

The purpose of this chapter has been to establish that research on media *content* plays a vibrant role in generating innovative insights into the social role of media *culture*. Showing how the proliferation of content around gaming affords fresh perspectives on the significance of screen violence has made this point. In this instance, the case has been made that those gaming journalists who lauded the creativity of *Valiant Hearts* also valorized imaginative violence as a means of evoking empathy from gamers. The fact that this point was made in relation to a game about the Great War is enormously significant, given that commemoration of that conflict has been a prime force in the politicization of culture since the early 20th century.

The point has also been made that the nature of gaming content has also moved debates on research methods in a positive direction. During the broadcast television era, scholars agreed that the purpose of content research was to demonstrate the political nature of television content, but couldn't agree on the best way to achieve this goal. In particular, sharp conflicts arose over the relative merits of quantitative and qualitative methods. These, in turn, reflected different views on whether 'content' referred to the particular themes of particular pro-grammes or to the general messages that crossed the entire medium. Arguments over this matter frequently focused on the meaning of violence.

Since gaming content permeates many social spaces, it also demonstrates the value of a mixed method approach. Non-gamers frequently encounter decontextualized images of violence, while experienced gamers, and profes-sional critics, have become adept at explaining why not all games containing violence are created equal. At any rate, academics who write about the genre have used a combination of enumerative and evaluative methods to explain the political significance of gaming violence as a vehicle that gamers use to contem-plate history and ethics – at least when it is done well. Nor have they been afraid to use the same methods to validate the impression that unimaginative violence reinforces oppressive social hierarchies. In doing so, it becomes clear that stud-ying gaming content, in all its forms, plays a significant role in structuring conversations over why we should take the genre seriously, as a cultural force that affects how gamers conceive and participate in society. This approach – comparing different kinds of content about the same title via a combination of qualitative and quantitative techniques – can be applied to other media subjects. In the next chapter, we will see how similar ideas can be put to use in understanding media audiences.

CHAPTER SUMMARY

- Media content comes in many forms.

- Studying the relationship between different types of media content gives useful insights into how media culture works.

- Gaming research demonstrates how mixed method, comparative approaches to content raise significant and innovative perspectives on the significance of screen violence.

- In doing this, gaming research has made a notable contribution to the debate on the relationship between quantitative and qualitative methods.

12

RESEARCHING MEDIA EVENTS

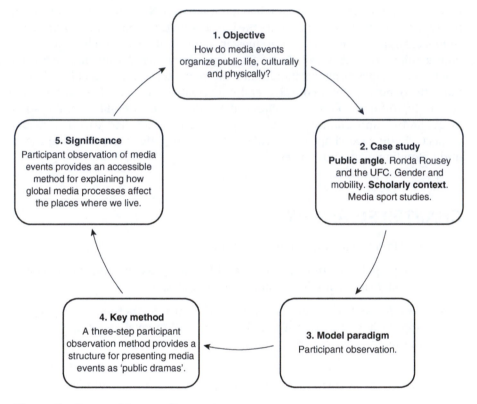

1. Objective
How do media events organize public life, culturally and physically?

2. Case study
Public angle. Ronda Rousey and the UFC. Gender and mobility. **Scholarly context**. Media sport studies.

3. Model paradigm
Participant observation.

4. Key method
A three-step participant observation method provides a structure for presenting media events as 'public dramas'.

5. Significance
Participant observation of media events provides an accessible method for explaining how global media processes affect the places where we live.

Figure 8 Researching media events

OBJECTIVE: DEVELOPING OBSERVATIONAL METHODS FOR ANALYSING MEDIA IN ACTION

This chapter explains how the relationship between culture and economy can be mapped by observing sport events in action, using participant observation techniques. The broader purpose is to show how theoretically informed field research can examine how media help to create meaningful social spaces. The presence of media affects how places are understood and managed. The production of 'media spaces' in turn creates opportunities to perform identities. Two consequences follow. First, media places become stages for social conflict. Second, they attract flows of human movement bearing all manner of economic and environmental effects. Global sporting contests are vivid examples of this process in action, as events that enact relationship between economy, media, culture and identity.

As a case study, the chapter explores how the Ultimate Fighting Championship (UFC) turned a stadium in Melbourne, Australia, into an arena for a battle over gender in November 2015. Celebrity athlete Ronda Rousey's fight with Holly Holm was not just another contest that just happened to be staged in Australia; it was a gendered drama deliberately staged at a key node in a competitive global sport economy. Melbourne's Etihad stadium was a sophisticated media place ideally suited to an event that aspired to change perceptions about women athletes. The fight animated the relationship between culture and economy. It was an exhilarating confirmation that sport turns on money, power, identity work and globalization. Much as the fighters and the UFC were relative newcomers to the global sport scene, they deserved attention for their keen appreciation of sport as an organized technological and economic activity that enervates the relationship between media representation and space.

Informed by these insights, the chapter then explains how participant observation explains why the Rousey fight was a landmark in the history of gendered media sport. Participant observation is a method for researching cultural 'scenes' – places where people interact in meaningful ways. It provides a structured method for investigating media events – occasions that demonstrate media's power to organize people, places and times. Here, attention is paid to how a press conference for Rousey's fight became a moment in the articulation of sport, place, gender and national identity, using a variety of strategically selected research materials to arrange observation of the event itself.

Finally, the chapter comments on what researching this sporting media event says about the significance of research about media places, and methods for conducting such studies. Ultimately, studies of media spaces allow us to appreciate the relationship between two kinds of communication: representation and movement. This connection is especially useful in appreciating media as a catalyst in consumer culture.

In summary, this chapter:

- Explains geographical media effects.
- Uses sport to relate media meanings to the management of space and identity.
- Maps a method for observing media places in action.

CASE STUDY: RONDA ROUSEY: SPACE, TRAVEL AND THE MEDIA SPORT STAR

Public angle: Ronda Rousey comes Down Under

When Ronda Rousey and Holly Holm fought before 56,214 fans in Melbourne in November 2015, they set a world record for Dana White's Ultimate Fighting Championship (Doyle, 2015). The fight was a sensation. The previously unde-feated, popularly feted Rousey lost to a short, sharp savage salvo of punches, elbows and a cruelly accurate roundhouse kick to the neck. Much as the out-come damaged the reputation of its best known star, the fight cemented the UFC's reputation as an innovative, mobile form of media sport that revelled in upsetting gender stereotypes.

Spectacular as the contest was, perhaps it is more remarkable that two months before their fight, Rousey and Holm held a press conference at the Etihad Stadium venue on a gloomy winter Wednesday afternoon that drew an extraordinary 5,000 spectators. Rousey arrived as arguably the most famous female athlete in the world. Pipping Serena Williams as the ESPN Women's Athlete of the Year 2015 had witnessed Rousey's arrival as the 'David Beckham' of the UFC: the fighter recognized by people who knew little about martial arts. She had appeared on the *Ellen Degeneres Show*, and had a cameo in the movie *Entourage* (2015). Her autobiography, published in the same year (Rousey, 2015), detailed a heartbreaking journey from childhood tragedy to sporting excellence. Rousey had a story to tell, and she didn't shirk in telling it. She was especially blunt on how her body confronted gender stereotypes, famously quipping: 'just because my body was developed for a purpose other than fuck-ing millionaires doesn't mean it's masculine. I think it's femininely badass as fuck because there's not a single muscle on my body that isn't for a purpose, because I'm not a do-nothing bitch'. Before a cheering crowd, Rousey explained why Australia was the ideal location for the biggest fight in the history of wom-en's martial arts. Australia was a perfect home for gender-breaking pugilism as a nation of tough people who like a good fight. But why would so many show up to hear predictable pre-fight puff drawing on well-worn national stereotypes, especially when most presumably had other things to do (work, school)? What was it about the athlete, her sport and the arena that gave people licence to take a break from normal midweek routines?

Rousey, Holm and the fans who attended on that day revelled in breaking rules. Parents in the crowd boasted of taking their kids out of school, and the fighters basked in levels of attention rarely enjoyed by women athletes. At the same time, this 'rebellion' was highly organized by an innovative sporting organization skilled in mining the interconnected resources of sport, media, entertainment and celebrity. As such, it is worth considering how observation of events like this, informed by sociological views on why sport is a key ingredient in media and consumer cultures, offer useful insights into the relationship between economy and culture.

Scholarly context: Media sport studies

Understanding how sport attracts public attention is a handy way of showing how media industries integrate consumption and cultural participation. Spectacular media events play key roles in development of social meanings and values. The analysis of how this happens is the core business of critical media sport studies. Serendipitously, this project started with the analysis of a controversial martial art.

When famous French semiotician Roland Barthes explained the political weight of popular culture in *Mythologies* (1972), he included an essay on professional wrestling. Barthes found wrestling to be wonderfully ironic. It entertained audiences by wilfully eschewing notions of unpredictability and fair play, thus raising fascinating questions about what sport is for. Other pugilistic pastimes, such as boxing and Judo, are premised on the idea that no one can predict the outcome of a contest of skill between matched opponents. Here, when the knockout blow is delivered, all attention switches to the victor, leaving the vanquished opponent to their bloodied humiliation. That seems natural. Not so in wrestling. Unfair fights lead to predictable outcomes where most of the attention is paid to wounded losers – eyes linger on bodies as they roll around the floor in agony, frequently as victims of egregious fouls conducted in plain sight. Poor justice, great entertainment and an indicator that to be popular, sport has to be about much more than skill and athleticism. Barthes admired the audacity of this unsporting sport. The fact that this 'aberration' went on to become a global triumph thanks to the WWF indicates that he was on to something; that understanding sport as spectacular drama above all else is the key to appreciating why it matters as the exemplar of culture in action *par excellence*. This is the essential idea behind the emergence of critical media sport studies.

Critical research on media sport has advanced Barthes' ideas by connecting the production of values through the staging of events to matters of justice raised by consumer culture. As David Rowe (2004a, 3) explains, media sport:

> occupies vast tracts of electronic, print and cyber media space; directly and indirectly generates a diverse range of goods and services ... and is strategically used by the political apparatus in the name of the people.

These are the characteristics of Rowe's 'media sport cultural complex'. This 'complex' folded elite athletics into the mechanism of globalization, defined as 'the enhanced flows of people, capital, ideas and technologies around the world' (Rowe, 2004b, 11). This transformation was achieved through the ingenious integration of 'personnel, services, products and texts which combine in the creation of the broad and dynamic field of contemporary sports culture' (Rowe, 2004a, xx). The connection with Barthes is this: wrestling was popular because it was meaningful and emotionally absorbing, and this has little to do with fairness and skill. For Rowe, this is why sport and media industries have become powerful allies in advancing global consumer culture.

The political gravity of media sport entertainment is underlined by the sustainability challenges prompted by mega-events like the Olympics and Football World Cup. Such occasions strain already overburdened urban environments. Rio de Janeiro's residents protested at the price paid by the city's poor as Brazil geared up for the World Cup and the Olympics (Schimmel, 2015). Such events create environmental challenges and exploit local cheap labour (Young, 2015). Brazilian tensions dragged global sporting events into debates around security and terror, locating such occasions as sources of anger, injustice and fear as much as pleasure (Jackson, 2015). The important point to note here is not that media are simply there to cover such tournaments, but that their arrangements as live spectacles suitable for global screen audiences become a driving force in their arrangement (Rowe, 2004a). Consequently, the mediation of sport creates an opportunity to explore how inclusion and equity function in a global consumer culture, since sporting events are occasions where tensions about the distribution of economic resources connect with the things that people care about – their identities and pleasures (Wenner, 2015).

All of this places studies of media sport squarely within the media studies tradition of viewing popular culture as the setting for social conflict and change. Often media sport reproduces power inequalities based on race, nation and gender (Wenner, 2015). On the other hand, the need to find new audience markets through sport also creates new identity. New media sports like snowboarding, skydiving and surfing show audiences women athletes who defy masculinist prejudices (Sisjord, 2015). According to Wheaton (2015), these extreme sports have come to matter because they offer alternative identities by being athletic in different ways, *and* they have shown the ability to find new media sporting audiences to satisfy the global television market. A quick example illustrates her argument. In 2014, Australian snowboarder Belle Brockhoff, while competing at the Sochi Olympics, criticized Vladimir Putin's stand on sexual politics. The world heard about this courageous act not simply because Brockhoff was an exceptional snowboarder who also happened to be gay, but because snowboarding had become a bright new feature of the Olympic brand.

The media staging of sport also determines how people interact with events through their own movements and performances. Sport helps media industries break new viewing markets by multiplying ways to engage with contests, teams and athletes (Hutchins and Rowe, 2013). For the same reason, it has also pioneered methods for synthesizing social and consumer identities. The foundation of this 'achievement' is constituted by the sheer ubiquity of sport in the media, which renders it as an easy topic of everyday sociality. The plethora of information about athletes, teams and likely outcomes of forthcoming competitions attracts people who wish to showcase their expertise in front of their peers (Rowe, 2015). Internet fan communities are obvious places where this can be seen in action, as fans try to win prestige by demonstrating their superior knowledge. Often, these discussions mutate into weighty discussions on race, gender and justice (e.g. Ruddock, 2005, 2013b, 2016; Millward, 2008; Cleland, 2014).

These developments can go in many directions. Some studies, for example, find that these fan practices end up shoring up the idea that sport is 'a man's game' (e.g. Ruddock, 2005; Palmer, 2009; Rowe, Ruddock and Hutchins, 2010). Wenner (2015) agreed, but argued that the real issue is how fan actions solder identity to consumption. Ubiquitous screens, global tournaments, celebritization and the explosion of sport commodities ensure that 'media sport coverage and sport anchored advertising have worked to align our fanship identities with our consumer identities. The hypercommodification that has infused our relations with both sport and media is now foundational' (Wenner, 2015, 631).

What this means is that the analysis of sporting events, as media spectacles that create meaningful places and identities, has to be premised on a clear identification of how that event addresses key academic themes, and how a specific method lends a unique perspective on how that event linked economy and culture. Bearing this in mind, there are four solid reasons why UFC193 was a mediated sporting event that was worth paying more attention to: the political economy or urban development, the formation of identities in relation to political economy, gender as a special example of this process in action, and how the nature of sporting competition is affected by mediated consumer culture. The next question is: What methods show these processes in action?

KEY PARADIGM: PARTICIPANT OBSERVATION

Participant observation: A three-step approach

Media sport literature conceives a close relationship among economy, culture and spectator experience. But what methods show that these arguments have some kind of relationship to how real people experience real sport events? One option is participant observation. Participant observation involves watching culture in action, as it happens. The goal is to 'share firsthand the environment, problems, background, language, rituals and social relations of a more-or-less bounded and specified group of people' (Van Maanen, 1988, 3). This can be done in a variety of ways, ranging from simple observation of events to more involved methods that include other techniques, such as interviewing. In *Tales of the Field* (1988), Van Maanen portrayed participant observation as a method based on the idea that culture is a thing that can be observed in action when people interact. This is because apparently mundane scenes from everyday life are 'rule'-governed events, structured by unspoken but widely shared understandings. Another way to say this is that 'macro' social forces matter most when they percolate all the way down to face-to-face interaction, and therefore observation of the small scenes of social life underline why the big questions matter. At face value, this suits the goals of critical media sport studies, which seek to understand how sporting events conjure consumer-based identities into action when people are gathered around a specific event.

An obvious challenge in this method is that it hinges on one person's account of what happened. Van Maanen argued that this could be compensated for by telling readers as much as possible about the research process. This, in his view, was a matter of differentiating between three different kinds of 'stories' that the participant observer tells. The first thing to do is to embrace the reality that participant observation is not an objective science, by engaging with 'confessional' tales. Confessional tales deal with the challenges posed by situations where 'findings' are intimately affected by the research process, rather than simply being dictated by the events that one observes. Hence, being 'confessional' means reporting in as much detail as possible on the factors that affect how one goes about research – from choosing a setting to methods for recording and interpreting data.

This sets the ground for the next stage: the production of 'realist' tales. Realist tales involve describing the events that one observes. Conventionally, this was done through the production of field notes, observations written down either during or as soon as possible after the event being observed.

The third kind of tale moves participant observation into analysis proper. 'Impressionist tales' are told by sifting through observations to find dramatic moments where the rule- and conflict-based nature of social life is manifested most vividly. The notion of observation has to be tempered against the fact that what one is often doing is testing out existing academic ideas about how life works; that is, you go into a scene looking for things that are especially relevant to a field of study. With Rousey, for example, the fact that gender identity is such a point of interest in critical media sport research, and the fact that gender was used as a major marketing tool in the fight, means that it makes sense to search for moments where gender erupts as an idea that affects how people related to the fight.

Being confessional means asking by what criteria one is to identify 'dramatic' moments for impressionist tales. One way to do this is to historicize the events that are observed, showing how they are related to sustained social formations. Hammersley and Atkinson (1995) call this 'casing the joint', using documents and archives about the place of study as a way of sensitizing oneself to what this 'event' might be about in terms of history and culture. For Rousey's fight, this could be done because both the stadium and the UFC were both sports innovations that understood that they were cogs in a global media sport cultural complex. Hence, foregrounding the participant observation in historical research, using newspaper archives to explain how Etihad and the UFC came to be and why they mattered to Melbourne and the World of Sport in general, provides a vital context that explains why the press conference and the fight were worth paying attention to, and speak to matters beyond the 'particulars' of that event.

Preparing for participant observation: Using archives to case map the terrain

Understanding the stadium

The challenge is to make a persuasive case that the Rousey/Holm press conference somehow dramatized conflicts around identity that result from the popularization of sport as a form of global entertainment. In terms of conflict and entertainment, it's tempting to think that much of the appeal of the fight derived from the UFC's audacity in using the home of Aussie Rules Football to showcase the quality and appeal of women's martial arts. However, a closer look at the history of the stadium and the Australian Football League (AFL) shows this to be far less of a contradiction than we might think, and in the end this affects how we should interpret what happened in the press conference.

The Etihad Stadium began life as the Docklands Stadium in the mid-1990s. The arena was explicitly designed to boost Melbourne through an urban planning strategy that would allow the city to establish itself as a key destination in the Australian and world sporting map. The new stadium was intended to showcase Melbourne and the Australian Rules Football League as key components in Australia's global economic ambitions. To be sure, the AFL lobbied hard to make itself the 'grand jewel' in the new venture (Linnell, 1997), but it was only too aware that this could only be achieved by literally moving with the times, relocating its operations and learning to share with competitors in the media sport market. Initially, the game attracted pride of place as the only vehicle that could promise a quick return for expensive investment in a pricey property market. That is, although the hope was that the stadium would serve as a lucrative hub for all manner of sport and music events, the Australian game was needed to make it happen (Davidson, 1997).

Looking at stories about the development of the stadium, a tale emerges where the AFL's 'story' moves from Melbournian suburbs to the city as a whole, and thence to the world. Here the identity of neighbourhood and city relied on the management of local economy and infrastructure with the goal of tapping into the local benefits of global media sport culture. For AFL clubs, claiming the right to play at the new stadium was a method for associating their franchise with the fan base of very particular suburbs of Melbourne with their own identities. In terms of mobility, being in Docklands was really about being elsewhere and giving fans a reason to travel from where they were to where they could be represented. Being in Docklands was a way to perform local identities to the rest of Melbourne, Australia and the world (Linnell, 1996). At the same time, it also created marketing pressures. Teams that shared the stadium were obliged to sell at least 40,000 tickets during designated 'home' games or face a fine (McMahon, 2009).

Economic managements also emerged as a consideration in terms of how stadia and franchises were to cooperate in managing Melbourne's value as an entertainment hub characterized by business synchronicities. For example, management of Melbourne's more famous, iconic Melbourne Cricket Ground welcomed Docklands as a partner that would help the city bid for multi-stage international media sport events. This is why the Rousey event succeeded a history of the AFL accepting the benefits it would reap by seeking synergies with the global sport media market (Linnell, 1997).

Media were key to infrastructural arrangements that would attract spectators to the ground, promoting the comfort and ease that it offered. Fans could travel from distant suburbs to a train station just a few hundred metres from the ground, and could enjoy the short promenade across a newly constructed pedestrian bridge. After their stroll, they could enjoy the game in a stadium free from fears of inclement weather or poor vision. In-seat TV screens were floated (Watkins, 1998), and a roof was installed to shelter crowds from the rain. Media muscle in managing the spectacle in the stadium was demonstrated in 2014, when local news station Channel 7 lobbied to have the stadium roof closed for all games, no matter the weather or time of day, since this made for a better screen experience (Murnane, 2014). In this way, Etihad's existence as a screened space became key to its physical management.

Significantly, athletes accepted the need to accede to audience experience. Because the pitch was laid over a concrete underground car park, AFL players quickly complained of injuries and longer recovery times inflicted by the playing surface. As one player put it, 'You would rather play at the MCG, you would rather play in Tassie, than at Telstra Dome. Cosmetically it might look good but it is still hard to play. Players are resigned to it, and clubs are adjusting' (Gleeson, 2006, 2).

All of this rather underlines the point that the social significance of sport is best demonstrated by regarding it as entertainment above all else. That players accepted painful playing surfaces spoke to this truth: Etihad was the hub of a sporting city where fans, players, clubs, sporting organizations, planners and politicians benefitted from the skilful blending of athletics, urban regeneration, tourism and global marketing. Guest sports helped the costs of expensive local investments. So athletes like Rousey and organizations like the UFC were welcome to pitch for the pitch, and therefore Etihad's history goes a long way to explaining why the Rousey fight attracted such attention, and why the press conference attracted so many people. Etihad is a major, easily accessible landmark in a city that has cultivated a sophisticated tourism and leisure market. When we add the UFC's role as a pioneer in global media sport, then it becomes even easier to see how the press conference became an event in itself.

Understanding the UFC

Analysis from the media industry trade press depicts the UFC as an ideal 'fit' for Etihad as the epitome of media sport. The organization has taken mixed martial arts from ridicule to respect, thanks to an understanding of what makes for successful entertainment. In a nutshell, the UFC's appearance in Melbourne underscored its canny understanding that live media events worked by spinning entertaining *stories* to diverse audiences, many of whom usually had little interest in sport. While sports like soccer are prone to grumble about how media erode the authenticity of the game, the UFC accepted the necessity of changing its game to suit alternative locations, publics and media platforms. Unlike sports with claims to lives before media, the UFC embraced its status as a child of convergence – an authentically mediatized sport, if you will. When it comes to space, the UFC's flexibility is reflected in a willingness to migrate across locations and screens. It has become adept at transforming sport places into UFC ones. As such, its Etihad event stands out from other occasions – AFL games, for example – as an instructive case study in what sport tells us about the politics of media and space.

Several themes picked up by the trade press support these interpretations. First, much of the UFC's significance can be attributed to the determination of its celebrity CEO, Dana White, to recreate the excitement that surrounded live television boxing during the 1970s and 1980s. Muhammad Ali became history's most famous boxer partly because his landmark bouts were broadcast live to huge international television audiences. Consequently, where many sports have concentrated on pursuing 'after television' opportunities (Hutchins and Rowe, 2013), White claimed that his ambition to secure the UFC as a broadcast television sport would signal its arrival as a true sport (Grossman, 2011).

To achieve this goal, White transformed the image of the UFC from an ultra-violent novelty to a television-friendly entertainment genre. When the franchise emerged from the mixed martial arts scene in the 1990s, it was beset by myriad legal and marketing problems (Maher, 2010). White responded by toning down UFC violence while amplifying its capacity to tell interesting stories about human characters. When the UFC made its prime time television debut on the Fox Network in 2011, it was with a one-hour show that featured just one minute of fighting – a headline heavyweight bout that lasted less than a round (Grossman, 2011). White's comments on what he most feared for the show were instructive. His biggest fear was that the bout would be 'a three-round war with one guy against the fence and he's cut and blood squirting all over the mat' (cited in Grossman, 2011, 14). In the same report, White noted the need to 'tone down the testosterone' (cited in Grossman, 2011, 14) in favour of story-driven content that would attract advertisers.

The UFC's commercial promise for television broadcasters was proven though its success in live pay-per-view events, and all of the corporate sponsorship that came with it (Miller, 2013). By 2012, UFC Fox broadcasts attracted commercial endorsements from the alcohol, movie and gaming industries (Lafayette, 2012b). At this point, the reason why Fox had fought off interest from other television companies to secure UFC rights became clear. The brand was a vital tool in Newscorp's digital television strategy, playing an essential role in the 'rebranding' of cable station 'Fuel TV', which aspired to capture the 18–34 male market (Lafayette, 2011).

The UFC has become a global sport because it understands that to do this you have to provide media content (Miller, 2013). It is now appreciated as a leading 'water carrier' for television interests (2013) because it has used its ownership of media content to integrate various television and streaming platforms, such as Xbox, PS3, Amazon, Facebook, YouTube and Apple iOS (2013).

Its willingness to 'travel' across media interests is matched by an enthusiasm for physically expanding into international markets. It has regional offices in Europe, Asia and South America, and an international chain of health clubs, including a branch in Sydney (Miller, 2013). The competition's embrace of media has put it on a par with the Superbowl as a world media event (Grossman, 2011). This can also be explained by White's appreciation of how social media and celebrity can recreate an earlier age of the superstar martial artists. According to the UFC, the advantage that his sport has over American football and baseball is its capacity to function as a personality-driven phenomenon, where people become attached to people, not teams. To this end, its athletes are encouraged to brand themselves through social media (Schrager, 2012). This is why the UFC is distinct from other sports as a child of mediatization. Where other sports have viewed the autonomy that social media affords athletes with suspicion, Dana White welcomes it as part of the show.

Putting all of these ideas together provides a justification for choosing the press conference for showcasing what media sport theory says about media, place and identity. The UFC sells itself as a sporting narrative driven by personalities. These narratives drive the pleasure of live events, carried across screens. The events themselves are often short. White prefers them this way. The real skill, White seems to realize, lies in building anticipation through writing detailed stories about athletes. In this sense, one can argue that the real work of the UFC is done before anyone enters its hexagon. This is why thousands of people arrived at Rousey's press conference, and this is why we can say that in many respects, what they saw was the real show, the place where Rousey and White appeared to explain why people should want to come to the November fight. Rousey was the ideal figurehead for an organization that was only too happy to change its game to suit the needs of global entertainment, as a person with a compelling personal story combined with the appeal of a gender identity breaker for a sport that was keen to embrace audiences who had traditionally taken little interest in martial arts. These ideas were confirmed by the drama of what happened on an otherwise drab midweek afternoon.

KEY METHOD: OBSERVING MEDIA EVENTS

Reprising the method, fieldwork was intended to recreate the experience of a media event by using an ordered approach to data gathering. This order distinguished three kinds of stories: the confessional, the descriptive and the impressionist. Essentially, this involves using ordinary observation to precede a carefully considered, analytically and theoretically informed account of how the press conference dramatized dynamics that media sport scholars have been writing about for some time.

A confessional account

Confession wise, pragmatic issues in research management affected the choice of case study and methodological approach to the same. I adopted a passive observation approach by visiting a press conference, where I spoke to no one and concentrated on the public comments, made for public consumption, by media professionals – Dana White, Rousey and her UFC peers, and journalists. Why this approach?

There was more at play here than the theoretical justification for the approach. Decisions were made based on the financial and administrative difficulties of researching media cultures where fascinating case studies appear in an instant. So here's the 'confession'. This book needed a chapter on media and sport. It needed to talk about the construction of media sport events. Given the importance of gender in media power, I was just as keen to write about female athletes. So, when the most famous woman athlete in the world shows up at a place that is a 15-minute train ride from your house, you can't ignore that.

Except that you can't just go. What about funding? Fight tickets cost $459 for good seats, and there was no time to apply for a grant. So the press conference solved that problem – it was free. But what *was* the press conference, as an event, and how did that affect the permissions I needed to study it? Its status as a 'live' thing involving other human beings carried ethical considerations. Once again, time was of the essence. With no time to apply for ethics clearance, I had to discover a way to observe ethically. So I contacted my university ethics office. The press conference, I argued, was a public performance. From an ethics perspective, it was equivalent to a film, or a speech, or a newspaper article – an event where the person who speaks claims no right to privacy. We agreed that no ethics requirements were necessary as long as I limited my work to the professional staging of the event and the verbal exchanges between journalists and UFC personnel. That is, no talking to the fans in attendance. These restrictions affected the focus of the following account, and explain the focus on the 'pure' observation of performers only. This focus also explains how the impressionist tale of 'gender drama' was developed.

A realist account

Let's move on to the descriptive aspect of the project. From media sport theory and local stories about what Etihad leisure represented as a leisure experience, it seemed best to start note-taking with a description of the journey to the stadium. This was harder than it sounds because it meant thinking about a journey that I'd taken many times. Usually, like most people, I spend most of my time on public transport trying not to think about where I am. Paying closer attention, it appeared that the ease of movement to the stadium expresses how smoothly it has blended into Melbourne's transport network and consumer culture, in such a way that it is quite a peculiar sporting place.

Describing the journey, the strangest thing about Etihad is that public transport users don't know they are there until they are almost at its gates. Alighting at Spenser Street Station, travellers are carried to a pedestrian walkway via escalators, at the top of which stands a new shopping mall with retail outlets and chain eateries. Turning left, they know from the signs that they are headed in the right direction, with their final destination standing just a few hundred metres away. But the only thing that they can see, directly ahead, is the black-glassed head office of the National Australian Bank. The 'presence' of a premier stadium in a premier sporting city is hardly awe-inspiring.

It's also worth noting, then, that the first thing you would have seen on that Wednesday, as you walked around the bank, were three red three-metre-high letters: UFC. Women clad in UFC-branded lycra handed out flyers, but they, and the letters, were all I could see at first. Suddenly my eye was drawn to a queue – it too had been obscured by the National Australian Bank, but as I walked and looked, I soon realized that the line of fans stretched for about 400 metres. It was later reported that a staggering 6,000 people had registered for the event on a nondescript Wednesday afternoon (Oates, 2015).

I took my place at the back of the queue. It was soon moving, as the crowd was ushered through turnstiles and security. As we entered Gate 3, we were quickly moved past a UFC tableau that had been set up for fan selfies. Ushers made it clear that it was for after the show. We were in the bowels of Etihad now, on the first of its three levels, the pitch-side seats that represent the most expensive tickets for the AFL and soccer matches that usually dominate. The crowd was corralled into a roped-off section on the pitch's half-way line. Fifty metres before us was the stage, which was set against a backdrop of pictures of the four women who would fight in November: Holly Holm, Joanna Jedrzejczyk, Valerie Letourneau and Ronda Rousey. It was 15 minutes before the combatants entered. Meanwhile, we were left to contemplate the fighters' skills, as videos of their bouts played on televisions next to the stage and on the enormous screens that are a permanent fixture in the upper tiers of the stadium. On the night, that will be the best view that fans will get of the action in the ring. We can tell because a real UFC octagon had been set up next to the stage. It's small, and will be barely visible from the 'cheap seats'. While everyone was waiting, local martial artists and journalists posed for photographs in the ring-to-be.

The fights on the screens were ferocious. Jedrzejczyk's opponent flinched in pain as the Polish champion rained endless jabs, crosses and hooks onto her bloodied nose. Letourneau's foe had a terribly damaged left eye. It was almost completely closed and there was a huge welt over her brow. It looked like a fractured eye socket to me, and I was amazed when a doctor waved the battle on after a quick, gloveless examination. I've watched boxing for years, but this made me wince.

Then the show was on, as the journalists were seated and Dana White took to the stage. For a guy who knows how to put on a show, he was pretty casually dressed – jeans, black t-shirt, shaved head, hulking frame. He looked like a retired boxer. Then he introduced each fighter, in this order: Letourneau, Jedrzejczyk, Holm and Rousey. The dress was smart casual. All were in tight jeans. Letourneau, Holm and Rousey wore six-inch heels. Their hair was long and down, in contrast to the tight bunching they wear during fights. Holm's hair reached to her waist. Unlike the other fighters, she eschewed a jacket on this chilly afternoon, and was wearing a sleeveless top that displayed enviously developed biceps and triceps. She looked like she was ready to fight that day. Jedrzejczyk bucked the trend a little. She wore wedges not heels, her hair was plaited and she wore an overcoat. In a genre where gender was high on the agenda, these details were worth mentioning, even if their significance was open to debate.

An Impressionist account

And then it was on, and at this point I switched to the impressionist approach, since developments enacted a drama that labelled this 'media event' as a story about gender. The press gallery included journalists from UFC partners, such as Fox Sport. But that didn't mean everyone was on the same page. The floor was opened to questions. The first three questions were directed at Dana White. Perhaps that was understandable. He had been widely credited as the author of the UFC's remarkable success. But it seemed rather odd that reporters weren't champing at the bit to talk to Rousey. It was hard to imagine the same thing happening to Mike Tyson, so perhaps White's analogy had its limits. When the fourth question was directed at Rousey, it was to ask how she felt about her appearance in the *Entourage* movie and being name-checked by Beyoncé.

Then an odd question was directed at Holly Holm, given Rousey's popularity: 'How does it feel to be the one who has to kill Bambi?' A puzzled Holm managed an answer. All of the other fighters seemed resigned to the fact that the show was about Rousey, but the ignoring of all of them, and the likening of a fearsome martial artist to a baby deer on ice, marked this event as different. Which indeed it was. This was going to be the most lucrative, most watched women's martial arts event of all time. Much as there was a determination to present this as a martial arts event (White tells us that Rousey demanded to be introduced as champion, not women's champion), the fact is that it was an event featuring a main cast of women. Rousey knew this, with her 'Do Nothing Bitch' comments, and the content and structure of the questions had a gendered tone: talk to the men first, liken Rousey to a creature who needs protection (albeit a male one).

But the gender issue really exploded when another journalist asked Rousey for her opinion on poor pay in women's professional soccer. The question was drowned out by boos from the crowd. Some fans got to their feet. A man yelled 'resign' at the reporter. Rousey restored order with a measured response. Whatever the sport, women would be paid the same as men when they could sell the same tickets for the same prices. If she sold out Etihad, she would have proved her status as an elite global athlete, regardless of her gender. That was why she was in Australia. Aussies were a tough bunch who liked a good fight, regardless of who was throwing the punches. That was why Melbourne was such a natural setting for the change that she was trying to bring. It was quite clear: her battle to be recognized as a truly great athlete by fighting through gender barriers had landed in Australia for a reason. In these comments, Rousey sold the fight as an occasion that would work because it brought the gender battle to the place where it had the best chance of a fair fight. Where else than the land of the 'fair go' that the nation's tourist industry had promoted so enthusiastically over the last generation?

Things simmered down after that, the fighters faced off against one another, and the mood was lightened as fans were invited down to take pictures with Rousey, who later walked into the crowd to happily pose for selfies. The question that remained was this: How could we explain why the most heated moment in a press conference for martial artists was not the traditional sparking point, where opponents face off, but in a question from a female reporter about pay in women's sports? In what way could this dramatic moment be connected to the location of Rousey and the UFC in the growth of media sport as an arena that combines sport, leisure, pleasure and media?

Returning to the opening ideas of the chapter, one can say that the flow of 6,000 people to the event had an impact on the conflict that erupted around gender during this event. The drama was produced not by the question, but by the reaction of the large crowd. Spectators were attracted by a smart media event hosted by a savvy sport in a cleverly designed stadium that was easy to access as part of a day out. If the ferocity of the reaction might have been unanticipated, the fact that gender emerged as a controversial issue was not surprising, given Rousey and the UFC confront gender questions head on in their efforts to take the leading edge in the global sports market. By placing this moment in the context of research on Etihad Stadium, the UFC and decades of work on the evolution of media sport as a form of entertainment, it is possible to make the argument that the Rousey conference dramatized media sport contests as places where identity conflicts are part and parcel of live social experiences.

SIGNIFICANCE: MEDIA EVENTS DRAMATIZE GLOBAL MEDIA PROCESSES RIGHT BEFORE OUR EYES

The point of studying popular culture is to show how important issues about identity and power come to life. These are moments where sociological forces are seen in action. The goal here is modest; it is simply to show that when controversies about things like gender crop up in the course of entertainment, as it did in the Rousey press conference, this reflects how popular culture is organized, performed and received. When it comes to sport, the economic role of mediated contests as drivers of tourism and urban regeneration make these complex, weighty matters indeed. At the same time they are possible to decipher, and research-based participant observation is a useful tool in this regard, not least because we all have access to media events.

The Rousey/Holm fight linked popular culture research to the matter of how media influence the economic management of geography. Recall, this was the basic question that motivated Innis (2008): the idea that culture involved a particular arrangement of physical resources that favoured some interests with others. We can see how this applied to Rousey by considering geographer David Harvey's *The Condition of Postmodernity* (1990), a highly influential analysis of how cultures make sense of the relationship between space, time and identity. Harvey extended Innis's ideas to consider how the management of space implicated people's bodies into politics, as a final destination where 'forces of repression, socialization, disciplining, and punishing are inflicted' (1990, 215). These forces mean we 'must either submit to authority ... or carve out particular spaces of resistance and freedom' (1990, 213). The co-determination of space and bodies 'become an essential ideological ingredient to social reproduction' (1990, 217).

Ronda Rousey certainly translated Harvey's thesis into a kinetic language that everyone could read. Rousey's press conference showed this process in action as the fighters fought to win acceptance as athletes, above everything else, by trying to tell a different story about gender. Well before the fight, Rousey had openly acknowledged the challenge that her body posed to gender stereotypes: the notion that she could be sexy without directing her look at that goal above all else. Such comments recognize that there is a difference in how men and women are treated as athletes; male martial artists are never asked how their fighting prowess and chiselled muscles complicate their sexuality. Plus, the competitive edge of the event was enhanced by the added challenge of proving that Rousey could draw a bigger crowd than UFC men. In a very real way, Rousey's physical presence in Melbourne became a catalyst for a debate on sport, gender and even Australia, the land of the 'fair go'.

Participant observation, using differentiated voices of description and analysis, was one way to explain how Rousey, the UFC and Etihad Stadium summoned debates about gender and media. An important part of the process, though, was in finding an explanation for what brought each entity together before 6,000 people. Had the crowd been smaller, and less ferocious in its reaction to the question about gender and pay, the moment would have been less dramatic. We have asked why so many people would show up, but perhaps it's better to ask how they *could*. Part of the reason, surely, is the appeal of the UFC and Rousey, but much is also about the fact that Etihad was designed as an accommodating place for athletes and audiences alike – a reachable landmark in a global sporting and entertainment economy.

As such, the event presented an opportunity to explore how media sport plays a role in the construction of place and identity. Given research, it was a fair bet that Rousey's appearance would be the site of some kind of gendered 'drama'. Further, theoretically informed participant observation provided a method for explaining why it is more than coincidence that a question about gender, sport and pay would have become a matter of controversy. The lesson is that an understanding of how participant observation can be used as a way of illustrating the connection between media, place and power vastly expands research opportunities since, in a mediatized world, we all have access to such events.

CHAPTER SUMMARY

- The role of media in making meaningful places is a key theme tying media research to the question of how economy and culture are related.

- Research on sport has done much to explain how the staging of contests integrates media industries' economic management identities.

- Theoretically informed participant observation is a useful tool in explaining how such events work.

- The UFC is a valuable case study in how gendered bodies become involved in the media-driven management of space.

13

BIG DATA: HOW CAN WE USE IT?

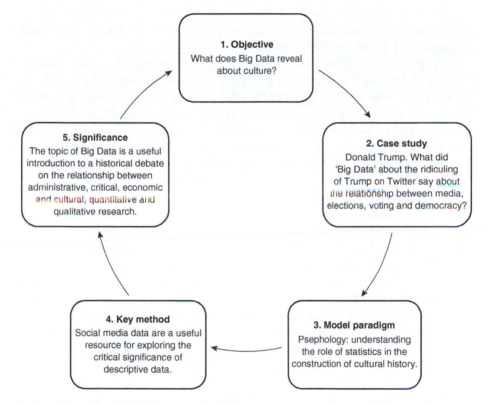

1. Objective
What does Big Data reveal about culture?

2. Case study
Donald Trump. What did 'Big Data' about the ridiculing of Trump on Twitter say about the relationship between media, elections, voting and democracy?

3. Model paradigm
Psephology: understanding the role of statistics in the construction of cultural history.

4. Key method
Social media data are a useful resource for exploring the critical significance of descriptive data.

5. Significance
The topic of Big Data is a useful introduction to a historical debate on the relationship between administrative, critical, economic and cultural, quantitative and qualitative research.

Figure 9   Using Big Data

OBJECTIVE: UNDERSTANDING HOW TO USE SOCIAL MEDIA DATA IN A CRITICAL FASHION

Big Data refers to 'continuous gathering and analysis of dynamically collected, individual-level data about what people are, do and say' (Couldry and Powell, 2014, 1). This chapter outlines the complexities of using Big Data in research by asking what descriptive, quantitative data really tell us about media culture. It also shows how these conceptual issues affect practical challenges in using social media data sets in qualitative data assessment (QDA) software. In particular, the chapter explains how to work through conceptual and methodological problems to find ways to develop valuable critical insights into the impact of social media on political participation from descriptive statistics.

The discussion is grounded in research on Twitter's role in Donald Trump's 2015–2016 campaign to win the US Republican Party's nomination as its candidate for the US Presidency. The case study has been chosen for the following reasons. The debate about what one can and cannot do with Big Data reflects the bigger question about how much information, especially qualitative information, tells us about how society works. Psephology – the study of voting behaviour – has played a leading role in this conversation. Current discussions about the difficulties of understanding voting preferences with Big Data echoes many conceptual and methodological issues that psephology raised. In 2015–2016 such discussions centred on Donald Trump, a political candidate whose appeal perplexed not only American but global media audiences. Social media played an enormous role in this international media drama. Trump was a prolific Twitter user, which exposed him to a great deal of voter feedback through tweets. As such, his candidacy provided an opportunity to assess how much social media data could contribute to critical understanding of modern politics. This is all the more so since, as a figure whose public profile was built in part through a reality television career, Trump's campaign was a landmark in the convergence between political communication and entertainment. Eminent psephologist Sir David Butler thought the transformation of elections into media dramas was the defining political 'fact' of the post-Second World War world. Trump's eventual election as President of the United States demonstrated two things: the prescience of these observations and the necessity of considering why most political experts failed to predict his success, despite access to sophisticated polling mechanisms and banks of data. In hindsight, the role that Twitter played in *obscuring* Trump's popular appeal, during the primaries, was a portent of things to come. It was an illustration of how Big Data can be seductively misleading because of its narrative flexibility.

So, Big Data provokes big questions about methods and mediatized politics. The chapter identifies and answers these puzzles as follows. First, it examines the public furore around Donald Trump's primary electoral campaign and Twitter's role in building his controversial persona. Second, it links confusion about the impact of

Twitter on Trump with academic observations over the ambiguous status of Big Data as a resource. Third, debates about Big Data and elections are connected to psephology, the science of voting behaviours. Here the work of Big Data analyst Nate Silver is compared with the career of Sir David Butler, the Oxford don who is famed as the founder of this field. The comparison shows that many questions about Big Data recycle earlier discussions on the difficulties of predicting voting action. Finally, the chapter translates scholarly observations about evidence, Big Data and mediated elections into practical steps for using Twitter data to pinpoint trends in media politics.

The key points of this chapter are that:

- Big Data concerns the value of numbers in understanding culture.
- This issue has taken on particular importance given the increasingly influential role of media in electoral politics.
- Big Data reveal more about the biases of media and information industries than the feelings and thoughts of media users.

CASE STUDY: BIG DATA, TWITTER AND THE 2015–2016 US PRESIDENTIAL ELECTION

Public angle: What is Big Data and why does it matter?

In 2015, a group of political scientists wrote a chilling *Washington Post* article on how Big Data corrupted American politics (McDonald, Licari and Merivaki, 2015). New methods for analysing voter registration records afforded granular understanding of the audiences for political messages, such that those messages could be tailored to suit a panoply of interests. Trouble was, some states charged for access to the data. Ergo, Big Data had turned elections into a game for rich people who could find out how to say the right things to the right people.

At one point during the US primaries of the same year, it seemed Donald Trump hadn't quite taken the point. That September, the celebrity mogul exposed himself to the popular scrutiny of Twitter, inviting the public to ask him anything they liked via the #Asktrump hashtag. Within hours media outlets like *Time* (White, 2015) and *The Huffington Post* (Satran, 2015) ridiculed the stunt as a débâcle. An avalanche of abuse crashed down – payback, it seemed, for a candidate for whom vitriol was a signature campaign move. Trump had called Mexican immigrants rapists and murderers, promised to build a wall along the US–Mexican border, and advocated a blanket ban on all Muslims entering the US. Twitter delivered a public backlash. Some of the more amusing/trenchant tweets were reported ('So a Muslim, a woman, and a Mexican walk in a bar, who's rights do you alienate first? #AskTrump'; Satran, 2015, no page). Trump was likened to an over-ripe vegetable. Twitter users had, it seemed, done far better than professional politicians or journalists to befuddle Trump's populist appeal. Here was the popular power of social media. Twitter's ability to capture historical snapshots in downloadable form also seemed to promise that if ordinary people can lay the mighty low, so too a wider spectrum of researchers could analyse how such feats worked.

Except Trump wasn't brought down by the incident; if anything, his social media outbursts became more impudent. Certainly, the incident showed what some people thought about the man. It also made the point that the last half-century has seen a media-driven shift in the nature of political communication, where today much campaigning is 'reactive' and responds to unexpected challenges thrown at candidates (McNair, 2006). Ed Miliband's disastrous tilt at the UK premiership in 2014 came at the end of a campaign where much was made of a photo of him struggling to eat a sandwich. But what's the evidence that these moments really matter, and if so, why do they matter? Especially given that Trump won. At the very least, one can say that the data generated around #AskTrump in fact said very little about his appeal. So what did it signify? The political biases of Twitter users? The entertainment value of electoral politics? The role of social media in cultivating smugness? The only thing we can be confident about is that the Trump phenomenon was an opportunity to reflect on the kind of knowledge that Big Data generates.

Scholarly context: Big Data

Across the humanities, resistance to quantitative methods reacts to the notion that the only knowledge worth having is that which comes from the value-free measurement of tangibles – like a person's decision to vote for a certain candidate (Kolakowski, 1992; Fay, 1993). This theme is picked up in the Big Data literature. Squabbles about what Big Data can and can't tell us reflect cornerstone enigmas in social research: 'puzzles about the locus and nature of human life, the nature of interpretation, the categorical constructions of individual entities and agents, the nature and relevance of contexts and temporalities, and the determinations of causality' (Wagner-Pacific, Mohr and Breiger, 2015, 1). So, Big Data is the latest instance of a familiar gambit, where quantitative methods are presented as value-free tools when their effective use depends on the ability to explain why they are nothing of the sort. The apparently automatic algorithms that capture data emerge from thoroughly human processes of scientific development utilizing the training and experience of people who apply their expertise to technical problems in specific ways (Wagner-Pacific et al., 2015).

What's new about Big Data?

Big Data has reignited discussions on the validity of statistics as a mode of cultural research. What is new is the ferocity of these debates, and the level of public interest that they elicit. David Beer (2015, 1) observed that 'general reliance on statistics and probability calculations ... have suddenly become a central part of culture'. Critics think Big Data has produced a 'change' where numbers become more effective because their use value doesn't have much to do with representing what people are really like. Big Data is attractive to media and businesses because it dispenses with the obligation to engage with viewers, readers and listeners on their own terms. For all the rhetoric of wanting to please the public, audiences are inconvenient realities for media companies (Bratich, 2005). Whether it's to attract advertising revenue or defend public subsidy on the basis of public service, media organizations have historically pursued more sophisticated methods to enumerate audience quantity and quality (Ang, 1991; Balnaves and O'Regan, 2010; Balnaves, O'Regan and Goldsmith, 2013). One way or another, commercial newspapers, radio and television interests used numbers to tell advertisers plausible stories about who was paying attention to their content, and this shackled numbers to representative obligations (Couldry and Powell, 2014). Social media have changed the game. Instagram, Twitter, Facebook, Snapchat, etc. still have to sell evidence about the size and spending power of their customers, but the data comes from those customers in the course of their usage. Social media don't have to 'ask the audience' what they are doing because their users *must* provide such data to be users at all.

Consequently, Big Data represents a profoundly changed mode of communication, expression and social existence. According to Couldry and Powell (2014), Big Data threatens the idea of common culture by altering media ecology. In the most dystopian of views, the technology and business models of mobile media oblige users to provide a constant stream of data about their habits and preferences, attenuated from notions of identity or expression, thus removing meaning and culture from the communication equation.

Worse still, Big Data's potential value is inaccessible to most media researchers. Cracking it can require collaboration with computer scientists, and it is often hard to connect their technical expertise to the purpose of cultural analysis (Shaw, 2015). Unsurprisingly, some conclude that Big Data has reinforced a new 'knowledge divide' (boyd and Crawford, 2012). Taking all of this into account, social media can be extremely poor research resources. Twitter is a case in point. Sure, it's great at archiving the quotidian and not-so-ordinary thoughts that pass through public conversation. Regrettably, the platform only makes a small sample of its tweets available. This data is, after all, the revenue stream of the platform, meaning that 'tracking the ongoing public activities of more than 5000 Twitter users at a time is now only possible by working with Twitter's licenced third-party API provider Gnip, at a cost well beyond the funding available to most research projects' (Bruns and Burgess, 2012, 4).

Lewis, Zamith and Hermida's (2013) research on Twitter's role in the 2011 Arab Spring is an interesting case study of how these tendencies turn into real strangleholds on knowledge. The researchers wanted to examine 'how social media, and more specifically Twitter, can offer a platform for the co-construction of news by journalists and the public', using the tweets of Andy Carvin. Carvin, who worked for America's National Public Radio, was a prolific tweeter credited with playing an important role in connecting the protestors with the outside world – a symbol, if you like, of Twitter's democratic potential. There was nothing democratic, however, about accessing data. The authors used several different kinds of software to harvest Carvin's tweets, but only gained access to the full data set when it was given to them by the man himself. More to the point, Carvin only had them because Twitter gave him the file, which belonged to them.

Even if you can access the 'firehose' and tools to make sense of it, it isn't clear the data are worth the effort. Media researchers seek rich explanations for how people live with media. Even researchers who do appreciate the value of studying Twitter as a new style of open political discourse admit that claims have their limits. Bruns and Burgess (2012), for example, qualified their study of the #ausvotes hashtag as a distinct political narrative in the Australian Federal Election of 2011 with the recognition that this conversation circulated among a minority of tech savvy, affluent 'political news junkies', where caustic comments directed at campaign messages 'can be understood as a mildly subversive, if largely inconsequential, form of speaking truth to power' (2012, 395).

For critics, then, Twitter is at the cusp of the argument that there are good reasons to ask whether Big Data does more harm than good when it comes to understanding the social world. In fact, there is almost an architectural desire to make that world disappear into bundles of data. Consequently, a good deal of effort has gone into detailing how Big Data builds barriers to knowledge: Twitter frequently features in exemplification. Twitter's capacity to obscure political conversations, and Donald Trump's prolific use of the platform, thus made the entrepreneur's political ambitions a significant historical moment in research on media, elections and democracy.

Big Data, Donald Trump and Nate Silver

This is all the more so given how one of Big Data's leading luminaries, Nate Silver, used Trump to explain the limitations of statistics in understanding voters. Nate Silver's '538' blog offered interesting reasons for why scientific polls using sophisticated surveying methods produced at best mystifying, and at worst downright misleading, accounts of Trump's appeal. Silver won renown as a precociously gifted statistician with almost supernatural predictive ability. Counterintuitively, he spent a lot of time bursting the bubble around statistical modelling methods. In *The Signal and the Noise* (2012), Silver warned that we are not enjoying an era of better predictions of everything from the weather to voting, and Trump's early 2016 standings in news polls were a case in point. More or less across the board, polls showed Trump leading the Republican race for months. However, primary campaign polls were historically bad at calling the winner. In these kinds of contests, popularity was one thing, voting was another. This was likely to be especially true of Trump, given the different reasons being propounded for his success. Was he a lightning rod for resentment against the political establishment? A symptom of a 'power failure' within the Republican leadership? The benefactor of wildly disproportionate media coverage? Whatever the answer, the lesson was that polls did a poor job of explaining America's political mood. Did Trump's poll success represent genuine popularity? And what had brought that about? Both questions remained mysteries (Silver, 2016a). Indeed, Silver fell victim to his own prediction. After months of dismissing Trump's nomination chances, the latter-day Nostradamus confessed The Donald's victory proved the limitations of his methods (Silver, 2016b).

Silver's criticisms represented profoundly important perspectives on the use of numbers to understand society through election case studies. Throughout the 20th century, scholars had used statistics to produce forensic explanation of voting behaviours, but were aware of two important qualifications in this pursuit. The first was that media were driving significant changes in what elections represented as events in cultural history. The second was that the use of numbers in political science was itself a form of cultural history, where the role of human interpretation and the biases in data collection, storage and use were factors to be considered at the analytical stage. No one claims that numbers provide an objective picture of what happens in elections. Nate Silver became important as a figure who applied the same argument to a new era of numbers with apparently impeccable objectivity credentials – the era of Big Data.

Silver's observations about Trump connect current debates on Big Data to a longer tradition where elections have been used to make sense of the power of numbers as tools for cultural historians. It is, in many respects, a variant on quarrels over the relative merits of quantitative and qualitative methods. It also relates to the question of how media affect political practice, where elections can be understood as events that either drive or exhibit the forces of mediatization in action. Finally, although Big Data does represent different modes of generating and analysing quantitative data about how culture works and how people behave, this knowledge is best understood through critical research principles that have been at play in media studies for several decades. In particular, the idea that media industries affect knowledge through the structure of their message systems is now an insight that reaches more visibly into the research process itself, given the deliberate space between the amount of data generated about media users and the amount of that data that becomes available to public scrutiny. In this respect, Big Data research is characterized by a remarkably clear view that any method of any value must be informed by well-developed theory. To put this more simply, the new Big Data era, and people like Silver, underline the counterintuitive position that knowledge begins with the detailed analysis of what isn't and can't be known, given the tools available to most analysts most of the time. To begin to understand, let's go back to post-war Britain.

KEY PARADIGM: PSEPHOLOGY

The birth of psephology

At the end of the Second World War, a young British Army lieutenant called David Butler returned to his studies in political science at Nuffield College, Oxford. Back at his desk, he commenced using statistics to provide sophisticated, multidimensional explanations for British voting patterns. He believed that new data methods could revolutionize understanding of how Britain voted (Butler, 1998). Butler's work came to the attention of none other than Winston Churchill. In 1950, Britain's most experienced parliamentarian asked the 25-year-old political scientist to explain the nation's post-war mood. Soon, Butler was recognized as the founder of psephology – the study of electoral facts (Ranney, 1976).

Butler was the Nate Silver of his day. His knack for analysis established him as the driving force behind the Nuffield election studies, 'one of post-war political science's most massive enterprises' (Ranney, 1976, 217). These studies became the authoritative accounts of British political facts. Part of their success was attributed to Butler's scepticism about statistical truths. Early on, Butler advised that a detailed understanding of why people voted as they did in the past did not translate into an ability to predict how they would do so in the future (see Bale, 2012). He regarded election research as an inherently 'messy' business, given that it involved the complicated intersection of cultural and institutional life. The combination of statistical skill combined with a critical awareness of the limitations of his art placed Butler at the centre of British television election coverage for 60 years. Retiring from media work in 2015, Butler did his best to avoid predicting the outcome of the British election of that year (Wallop, 2015). The question missed the point of his life's work.

Psephology and Big Data

The Butler/Silver analogy ties the new interests in Big Data to key themes in studies of media and power. Butler and Silver shared the view that statistics offer valuable tools for building intricate cultural histories. Silver was unashamedly 'pro science and pro-technology', but added 'numbers have no way of speaking for themselves. … We imbue them with meaning … we may construe them in self-serving ways that are detached from their reality' (Silver, 2012, 8). Butler was similarly smitten with the new explanatory power of post-war social statistics. The post-war provision of social housing in the UK, for example, provided a wealth of unprecedented data on lifestyle gradations within the working classes that could break voting patterns down into finer classifications (Butler, 1955). Yet the key to locking this potential lay in subordinating numbers to the broader dictates of cultural history:

> I have … wondered at the complex of family history and neighbourhood pressure, of house ownership and class status, that has determined their

vote. ... I have always been conscious of the gaps in my knowledge of British economic geography and local history. (Butler, 1983, 15)

Butler wanted to dismiss electoral 'myths', by which he meant contestable simplifications of voting behaviours, but warned there was more to the project than making sophisticated statistical associations between voting and demographic factors. To take such a view was to lose sight of elections as historical snapshots. Butler feared that the very science he was pioneering ran the risk of writing self-defeating cultural histories with no people in them.

A second sentiment shared by Silver and Butler was that media had changed elections, complicating data analysis in the process. Silver complained that television encouraged data analysis that served dramatic effect more than edification. This had more to do with the transition of politics into a form of media entertainment than it did with the improved powers of polls (Silver, 2012). Asked to define landmarks in post-war electoral politics, Butler named the arrival of television and the rise of public relations. Butler's interest in PR presaged many of the themes that were to characterize Silver's intervention in the Big Data arena. The former had been struck by the 1997 Labour Party's innovative understanding of how detailed surveillance of the media scene, accompanied with data from qualitative and quantitative voter research, produced a nimble campaign where opposition messages were rapidly countered with crowd-pleasing counter-arguments. Labour's spectacular rebranding in the public mind was produced by Big Data and small data. It used qualitative data to listen to audiences, in focus groups, but it also kept a forensic eye on opposition press coverage and learned to rebut criticisms as soon as they were made. The main effect of this, however, has been to make performative politics the supreme measure of campaigning.

Butler believed media had changed elections as historical events. He considered elections as events that made the mechanics of politics more visible by placing them 'under strain'. By the late 20th century, media had become central to campaigning practice, and elections displayed the media's political role in full flow. During elections, societies consciously put their full sense-making capacities to political use, and media had become key ingredients in this process (Butler, 1998). Consequently, the study of elections was more about making sense of this change, rather than simply predicting winners and losers.

So Butler's psephology defined elections as political, historical and cultural rituals, wherein the scholar's role was to explore the complexity of voting behaviours. In a similar vein, Silver argued that media harnessed sophisticated data-gathering methods to manufacture the very myths that Butler abhorred. Silver feared that the spectacular nature of media elections transformed data into something that was used to tell stories, rather than the truth. So the new topic of Big Data reflects old ideas about the role of media in the production of knowledge, and the role of media studies as a topic that plays close attention to how political truth is created and shared in society. Silver used Trump as an exemplar. There's a world of difference between saying that Donald Trump was ahead in the polls and concluding that he was a person that a sizeable portion of

American voters actually liked. In the early 21st century, this was a media matter since poll stories are a staple of political news.

When we add into the mix how media users contributed to the data explosion through social media reactions to candidates, and how these reactions became part of the media story about how audiences read elections, as it did in #Asktrump, then we are left with an intriguing convergence between psephology and Big Data. The staging of elections as media events has affected the use of statistics in understanding voters. We might say, for example, that Silver's comments about the mystery of Trump's popularity were an example of the myth making that Butler deplored. At any rate, there are dangers at play in how media and statistics collude to conjure impressions of media reality, and the provision of Big Data by social media users adds to the confusion, not least because it conflates the identities of citizen, audience and participant. But the point is not to dismiss the value of Big Data; it is to appreciate how knowing what we can say with it starts by thinking about what it can't do.

KEY METHOD: CAPTURING AND ANALYSING TWEETS

Fortunately, the alliance between Big Data and QDA software makes it pretty easy to see how these conceptual observations transfer into research practice. NVivo, for example, easily seduces with its power to automatically capture, sort and analyse social media data with the tick of a box. Evidently, the lesson so far is that there's no point in producing word clouds, charts and the like unless we think carefully about what this information says. To see how this works in practice, let's consider what following NVivo guidelines for analysing social media content tells us about the media relationship that Trump established with the rest of the world.

Choosing a case study

The first step in using Big Data is to think about what to look at. Given the plethora of evidence, it is important to get the story straight on how a particular data set relating to a particular event has been selected. When it comes to elections, if we follow Butler's advice then the task is to choose evocative historical snapshots of the cultural mood at a significant moment. With that in mind, the data set we are going to work on is the reaction to a tweet that Trump sent shortly after it became clear that he had won the race as Republican nominee.

On March 5, 2016 Trump tweeted a picture of himself eating a taco alongside the legend 'Happy #CincoDeMayo! The best taco bowls are made in Trump Tower Grill. I love Hispanics!'. The tweet met a wave of criticism as a crass effort to win over Hispanic voters, given his racist attack on Mexico. The message seemed to glory in ignorance. Far from seeking forgiveness, Trump revelled in his victory by promoting his commercial interests, appropriating the very culture that he had gone out of his way to malign (Parker, 2016).

So, here was an incident where it was possible to see what social media users thought about Trump at a key moment when criticisms about his campaign came to a head in public. Trump's victory in the face of unapologetic racism evoked the possibility that his campaign had worked beyond expectations because of his bigotry. The decision to celebrate a political milestone by basking in racism seemed to support this view. But what would Twitter users make of it, and what could we say about this political moment by capturing tweets?

Capturing and making sense of tweets

Having selected a plausible case study, the next step is to figure out how to load it into NVivo. Here, we encounter a series of good news/bad news scenarios. Positively, there are a range of tutorials on YouTube that will teach you how to catch tweets, then load them into the software. Negatively, two problems immediately emerge. The first is that we discover that the PC version of the software has more functionality than the one available to Mac users. The second is that whatever the platform, Twitter controls the amount of tweets that it is possible to capture, so at base one can only view about 1% of the chatter about the event, and there is no way of telling how these tweets are selected. So, the very first practical issue one faces isn't figuring out the technology, but figuring out the point of engaging with research so confined by the proprietorial interests of media, software and hardware companies.

Here, the strategy is to go for the PC option, based on techniques outlined in NVivo's tutorials (QSR International, 2015). Following instructions, this study did a Twitter search for the hashtag #trumptaco, captured those tweets via a plug-in called NCapture, then loaded the captured tweets as a data set into NVivo for PC. This process captured 11,099 tweets. The next task was to infuse this data with meaning. The key lies in using descriptive statistics to ask questions as well as find answers. Once we understand that, the simplest features of NVivo's descriptive analysis in fact represent useful tools for addressing the limitations of mediated democracy and our ability to fathom how it works.

Critically visualizing descriptive data

Remember, the idea is to critically evaluate evidence by placing it in a theoretical context. So the analysis here confines itself to considering the complexity of descriptive data. The process described above gathers what looks like an impressive data set, ordered to produce instant information, and provides an architecture for further study. Captured tweets identify the tweeter and his or her location. Locations are mapped, meaning that we can either look at global pictures or drill down into specific localities, or indeed take a comparative look at reactions in different places. We can start all of this by simply hitting a 'map' tab in NVivo. The program also 'clusters' bundles of linguistically similar tweets.

NVivo produces tree diagrams that map together Twitter user names according to similar content. Other information includes the biographies attached to each Twitter handle, and of course the tweets themselves.

There's no doubt that this gathering and sorting function is useful, but it's just as clear that the harvested and sorted data mean nothing without critical reflection. There's no way of knowing why these tweets in particular were selected (QSR International, 2015). Also, if you try repeating this exercise over a number of days, you'll get different results. Try a Twitter search ncapture for 'Trump' and 'taco' right now, and you'll see what I mean. The 'wow' factor of the map also dissolves once you realize that Twitter users can edit their location if they want to (QSR International, 2015).

So we're faced with a filtering process that we can't control, which makes it incumbent on us to consider how the choices that we do make, as researchers, might aggravate this problem. Let's go back to the beginning of the chapter, and the fact that political journalism about Trump-related Big Data probably told us very little about what was going on in the Republican primaries. Here, again, it would be possible to research how people attacked Trump's chutzpah. We could do this by using a word search. In this case, I ran a search for the 50 most used words in the sample, setting the minimum word length to four letters (to suit taco; anything less would have missed out a key term). 'Racism' occurs 828 times, with 'racist' making a further 506 appearances. So we could discuss how Trump's tweet made the issue of racism visible. Except we'd quickly notice, looking at these tweets, that it's very difficult to assess how racism entered the public vernacular. Almost 600 of those references are retweets of a CNN tweet about US Senator Elizabeth Warren accusing Trump of basing his campaign on pure racism. We might also note that 'racism' is 29th in the list of 50 most used words, and along with 'racist' is one of only two key words that gives any hint at any real political content. We are reminded that we are dealing with algorithms, not content, here by the fact that numbers one, two and three in the list are 'https', 'trump' and 'taco'.

It's tempting to say that descriptive data gained from the combination of Twitter and NVivo doesn't tell us much about anything other than what happens in Twitter and NVivo. Unless, of course, we want to think about how Big Data contributes to the transformation of mediatized politics into an exercise in entertaining myth making – the critical line of inquiry introduced by Butler and continued by Silver. If that is the case, then simple descriptive Big Data from Twitter demonstrates why Big Data makes it harder to figure out what people make of politics.

Something interesting happens with this data set if we use the chart function, tabulating the Twitter users and hashtags that dominated the conversation. Producing a three-dimensional chart produces a picture that can be related to critical views on the alienating aspects of electoral politics (see Figure 10).

The immediate impression is telling. @the realdonaldtrump stands like a skyscraper surveying the rest of the Twitterverse. For all the media controversy about the tweet, the main thing you could capture from Twitter in the

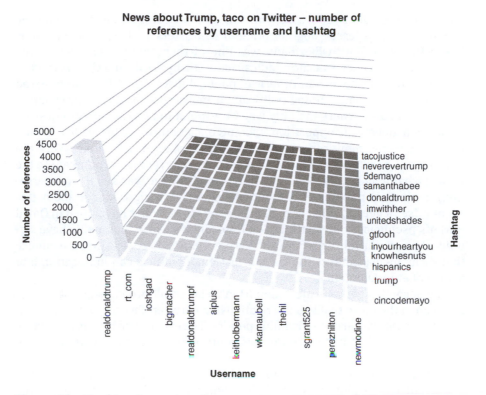

News about Trump, taco on Twitter – number of references by username and hashtag

Figure 10 Tracking Trump tweets

days afterwards was the voice of the man himself – his unapologetic micro-blogged advertorial accounted for almost 50% of the traffic captured. To be sure, the hashtags signal dissent (#inyourheartyouknowhesnuts, #never-trump). But looking at the top sources, it's hard to see a connection with popular resentment. Other listed tweeters included comedians Josh Gad and Jeff Dwoskin, broadcasters W. Kamau Bell and Keith Olbermann, news source *The Hill*, and celebrity blogger Perez Hilton. So, the evidence tells us this: if you used Twitter to figure out the political mood in America at the time when the world realized that Donald Trump would be the Republican's official candidate for President, then what you would have seen is a public conversation dominated by the man himself, where the most visible opposition came from other parts of the media sector, including significant contributions from the entertainment world.

In spite all of the reservations about what Big Data really says, and the admitted limitations of methods for importing and analysing this evidence, this is a pretty interesting finding that can ground some useful questions. The first is that, for all the advent of social media, televised people's forums and the like, political communication remains an elite game dominated by the logic of media businesses that want to enrapture audiences. If you looked at Twitter four days after the tweet, what you saw was a conversation dominated by Trump and, to a lesser degree, other broadcasters and entertainers. It is interesting that Keith Olbermann was one of them. Four years earlier, the famous American news anchor had caused a stir by criticizing the prevalence of aggressive hate speech in American political discourse. Olbermann feared that the effect of entertaining political journalism had turned politics into a gladiatorial sport, where the only way to respond to criticism was to destroy rather than debate the opposition. Trump's open taunting of his critics seemed to underline the significance of Olbermann's earlier observations. What the data did say, as mapped in Figure 10, was that whatever the event meant to the public, what it looked like when filtered through NVivo was an elite conversation/row between media elites. In that respect, this Big Data set about this event raises a question that complements the interest first developed in David Butler's psephology and continued in Nate Silver's work: that media have significant effects on politics. There are two possibilities here. The first is evidence that social media enhance the transformation of political communication into a form of entertainment.

The second is perhaps more important. This small project suggests a 'big' problem in the sense that it is the relationship between Twitter and NVivo that 'describes' this vision of entertaining politics. The experience here is one where the descriptive first impression of this controversy was that it was, above all else, a drama born of well-established media industries where news, theatrics and comedy coexist. In the context of critical debates about Big Data, it is important to consider the factors that indicate that this 'impression' is the product of the creation, harvesting and analysis of Big Data. In that sense, the fact that Big Data told us virtually nothing about how ordinary people felt about Trump's taco is really quite useful. If nothing else, it contributes to the conversation on why his victory was so surprising, and dismaying to so many: it was just too easy to write evidence-based stories about why it would never happen.

SIGNIFICANCE: BIG DATA ALERTS US TO THE TENSIONS BETWEEN DIFFERENT KINDS OF KNOWLEDGE

Big Data prompts considerable social unease. Our reliance on mobile and social media means that we generate rafts of personal information without meaning to or understanding where it goes and what it does. These technologies make an 'always on' world. We announce where we are, what we like and what we do to those interested in managing such things for political and/or economic reasons. Hence the public debates on cyber security and privacy. Clearly, Big Data has become a focus for research on the intersections of media technologies, media users and political power, and it is incumbent upon us, as media researchers, to consider what we can – and can't – do with it.

When making sense of what Big Data means for society and media research, one useful place to start is by thinking critically about a sense of optimism on social media and participatory culture. Twitter, for example, has been celebrated as a method that ordinary people can use to humiliate powerful people. When they do, they generate masses of information that can be easily downloaded into QDA software. This allows us to gather and analyse evidence about key media events, like elections, in completely new ways. The data, and the tools, are remarkably accessible: the data is public and the software is relatively easy to use to produce results. One of NVivo's key features, for example, is the capacity to download and analyse social media content from Twitter and Facebook. This capacity promises a unique insight into media events, as they happen. Not only can citizens do more, but researchers can say more about them.

The generation and capturing of Big Data has certainly changed what we can say about media users. However, figuring out what Big Data from social media says is incredibly difficult in practice – impossible, in fact, without critical insights. What looks like a flood of data is really a trickle that is controlled by the technologies of social media and analytical tools. In this sense, research using Big Data is subjected to a kind of media dependency that is itself unique. If researchers have never been so data rich, they have also, arguably, never been so tied to media message systems, broadly defined. According to some critics, Big Data is the latest version of a myth where systematic methods of gathering and ordering data reflect an objective system of data gathering and analysis that is unaffected by any kind of human bias (boyd and Crawford, 2012). The political consequences of this myth become more profound when it is tied to the commodification and gatekeeping power of the private media platforms that gather and selectively share Big Data.

That said, researchers who have revolutionized the applications of statistics to understanding elections have directed a considerable amount of time working through these issues, and their insights into what you can't claim for numbers and Big Data are a valuable position from which to generate critical insights into media politics that *leverage* the limitations of empirical analysis. When it comes to Twitter, and NVivo, bearing these points in mind makes simple descriptive analysis a useful means of demonstrating the transformation of electioneering into a form of media entertainment, and resisting the temptation to create an image of widespread popular participation in those politics by cherry-picking the odd satirical quote that the odd member of the public might direct at elite politicians. In this sense, this 'simple' use of Big Data poses a very big question for media and democracy. Does the ability to critique the political establishment in very public ways through social media disguise ongoing imbalances, where electoral politics remains an elite sport? And if so, what does this say about the degree of participation that happens in media cultures? These questions are further explored in the following chapters on policy and audiences.

CHAPTER SUMMARY

- Big Data reminds us that all forms of evidence about media influence have to be interpreted through well-established critical insights into the relative merits of quantitative and qualitative methods.

- Big Data is not simply evidence, but is the product of message systems. It is a form of media representation that has to be interpreted.

- Using simple descriptive methods is a useful way to demonstrate how Big Data works as a narrative about new modes of media power.

- Used this way, Big Data is also a useful tool to assess levels of popular participation in media culture.

14

RESEARCHING MEDIA POLICY

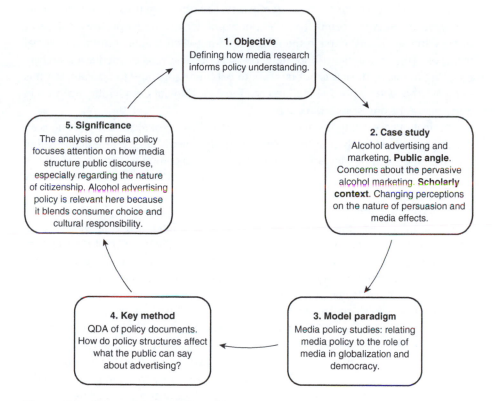

Figure 11 Researching media policy

OBJECTIVE: DEFINING HOW MEDIA RESEARCH INFORMS POLICY UNDERSTANDING

Since the turn of the century, events like the UK's Leveson Inquiry into intrusive journalism have piqued international interest in media standards: what they are and who should enforce them (Maras, 2014). Media policy is now recognized as a public well-being issue, and a wealth of information on policy-making processes is now in the public domain. In this chapter, we will see how qualitative data assessment (QDA) methods can interpret policy documents in relation to themes of citizenship, consumption and the role of media in democracy. The objective is to show how media policy builds ways of seeing that affect how politicians, media professionals, academics and the public explain the relationship between media content and social inclusion. This indicates an important point about the role of media research in directing media futures. It is not our task to tell the media how to operate, but it is our job to show how policy initiatives can move notions of democratic inclusion in particular, and contestable, directions.

UK alcohol advertising is the case study. The regulation of alcohol marketing is an evocative topic *vis-à-vis* the general challenges of media policy research. Alcohol advertising is an enthralling art, ingeniously integrating commercial messages, leisure sites and pleasure. As such, it exemplifies intimate connections between media policy and broader experiences of living in societies where citizenship is often understood in terms of consumption.

To make this point, the chapter pays particular attention to the work of Peter Lunt and Sonia Livingstone, scholars who have deftly related the practice of media policy making to global political trends. Lunt and Livingstone's (2009) work relates policy issues to changed understandings of media influence, and the role of media in forming public life. In particular, they note how media policy has become a testing ground for efforts to define citizenship in terms of consumer rights.

Lunt and Livingstone (2009) argue that UK media regulation shows that it is hard to mobilize an effective consumer-led regulatory regime. While the notion of 'customer satisfaction' is attractive and comprehensible, its relationship to citizenship and political rights is less so. Ironically, sophisticated policy mechanisms giving the public a say on media content make it hard to talk about the complexities of commercial speech. This is all the more so since responsible, consultative media policy is by definition slower to respond to changing media landscapes than are advertising and marketing strategies.

To test these ideas, the chapter explores a study analysing complaints made to the UK Advertising Standards Authority about alcohol advertising between 2010 and 2015 (Ruddock, 2017, in press). The study translated concepts on the risks of advertising and the effectiveness of media regulation into a set of thematic indicators for analysing publicly available materials on offensive advertising. The study used thematic analysis to identify patterns in policy documents and to explain the significance of those patterns in relation to contemporary media policy theory.

In summary, this chapter:

- Explains why the topic of alcohol marketing encapsulates changing understandings of persuasion, behaviour and influence, and how those changes are a policy challenge.
- Locates the significance of Lunt and Livingstone as key figures who integrate media policy within the general management of risk in consumer society.
- Shows how regulatory regimes have generated research data that can be analysed by theoretically-informed thematic analysis.

CASE STUDY: ALCOHOL ADVERTISING AND MARKETING

The management of alcohol advertising and marketing reflects global concerns about ensuring public interest through media policy, and is therefore a useful lens to identify globally recognizable challenges. Bearing this in mind, policy interventions in one part of the world – in this instance the UK – can contribute to the understanding of media issues elsewhere. To make this case, it is important to find evidence of such global concerns, alongside similarly worldwide patterns of academic takes on how advertising and marketing work as a threat to the public – if, indeed, that's what they do.

The public face: Media sport, alcohol and kids

2016 saw a wave of new concerns about alcohol and marketing during televised sport events. In Australia, medical bodies called for a ban on alcohol advertising during televised cricket and rugby league games, given the likelihood that children would be exposed to them. Elsewhere, politicians expressed incredulity at the fact that the national cricket team wore the logo of a beer manufacturer on its uniform. Cricket is the game closest to the heart of Australian national identity, and cricket players have been aspirational figures since the early 20th century (Hutchins, 2005), so turning them into beer billboards bordered on a national insult.

Things weren't much better in Europe. The European Football Championship tournament of that year, sponsored by Danish brewer Carlsberg, televised matches that featured digital billboards next to pitches. As a result, it was estimated that viewing audiences were exposed to a Carlsberg slogan once every 72 seconds (Moss, 2016). Games, in a sense, became extended commercials.

There is an obvious contradiction between sporting tournaments that champion physical fitness and the promotion of a carcinogenic drug. Drinking and driving is another idea that doesn't work, and so it is unsurprising that Dutch brewer Heineken's sponsorship of Formula 1 motor racing fell foul of the same criticism (Reuters, 2016). Given new knowledge on the health risks associated with alcohol, it made sense, so the story went, to take just as tough a line on drinks sponsorship as had been applied to the tobacco industry.

And this wasn't just a European thing. Drinks marketing experts noted that the sponsorship targeting of soccer and F1 was really aimed at Asian markets. This was where brewers sought new markets. Hence F1's similar desire to expand its fan base by staging events in Malaysia, Singapore and China provided just the 'Trojan Horse' that companies like Heineken needed (Grand Prix 247, 2016).

Cumulatively, these observations nodded towards a changed model of media marketing, one that recognized the mobility of media events, media consumers, and the integration of media and leisure experiences. To see what this means, let's sojourn to the Caribbean. In that same year, a much less well-known, exclusive sporting entertainment event gave a clue about the magnitude of the changes afoot. Appleton Estate Jamaican rum teamed up with digital media provider Digicel to sponsor a four-day party to promote the Caribbean Hero Premier League T20 cricket tournament (The Gleaner, 2016). The event was notable for an especially clear articulation of how alcohol marketing cleverly blends with ideas about entertainment, pleasure, tradition and even politics, embodying the idea that the identities of the consumer and the citizen can happily coexist. An Appleton spokesperson put it like this: 'We are rum people and we love cricket! … The party stand will show the world how Jamaicans party!' (The Gleaner, 2016, no page). More soberly, Digicel observed 'we have combined two essential passions, music and sport, and use it to unite people across the region' (2016, no page).

Appleton embraced transformed relationships among drinks marketing, media and sport, and the drift of citizenship towards consumption. These changes turn a Venn diagram into a circle, taking spheres of media, business and culture and widening their 'overlap' to a point where it is hard to see anything more than one great big bubble of fun. The idea was to blend symbolic action and material experience to help people *feel* the benefits of citizenship as consumption. The aspirations to turn national cultural life into a commercial opportunity speaks to the political significance of advertising regulation.

Scholarly context: Putting consumers to work

Research validates the notion that these ambitions are global. O'Brien et al. (2015) validated qualms about sport by counting alcohol advertising on Australian screens. They found that 87% of daytime alcohol promotions were carried by sporting programmes, and 86% of evening alcohol ads were also carried by sports content. They concluded that sport was central to the problem of responsible advertising because it carried positive images of drinking to daytime audiences, including children.

You might point to the controversy about the correlation between exposure and behaviour when it comes to the effectiveness of alcohol marketing (see for example, Gunter, Hansen and Touri, 2011). But that really isn't the point. The study noted material changes in the formal language of advertising, and the extent that these shifts quickly challenged policy. O'Brien et al. (2015) simply observed that contemporary Australian sport, as a day and night free-to-air television staple, effortlessly violated the principle that children should be shielded from alcohol promotions. Remarkably, nobody appeared to notice or mind that much.

The Australian evidence joins with other studies noting that evolving media practices outpace efforts to regulate them when it comes to selling alcohol (Nicholls, 2012; Carah, Brodmerkel and Hernandez, 2014; Uzunoğlu and Öksüz, 2014; Alhabash et al., 2015). In particular, social media let drinkers say all kinds of things about drinking and fun that regulation prohibits in advertising (Nicholls, 2012; Carah et al., 2014). Crucially, this shifts the attention from drinking behaviour to communication behaviour as an advertising effect. According to some accounts, alcohol marketing mainly 'wins' by naturalizing associations among drinking, pleasure, sociality and tradition (Nicholls, 2006). In doing so, the alcohol topic frames the 'problem' of marketing as a 'problem' of democracy, and the forms of communication that democracy needs. This prob-lem is especially related to a trend toward discussing rights, such as the right to buy (Lunt and Livingstone, 2007, 2009).

Public and scholarly concerns about the role of alcohol marketing in sporting events speak to new modes of advertising, new understandings of the behav-iours that such communication may encourage, and new views on the politicization of consumer culture. Traditionally, the question has been whether exposure leads to drinking, a possibility that is the cornerstone of efforts to reg-ulate what advertisers can say (Sjøvaag, 2014). Critical advertising research suggests the main effect of commercial messages has been to equate consump-tion and happiness in the social imagination (Leiss, Kline and Jhally, 2002). Initially, this was achieved through modes of advertising where products blended into stories that 'sold' lifestyles (Leiss et al., 2002). What was being sold was less the product and more the idea that consumption and well-being went hand in hand. Contemporary scholarship notes an evolution; now advertising and marketing organize the material structure of leisure, based around the consumption of product-centred events.

Consider Appleton again. The rum makers sought to popularize their product by getting their customers to promote it – and even pay for the pleasure. Cricket and music fans were charged around US$40 to access a VIP area of a Jamaican cricket ground, where they would embody the links between sport, music, drinking, fun and Jamaican national identity. Thus, where the focus of advertising policy has been on content – the way that ideas are presented to consumers – advertising strategies are more about encouraging consumer behaviours that create commercial messages. Consumers are not just persuaded, but are also persuaded to persuade.

Concerns about advertising, media, sport and drinking, then, crystallize into a broader shift where advertising becomes integrated into material culture through a blend of media practices, many of them place-based, where the commercial language becomes something that is used as well as received. This idea – that advertising has in some ways determined the very language that we use to make sense of the form itself – is the crux of the policy challenge.

In their book on the changing vista of advertising practice, Carah and Brodmerkel (2016) explained how the practices criticized in sport gestured to innovations across the leisure sector. The pleasures of drinking are routinely blended into experience through interactions between space and social media. Their work on this synthesis was a particularly lucid account of why media policy is so difficult to formulate and activate in the face of fluid communications practices, and how, as a result, the policy forum is one that graphically outlines the difficulties of making inclusive cultures in the face of the synthesis between consumer logic, media practices and lived experience.

If it's hard enough to regulate advertising content (e.g. Ruddock, 2013, 2017), what can you do when an entire island, and all the people on it, become living commercial endorsements? This is the issue Australia faced when a brewery leased an entire island off the country's north coast, and changed its name to 'XXXX'. During a four-year rental, the brewery first invited its customers – mostly male – to share through social media their ideas about how to turn the place into their ideal holiday destination, and then invited them to come and 'live the dream' at a real location. This wasn't your common 'men 'n' beer' fantasy, though. XXXX also turned its attention to concerns about sustainability and environmentally-friendly tourism, placing a benign twist on familiar themes (Carah and Brodmerkel, 2016).

Looking at social media content generated around the place, Carah and Brodmerkel (2016) noted that this even became a place where men could revel in sexism. When male drinkers discussed it online, XXXX was broadly imagined as a space where women were either absent, barely dressed and/or servile. There was plenty of evidence that women found this offensive and engaged in social media in vigorous criticism, but the architecture of the furore stepped outside the advertising regulation framework altogether. If XXXX had been advertised as a place of gender apartheid, it could have been subjected to formal complaint and redress. By asking its customers to share their ideas, though, the same idea emerged from social media storms that appeared private. The outcome was an impression that the island was a place where boys could be boys, thanks to beer. Carah and Brodmerkel thought this epitomized the frightening potential of contemporary alcohol marketing. 'XXXX Island' was a real place built by untrammelled commercial speech, spoken by consumers. The interface between people, places, social media and consumption created a social discourse about drinking far beyond the reach of any regulation.

Overall, alcohol marketing vividly demonstrates how advertising creates a rich language through which users express a range of ideas about pleasure and identity. This ability to encroach on common sense encapsulates the challenges of regulation. But there's more at stake here. When 'XXXX Island' leveraged public sympathy by addressing sustainability, it ingeniously married consumption with progressive citizenship. This counts because associations between citizen and consumer identities are the nub of 21st-century media policy. Hence, the matter of alcohol advertising, in terms of its changing practices and modes of influence, can be used to examine key practical challenges in formulating media policy. To flesh this idea out, we can ask a simple question. Do policy mechanisms create as rich a language to complain about commercial messages as advertising does to celebrate and legitimate the value of consumption? Such a focus poses the idea that consumption is a powerful political language still further. It asks this question: What do we learn about the nature of political participation through media by looking at how policy includes the public in conversations about how the media should work?

KEY PARADIGM: CITIZEN-CENTRED POLICY STUDIES

Academics on the 'problem' of media policy

Just as we might see alcohol advertising as a 'cutting edge' in the evolution of commercial speech, and its effects, so too reflections on media policy carry insights into the role of media in global governance. Sonia Livingstone and Peter Lunt have been especially effective in explaining this shift. Their work will be described in greater length a little later, but for now it's worth noting that Lunt and Livingstone characterize media policy as part of a general trend where states turn greater attention to managing the risks of global economic and technological change. Media policy is a component of general efforts to organize social and economic life within the parameters of a key historical shift (Lunt and Livingstone, 2009).

So media policy studies exist within the recognition that global media industries contribute to the metamorphosis of democracy and citizenship, communication-driven entities that are affected by the operation of media industries (Blumler and Coleman, 2015). Consequently, the extent to which a national policy framework creates the possibility for anybody who wants to complain, about, say, the perceived sexism in the promotion of 'XXXX Island', reflects how effectively a democracy is working. It is about much more than advertising.

Along these lines, scholars have noted several encumbrances on policy initiatives that wrestle with more agile commercial communication networks. In Europe, criticisms have been made that states have struggled to even understand structural changes in media industries, much less to manage them (Coastache and Llorens, 2015; Evens and Donders, 2016). Added to this are difficulties of coming to terms with diversity and its relationship to inclusion. Too often, critics say, diversity is equated with the number of content choices audiences have, with too little attention being paid to the role of media in facilitating dialogue (Gibbons, 2015). The notion that commercial media environments popularize languages that can't express many ideas is important to the following analysis.

It is tempting to compare the fight between advertising and policy to an unfair boxing bout: in one corner, athletic alcohol marketing, hitting audiences with dizzying combinations of consumption, media and a life worth living; in the other corner, ageing heavyweight media policy, sluggishly struggling to get off its stool. Things get worse when you consider the argument that the mismatch expresses a fundamental flaw in western media. Pickard (2014) argued that the palpable failure of commercial systems to serve the public interest is literally unspeakable – it is impossible to conceive, and even harder to find a language to express, given that our language is dominated by the interests that policy seeks to counter.

These conversations signal international interest in how media regulation challenges are tied to the future of global democracy. Indeed, the fear is that foxes have been left to care for chickens. Regulation has to work with the systems of commercial speech and thought that it is supposed to manage.

Lunt and Livingstone: Using UK media policy to understand the global media challenge

When trying to make sense of all of these changes, within the understanding that there are common conceptual themes that drive questions about media policy in different parts of the world, Lunt and Livingstone's analysis of the formulation of the UK's 2003 OFCOM Act served as a handy statement on key principles.

The 2003 OFCOM Act tried to create an effective mechanism for including public opinion in the policing of advertising standards. Lunt and Livingstone's review of the background to the Act is vital in establishing how looking at British alcohol advertising regulation reflects global policy matters. Indeed, Livingstone and Lunt (2007) characterized the Act as a microcosm of regulatory challenges crossing western nations, most of which struggled to define the state's role in preserving public interest media in an environment that generally favoured *de*regulation and the empowerment of media choice. The logic of this patently contradictory strategy – protecting people by doing less centralized policing of media – was twofold: to create regulatory agility and to bring media relations in line with other forms of risk management. The common ground was the idea that equity and justice frequently converged around consumer choice (Lunt and Livingstone, 2009). In other words, here was an historical juncture where long-running debates on the nature of democracy – the balance to be struck between individual liberty and collective welfare, and the extent to which the latter could be realized through the former – were squarely located at the centre of media policy.

By reviewing the drafting and implementing of the policy, interviewing both the public and key people involved in making the legislation, Lunt and Livingstone were able to point out that 'agile' policy is inherently difficult to realize. Properly considered public policy makes genuine attempts to consult diverse groups. So, good policy can never be as dynamic as commercial media. Consultative policy has to be slow. That said, one of the things that slowed down the OFCOM Act, and continued to dog its implementation, was the controversial effort to treat citizens' rights as synonymous with consumer rights.

The notion that citizen and consumer were synonyms was the topic of heated disagreements at the drafting stage. The House of Lords saw vociferous rows between those who wanted to preserve a notion of citizenship that was innocent of economic markets and others who favoured consumer as a practical, modern identity that reflected how people actually understood their place in life. When it came to the public, Lunt and Livingstone's research on popular attitudes found evidence to support both sides. People liked the idea of being responsible for their own choices, but still wanted protection from market forces that they did not understand. A preference for either more or less central regulation depended on the topic of conversation. People liked the idea of being able to choose what to watch, but wanted heavy regulation in areas like the financial services, areas where, the perception was, it was very hard to make informed consumer choices.

Consequently the 2003 OFCOM Act was a microcosm of global trends in risk management, where individual empowerment was preferred to state influence. Naturally, this also made it a case study in how media regulation was enveloped in general issues of social management. In practice, OFCOM has been given the job of reconciling identities, arguably irreconcilable identities. Lunt and Livingstone concluded that in effect OFCOM has deferred to consumer identities. This makes sense in that the public have a better sense of what it means to be a consumer. However, in Lunt and Livingstone's view, the outcome has made OFCOM an economic rather than cultural regulator. Its mechanisms for protecting public good assume that audiences are rational, motivated, informed individuals who know how to act appropriately (Lunt and Livingstone, 2009).

So, how accurate is this picture? One way to find out is to look at how a complaints-based system works. In this regard, complaints about alcohol marketing and advertising, made under the OFCOM framework, represent a useful case study. Concerns about the effects of alcohol advertising, especially when they are directed at minors, have been widely noted (see for example, Nicholls, 2012). OFCOM established an architecture allowing the public to have their say on the issue. So, what did they say, and what did their speech tell us about the richness of language that a consumer-based regulation system affords? Is policy as adept as advertising in facilitating public talk that we can all hear and participate in?

KEY METHOD: QDA ANALYSIS OF COMPLAINTS ARCHIVES

In 2010, OFCOM appointed the Advertising Standards Authority (ASA) to regulate UK advertising (OFCOM, no date). The ASA develops good conduct codes, advises advertisers on compliance issues, and fields complaints about all forms of advertising deemed to violate these standards. When a complaint is filed, it is put before a panel comprising advertising industry executives, media experts, and others with knowledge of media public interest issues. They adjudicate every complaint and, since 2010, each has been recorded in an online archive.

In a study on complaints made to the ASA about alcohol marketing (Ruddock, 2017, in press), I took the position that the body's online archive provided data that could be used to identify 'speech patterns' in the public voice on advertising. The topic of alcohol was selected for several reasons. First, in the UK, the issue of alcohol abuse has articulated bigger political ideas around free choice, responsibility, and the state's responsibility to save weak citizens from themselves (Nicholls, 2006). Indeed, there is a striking parallel between the quarrels over the consumer/citizen relationship and ideas of freedom and paternalism that have characterized alcohol legislation for centuries (Nicholls, 2006). For this reason, adjudications on alcohol advertising represented a defensible way of sampling complaints from an organization that receives 30,000 complaints every year. It is possible to tell a story about what they are about in general, cultural terms. Additionally, the perception that alcohol marketing has been especially innovative in its modes of evading regulation made this data set an ideal place to weigh up the position that media regulation was implicated in broader risk assessment regimes, which are the cornerstone of governance modes throughout the west.

Eighty-six complaints adjudicated by the ASA from 2010 to 2015 were loaded as PDFs into NVivo and were coded using criteria designed to address the diversity of the debate. To examine how far this mechanism provided the public with a sophisticated voice that could address a variety of concerns, the following thematic codes were used:

- Who lodged the complaint (private consumer or public body)?

- What kind of 'risk' did they complain about (encouraging 'bingeing', linking alcohol with success, exposure of minors or appeal to minors, offensiveness, misleading claims)?

- What medium was involved (television, social media, below-the-line promotion, radio, press and cinema ads)?

- What kind of organization prompted the offence (alcohol manufacturer, media company or retail outlet)?

- What was the outcome of the complaint?

- How did the defendant respond (did they apologise or mount defences based on disputed readings of ethical practices)? (Ruddock, 2017, in press)

As with the social media chapter, the approach here combined quantitative and qualitative methods (a) to discover general patterns of response, finding out who tended to complain and about what, and (b) to develop a rationale for exploring particular case studies in more depth. Since it was possible for more than one person or organization to complain about campaigns that could cross many media and could be perceived as objectionable for several reasons, the coding scheme provided an organized way to identify rich cases touching on multiple themes.

The first stage in the analysis was to look at indicators from simple statistics. Initially, modal responses were identified by looking at the top answers for each category. In this case, the modal complaint came from an individual about a television advertisement, and the commonest objection was that the ad would reach or appeal to minors (although many also complained about the linking of drinking with various modes of social success). Alcohol companies usually contested these complaints, but typically lost.

These numbers suggested a few things. First, if the focus on alcohol marketing had moved online and into physical spaces, the focus of public attention remained onscreen. Second, the thing that people cared about the most was protecting young people, hence the prescience of studies that would show how pro-drinking messages were 'leaking' into sporting media events that minors could access. Third, prospects for successful complaints were relatively good, although very few people bothered to make them. So, the public could speak effectively through policy, but few did and in the main their discussion evaded the more innovative edge of marketing.

In addition to typical cases, quantitative coding also helped identify others that were unusual in that they attracted diverse complaints from diverse communities about campaigns that used more than one medium. These cases, small in number though they were, were worth scrutinizing as examples of how complaints worked when public interest was attracted to the ingenuity of modern marketing.

As we have seen, each case was coded according to six criteria, understanding that each case could accrue multiple 'points' (most obviously, being objectionable for more than one reason). Most items scored 6 or 7, but 9 complaints stood out by accruing 10–11 points. These were multimedia campaigns prompting concerns from citizens and public bodies for more than one reason. Most of these cases (seven) involved social media. While all of these did involve complaints that such ads could be seen by minors, five also objected to connections between alcohol and sex, and four criticized the targeting of students.

These coding patterns allowed a specification of the kinds of cases where alcohol complaints could be connected to broader observations about changing modes of alcohol marketing that (a) push alcohol further into social life and (b) address notions of citizenship and rational consumption. An ideal test case would be an ad that used more than one medium, and that was complained about by more than one body for more than one reason.

Enter the 2012 ASA ruling on 'Eat My Disco' (Advertising Standards Authority, 2012). An entertainment company called Eat My Disco (EMD) promoted a student-themed club night in the Northern English city of Sheffield. They did so with flyers and a Facebook page promising all kinds of attractions: 'GET LAID!

EVERY TUESDAY AT REPUBLICA 20TH SEPT FRESHERS SHUTTER SHADES RAVE! FREE SHUTTER SHADES FOR ALL! £1.50 DRINKS ALL NIGHT'. In the ad, a speech bubble appeared from the shorts of a young woman promising 'YOU'RE GOING TO GET LAID!'

A consumer complained that the ad featured people who appeared underage, and that it was also offensive. The ASA itself agreed with the former qualm, adding that the ad connected drinking and sex. However, the ASA panel did not agree that the ad was offensive. This was because of the media that carried it and the population it reached. EMD maintained that the ad was not offensive because its distribution methods – student union flyers and Facebook pages that only adults were supposed to access – should have kept the message to the student audience to whom it was aimed. This audience, so the company reasoned, would understand that the copy was tongue in cheek, not a promise. On this matter, the ASA agreed: 'the vast majority of recipients would be adult students who could choose whether or not to accept the flyer ... the ad did not contain any sexual imagery or graphic content and considered that its content, while likely to be distasteful to some, was unlikely to cause serious or widespread offence to the student audience at whom it was targeted' (Advertising Standards Authority, 2012, no page).

The significance of this adjudication is that it represented the contestable logic of a regulatory system premised on the notion of rational consumer choice. That's not to say the adjudication was wrong, but it is to say that it fit with the view that media policy works best by empowering consumers, although the history of the 2003 OFCOM Act tells us that policy makers and citizens alike are torn on this view. Aside from the risible argument that only adults access Facebook (and the implied assumption that minors who do so are victims of bad parenting), the idea that students are adequately protected by the right to say no to potentially offensive flyers, and that those who are offended somehow don't get the joke, is equally problematic. Should drinks companies be able to exploit student unions as advertising spaces? Should students be in positions where they have to say no in any case when they are going about their business as students? Open questions, to be sure, but ones that can be asked given broader trends where alcohol advertising turns places that are meant for one thing – sports events, concerts, student unions – into marketing opportunities that naturalize the relationship between drinking, culture, leisure and, in this case, even work.

SIGNIFICANCE: MEDIA POLICY *CREATES* CITIZENS

In a world of proliferate media experiences, it is frighteningly easy to find evidence supporting pretty much any argument you like about how media harm or help society. Generally speaking, then, presenting a case that teaches something worth knowing about media work means explaining how one arrives at the topic at hand. In this case, what do flyers and a Facebook page that circulated around a British university campus in 2012 have to do with global media policy, and what method charts the journey from one to the other?

The narrative linking Eat My Disco and policy *per se* goes like this. Media policy debates have been energized by appreciation of media's contribution to social well-being, and efforts to secure this function by harmonizing cultural, political and consumer rights. These efforts encounter conflicts over the relative merits of individual autonomy versus centralized protectionism. Difficult as these clashes are to resolve, they nevertheless underscore the amalgamation of media and political rights.

Historically, alcohol, like media content, is another product that has animated social debate about how far people should be left to govern their own environment. So it isn't surprising that regulating alcohol marketing and advertising produces rich evidence about what happens when one tries to direct media and consumption at the same time. Alcohol companies have found innovative methods to pervade social and media spaces with positive messages about drinking. More significantly, they have become adept at encouraging drinkers to speak a commercial language. Sometimes drinkers speak ideas that advertisers cannot articulate, and concretize the links between drinking and fun in embodied experiences. When it comes to the impact of media policy on alcohol advertising, then, we find a 'double dose' of the notion that policy is intimately connected to how we imagine and practise citizenship.

Because policy makers leave public archives recording their work, we can find evidence of how the conceptualization of the political nature of media policy translates into actual decision making. OFCOM's record of alcohol adjudications represents a valid archive in this regard, partly because of scholarly work on how the institution's history echoed with the dilemma of twin citizen and consumer responsibility. A logical question, faced with this evidence, is to ask whether regulation provides as rich a language as advertising for public expression. One way to test this is to look at how complex the OFCOM adjudications are. Can the same ads be seen as reflecting different aspects of what advertising means, as a social discourse? By and large, the answer is no. Most people complain about simple exposure issues.

However, if we are looking for complexity, then the ambiguities of the Eat My Disco adjudication are notable. On the one hand, having a speech bubble shouting 'get laid!' coming from a woman's shorts was offensive, but that the target audience could be trusted to laugh it off or ignore it echoed similar differences among legislators and the public, who weren't sure whether they wanted to think of people as citizens or consumers, or live in a society with more or less regulation. But more than this, the Eat My Disco adjudication also spoke to the normalization of celebrating alcohol. It was one of the more complex cases in a relatively small number of complaints that have been made by a pervasive media phenomenon, where the predominant sentiment is simply 'not in front of the children'.

Naturally one can contest these conclusions, but at least they have a procedure. That procedure is based on translating theoretical debates into material indicators that can be applied to a coherent sample of evidence, with a traceable history. The key here is not the number of cases, but the fact that the cases can be defensibly presented as a significant part of something. The argument is not that the OFCOM archive says all there is to know about alcohol marketing as a subset of media regulation, but it *is* that trends in these adjudications can be explained within the politicization of media policy and the codetermined advances of consumer society and popular media practices.

CHAPTER SUMMARY

- Scholars identify media policy as a key battleground in managing the political impact of consumer culture.

- The regulation of alcohol advertising provides a valid case regarding how citizens are invited to participate in media culture, both through the production of media content and contributions to policy debates.

- Recorded complaints decisions allow us to research patterns in public speech about advertising and comment on the fluency of popular speech on media regulation.

15

RESEARCHING AUDIENCES

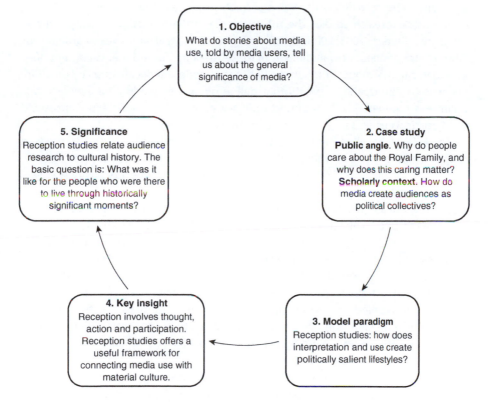

1. Objective
What do stories about media use, told by media users, tell us about the general significance of media?

2. Case study
Public angle. Why do people care about the Royal Family, and why does this caring matter?
Scholarly context. How do media create audiences as political collectives?

3. Model paradigm
Reception studies: how does interpretation and use create politically salient lifestyles?

4. Key insight
Reception involves thought, action and participation. Reception studies offers a useful framework for connecting media use with material culture.

5. Significance
Reception studies relate audience research to cultural history. The basic question is: What was it like for the people who were there to live through historically significant moments?

Figure 12   Researching audiences

OBJECTIVE: NARRATING MEDIA INFLUENCE WITH THE STORIES THAT AUDIENCES TELL

The book began by discussing how people live with media. There are, it was argued, social and historical stories behind personal media experiences. We close with the same point, exploring how audience research sharpens the analysis of media power by looking at how that power is explained by audiences, in their own words. In particular, the chapter shows how qualitative reception research explains how media power thrives through *diversity* among users and audiences. Prioritizing diversity and context helps to define the value of small-scale qualitative studies.

Audience research studies the role of media in the formation of historical consciousness (Butsch, 2003, 2008). It connects grand historical narratives to ordinary life. Finding stories about how audiences make sense of media and media content offers an organizational model of media power. In this model, media affect us by providing chances to participate in events that define our public world. This power model emerges from methods that connect ordinary, even boring, media experiences with vivid political conflicts and moments of historical change.

To explain what all of this means, the chapter takes us back to 1981, and the wedding of Charles, Prince of Wales, and the then Lady Diana. The wedding was at once a political ritual, public holiday and media event, being the subject of a widely viewed live broadcast, watched by millions given the day off work. We know a bit about public reactions to the Royal union because a project called the 'Mass Observation Exercise' collected diary accounts of what ordinary Britons did on the day, and eight of these stories have been released into the public domain. The data do not definitively say what the whole nation was thinking, but they do explain how an elite political ceremony (bound, as it was, to discussions about the place of monarchy in a changing, conflicted society) became relevant to ordinary people, and how media weaved the trappings of archaic pageantry into modern rituals – eating, drinking, catching up with family and watching TV. The case study connects audience studies with a foundational research enigma: What do small sets of qualitative data tell us about 'big' cultural questions?

The particulars of the Royal Wedding evidence, scant as they are, serve several functions. They capture the purpose of qualitative audience research, clarify how careful attention to core research principles enable us to capitalize on evidence about media influence that is readily available to all, and identify the contribution of qualitative audience studies to explorations of media power. All of this is explained through the following steps. First, the chapter makes the case that media representations of Royalty reflect how media facilitate popular political thought, and in this sense become a part of common cultural history. Next, audience research is introduced as a field that inherits the interests of cultural history. It studies how ordinary media experiences play a part in forming political moods in historically significant moments. Third, reception research is introduced as a useful method for approaching qualitative data about these processes in an organized way.

Finally, the chapter shows how to apply reception theory to a data set, using the Royal Wedding accounts. The purpose is to show how small qualitative data sets reflect modes of media power and media engagement that can be applied to other situations.

In summary, this chapter:

- Explains the value of qualitative audience research as a form of historical inquiry.
- Shows how models of audience reception provide useful guides for approaching diverse qualitative data in an organized way.
- Explains how it is possible to combine the analysis of media interpretation with that of media use.

CASE STUDY: MEDIA, THE ROYAL FAMILY AND THE BRITISH PUBLIC

The public face: Brexit, the monarchy and national identity

In 2016, international television audiences saw two Britains. One was bitterly divided over 'Brexit', the referendum where 17 million people elected to leave the European Union, defying the 16 million 'remainers'. The other loyally rallied around the Queen. Even as the leave/remain camps indulged in bitter disputes, news outlets reported that three-quarters of the public approved of the monarchy (Herald Scotland, 2016).

As opposing Brexit forces struggled to win majorities, they probably envied the Royal Family's aplomb in seducing the public. At the Opening Ceremony of the 2012 London Olympic Games, the Queen wowed the world by 'parachuting' into the stadium alongside James Bond. The secretive stunt was dreamed up between Buckingham Palace, Daniel Craig and the Ceremony maestro, film director Danny Boyle. The wedding of Prince William and the Diamond Jubilee, marking Elizabeth II's 60 years on the throne, quickly followed. But it wasn't all about pageantry. In 2016, Prince Harry opened up about the personal difficulties of being a boy who lost his mother in childhood, and having no one to talk to about it, as part of his patronage of mental health issues.

So, if the Brexit vote was a highly mediated political event that painted an ugly picture of Britain, it made sense that the nation would turn to the Royals as a palatable vision. Apart from anything else, Royalty-based media events let people 'do' Britishness for global audiences. When it rained on Jubilee day, thousands turned out for the celebrations in London, with a defiance quickly attributed to a national tenacity that only the Queen could inspire. This underlined an important, recent point in media research: being an audience is about doing things; performing, if you will, for other audiences

(Abercrombie and Longhurst, 1998; Couldry, 2004). It is this intersection between thinking, doing and the creation of cultural history that is the object of critical audience research.

Scholarly context: Royalty, media and cultural history

When future historians contemplate what it felt like to live in the UK in the early 21st century, attitudes towards the monarchy will be a significant indicator. Additionally, the question of how these thoughts were arranged in relation to media industries and ordinary media habits is one that our future antiquarians will do well to consider, because media scholars of Royalty have used Royalty to outline how media *create* powerful impressions of public opinion, succinctly affecting how we think most people feel, in a way that carries genuine political repercussions.

Princess Diana featured prominently in work on Royalty's audiences. Much has focused on her passing and funeral. Scholars have analysed how emotional reactions to her death were shaped by media coverage (Bishop, 1999; Montgomery, 1999; Shome, 2001; Marriott, 2007). The most significant work here was James Thomas's *Diana's Mourning: A People's History* (2002).[1] Media coverage of the Princess's demise and funeral painted a picture of an entire nation in mourning. Thomas wanted to know a bit more about this picture. Was this simply a media impression? Why were people mourning? Were there patterns of diversity amid the general despair? Was there evidence that the sense of general despair was largely a media story?

Thomas pursued these questions by examining accounts of what people did on the day of the wedding, from the University of Sussex's Mass Observations Archive. The Mass Observations Archive had been collecting accounts of public reactions to key events since the 1930s. Back then, anthropologists asked panels of 'observers' to write about their experiences of social events. This bequeathed a huge archive of public life in 20th-century Britain, as told by ordinary people. Naturally, one could quibble about the typicality of the stories. Nevertheless, this archive gives us a unique glimpse of how British citizens have understood historical changes. Observations about the role of the media often feature in these stories (Thomas, 2002).

Thomas was faced with a familiar challenge – having to deal with valid research data while knowing that this data could not be generalized, in the usual sense of the word. There was no question of using a self-selected sample to try to fix, once and for all, what Diana's death meant to the British public. What it was possible to do, however, was to use the evidence as a testimony to the complexity of the event. If cultural research is interested in conflict, then there was

---

[1]Thomas also produced a valuable shorter version of his research in a special paper for the Mass Observations Archive entitled *Beneath the Mourning Veil: Mass-Observation and the Death of Diana* (2002).

value in highlighting differences, ambiguities and puzzles in the only archive of public responses that we have. Proceeding in this spirit, Thomas found real grief, accompanied by much confusion. Many were not sure what to make of the Princess, as a person who seemed ordinary, while clearly being nothing of the sort. She was the first Royal celebrity who lived a life of unimaginable glamour, publicity and pressure. And the image of a nation in mourning was equally confusing. Media concoction? Reality? A bit of both? Some writers had intense difficulty putting their finger on exactly what to say about their feelings. To some, the sudden outpouring of public grief seemed somehow unBritish – whatever that meant. The idea of 'unBritishness' seemed to be a code for a shift in public sentiments that was difficult to encapsulate in words. But the most significant trend, Thomas thought, was that people were reticent to express indifference to the event because when they turned on the television they saw a nation in mourning, and believed this to be an accurate depiction of how other people felt.

Such discomfort directed Thomas to sharp criticisms about what audiences revealed on the relation between media and democracy. Where media were full of popular mourning scenes – visiting sites of commemoration, signing condolence books, that sort of thing – evidence that this had been a common reaction was unconvincing. Most people didn't participate, and mass observers talked about other reactions. Bemusement and indifference seemed more to the fore than sadness. However, when it came to perceptions of how others felt, the tendency to think that 1997 was a time of national mourning was evident. Thomas concluded that in failing to report on perplexed publics, the media had failed in its duty to reflect all shades of public opinion. Later in his career, Thomas (2008) came to see this as a harbinger of the phenomenon of celebrity mourning, a media device that, among other things, endeavours to suppress social conflicts over different social values.

In reaching these conclusions, Thomas offered an intriguing, accessible vision for the role of audience research. In a world where it is difficult to encounter all shades of public feeling through the media, it is important to develop methods for exploring audience diversity. This has a political function. It is a way of avoiding the tendency to reduce complicated social conflicts to a few simple positions, thereby prematurely closing debates. Thomas believed the Mass Observations Archive data were a valuable resource in outlining the unique purpose of reception studies – to examine how people establish complicated emotional ties to public events in relation to media coverage.

Thomas confessed that the ambition to marshal Mass Observation reports – personal narratives – into a coherent observation about media power was an inherently messy business. What follows, then, builds on his work to suggest how similar accounts of another Royal event can be explained by using methods from the encoding/decoding tradition. To exemplify, let's go back further, to use the Mass Observations database to look at the moment when the Diana phenomenon began as a national media holiday: the Royal Wedding of 1981.

KEY PARADIGM: RECEPTION STUDIES

Audiences and the making of history

History and audience studies share similar perspectives on the nature of the political. For the historian, rich accounts of political history include considerations of how people were motivated in those moments by things that were not political, in the strictest sense (Thompson, 1963). Similarly, audience researchers recognize that media content becomes political, ironically, because very often it isn't seen as such. That is, you can't make sense of popular content by seeing it as nothing but a conveyor belt for a series of ideas about power, where all that audiences do is decide whether or not they buy into the visions of reality paraded before them.

Audience studies and cultural history are linked because media make history by attracting audiences. Evidence shows that if you want to know how people were feeling during key historical periods, looking at how they used media is often a handy place to start. This is true from the pressing political crises that are the stuff of conventional history to the rhythms of everyday life that often go unrecorded – much to the historian's chagrin.

With regard to the former, it's the organizing power of media that links history with popular culture. In Germany, after the Second World War, Allied radio provided one of the first signs of social reconstruction. Germans remember the return of radio broadcasting as a sign that post-war life was improving, alongside other events such as the return of foods that had disappeared during the conflict. The world remembers the war in terms of its key battles and elite figures. Yet ordinary Germans, so the research suggests, tended to tell it in terms of everyday experiences, and the return of radio was recalled as a symbol of progress (Badenoch, 2005).

The idea that interactions between media and audiences contribute to national construction is hardly controversial. In Europe, 'public service' principles conscripted television to cultivate national identities (Bourdon, 2000). However, histories of how such strategies worked on the ground among audiences demonstrate how precarious such ambitions were. In Portugal, for example, when 1950s catholic TV broadcasts aspired to reconcile women with a patriarchal political dictatorship, communal viewing habits went off message. In one memorable incident, women reported being marched to local taverns to watch a Papal visit – being taken to the very 'male spaces' that they were not supposed to visit. An event that was supposed to show the world in one way ended up teaching how it could be different (Portovedo, Tomás and Carvalheiro, 2015). Viewing habits intended to reinforce patriarchy ended up letting women into a conventionally men-only space.

Broadcasting also affected the definition of famous historical incidents that shaped national political agendas. Radio's distinctive capacity to capture senses of intimacy and immediacy, for instance, was dramatically experienced in the United States through the Lindbergh kidnapping drama in 1932. The infant son of famed America aviator and national hero Charles Lindbergh was kidnapped and murdered. Listeners avidly followed the news as it happened, and the collapse in space between events happening and news being made lent the event an unprecedented emotional impact, bearing significant changes in how audiences felt about public safety (Howell, 2012).

The notion here was that media were doing more than recording and showing history to audiences; they were also letting them experience history as history, feeling they were part of important events as they were happening. Thirty years after the Lindbergh kidnapping, viewer reactions to TV coverage of John F. Kennedy's assassination showed a savvier, but no less moved public who seemed more aware of the historical significance of audience experience. Reacting to the coverage, many viewers wrote to television stations to express not only their grief, but also their observations of how that grief was structured by the viewing experience (Bodroghkozy, 2013).

Such effects are not limited to news. Researchers have also found instances of audiences using media to negotiate social reality in historical accounts of reactions to popular entertainment – for instance, crime. Shows about crime have been a staple of television entertainment for decades. Talking to people about these shows, scholars have found that viewers commonly contemplate social and moral changes in their evaluation of this screen perennial. The discourse of fictional crime parallels the discourse of real social change, serving as a handy metaphor (Livingstone, Allen and Reiner, 2001; Chapman, 2006). *Dexter*, for example, the innovative drama featuring the eponymous serial killer as its hero, was interpreted by its fans as a discourse of the complications of good and evil (Tager and Matthee, 2014).

So, talking to audiences puts ordinary voices at the heart of understandings of what it was like to live through key moments (Livingstone et al., 2001). Audiences are integral to cultural history because they leave a lot of evidence about what they do and think, and their experiences can be reconstructed through archival methods. This brings us back to the Royal Family. What we are trying to get at is how media affect politics through their impact on audiences and social institutions. This impact, so evidence suggests, reflects media's power to organize audiences in relation to historical shifts, sometimes in ways they actually create those shifts. One must ask, for example, whether the JFK assassination would be recalled as such a watershed in the absence of the millions who felt it through television. At any rate, if the Royal Family are an institution that the public use to 'think' Britain, and if that thinking, and the institution itself, is increasingly experienced as a media event, then how can we use the reception of Royal media to assess media power to make identity, society and history? Like good historians, we have to use what we have to hand. Like good audience scholars, we must have a method for analysing gathered evidence. In this instance, the question is explored by looking at the archived response to the Royal Wedding of Charles and Diana in 1981, using categories of audience activity derived from Carolyn Michelle's development of the encoding/decoding model (Michelle, 2007; Michelle, Davis and Vladica, 2012).

Evidence and method: Applying audience theory to Mass Observation directives

In 2007, New Zealand researcher Carolyn Michelle developed a 'Composite Multi-Dimensional Model of Audience Reception'. Her model was significant as one that inherited the ideas of the encoding/decoding model in a form that allowed for multiple kinds of audience reactions and uses.

The encoding/decoding was developed by Stuart Hall (1980) and David Morley (1980, 1992, 2006) as a means to conceive the relationship between media representation and social sense making. Its premise was that media reception connected audiences to political life. The notion was that popular culture was implicitly 'coded' with political values, and that to be entertained or informed by the content was also to take a position on these values – classically, to accept, negotiate with or reject the vision of the world that they proffered.

Michelle's model drew on a history of reception studies to posit three 'levels' of textual encounters, each of which contributes to differing modes of reality effects. Using semiotics, Michelle suggested that media use can be understood on denotative, connotative and evaluative terms. In one sense, this was a continuum that runs from the least to most political. Denotative relations imply a functional relationship to the media – we look at the news simply to find out what is going on, or we watch a TV drama because we want to be entertained. Here, there isn't much of a sense that anything is being 'done' to us, or indeed that we are doing anything significant. That said, we may see parallels between the content we watch and the lives we live – seeing media as a useful sounding board to talk about things that matter to us. Or we might have feelings about the form of that content. We might find a drama especially believable, or not, for example, but there's little sense that this bears much weight in the greater scheme of things.

Connotative reactions involve seeing media content as something that *is* trying to elicit certain reactions. This aspect of the model applies to those moments where we see the media as trying to do something, evaluate how effectively they are doing their job, and react to it in one of three ways: we can accept what is being offered to us – in the model, this is to make a 'dominant' reading; we can 'negotiate' our reactions, taking some things on board and rejecting others; or we can take an 'oppositional' stance, which rejects the ideas being offered to us. These are the classic types of audience reaction that were set out in Hall's original model (1980) and David Morley's work (1980, 1992).

Let's explain how an oppositional reading works by examining how people think about Royalty in relation to television. Consider an episode of *Gogglebox Australia* that featured audience reactions to a dramatized account of the romance between Denmark's Prince Frederik and his Australian-born wife, Princess Mary (Gogglebox Australia, 2015). *Gogglebox* is a television show about watching television. Its 'stars' are the friends and families who sit down to interact with television. The show is popular because it knows that television is something we do, not something we watch. We watch the watchers because they are performers, who use the sounds and images on their screens as raw materials for comedic and empathetic performances, where they reflect on the nature of television, the world and their relationships with the people they love.

Princess Mary shows how to understand the show's appeal in connotative terms. It features reactions to a scene where, on Frederik and Mary's first date, the dashing Prince strips naked on a beach before delivering the couple's first kiss. The Goggleboxers interpret this as a hilariously failed moment of romantic drama: 'It's really funny because that looks really romantic, but at the bottom, he's just hitting her with his penis!' That's an oppositional reading.

The model's third level refers to 'evaluation'. 'Evaluations' are text-related activities where we read society through media lenses, triangulating between media, personal experience and cultural politics. In this sense we are taking a position on the world, not just the media. This is where popular culture gets serious. Let's explain in relation to *Gogglebox* again. At the level of evaluation, we would think more carefully about laughter as a response. Prima facie, there's a playfulness in the audience reactions. The idea is that the main appeal of *Princess Mary* is that it was all a bit silly. A real story is rendered farcical by hilariously misjudged dramatic devices, at least that's what the Goggleboxers think.

But to some Australians, monarchies aren't funny at all. Australian republicans object to the fact that Queen Elizabeth II is the head of state. These people might worry about dramas that glamorize and humanize European Royalty – they're really nice and hey, who wouldn't want to join them? Then, of course, there's the whole princess myth thing. Parents with daughters know that their kids are bombarded with tales of girls waiting to be rescued by boys, and might have seen *Princess Mary* as a boring elaboration on a tired theme that girds gender inequality. At any rate, evaluation refers to how audiences use media to read society, recognizing entertainment as something that is related to power. Here, we look for how audiences talk about society – how it is and how they would like it to be, in relation to media. Here we also engage with how audiences evaluate matters of equality in relation to the media. Do they like the way things are, or would they like things to change?

There are two aspects that made Michelle's (2007) model a useful addition to the work on encoding/decoding and reception. The first is an agnostic take on power. The encoding/decoding tradition had been criticized for conceiving social power in terms of dominance. The model had its origins in a moment when its founders were heavily invested in researching how media affected society because of cultural affinities shared across the elites that managed social, political and media institutions. The question, at that time, was how complicated production processes nevertheless tended to 'prefer' views of social reality that corresponded with those who already held the reins of power.[2]

---

[2]The best example is Hall, Jefferson and Critcher's *Policing the Crisis*, which outlined how British media framed crime in certain ways because of news routines and unspoken cultural affinities between elite politicians, police officers, members of the judiciary and journalists.

The problem this established was the temptation to view media content as an apology for sexism, racism and classism. Such a view wasn't good at recognizing the complexity of social conflict or the role of media therein. There are many issues where it is hard to discern a dominant perspective, in either media or society. Michelle's model averted this temptation by explaining how the 'levels' of encoding and decoding could be imagined in a non-hierarchical way. The point is to find methods for appreciating the diversity of media use by establishing the multiple modalities that characterize media use. The goal is not to put audiences into one of the model's boxes, but rather to understand how people can move across all of its levels in the same event, and to place value in what had previously been thought of as more 'passive' reactions.

Let's think about the *Princess Mary* Goggleboxers again to flesh out what this means. A married couple, husband and wife, are shown watching the first kiss scene. They compare the vignette to their own first encounter. The wife asks why she didn't meet a prince in a bar. The husband replies that she went to the wrong pub on the night that they met, and the couple share a laugh. The interaction is worth considering as one that reflects how fluid and fascinating 'denotative' interactions can be, and how Michelle's typology provides a way of explaining how such humdrum encounters with popular culture matter to people. Denotatively, *Princess Mary* is understood as a 'transparent' form of popular entertainment that becomes the basis for an intimate moment where the couple can reflect on their life together. The show is used as a conduit to intimacy, as something that can be made to run parallel to life in two ways: as a part of a familiar shared ritual of watching television, and as a medium to affirm the longevity of the couple's relationship. The question of how the show did this or that to make the couple think this or that is never discussed because it is not relevant, although the role of television in supporting a shared history in general clearly is. Hence the ability to 'flow' between different kinds of denotative activity isn't simple or passive in any way.

So Michelle's model usefully dispensed with the notion that sorting audience reactions along a line from denotation to evaluation was akin to deciding who was active and who was passive, which implied that some audiences are smarter than others. As Michelle noted, an important aspect of audience research is to explain how denotative action becomes the basis for political engagement. To be sure, there is more at stake here than finding shows that either do or don't reflect the views of the powerful, and audiences who accept, reject or rework what they see. It is quite another to say that media don't contribute in significant ways to political perception. So what we need are models that allow us to explore the diversity of audience experiences, understanding them on their own terms while remaining sensitive to how media can 'pull' this diversity in a particular direction, for example creating the general impression that one is experiencing a historically significant moment alongside millions of others, even if what you make of that moment might differ.

One way to do this is to consider how Michelle's model can be adapted to include media use as well as interpretation, to suggest that 'reading' texts denotatively, connotatively and politically can relate to interactions between patterns of the material things that we do in relation to media. The suggestion here is that the attitude we adopt to media, and to society in relation to media, depends not only on how we feel about what we watch, read, listen to and play, but on how we do it – when, where, with whom, and accompanied by what else? Take a moment to reflect on Barker and Brooks' (1998) work on cinematic pleasure. The ease with which we find ourselves immersed in cinematic block-busters is as physical as it is aesthetic. It is simple to get lost in epic narratives and effects when slumped in a reclining chair, surrounded by food, warmth, immersive sound and darkness (Barker and Brooks, 1998). These too are deno-tative pleasure. We don't ask why they are there, *but* we go to great lengths to get to them. If they fail to deliver, however, or if we find ourselves in the wrong crowd – people who talk too much, for example – then the illusion breaks down. Hence there are 'use' aspects of denotation and connotation.

Bearing this in mind, the value of Michelle's model can be developed by applying denotation, connotation and evaluation to media use as well as recep-tion. The overall value of this model is that it recognizes that audiences don't fall into types, but instead audience is an idea that refers to different ways of relat-ing to media through changing circumstances, both textual and contextual. To exemplify what this means, let's move to the Royal Wedding data.

KEY METHOD: USING ENCODING/DECODING TO MAKE SENSE OF AUDIENCE DIARIES

This is where we are: reception studies seek to explore how media place audi-ences in history. We know from James Thomas's work that mediated events around the British Royal Family have demonstrated this in action. We also know that the Mass Observations Archive is a valuable resource that tells us what it was like for people to live within historical media moments. This leads to the question: Can accounts of Royal encounters be used to explain how the diversity of audience experience enriches the political significance of media use, using a structured model of audience action – such as Michelle's composite model? And what are the options for developing this model to include media use as well as media reception?

To answer these questions, Mass Observations accounts, where observers reported what they did on the day of the 1981 Royal Wedding, were loaded into NVivo for analysis. The first step in the study was to think about what these accounts represented. There were just eight of them, so the goal, following Schrøder's view on the exploratory value of audience research (Schrøder, 2013), was to looks for *patterns of diversity*. That is, the reports were regarded as accounts of an enforced social experience, where media played a part. The Royal Wedding was a public holiday, characterized by an unusual event – a real-time media broadcast on television. The intersection is significant, given that watching broadcast television was a major leisure pursuit of the age.

We can't use the accounts to consider what all Britons were doing with this holiday, but we can use them to look for the things that explained how people engaged with these sociological facts in particular ways. This promised insights into how a medium like television was 'realized' as a cultural fact in a way that defined a key historical moment.

Step one: Sensitizing evidence

Michelle's model provides a series of sensitizing concepts that can define a procedure for finding 'signposts' to how this happened among the unstructured data. Broadly speaking, this involves negotiating between the model and the data to identify moments of diverse denotative, connotative and evaluative reactions at the level of what people thought *and did* around the wedding. This was achieved by the following process. First, in accordance with standard practice in qualitative analysis (Gray, 2003; Stokes, 2013), the reports were read several times to get an overall impression of what the wedding was like for respondents. This impression was, inevitably, informed by understanding how audience research approaches matters of media interpretation and use. Notes were then taken on the overall impression gained. Thomas's work was used as a guide here. Thomas's unique contribution to the understanding of Diana's death was that where many were lost in a row about whether most people were or were not grieving, there was much to be gained in exploring how the event was simply confusing, looking at those who had a hard time figuring out whether they were one of the other, or whether it really mattered on any level, and if so why.

The idea that if we have to reduce any media event to an essence then the best one is probably confusion, was useful in gaining an overall impression of the Royal Wedding accounts, and indeed justifying the value of thinking 'big' media power in relation to a small number of highly personal recounts. To put this into action, where the encoding/decoding model looks ultimately for political engagement, the emphasis was on highlighting *emotional* engagement: pleasure, disappointment, joy, sadness or even apathy. This process highlighted elements of the data that prompted further thinking on complexity that, in turn, indicated a method for further investigation.

Consider this quote: 'Neither of us hungry but Jay insists I go ahead as planned with special three course menu hors d'oeuvres panfried trout in mushroom cream sauce with sauté potatoes and courgettes and a bought cream gateau. Washed down with a better than usually afforded It was, bottle of white wine' (R470, no page). This is an excerpt from a female correspondent for whom the Royal Wedding fell in the midst of an upsetting family crisis, involving the illness of a parent. A common theme across the eight accounts was the role of food and television in marking the day out as special. Some accounts described having lavish lunches to accompany the wedding ceremony. It was, in this sense, an occasion casting a spotlight on the intersection between nation, leisure and media, and how that intersection *forced* participation in a thing called Britishness. R470's note is a tangible example of what this meant in practice for real people: gulping down elaborately prepared food in the absence of hunger or pleasure because the special nature of the day as a public event overrode another way in which the time was special – the period of a painful family crisis.

In this project, this quote was used as a conceptual anchor; it was a reminder of the core research problem. One of the main challenges in qualitative research is justifying the reporting of data. Faced with a mass of unstructured comments people have made about this, you choose to report something in particular. The reader is entitled to ask what justifies the choice. What criteria have selected this quote rather than another? In this case, the quote notably reflects the imperative to account for thought and action in making sense of audiences. There is no doubt that the Royal Wedding was a political event. There is no doubt that, as a political event, it encouraged people to react to an institution that few usually think about. Broadcast television made Royalty part of the furniture – as we shall see, television was a common reference points in all accounts. But television achieved this power by blending with social routines and personal histories. The quote reminds us that political sense making involves a series of thought processes and practices. If television and politics were important, so too were other things like emotional states and domestic labour. Hence the importance of coding frames that account for shifting positons on the event that happen in relation to both interpretation and action. Hence also a need to consider how one response to the event could reflect different modes of engagement.

Again, this quote clarifies the point. Michelle's model broadly contrasts moments where *media* rather than audience are *regarded* as 'active' or 'passive' – things that are or are not trying to do something. Passive is used somewhat ironically, as it is in the very assumption that media are simply there as the natural complement to everyday life that explains much of their purchase. R470's evening meal came at the end of a day during which the family had been 'Glued to the set so to speak from 10:30 AM onwards with a glass of Sherry sometimes', interspersed with heartbreaking hospital visits. Hence the account outlines a series of contradictions between actions and feelings – sets of celebratory practices carried out in the presence of a mood that was anything but. At one part of the proceedings, the author reported that her husband was so depressed that he went to bed in the afternoon. On the one hand, there is no sense that the national television holiday let the couple 'escape' their plight, but it is interesting that they did things that wouldn't usually be associated with times of distress. This called for a coding scheme, based on Michelle's model, that allowed for the analysis of evaluative practices, including interpretation and action. The purpose of this is not to place people in fixed categories, but rather to show how Michelle's categories serve more as reference points in descriptions of fluid cultural experiences.

Coding denotative practice

Denotative analysis can be taken to mean a largely descriptive approach that sets out how people related to the wedding as a media event. However, this is more interesting and complicated than it seems. The Mass Observation accounts allow us to see how that event fit into an entire context, including family life, gender relationships, domestic labour and a panoply of leisure activities. Seven of the eight accounts are provided by women. All worked really hard on this 'holiday', preparing meals, looking after kids, and in one case going to work after cooking breakfast and lunch. Men were largely 'absent' in a number of ways: they did the gardening (N403), played sport (W633), pursued hobbies (C108), and sometimes professed no interest in the wedding and then enjoyed watching it (G226). So denotatively, these accounts did accord with the argument that media use is implicated in the politics of domestic labour and leisure (Press, 1991; Seiter, 1999); some had more of a holiday than others. This is a significant context for making the case that denotative details about reception and action in fact reveal quite a lot about the workings of culture and the place of media therein.

This established a base for examining the component of denotative relationships. Coding looked for descriptions of a 'transparent' relationship to the event. This could be seen in moments where observers wrote as if they had been at the wedding itself, or treated the television as one of the family – another guest at the table. Regarding the former, we have this:

> Just in time to see the end of the service and the return journey my husband arrived back for lunch. All three men were really taken with the bride's dress and the bridesmaids outfits. My father summed it up by saying that the bride was bringing prettiness back into clothes. All three have also been impressed by her ready smile. (W633)

This can be taken as a 'denotative' reaction in so far as there is no indication that the men are actually watching television. Contrast this with the following account of a denotative *practice*:

> We sat and watched the wedding until 12:30 PM when we had lunch after the washing up at 1 PM we then saw the TV until the happy couple left the balcony to have their wedding breakfast. My husband went to a Bowls match, and I sat in the garden reading a book, I switched the TV on again at 3:45 PM to see the happy couple go to and on the broad lands. That TV stay on until we went to bed. (N403)

Here the thing that is most apparent is the role that broadcasting played in arranging the day. Other things the families wanted to do – eat, play sport, read – were fit around televised events: the wedding ceremony and the departure for the honeymoon. So, from these accounts, we can tell that denotation was experienced in different ways: in relation to the content of the event itself, and in relation to the general organizing principle that watching television played as the hub of leisure activities. This is notable because it suggests that the pulling power of the wedding had to do with the intersection between the content generated by an extraordinary occasion and the quotidian appeal of television as a point of daily reference. The medium's role as a constant touchstone in the midst of other pastimes was rarely questioned.

The Mass Observations evidence underlines Michelle's point that there's nothing simple about 'denotative' media uses. The data vividly recall an age when watching television was still special, and people were willing to work hard to 'switch off'. One participant mentions renting a colour television for the occasion (S496). Another planned to visit her father in a distant city, simply because he too had a colour television (G226). When plans fell through, she was disappointed to miss the 'full experience' (G226). So when viewed as a series of practices, denotative media use is quite complicated and interesting, sociologically and historically. It reminds us that once people had to put a lot of effort into watching television. Indeed, as one writer explained, television was crucial to those whose lives were bereft of much pleasure:

> Phoned elderly aunt. She had had a very quiet day. Not even a neighbour popped in. She watched a bit on TV but has glaucoma so can't see much and was widowed this year so is somewhat depressed. Loved the wedding though. (C108)

Coding connotative practice

Having considered how the event was encountered, the next step was to code how it was judged as a media experience. This evaluation took on forms that included the broadcast itself and other events that were built around it.

Again, it helps to give a contextual note to reasons why, in general, people were invested in having a good time around the Royal Wedding. The archive contains other materials showing that the wedding was also a community event that people wanted to be successful. The town of Newton Abbott arranged an evening of entertainment, including military parades, displays, music and keep fit classes. The town's Mayor implored people to enjoy all of this as a break from 'a time of so much doom and gloom'. The pamphlet was full of ads from local businesses, which hoped to drum up trade – butchers, garages, printing works, and a hairdresser offering what looked like trademark Lady Diana cuts.

Communities wanted the televised wedding to be a successful social event. Perhaps this partly explains why writers put so much effort into the day. According to the following account, a motivation behind this was that it provided a chance to see community life at its best:

> Myself three daughters a grand daughter and son-in-law walked the 1 ½ miles to see her Majesty band of the Royal Marines march through the town. Thousands of people in town all friendly like Christmas. (S496)

One question you might ask is in what way is this an evaluation that responded to the occasion as a message about something? On this, it was apparent that some writers anticipated the criticism that their enjoyment at the festivities was somehow foolish, a cheap distraction from things that really mattered. As one put it:

> The royal wedding was a good excuse for some fun and games a get together and an escape from depressing times we are going through. ... If it wasn't spent on royalty it would be spent on the bombs. ... People know and can relate to members of the royal family... . Working people I know did not find it a bore. (S496)

Yet others were let down by the whole thing. H260 describes a day spent at a holiday camp where her best efforts to become part of the occasion were ruined by lacklustre contributions from fellow holidaymakers:

> The atmosphere was not electric. In fact, I felt a little let down as my daughter and I had dressed in our red white and blue T-shirts, but others had not bothered ... perhaps we had hoped for too much. (H260)

W632's account stands out as the only person who neither watched the wedding on television nor did anything to celebrate. She was a mother of four whose husband was working away. She cooked a special meal, but otherwise spent the day gardening, listening to classical music, reading the newspaper and visiting the pub. The only mention of the broadcast came here:

> Sat outside Reading 1984 George Orwell hate week preparations reminded of wedding. Fantasy. Wedding services blaring from someone's television. (W632)

When W632 had time to relax, she turned to music, books and newspapers, staying away from the television, although never *quite* being able to do so completely. This itself is a form of practice-based evaluation – her judgement on the wedding was conveyed by actions that kept the wedding at arm's length, making this just another public holiday.

Coding evaluative practice

As W632's account reveals, the evaluation of media events can slip into overt political thinking about the state of society. The 'hate week' quote likens the wedding celebrations to the political carnival described in Orwell's dystopian novel, where citizens of Oceania are invited to participate in propagandistic displays of hatred against the nation's enemies. In classical encoding/decoding terms, this is an oppositional reading, one where the viewer interprets broadcasting's efforts to invoke feelings of national pride as a sinister political ritual that is more frightening than joyous.

So, some did see the day as an injunction to think about the political state of the nation. However, in this regard, the value of these accounts is that they present a chance to explain the importance of 'non-hierarchical' approaches to reception. W632 clearly put a lot of thought into her political reading of the day.

But others worked just as hard to politically justify the fun they had. Take this from the only male contribution to the collection:

> I was decorating on the day, but work my schedule to watch all that major parts on TV. Although I am a leftist, I believe that it is cheaper to breed heads of state than elect them, they cost no more to keep, and you don't get lumbered with geriatric actors. Most important they don't actually meddle in the running of the country. (R470, no page)

Naturally, the writer was aware that his story was going into a public archive recording the national mood. So it's interesting that he went to the trouble of explaining how a 'leftist' can be a monarchist too. This is presented as a pragmatic political position, that recognizing the republicanism does not instantly solve problems of political management (the reference to being lumbered with actors is presumably a reference to the USA, where ex-Hollywood star Ronald Reagan held the Presidency).

If we hold these two different readings of the day together, we can see that one does just as much mental labour as the other. There's no sense that the Royal Wedding was 'easy' to enjoy for R470. In fact, one could argue that his pleasure was harder to achieve than W632, who spent the day cooking, reading, drinking and listening to music, secure in her conviction that the whole thing was ludicrous, and never encountering anything that might make her think otherwise. R470, however, has to balance decorating, the desire to watch what's going on, and the faint suspicion that this desire contradicts who he thinks he is as a political person. It was possible to accept the preferred meaning of the day – and recognize that meaning as contentious.

Four principles in reception

Comparing these two quotes as instances of political labour establishes key points on the value of reception studies, as they are enabled by Michelle's multi-composite model. These are:

- Typologies are useful markers of ambiguity and diversity. Establishing typologies of response doesn't mean fitting audiences into fixed categories. N602 accepted the 'preferred meaning' of the wedding, but the route to this acceptance was not straightforward.

- 'Preferred readings' can be just as complex as their oppositional or resistive cousins.

- Political evaluation is a matter of thinking and doing things in relation to media over a long period of time.

- Even casual media engagements are culturally complicated. Denotative media uses are not transparent or functional. There is much to say about the ordinary things that ordinary people do around media. That said, extraordinary events that disrupt business as usual are useful for displaying this with greater clarity.

SIGNIFICANCE: AUDIENCES AS HISTORY MAKERS

Since the 1970s, qualitative research into what audiences think about and do with media has been subjected to all manner of criticisms about its value. Social scientists think it does little more than provide anecdotes that are at best pilot clues to big questions about what media do to most of the people most of the time (Schrøder, 2013). The encoding/decoding model has been criticized as a clumsy effort to sort media content and media audiences into fixed political positions, in a manner that vastly underestimates the complexity of politics, media artefacts and processes of identity (Morley, 2006). Studies noting how audiences critique what they perceive as dominant ideological positions in media, society, or both, have been criticized for vastly overestimating the political significance of popular culture, and the people who use it to laugh at or argue with elite cadres (Morris, 1996; Bird, 2011). None of this means that it is no longer worth examining how particular people engage with particular ways in particular times and places.

Humility is the key. The goal isn't to fix the truth of media culture; it is to find those moments in life when media really matter to particular people in particular ways for particular reasons. It's one thing, for example, to scoff at the validity of small-scale qualitative audience studies, and quite another to dismiss the view of a North Korean who describes risking their life to watch South Korean television just to keep their hopes of freedom alive (Yoon, 2015). Media matter to people for reasons that count, and figuring out how has become an important pursuit in cultural history, where memory and media experience are entwined. At stake here is the pursuit of complexity, not certainty, in the interests of social inclusion. When historical memory relies on media coverage, and as memories are made through activities including media use, then to research how people make sense of what they see, hear and read becomes an important part of understanding how history itself unfolds. This historical understanding of audiences is an important component in framing the unique significance of media research as a mode of social inquiry.

CHAPTER SUMMARY

- Qualitative audience research contributes to understanding of the relationship between media use and historical consciousness.

- The encoding/decoding tradition has developed valuable structures for making sense of diverse forms of media use.

- This involves processes of interpretation and habit.

- Using this framework shows the rich and complex histories behind apparently simple media experiences.

- By using resources such as the Mass Observation Archive, it is possible to see how audience reception operates as an historical force that defines moments of political significance.

CONCLUSION: HISTORICIZING MEDIA RESEARCH – AND THE PEOPLE WHO DO IT

Exploring Media Research starts and ends with people – the ones who want to do media research and the others who sit at the receiving end of the political forces that media release into the public realm. The book's trajectory frames media research as an historical pursuit tasked with explaining how political consciousness is constructed and experienced through media practices. In conclusion, media studies historicizes a chaotic present, where we are surrounded by all kinds of people doing all manner of things with an exotic array of media devices and genres. By paying close attention to basic questions about how media make reality, and how we can gather diverse evidence of the process in action, it is possible to explain the provenance of media phenomena that appear novel to the public eye – like Wikileaks. This historical capacity draws attention to the political foundations and consequences of media practices in an age where political thought and historical memory are heavily reliant on the production and circulation of mediated stories. At base, media research addresses the core theme in cultural history: how historical political change permeates daily experiences, and how traces of these momentous changes can be found in the evidence of them.

For sure, you could have made this argument at any time in the short history of media and cultural studies, but there are reasons for thinking that it has a special relevance to a 21st-century context. Changes in media industries, societies and universities (as both educational institutions and global business operations) all prompt introspection on media research. Such conversations take many forms, but in this conclusion I want to consider how an historical perspective informs an understanding of media education as a research practice involving partnerships between teachers and students.

THE POLITICIZATION AND PERSONALIZATION OF MEDIA RESEARCH

Theorizing media studies as history

Great historians like E. H. Carr and E. P. Thompson were keen to overcome the misperception that there are two kinds of people in history – those who make it and others who deal with the consequences. The trick of the historian is to explain how these binary opposites are nothing of the sort, that they share more than common sense would have us believe. Objecting to 'Bad King John' theories of historical change, Carr warned that it is important to regard those who apparently change the world, single-handedly, by skill, intelligence, wisdom and evil, as the products of historical forces. To exemplify in relation to the book, if he was around today, Carr would probably say that it is far more useful to examine Donald Trump as the product of shifts in American Republicanism and media industries than spend time figuring out how xenophobic and sexist he really was. Equally, Thompson objected to seeing ordinary people as victims of history; British socialism changed the direction of British history thanks, in large part, to the diverse ways that ordinary people learned to cope with the tumult of the industrial revolution (Thompson, 1963).

It's easy to see how this translates to theorizing the media. Industries, and those who run them, aren't puppet masters in any simple sense, and their ambitions, if they can articulate such things, often have little to do with what media end up doing. So, too, audiences and users are not simple victims of message systems beyond their comprehension. These points have been made many times. But what about another powerful binary, the one between academics and students, the people who do media research and the others who learn about it? How can we break this binary down, and what do we stand to gain from doing so?

Media studies in the news: The firing of Melissa Click

The notion that there's a close connection between teaching and learning about media research, or at least that the people who teach and learn about it share much in common, was played out to global media audiences in 2016 when a media scholar called Melissa Click was fired from her job as Assistant Professor at the University of Missouri. Click was filmed confronting two student journalists as they attempted to interview fellow students who were protesting against on-campus racism. A report written on the case by Click's union, the American Association of University Professors (AAUP) (2016), explained the events in the following way. In August 2016, African American students at the University of Missouri formed an organization called Concerned Student 1950. Their goal was to protest about the absence of a university response to the police shooting of Michael Brown, an unarmed African American teenager, in the nearby town of Ferguson, and its failure to address on-campus racism. One of their number began a hunger strike on one of the university's quadrangles. The hunger striker was soon joined by '1950' colleagues and their supporters. At this point, the group decided that they did not wish to speak to journalists, and erected 'no media' signs around the encampment.

As the report noted, it was hard to differentiate between the protest and the national cultural climate in the United States, created by widespread media coverage of Brown's killing and the protests about racism that followed. And it was in this context that Click joined protestors in a show of her support, confronted the journalists who were trying to interview Concerned Student 1950, and eventually agitated to have one of them physically removed from the camp. She had no authority to do so – the reporters had every right to be where they were – and later apologized.

As the report detailed, there was never any question that Click had erred, and she justifiably faced disciplinary action for doing so. What the union objected to was the politicization of her case. Media, and media studies, were at the hub of their argument that Click's actions were not judged fairly in the university's dismissal decision. To begin, the confrontation was filmed and released on YouTube, attracting millions of views and being frequently replayed on television news stories. Additionally, political pressure was brought to bear on the university to fire Click not just because of her actions, but also because of her research. As the AAUP detailed, Missourian legislators eventually threatened to withhold state funding from the university unless Click was terminated. But in a letter released by The Missouri General Assembly, Republican legislators decided to offer their views on Click's scholarly credentials.

> The public Spotlight that is now shining on Click because of her behavior has also revealed some of the research she is conducting at the University. Our constituents have expressed outrage at the fact she is using taxpayer dollars to conduct research on Shades of Grey, Lady Gaga, and Twilight. (AAUP, 2016, 5–6)

The investigation into Click had revealed nothing of the sort. Details of her publications and interests had been publicly available for years through her university profile. But while the letter acknowledged there 'was some value in popular cultural studies', it nevertheless questioned whether publicly funded institutions are places where people should be able to research or learn about media and culture. If we are speaking of historical figures as those who earn fame as conflict symbols, then Click had become the personification of media studies as a Mickey Mouse subject.

But elsewhere, Click won significant support. In the summer of 2016, lauded film director Spike Lee made *Two Fists Up*, a documentary about how Missouri students eventually forced University President Tim Wolfe to resign, after accusations of inaction on campus racism. The Concerned Student 1950 movement received a fillip when the university football team refused to play an upcoming game unless Wolfe left. American college football is a lucrative income stream for universities, especially as the game draws huge television audiences. However, Lee's documentary stressed how the high-profile actions of student athletes who are, in effect, elite sports personalities were far less significant than the determination of other 1950 members who skilfully played a media game, in which Click acted a weighty cameo.

Talking about the incidents that led to Click's dismissal, students explained how the media studies professor's actions had been decontextualized and misframed. Shortly before Click had called for 'muscle' to eject a journalist from the 1950 occupation, she had herself been manhandled by a camera operator. Similarly, while much had been made of other footage showing Click telling a police officer to 'get your f******* hands off me' as she joined protestors who blocked a parade attended by Wolfe, less had been made of the fact that Click had tried to protect African American students at the protest as they were jostled by drunken crowds. As one student said, 'she was one of the few people who stood up for them [the student protestors] while our President [Wolfe] sat in his car and wouldn't even look at them' (Lee, 2016).

Eventually, Concerned Student 1950 succeeded in making their point that the specific concerns about racism at the University of Misouri were part of more general fears about social inequality, expressed elsewhere through protests about the Brown killing. If state legislators questioned Click's contribution to campus life, Concerned Student 1950 members had no such qualms.

But what did this have to do with media teaching and research? Let's answer this with another question: Can we figure out why Click would jump to the defence of African American student protestors as they were jostled by drunken white men, by looking at her research? Is there a through line between the research and the action? The answer is yes.

The scholarly and cultural context of the Click Case

Two years earlier, Click was lead author in a study of audience reactions to depictions of masculinity in the TV series *Entourage* (Click, Holladay, Lee and Kristiansen, 2015). The study found that 33 interviewees, 25 of whom were men, responded most favourably to a character in the show who displayed conventional qualities of 'hegemonic' masculinity. The show, based on the experiences of super-buff Hollywood star Mark Wahlberg, features numerous versions of being a man. The most popular character among the group, however, was 'Ari', a muscular, aggressive agent prone to outbursts of sexism and homophobia. Interviewees either laughed off these outbursts as inconsequential aberrations, or else justified them as part and parcel of an aggressive environment where Ari remained 100% focused on doing right by his friends.

Click and her colleagues concluded that *Entourage* appealed because it allowed straight men to recall the days when they could say and do as they pleased without being called to account. Further, this appeal was not just about the pleasures of comedy, but was an expression of a masculinity 'crisis', where it was reasonable to note connections between how certain men enjoyed certain depictions of masculinity and the way that they wanted reality to be.

An organization called the Media Education Foundation (MEF) had been addressing this crisis since the early 1990s. Founded by Professor of Communications Sut Jhally, the MEF produced a series of educational videos and DVDs on how masculinity is represented and lived in American culture. Sociologist Robert Kimmel's *Guyland* (2015) argued that American college campuses were the epicentre of the masculinity crisis. Men in the 16–25 year age group were, he argued, trapped in a culture of 'adultolescence', grounded in the difficulties of achieving economic and social independence. The net result was that universities had become places where young men were trying to break the dependency mould by performing masculinity in aggressive and dangerous ways, with the net effect that campuses were marked by alarming gender inequalities.

MEF had been tracking how media articulated this crisis for over a decade. In *Tough Guise* (1999), Jackson Katz charted connections between violence and homophobia, masculine culture and the reliance of that culture on the glamorization of aggressive straight masculinity – the kind of thing that Click and her colleagues later found appealed to *Entourage* fans. If you're tempted to dismiss Katz's work as the typical kind of argument you might expect to come from media studies, consider this: the United States Marine Corps uses his work in training their recruits how to behave properly.

So, the incidents where Click clashed with men during the Missouri protests came in the context of research on how media stoked on-campus social inequality and intimidation. Concerned Student 1950 acted because African American students studied in a climate where culture screamed that their grievances about racism didn't matter, and this echoed a bigger problem, brutally encapsulated by the Brown shooting, that black lives mattered less than white ones. Of course we know that George Gerbner's cultivation analysis made the case that the dominant 'story' told by American broadcast television in the 1970s was that the world belonged to middle-class white men, and that media entertainment popularized this myth. According to *Two Fists Up*, little had changed.

Wherever you stand on these ideas, it was clear that for Click, the Missouri University campus was not just a place to teach about things that happened elsewhere; it was a microcosm of the media-related cultural processes that she studied. Similarly, members of Concerned Student 1950 were engaged in their own media experiences that would eventually become part of the historical record of how America dealt with renewed civil rights conflicts. Teaching about media research had eventually shoved Click into the middle of the processes that she analysed, and she came to share a real experience of media reality making with her students.

DEPERSONALIZING PERSONALIZED MEDIA STUDIES

The point is that it pays to regard media studies as a research practice that helps us to understand universities as economic, social, cultural and media places, or where at least doing media research is a way to understand how these spaces work as a reflection of global historical and political moments.

A consistent feature of my career has been an awareness that students live with media issues that affect them, although how this works changes with time and place. Click's experiences reminded me that teaching about the politics of popular culture on North American campuses in the early 1990s was quite easy, in the sense that the connections between media, race and power were topics of popular debate outside the classroom. Back then, race was high on the entertainment agenda. *The Cosby Show* was wildly popular; filmmakers like Spike Lee and John Singleton, and rap groups like Public Enemy and NWA, and even other television comedies like *In Living Color* and *Roc*, openly addressed the longevity of racism and poverty. While studying at the University of Massachusetts, two of my advisors, Sut Jhally and Justin Lewis, published *Enlightened Racism* (1992), a book about Cosby which argued that television was doing a great deal to obscure the reality of racism. Their argument was that American television failed US democracy by depicting a world where upward mobility knew no colour, in an age when most African Americans families were becoming poorer. Underlining the prescience of this political argument, the book was published in the week of the Los Angeles riots, caused by the acquittal of police officers who had been filmed gang-beating an unarmed black motorist, Rodney King.

Re-invented media?

So Click's experience was not personal inasmuch as it echoed core questions about media, people, societies and power that have been in play for some time. Graeme Turner thought these issues through in his book *Reinventing the Media* (2015). Turner's title was a little ironic, because his point was that basic questions about the reach and nature of centralized power had changed little through the history of media research. Additionally, his concern was that media studies had shot itself in the foot by recreating the very sort of relationships between media scholars and media industries that had inhibited critical thinking in the mid-20th century. Earlier in this book, we encountered the distinction between administrative and critical research. The accusation was that the power of governments and media industries to fund media research in the mid-20th century had seduced researchers into pursuing research questions that addressed industry needs – how does persuasion work? – but said little about the more significant question of how media industries in general had pervasive political effects. Turner argued that too many 21st-century media scholars effectively made the same mistake by viewing traditional questions about power and politics as matters that only applied to 'legacy' media – television and the like.

The problem with this view was that it pushed the future of media research in a direction where the bulk of attention was directed towards asking unhelpfully dehistoricized and therefore depoliticized questions about what media do. Eventually, these were more use to industries than the public – the thing that had been reinvented was a new era of administrative research. This was a problem, according to Turner (2015), because the main thing that had been reinvented was a new brand of agnostic media power. Essentially, Turner argued that the profit motive of media industries had evolved such that they had lost interest in what audiences think. Their goal is to exploit the commercial opportunities created by flexible state–media relations and market conditions. Here the monetization of attention, use and audience labour are the targets, and any ideological consequences are a sort of 'collateral damage'. The fascinating thing about this is that it suggests a reversion to an interest in what people do in relation to media, rather than what they think about it, although the doing here refers to cultural actions rather than behaviours.

Turner's conclusion was that at a time when media industries have never been nimbler in changing their operations, it is incumbent to reinvent media studies around historical power questions that are independent of technologies. We should be paying more attention to big questions about the practice of political power under given political and economic conditions, to the histories of those conditions, and to the methods that we can use to make useful sense of ever-changing pictures. This scholarly analysis helped to explain why the Click story had become an historical event worth paying attention to; it was a reminder that old power questions still drove new media cultures. Hence there is the need to reflect on how Turner's observations affect the daily practice of media education as a research exercise.

Reinvention strategies

Turner has led the development of media studies as a global institutional reality. So it's important to consider his argument – but it's just as vital to do it in a positive spirit. There's a danger that the other thing that his book 'reinvented' was a tendency to divide media research into two camps: one that thinks the media wield excessive political power versus another that sees such claims as overblown and dismissive of the creative energy in ordinary culture. Let us proceed instead from the premise that historically-informed, method-sensitive analyses of how media and political power are synthesized are the hallmark of critical media research, no matter the place or platform. How do we set about doing this work?

The task seems insurmountable; but it isn't, and we can appreciate this by returning to the theme of this book – that the reach of media power means we can easily gather evidence about its operations, as long as we know where and how to look. To start, consider how Turner's view helps explain why the Click incident was so impactful. To approach platform neutrality, it is clear that to explain the incident in terms of social media – the fact that the story started when a student report posted a mobile phone film clip to YouTube, which then went viral – is to grossly underestimate how the story reflected the complexity of the American and global media market. Legacy media – television, the press and radio – played a major role in asking the story what it was.

The event becomes more complex and interesting if pursued in terms of power, rather than technologies. Instead of getting lost in fairly pointless and ultimately unanswerable debates over whether mobile and social media made the world more or less democratic – because either side built its arguments through differently edited versions of mobile media footage – it's more interesting to observe the new cross-platform alliances it bequeathed. On one side, the story was a boon to stalwarts of the 'shock jock' radio and television era – the infamous American conservative broadcaster Rush Limbaugh pilloried Click (Limbaugh, 2015). On the other hand, it was stalwarts of the television and film industry that eventually defended the professor. Lee's *Two Fists Up* (2016) was produced by American television sports giant ESPN, except that's not quite right because one of the student journalists whom Click confronted, Tim Tai, was on assignment from … ESPN (Friedersdorf, 2015). ESPN's foot in both camps epitomized Turner's notion of agnostic power. There was no contradiction between lending Click a sympathetic ear and being at the heart of the furore in the first place, because all that really mattered was telling the story. Not to mention the fact that it was able to do this because mobile media created cheap local labour, in the form of student stringers. Seeing the Click story as a tale of power, rather than new media, allows a more complex account of the contradictions in the event. Here we are not trying to find its truth – to determine who was right or wrong or to sort the players into victims and villains – but simply to chart historical continuities where convergent media placed new spins on familiar stories. Twenty-six years after *School Daze* (1990), Lee's movie about campus race politics, here he was again. The continuity is more important than the technological new kid in town's role in the altercation.

The lesson is that, for some at least, media studies uses evidence to open social conversations about the nature of power. *Exploring Media Research* has offered a model for doing so, modelled on historical thinking. In my view, Click's actions and reactions to her situation were motivated by the perception that questions of race, equality and media still centred on notions of power and representation, the likes of which would have been familiar to earlier generations of scholars. Regardless of the changes in how people make and receive media, the question of how particular versions of reality are created, shared, popularized and converted into common sense remains the lifeblood of media research. The issue of social inclusion establishes a basis for research that privileged neither 'good' nor 'bad' biases, but rather a set of foundational questions that can be applied to any topic. These are an elaboration of the research cycle, described in the introduction. So, having started with that cycle, let's end by elaborating on how it can be mobilized through asking more detailed questions.

Explaining reality effects, and why they matter

Click's story tells us that although media influence is clearly ingrained into everyone's experience – even as we teach and research it – it is terribly difficult to get people outside the field to take this seriously. Turner (2015) thought this is partly because we tend to shoot ourselves in the foot by not viewing new research problems historically. However, he also does so in a way that threatens to continue to divide a field prone to in-fighting between different camps who, broadly speaking, tend to focus on industry versus popular power. One way out of the conundrum is to identify essential research questions that imply no a priori bias in either direction.

First, it is important to explain how a topic relates to a particular media 'reality effect'. Our task is to demonstrate material *effects*: how media give social, political and cultural life a specific shape. In 'big picture' terms, we can define this reality effect as involving:

- How media create and normalize politicized versions of social reality.

- How media users do the same thing in the way that they connect media use, identities and relationships.

- The blending of media, political, economic and social life, such that it is very difficult to 'do' any of these things without also 'doing' media.

Second, we must have a clear sense of why a topic matters. Several elements come into play here. First, why does it matter to *you*? Thinking about why you care about a question can be a useful way to figure out why it matters to everyone else. Or putting this another way, if you can't figure out why you find something interesting, then you aren't going to be able to get the reader's interest either.

Another useful strategy is to think about why the topic matters to *society*. You can figure this out by looking at how it features in news media, and how scholarly perspectives would improve the quality of the public debate. Closely aligned to this are ethical considerations. A good research question should be able to explain its relevance to social well-being. Finally, a good research question attempts to intervene in existing academic conversations, developing their arguments and indicating future research directions.

Next comes generalizability. Media communication is a social process, involving media industries, media people, markets and media users. All projects enter this circuit at a certain point that affects what is seen. What point in the circuit of communication are you observing, and what kinds of insights can it give you? Although the field has traditionally approached these questions in terms of audiences, texts and markets, it is now possible to be a little more forensic. Media studies is usually divided into studies of industries, texts and audiences. Part 3 of this book has suggested this traditional tripartite into media people, media markets, media content, media places, Big Data, media policy and media audiences. The purpose here is to show how we can get better at doing big research on big questions by getting smaller, learning how to explain the complexities of media power in persuasive terms by analysing specific media experiences with traceable histories rooted in global shifts.

Generally speaking, this involves being as specific as we can about how our research carves out 'slices' of media culture that are worth regarding for their specificity, which is the key to their generalizability. Here, modes of historical thinking are handy. What we do is akin to the historical process of establishing historical facts, as that process was explained by E. H. Carr (1961). Carr characterized history as an inherently messy business that extrapolated plausible arguments from piecemeal evidence. The method here is to explain in as much detail as possible why the evidence you have is worth knowing about, even if it is not the kind of evidence that you would ideally want. This involves infusing evidence with meaning, by explaining how its occurrence could only have happened given the intersection of identifiable historical forces. Method, here, involves telling a credible story and telling your peers how that story has come about, thus letting readers evaluate not only what your argument is, but also how it is made (Carr, 1961).

The same is true of media research. Moreover, understanding this makes teaching and learning more interesting, as a research process that constitutes the historical fact of media studies as a global intellectual pursuit. This is explained in the next section.

Researching and teaching: Scholars as historical facts

As an export business, media education can say big things with small projects centring on the media education experience. This, in turn, benefits from insights into the historical development of media research, as an interdisciplinary, mixed-method pursuit. Mass market media education has created concentrated pools of diverse media experiences that promise to tell fascinating stories about changing media histories. Let's go back to Chapter 15 on audiences. In the United Kingdom, since the 1930s the Mass Observations Archive has proved the value of telling stories about being on the inside of history. It doesn't take much imagination to realize that media teachers and students are in the same position to create archives of what it has been like to live the history of mediatization. Let me give you an example from my own teaching.

To give people a taste of what it's like to deal with historicized evidence about media influence, I have students write and share stories about significant media encounters. They are given three options: 'First encounters' with television, the internet, mobile phones, movies, video games and social media; 'Emotional experiences', where using media invoked feelings of joy, fear, inspiration and/or hope; 'Media events' asks about experiences with 'special' media occasions, such as meeting celebrities, attending televised events, or the broadcasting of special television events, for example the final of a television talent show. These are just prompts, but as a researcher, you only have to do this once to discover that the people in your classes have lived through momentous times in media history. They have experienced the explosion of new popular cultures in Asia; they have felt the ups and downs of media mobility in vivid, often surprising ways; because of this, they can sometimes tell you what it was like to be on the inside of live news events that captured international attention. And when you put all of this together, you realize that educators and students, as researchers, are in a unique position to create an historical record of how media worked in the early 21st century. We have seen an example in Melissa Click, whose story is really about how media studies and racial politics intersected through media, and the reasons why this was not an accident, since the analysis of race has been a mainstay of critical media research. The lesson is that we too live in these intersections, and by following a few basic principles about how to set about doing historically-informed, methodologically-sensitive media research, we are in powerful positions to create knowledge about the global political impact of media culture. By understanding our roles as historians of the present, we can combine the activities of teaching, learning, theory and method into a global practice of doing media research.

REFERENCES

Abercrombie, N., & Longhurst, B. (1998). *Audiences: a sociological theory or performance and imagination*. London: Sage.

Advertising Standards Authority. (2010). ASA Ruling on THQ (UK) Ltd [Press release]. Retrieved from www.asa.org.uk/Rulings/Adjudications/2010/12/THQ-(UK)-Ltd/TF_ADJ_49483.aspx#.Vt5TiJN95Bx

Advertising Standards Authority. (2012). ASA Ruling on Eat My Disco. Retrieved from www.asa.org.uk/Rulings/Adjudications/2012/1/Eat-My-Disco/SHP_ADJ_171330.aspx#.VmzGEt8rLFw

Advertising Standards Authority. (2014). ASA Adjudication on Entertainment One UK Ltd [Press release]. Retrieved from https://www.asa.org.uk/Rulings/Adjudications.aspx

Akira, A. (2014). *Insatiable porn: a love story*. New York: Grove Press.

Al-Rawi, A. K. (2010). Iraqi women journalists' challenges and predicaments. *Journal of Arab & Muslim Media Research*, *3*(3), 223–236. doi:10.1386/jammr.3.3.223_1.

Albury, K., & Crawford, K. (2012). Sexting, consent and young people's ethics: beyond Megan's story. *Continuum: Journal of Media & Cultural Studies*, *26*(3), 463–473.

Alhabash, S., McAlister, A. R., Quilliam, E. T., Richards, J. I., & Lou, C. (2015). Alcohol's getting a bit more social: When alcohol marketing messages on Facebook increase young adults' intentions to imbibe. *Mass Communication & Society*, *18*(3), 350–375. doi:10.1080/15205436.2014.945651.

Allen, R. (2011). The unreal enemy of America's army. *Games and Culture*, *6*(1), 38–60.

Altheide, D. (2009). The Columbine shootings and the discourse of fear. *American Behavioral Scientist*, *52*(10), 1354–1370.

American Academy of Pediatrics (AAP). (2009). Policy statement – media violence. *Pediatrics*, *124*(5), 1495–1503.

American Association of University Professors (AAUP). (2016). *Academic freedom and tenure: University of Missouri*. Retrieved from www.aaup.org/report/academic-freedom-and-tenure-university-missouri-columbia

Anderson, C.A., Shibuya, A., Ihori, N., Swing, E.L., Bushman, B.J., Sakamoto, A., Rothstein, H.R., & Saleem, M. (2010). Violent video game effects on aggression, empathy, and prosocial behavior in eastern and western countries: a meta-analytic review. *Psychological Bulletin*, 136(2), 151–173.

REFERENCES

Anderson, D. (2005). *Histories of the hanged: Britain's dirty war in Kenya and the end of Empire*. London: Orion Books.

Andrejevic, M. (2013). *Infoglut: how too much information is changing the way we think and know*. New York: Routledge.

Ang, I. (1991). *Desperately seeking the audience*. London: Routledge.

Attwood, F. (2014). Immersion: 'extreme' texts, animated bodies and the media. *Media, Culture & Society, 36*(8), 1186–1195. doi:10.1177/0163443714544858

Austin, T. (1999). Desperate to see it: straight men watching *Basic Instinct*. In M. Stokes and R. Maltby (Eds.), *Identifying Hollywood audiences* (pp. 147–161). London: BFI.

Babbie, E. (1990). *The practice of social research*. Belmont, CA: Wadsworth.

Badenoch, A. (2005). Making Sunday what it actually should be: Sunday radio programming and the re-invention of tradition in occupied Germany 1945–1949. *Historical Journal of Film, Radio & Television, 25*(4), 577–598. doi:10.1080/01439680500262975.

Bale, T. (2012). *The Conservatives since 1945: the drivers of party change*. Oxford: Oxford University Press.

Balnaves, M., & O'Regan, T. (2010). The politics and practice of television ratings conventions: Australian and American approaches to broadcast ratings. *Continuum: Journal of Media & Cultural Studies, 24*(3), 461–474. doi:10.1080/10304311003703090.

Balnaves, M., O'Regan, T., & Goldsmith, B. (2013). *Rating the audience: The business of media*. London: Bloomsbury.

Bandura, A. (2009). Social cognitive theory of mass communication. In J. Bryant & M. B. Oliver (Eds.), *Media effects: Advances in theory and research* (3rd ed.) (pp. 94–124). New York: Lawrence Erlbaum.

Barker, M. (1997). Taking the extreme case: understanding a fascist fan of Judge Dredd. In D. Cartmell, H. Kaye, I. Hunter, & I. Whelehan (Eds.), *Trash aesthetics: Popular culture and its audience* (pp. 14–30). London: Pluto.

Barker, M., & Brooks, K. (1998). *Knowing audiences: Judge Dredd, its friends, fans and foes*. Bedford: University of Luton Press.

Barker, M., & Petley, J. (1997). *Ill effects: the media/violence debate*. London: Routledge.

Barthes, R. (1972). *Mythologies*. New York: Hill and Wang.

Battaglio, S. (2015). Prospects fading for 'NBC Nightly News' anchor Brian Williams' return. *Los Angeles Times*. Retrieved from www.latimes.com/entertainment/envelope/cotown/la-et-ct-brian-williams-return-nbc-nightly-news-20150428-story.html

BBC News. (2013). Hannah Smith death: sister Joanne warns Ask.fm is addictive. *BBC News Online*. Retrieved from www.bbc.co.uk/news/uk-england-leicestershire-23825049

BBC News. (2014). How social media woke up Bhutan. *BBC News Online*. Retrieved from http://www.bbc.com/news/world-asia-25314578

BBC News. (2015). NBC news anchor Brian Williams suspended for six months. *BBC News Online*. Retrieved from www.bbc.com/news/world-us-canada-31398866

Beck, C. S., Aubuchon, S. M., McKenna, T. P., Ruhl, S., & Simmons, N. (2014). Blurring personal health and public priorities: an analysis of celebrity health narratives in the public sphere. *Health Communication, 29*(3), 244–256.

Becker, A. B. (2012). Engaging celebrity? Measuring the impact of issue-advocacy messages on situational involvement, complacency and apathy. *Celebrity Studies, 3*(2), 213–231.

Becker, H. (2005). *Tricks of the trade: how to think about your research while you're doing it.* Chicago, IL: University of Chicago Press.

Beer, D. (2015). Productive measures: culture and measurement in the context of everyday neoliberalism. *Big Data & Society*, January–June, 1–12.

Beyer, J. (2014). The emergence of a freedom of information movement: Anonymous, WikiLeaks, the Pirate Party, and Iceland. *Journal of Computer Mediated Communication, 19*, 141–154.

Bhutan Centre for Media and Democracy. (n.d.) Retrieved from http://bcmd.bt/

Bird, E. (2003). *The audience in everyday life: living in a media world.* New York: Routledge.

Bird, E. (2011). Are we all producers now? Convergence and media audience practices. *Cultural Studies, 25*(4–5), 502–516.

Bird, E., & Ottanelli, F. (2011). The history and legacy of the Asaba, Nigeria, Massacres. *African Studies Review, 54*(3), 1–26.

Bishop, R. (1999). From behind the walls: boundary work by news organizations in their coverage of Princess Diana's funeral. *Journal of Communication Inquiry, 23*(1), 90.

Blood, W., & Holland, K. (2004). Risky news, madness and public crisis: a case study of the reporting and portrayal of mental health and illness in the Australian press. *Journalism, 5*(3), 323–342.

Blumler, J. G., & Coleman, S. (2015). Democracy and the media – revisited. *Javnost – The Public, 22*(2), 111–128. doi:10.1080/13183222.2015.1041226.

Bodroghkozy, A. (2013). Black weekend: a reception history of network television news and the assassination of John F. Kennedy. *Television and New Media, 14*(6), 560–578.

Bourdon, J. (2000). Live television is still alive: on television as an unfulfilled promise. *Media, Culture & Society, 22*(5), 531–556.

Bourke, J. (1999). *An intimate history of killing: face to face killing in twentieth century warfare.* London: Basic Books.

boyd, d. (2014). *It's complicated: the social lives of networked teens.* New Haven, CT: Yale University Press.

boyd, d., & Crawford, K. (2012). Critical questions for big data. *Information, Communication & Society, 15*(5), 662–679.

Bratich, J. (2005). Amassing the multitude: Revisiting early audience studies. *Communication Theory, 15*(3), 242–265.

Bridges, A. J., Wosnitzer, R., Scharrer, E., Sun, C., & Liberman, R. (2010). Aggression and sexual behavior in best-selling pornography videos: a content analysis update. *Violence Against Women, 16*, 1065–1085.

Brock, A. (2011). 'When keeping it real goes wrong': *Resident Evil 5*, racial representation, and gamers. *Games and Culture, 6*(5), 429–452.

Brodmerkel, S., & Carah, N. (2016). *Brand machines, sensory media and calculative culture*. Basingstoke: Palgrave Macmillan.

Bruns, A. (2007). Produsage.org: from production to produsage: research into user-led *Content Creation*. Retrieved from http://produsage.org/node/9

Bruns, A., & Burgess, J. (2012a). Researching news discussion on Twitter. *Journalism Studies, 13*(5–6), 801–814. doi:10.1080/1461670X.2012.664428.

Bruns, A. & Burgess, J. (2012b). (NOT) THE TWITTER ELECTION: the dynamics of the #ausvotes conversation in relation to the Australian media ecology. *Journalism Practice, 6*(3), 384–402.

Buckingham, D. (1988). *Public secrets: Eastenders and its audience*. London: BFI.

Buckingham, D. (2006). *Media education: literacy, learning and contemporary culture* (4th ed.). Cambridge: Polity Press.

Buckingham, D. (2013). Teaching the creative class? Media education and the media industries in the age of 'participatory culture'. *Journal of Media Practice, 14*(1), 25–41.

Buckingham, D., & Bragg, S. (2004). *Young people, sex and the media: the facts of life?* London: Palgrave Macmillan.

Buckingham, D., & Sefton-Green, J. (2003). 'Gotta catch 'em all: Structure, agency or pedagogy in children's media culture'. *Media, Culture & Society, 25*(3), 379–400.

Bushman, B. J., & Huesmann, L. R. (2014). Twenty-five years of research on violence in digital games and aggression revisited. *European Psychologist, 19*(1), 47–55.

Bushman, B. J., & Pollard-Sacks, D. (2014). Supreme Court decision on violent video games was based on the First Amendment, not scientific evidence. *American Psychologist, 69*, 306–307.

Butler, D. (1955). Three styles of psephology. *Political Studies, 3*(2), 143–152.

Butler, D. (1983). Reading the entrails. *The Spectator*, April 22, 15.

Butler, D. (1998). Reflections on British elections and their study. *Annual Review of Political Science, 1*, 451–464.

Butsch, R. (2003). Popular communication audiences: a historical research agenda. *Popular Communication, 1*(1), 15.

Butsch, R. (2008). *The citizen audience: crowds, publics, and individuals*. London: Routledge.

C108. (1981). Mass Observations Correspondents PDfs 1981 Royal Wedding. Retrieved from https://drive.google.com/drive/folders/0Bz-9hs_TdzGPU kYzYlFMMG9Hak0

Cammaerts, B. (2013). Networked resistance: the case of WikiLeaks. *Journal of Computer-Mediated Communication, 18*(4), 420–436.

Caputo, N. M., & Rouner, D. (2011). Narrative processing of entertainment media and mental illness stigma. *Health Communication, 26*(7), 595–604.

Carah, N., Brodmerkel, S., & Hernandez, L. (2014). Brands and sociality: alcohol branding, drinking culture and Facebook. *Convergence: The Journal of Research into New Media Technologies, 20*(3), 259–275. doi:10.1177/1354856514531531.

Carey, J. (1983). The origins of the radical discourse on cultural studies in the United States. *Journal of Communication, 33*(3), 311–313.

Carey, J. (1989). *Communication as culture.* Boston, MA: Unwin Hyman.

Carey, J., & Kreiling, A. (1974). Popular culture and uses and gratifications: notes toward an accommodation. In J. Blumler & E. Katz (Eds.), *The uses of mass communications: current perspectives on gratifications research* (pp. 225–248). Beverly Hills, CA: Sage.

Carman, E. (2012). 'Women rule Hollywood': ageing and freelance stardom in the studio system. *Celebrity Studies, 3*(1), 13–24.

Carr, E. H. (1961). *What is history?* Cambridge: Cambridge University Press.

Carroll, B., & Landry, K. (2010). Logging on and letting out: using online social networks to grieve and to mourn. *Bulletin of Science, Technology & Society, 30*(5), 341–349.

Carroll, R. (2015). Porn industry groups cut ties to star James Deen amid sexual assault claims. *Guardian Online,* November 30. Retrieved from www.theguardian.com/us-news/2015/nov/30/james-deen-sexual-assault-accusations-stoya-porn-industry

Carusi, A., & De Grandis, G. (2012). The ethical work that regulations will not do. *Information, Communication & Society, 15*(1), 124–141.

Carvalho, V. M. (2015). Leaving Earth, preserving history: uses of the future in the mass effect series. *Games and Culture, 10*(2), 127–147.

Cashmore, E. (2014). *Celebrity culture* (2nd ed.). London: Routledge.

Chaffee, S. (1975). *Political communication.* Beverly Hills, CA: Sage.

Chapman, J. (2006). 'Honest British violence': critical responses to Dick Barton – Special Agent (1946–1951). *Historical Journal of Film, Radio & Television, 26*(4), 537–559.

Charlesworth, A. (2012). Data protection, freedom of information and ethical review committees. *Information, Communication & Society, 15*(1), 85–103.

Charlesworth, D. (2014). Performing celebrity motherhood on Twitter: courting homage and (momentary) disaster – the case of Peaches Geldof. *Celebrity Studies, 5*(4), 508–510.

Cho, S. (2006). Network news coverage of breast cancer, 1974 to 2003. *Journalism & Mass Communication Quarterly, 83*(1), 116–130.

Christensen, C. (2011). WikiLeaks and celebrating the power of the mainstream media: a response to Christian Fuchs. *Global Media Journal: Australian Edition, 5*(2), 1–3.

Cleland, J. (2014). Racism, football fans, and online message boards: how social media has added a new dimension to racist discourse in English football. *Journal of Sport and Social Issues, 38*(5), 415–431.

Click, M. A., Holladay, H., Lee, H., & Kristiansen, L. (2015). 'Let's hug it out, bitch': HBO's entourage, masculinity in crisis, and the value of audience studies. *Television and New Media, 16*(5), 403–421.

Clough, M. (1998). *Mau Mau memoirs: history, memory and politics.* London: Lynne Rienner.

CNN (Producer). (2015). Angelina Jolie cancer choice expert reaction. April 16. Retrieved from www.youtube.com/watch?v=U5bbatqXghg&spfreload=1

Cobain, I., Bowcott, O., & Norton-Taylor, R. (2012). Britain destroyed records of colonial crimes. *The Guardian,* April 18. Retrieved from www.theguardian.com/uk/2012/apr/18/britain-destroyed-records-colonial-crimes

Coleman, L., & Held, J. (Eds.) (2014). *The philosophy of pornography: Contemporary perspectives.* Lanham, MD: Rowman & Littlefield Publishers.

Coleman, S. (2012). Believing the news: from sinking trust to atrophied efficacy. *European Journal of Communication, 27*(1), 35–45. doi:10.1177/026732 3112438806.

Comella, L. (2011). From text to context: feminist porn and the making of a market. In T. Taormino, C. P. Shimzu, C. Penley, & M. Miller-Young (Eds.), *The feminist porn book.* New York: The Feminist Press.

Comella, L. (2014). Studying porn cultures. *Porn Studies, 1*(1–2), 64–70.

Consalvo, M. (2003). The monsters next door: media constructions of boys and masculinity. *Feminist Media Studies, 3*(1), 27.

Costache, A. M., & Llorens, C. (2015). A bridge too far? Analysis of the European Commission's new developments on media policy and media freedoms through the concept of soft regulation. *International Journal of Media & Cultural Politics, 11*(2), 165–181. doi:10.1386/macp.11.2.165_1.

Cottle, S. (2008). 'Mediatized rituals': a reply to Couldry and Rothenbuhler. *Media, Culture & Society, 30*(1), 135–140.

Couldry, N. (2003). *Media rituals: a critical approach.* London: Routledge.

Couldry, N. (2004). Theorising media as practice. *Social Semiotics, 12*(2), 115–132.

Couldry, N. (2013). Living well with and through media. In N. Couldry, M. Madianou, & A. Pinchevski (Eds.), *Ethics of media* (pp. 39–55). Basingstoke: Palgrave Macmillan.

Couldry, N. (2015). Illusions of immediacy: rediscovering Hall's early work on media. *Media, Culture & Society, 37*(4), 637–644. doi:10.1177/0163443 715580943.

Couldry, N., Madianou, M., & Pinchevski, A. (Eds.) (2013). *Ethics of media.* Basingstoke: Palgrave Macmillan.

Couldry, N., & Powell, A. (2014). Big Data from the bottom up. *Big Data & Society, 1*(2), 1–5.

Coverdale, J. H., Coverdale, S., & Nairn, R. (2013). 'Behind the mug shot grin': uses of madness – talk in reports of Loughner's mass killing. *Journal of Communication Inquiry, 37*(3), 200–219.

Crawford, G. (2012). *Video gamers.* Hoboken, NJ: Taylor and Francis.

Custers, K., & Van den Bulck, J. (2013). The cultivation of fear of sexual violence in women: processes and moderators of the relationship between television and fear. *Communication Research, 40*(1), 96–124.

Davidson, K. (1997). Private ball game in Docklands stadium. *The Age,* February 20, p. 1.

Davis, H. H. (2003). Media research: whose agenda? In J. Eldridge (Ed.), *Getting the message: news, truth, and power* (pp. 35–49). London: Routledge.

Davison, W. (1983). The third person effect in communication. *Public Opinion Quarterly, 47,* 1–15.

Delaney, S. (2009). HBO: television will never be the same again. *The Telegraph.* Retrieved from www.telegraph.co.uk/culture/tvandradio/4733704/HBO-television-will-never-be-the-same-again.html

Deming, C., & Jenkins, M. (1991). Bar talk: gender discourse in *Cheers*. In L. Vandeberg & L. Wenner (Eds.), *Television criticism: approaches and applications* (pp. 47–57). White Plains, NY: Longman.

DeNora, T. (2000). *Music in everyday life*. Cambridge: Cambridge University Press.

DeSantis, A. (2002). Smoke screen: an ethnographic study of a cigar shop's collective collective rationalization. *Health Communication*, *14*(2), 167–198.

DeVane, B., & Squire, K. (2008). The meaning of race and violence in *Grand Theft Auto: San Andreas*. *Games and Culture*, *3*(3–4), 264–285.

Dickinson, R., Matthews, J., & Saltzis, K. (2013). Studying journalists in changing times: Understanding news work as socially situated practice. *International Communication Gazette*, *75*(1), 3–18. doi:10.1177/17480485 12461759.

Dines, G. (2010). *Pornland: how porn has hijacked our sexuality*. Boston, MA: Beacon Press.

Donofrio, T. (2010). Ground Zero and place-making authority: the conservative metaphors in 9/11 families' 'Take Back the Memorial' rhetoric. *Western Journal of Communication*, *74*, 150–169.

Dorfman, A., & Mattelart, A. (1984). *How to read Donald Duck: imperialist ideology in the Disney comic* (2nd ed.). Santiago: International General.

Dorji, G. (2013a). Threats posted on website. *Kuensel Online*. Retrieved from www.kuenselonline.com/threats-posted-on-website/#.UvwRHUKSyw4

Dorji, G. (2013b). Anything online is there forever. *Kuensel Online*. Retrieved from www.kuenselonline.com/anything-posted-online-is-there-forever/#.UvwaKEKSyw4

Dorji, G. (2013c). On whom does the onus to protect the innocent fall? *Kuensel Online*. Retrieved from www.kuenselonline.com/on-whom-does-the-onus-to-protect-the-innocent-fall/#.VYplbhOqpBc

Dorji, G. (2013d). Fashion page raises furore. *Kuensel Online*. Retrieved from www.kuenselonline.com/fashion-page-raises-furore/#.VYpkUxOqpBc

Doyle, D. (2015). UFC 193 crowd of 56,214 sets company attendance record. *MMA Fighting*. Retrieved from www.mmafighting.com/2015/11/15/9737660/ufc-193-crowd-of-56214-sets-company-attendance-record

EA Games. (2014). EA Outreach. Retrieved from www.ea.com/outreach

Eldridge, J. (2003). News, truth and power. In J. Eldridge (Ed.), *Getting the message: news, truth and power* (pp. 3–33). London: Routledge.

Eldridge, J., Milne, A. and Philo, G. (1985) Letters retrieved from http://www.glasgowmediagroup.org/images/stories/pdf/lettersbbc.pdf

Eliasoph, N. (1988). Routines and the making of oppositional news. *Critical Studies in Mass Communication*, *5*(4), 313–334.

Elkins, C. (2006). *Imperial reckoning: the untold story of Britain's gulag in Kenya*. New York: Henry Holt and Co.

Elkins, C. (2011). Alchemy of evidence: Mau Mau, the British Empire, and the High Court of Justice. *The Journal of Imperial and Commonwealth History*, *39*(5), 731–748.

Elson, M., & Ferguson, C. J. (2013). Does doing media violence research make one aggressive? *European Psychologist*, *19*(1), 68–75.

Endres, F. (1978). The pit-muckraking days of *McClure's Magazine*, 1893–1901. *Journalism Quarterly*, *55*(1), 154–157.

Engelhardt, C. R., Bartholow, B. D., Kerr, G. T., & Bushman, B. J. (2011). This is your brain on violent video games: neural desensitization to violence predicts increased aggression following violent video game exposure. *Journal of Experimental Social Psychology*, *47*, 1033–1036.

Erdur-Baker, O. Z. R. (2009). Cyberbullying and its correlation to traditional bullying, gender and frequent and risky usage of internet-mediated communication tools. *New Media & Society*, *12*(1), 109–125.

Evens, T., & Donders, K. (2016). Mergers and acquisitions in TV broadcasting and distribution: challenges for competition, industrial and media policy. *Telematics & Informatics*, *33*(2), 674–682. doi:10.1016/j.tele.2015.04.003.

Ewen, S. (1983). The implications of empiricism. *Journal of Communication*, *33*(3), 219–225.

Fay, B. (1996). *Contemporary philosophy of social science*. London: Blackwell.

Ferguson, C. (2007). The good, the bad and the ugly: a meta-analytic review of positive and negative effects of violent video games. *Psychatric Quarterly*, *78*, 309–316.

Ferguson, C. (2011). Video games and youth violence: a prospective analysis in adolescents. *Journal of Youth Adolescence*, *40*, 377–391.

Ferguson, C. (2013a). Violent video games and the Supreme Court lessons for the scientific community in the wake of Brown v. Entertainment Merchants Association. *American Psychologist*, *68*(2), 57–74.

Ferguson, C. (2013b). *Adolescents, crime, and the media: a critical analysis*. New York: Springer.

Ferguson, C. (2014). A way forward for video game violence research. *American Psychologist*, *69*(3), 307–309.

Ferguson, C., & Ivory, J. (2012). A futile game: on the prevalence and causes of misguided speculation about the role of violence video games in mass school shootings. In G. Muschert & J. Sumiala (Eds.), *School shootings: mediatized violence in a global age* (pp. 47–68). Chicago, IL: Emerald.

Ferguson, C., & Olson, C. (2014). Video game violence use among 'vulnerable' populations: the impact of violent games on delinquency and bullying among children with clinically elevated depression or attention deficit symptoms. *Journal of Youth and Adolescence*, *43*, 127–136.

Feuer, J. (1992). Genre study and television. In R. Allen (Ed.), *Channels of discourse, reassembled* (pp. 138–160). London: Routledge.

Fischoff, S. (1996). Sources of stereotyped images of the mentally ill. *Journal of Media Psychology*, *1*(1), 4–11.

Fiske, J. (1987). *Television culture*. London: Methuen.

Fiske, J. (1993). *Power plays, power works*. London: Verso.

Fiske, J., & Hartley, J. (1978). *Reading television*. London: Routledge.

Friedersdorf, C. (2015). Campus activists weaponize 'safe space'. *The Atlantic*. Retrieved from https://www.theatlantic.com/politics/archive/2015/11/how-campus-activists-are-weaponizing-the-safe-space/415080/

Fuchs, C. (2011). WikiLeaks. Power 2.0? Surveillance 2.0? Criticism 2.0? Alternative media 2.0? A political-economic analysis. *Global Media Journal: Australian Edition*, *5*(1), 1–17.

Fuqua, J. V. (2011). Brand Pitt: celebrity activism and the Make It Right Foundation in post-Katrina New Orleans. *Celebrity Studies*, *2*(2), 192–208.

G226. (1981). Mass Observations Correspondents PDfs 1981 Royal Wedding. Retrieved from https://drive.google.com/drive/folders/0Bz-9hs_TdzGPUk YzYlFMMG9Hak0

Gao, F., & Martin-Kratzer, R. (2011). Gender differences in Chinese journalists' blogs. *Chinese Journal of Communication*, *4*(2), 167–181. doi:10.1080/17544 750.2011.565675.

Garnham, N. (1983). Toward a theory of cultural materialism. *Journal of Communication*, *33*(3), 314–329.

Gauntlett, D. (2011). *Media studies 2.0, and other battles around the future of audience research*. Retrieved from www.theory.org.uk/david/kindle. htm

Gellman, B. (2010). Person of the year, 2010. *Time*. Retrieved from http:// content.time.com/time/specials/packages/article/0,28804,2036683_2037 118_2037146,00.html

Gerbner, G. (1958a). The social anatomy of the romance – confession cover girl. *Journalism and Mass Communication Quarterly*, *35*(3), 299–306.

Gerbner, G. (1958b). On content analysis and critical research in mass communication. *AV Communication Review*, *6*(2), 85–108.

Gerbner, G. (1960). The individual in a mass culture. *Saturday Review*, June 18, 11–37.

Gerbner, G. (1966). An institutional approach to mass communications research. In L. Thayer (Ed.), *Communication: Theory and research*. Spingfield, IL: Charles Thomas.

Gerbner, G. (1969a). Toward 'cultural indicators': the analysis of mass mediated public message. *AV Communication Review*, *17*(2), 137–148.

Gerbner, G. (1969b). The film hero: a cross-cultural study. *Journalism Monographs*, *13*, 1–54.

Gerbner, G. (1973). Cultural indicators: The third voice. In G. Gerbner, L. Gross, & W. Melody (Eds.), *Communications technology and social policy* (pp. 555–573). New York: John Wiley.

Gerbner, G. (1983). The importance of being critical – in one's own fashion. *Journal of Communication*, *33*(3), 355–362.

Gerbner, G. (1993). Images that hurt: mental illness in the mass media. *Journal of the California Alliance for the Mentally Ill*, *4*(1), 17–20.

Gerbner, G. (1994). The politics of media violence: some reflections. In C. Hamelink & O. Linne (Eds.), *Mass communication research: on problems and policies* (pp. 133–146). Norwood, NJ: Ablex.

Gerbner, G. (1995). The cultural frontier: repression, violence, and the liberating alternative. In P. Lee (Ed.), *The democratization of communication* (pp. 153–172). Cardiff: University of Wales Press.

REFERENCES

Gerbner, G. (1998). Cultivation analysis: an overview. *Mass Communication and Society*, *1*(3–4), 175–195.

Gerbner, G. (2001). If Adolf Hitler … *Znet*. Retrieved from http://web.asc.upenn.edu/Gerbner/Asset.aspx?assetID=2794

Gerbner, G., & Gross, L. (1979). A reply to Newcomb's 'Humanistic Critique'. *Communication Research*, *6*(2), 223–230.

Gerbner, G., Gross, L., Jackson-Beck, M., Jackson-Fox, S., & Signorielli, N. (1979). Cultural indicators: violence profile #9. *Journal of Communication*, *28*(3), 176–207.

Gerbner, G. & Tannenbaum, P. (1961). Regulation of mental illness content in motion pictures and television. *Gazette: International Journal for Communication Studies*, *6*, 365–385.

Gerbner, G., Gross, L., Morgan, M., & Signorielli, N. (1980). The "mainstreaming" of America: violence profile #11. *Journal of Communication*, *30*, 10–29.

Gibbons, T. (2015). Active pluralism: dialogue and engagement as basic media policy principles. *International Journal of Communication*, *9*, 1382–1399.

Gitlin, T. (1978). Media sociology: the dominant paradigm. *Theory and Society*, *6*(2), 205–253.

Gitlin, T. (1987). Prime time ideology: the hegemonic process in broadcast television. In H. Newcomb (Ed.), *Television, the critical view* (4th ed., pp. 507–532). New York: Oxford University Press.

Gleeson, M. (2006). Players feel pain of giving rivals the slip at Docklands stadium – FOOTBALL. *The Age*, August 10, p. 2.

Gogglebox Australia (Producer). (2015). *Princess Mary*. Retrieved from www.youtube.com/watch?v=M7gLZU6s970

Goodman, A. (2014). 'Women are being driven offline': Feminist Anita Sarkeesian terrorized for critique of video games. *Democracy Now*. Retrieved from https://www.democracynow.org/2014/10/20/women_are_being_driven_offline_feminist

Görzig, A., & Ólafsson, K. (2013). What makes a bully a cyberbully? Unravelling the characteristics of cyberbullies across twenty-five European countries. *Journal of Children & Media*, *7*(1), 9–27.

Granatt, M. (2004). On trust: using public information and warning partnerships to support the community response to an emergency. *Journal of Communication Management*, *8*(4), 354–365.

GrandPrix 247. (2016). Heineken want more F1 races in Asia Pacific, 2016. *GrandPrix247*. Retrieved from http://www.grandprix247.com/2016/09/26/heineken-want-more-f1-races-in-asia-pacific/

Gray, A. (2003). *Research practice for cultural studies*. London: Sage.

Gross, K., Aday, S., & Brewer, P. R. (2004). A panel study of media effects on political and social trust after September 11, 2001. *Harvard International Journal of Press/Politics*, *9*(4), 49–73. doi:10.1177/1081 180X04269138.

Grossman, B. (2011). Dana White. *Broadcasting and Cable*, *141*, 10–16.

GUMG (Glasgow University Media Group). (1976) *Bad news*. London: Routledge and Kegan Paul.

GUMG. (1980) *More bad news*. London: Routledge and Kegan Paul.

GUMG. (1985) *War and peace news*. Milton Keynes: Open University Press.

Gunter, B. (2008). Media violence: is there a case for causality? *American Behavioral Scientist, 51*(8), 1061–1122.

Gunter, B., Hansen, A., & Touri, M. (2010). *Alcohol advertising and young people's drinking*. Basingstoke: Palgrave Macmillan.

H260. (1981). Mass Observations correspondents PDfs 1981 Royal Wedding. Retrieved from https://drive.google.com/drive/folders/0Bz-9hs_TdzGPU kYzYlFMMG9Hak0

Hald, G., & Malamuth, N. (2008). Self-perceived effects of pornography consumption. *Archives of Sexual Behavior, 37*, 614–625.

Hall, S. (1978). *Policing the crisis: mugging, the state, and law and order*. London: Macmillan.

Hall, S. (1980). Encoding/decoding. In S. Hall (Ed.), *Culture, media, language: working papers in cultural studies* (pp. 129–138). London Hutchinson.

Halton, B. (1998). *Saving Private Ryan* is too real for some. *Florida Times-Union*. Retrieved from http://jacksonville.com/tu-online/stories/081598/met_ 2a1priva.html#.WAgEQ5h95Bw

Hammersley, M., & Atkinson, P. (1995). *Ethnography: principles in practice*. London: Routledge.

Hanitzsch, T., Hanusch, F., Mellado, C., Anikina, M., Berganza, R., Cangoz, I., & Yuen, E. K. W. (2011). Mapping journalism cultures across nations: a comparative study of 18 countries. *Journalism Studies, 12*(3), 273–293. doi:10.10 80/1461670X.2010.512502.

Hardaker, C. (2010). Trolling in asynchronous computer-mediated communication: from user discussions to academic definitions. *Journal of Politeness Research: Language, Behavior, Culture, 6*(2), 215–242.

Harper, S. (2005). Media, madness and misrepresentation: critical reflections on anti-stigma discourse. *European Journal of Communication, 20*(4), 460–483.

Hartmann, T., Toz, E., & Brandon, M. (2010). Just a game? Unjustified virtual violence produces guilt in empathetic players. *Media Psychology, 13*(4), 339–363.

Harvey, D. (1990). *The condition of postmodernity: an enquiry into the origins of cultural change*. Oxford: Blackwell.

Hasian, M. (2012). Watching the domestication of the Wikileaks helicopter controversy. *Communication Quarterly, 60*, 190–209.

Hasinoff, A. (2013). Sexting as media production: rethinking social media and sexuality. *New Media & Society, 15*(4), 449–465.

Heemsbergen, L. J. (2013). Radical transparency in journalism: digital evolutions from historical precedents. *Global Media Journal: Canadian Edition, 6*(1), 45–65.

Henderson, L. (2008). Slow love. *Communication Review, 11*, 219–224.

Hepp, A. (2013). *Cultures of mediatization*. Cambridge: Polity Press.

Herald Scotland. (2016). Poll finds most Brits support the monarchy. Retrieved from http://www.heraldscotland.com/news/14430937.Poll_finds_most_ Brits_support_the_monarchy/

Hesmondhalgh, D. (2004). *Cultural industries*. London: Sage.

Hesmondhalgh, D. (2009). Politics, theory and method in media industries research. In J. Holt & A. Perren (Eds.), *Media industries: history, theory and method* (pp. 245–255). Chichester: Wiley-Blackwell.

Hesmondhalgh, D., & Baker, S. (2013). *Creative labour*. London: Routledge.

Hess, A. (2007a). In digital remembrance: vernacular memory and the rhetorical construction of web memorials. *Media, Culture & Society*, *29*(5), 812–830.

Hess, A. (2007b). 'You don't play, you volunteer': narrative public memory construction in *Medal of Honor: Rising Sun*. *Critical Studies in Media Communication*, *24*(4), 339–356.

Hess, A., & Herbig, A. R. T. (2013). Recalling the ghosts of 9/11: convergent memorializing at the opening of the National 9/11 Memorial. *International Journal of Communication*, *7*, 2207–2230.

Higgins, M. (2010). The 'Publicinquisitor' as media celebrity. *Cultural Politics*, *6*(1), 93–110.

Higgins, M., & Smith, A. (2010). Not one of us: Kate Adie's report of the 1986 US bombing of Tripoli and its critical aftermath. *Journalism Studies*, *12*(3), 344–358.

Highfill, S. (2014). 'Bates Motel' postmortem: EP on Norman's memory, Dylan's [spoiler!], and 'burning flame' between Norma and Romero. *Entertainment Weekly*. Retrieved from http://insidetv.ew.com/2014/04/28/bates-motel-postmortem-season-2-penultimate/

Hill, A. (2005). *Shocking entertainment: viewer response to violent movies*. Bedford: University of Luton Press.

Hine, C. (2000). *Virtual ethnography*. London: Sage.

Hinnant, A., & Hendrickson, E. M. (2014). Negotiating normalcy in celebrity health behavior: a focus group analysis. *Journal of Magazine & New Media Research*, *14*(2), 1–20.

Hitchens, M., Patrickson, B., & Young, S. (2014). Reality and terror: the first-person shooter in current-day settings. *Games and Culture*, *9*(1), 3–29.

Hjarvard, S. (2013). *The mediatization of culture and society*. New York: Routledge.

Hoffner, C. A., & Cohen, E. L. (2012). Responses to Obsessive Compulsive Disorder on *Monk* among series fans: parasocial relations, presumed media influence, and behavioral outcomes. *Journal of Broadcasting & Electronic Media*, *56*(4), 650–668.

Hoggart, R. (1976). Foreword. In G. U. M. Group (Ed.), *Bad news* (pp. ix–xiv). London: Routledge and Kegan Paul.

Höijer, B., & Rasmussen, J. (2007). Making sense of violent events in public spaces. *Nordicom Review*, *28*(1), 3–15.

Hong, S.-H. (2015). When life mattered: the politics of the real in video games' reappropriation of history, myth, and ritual. *Games and Culture*, *10*(1), 35–56.

Horner, J., & Minifie, F. D. (2011). Research ethics I: Responsible Conduct of Research (RCR) – historical and contemporary issues pertaining to human and animal experimentation. *Journal of Speech, Language & Hearing Research*, *54*(1), 303–329.

Houston, J. B. (2013). Long-term sociopolitical effects of 9/11 television viewing, emotions, and parental conversation in U.S. young adults who were children in 2001. *Communication Research Reports*, *30*(3), 183–192.

Houston, S. L. (2014). About Pink and White Productions. Retrieved from http://pinkwhite.biz/about/

Hovland, C. (1959). Reconciling conflicting results derived from experimental and survey studies of attitude change. *American Psychologist, 14*(1), 8–17.

Hovland, C., Lumsdaine, A., & Sheffield., F. (1949). *Experiments on mass communication. Vol. III of studies in social psychology in World War II*. Princeton, NJ: Princeton University Press.

Howell, P. (2012). Early radio news and the origins of the risk society. *Radio Journal: International Studies in Broadcast & Audio Media, 10*(2), 131–143. doi:10.1386/rjao.10.2.131_1.

Huffington Post. (2013). 'Bates Motel' renewed for Season 2 on A&E. *Huffington Post*. Retrieved from http://www.huffingtonpost.com/2013/04/08/bates-motel-renewed-season-2-a-e_n_3039230.html

Hutchins, B. (2005). *Don Bradman: challenging the myth*. Cambridge, UK: Cambridge University Press.

Hutchins, B., & Rowe, D. (2013). *Sport beyond television: the internet, digital media and the rise of networked media sport*. London: Routledge.

Innis, H. (2007). *Empire and communication*. Toronto: Dundurn Press.

Innis, H. (2008). *The bias of communication* (2nd ed.). Toronto: University of Toronto Press.

Jackson, S. (2015). Assessing the sociology of sport: on media, advertising and the commodification of culture. *International Review for the Sociology of Sport, 50*(4–5), 490–495.

Jamal, A., & Melkote, S. R. (2008). Viewing and avoidance of the Al-Jazeera satellite television channel in Kuwait: a uses and gratifications perspective. *Asian Journal of Communication, 18*(1), 1–15. doi:10.1080/01292980701823732.

Jebril, N., Albæk, E., & de Vreese, C. H. (2013). Infotainment, cynicism and democracy: the effects of privatization vs personalization in the news. *European Journal of Communication, 28*(2), 105–121. doi:10.1177/0267323112468683.

Jenkins, H. (2006). *Convergence culture: Where old and new media collide*. New York: New York University Press.

Jensen, R. (1998). Pornographic dodges and distortions. In G. Dines, R. Jensen, & A. Russo (Eds.), *Pornography: The production and consumption of inequality* (pp. 1–8). New York: Routledge.

Jhally, S., & Lewis, J. (1992). *Enlightened racism: The Cosby Show, audiences, and the myth of the American dream*. Boulder, CO: Westview Press.

Jo, S. (2005). The effect of online media credibility on trust relationships. *Journal of Website Promotion, 1*(2), 57–78. doi:10.1300/J238v01n02•04.

Johnson, D. A. (2008). Managing Mr. Monk: control and the politics of madness. *Critical Studies in Media Communication, 25*(1), 28–47. doi:10.1080/15295030701851130.

Jolie-Pitt, A. (2015). Angelina Jolie-Pitt: Diary of a surgery. *New York Times Online*. Retrieved from https://www.nytimes.com/2015/03/24/opinion/angelina-jolie-pitt-diary-of-a-surgery.html

Jones, D. A. (2004). Why Americans don't trust the media. *Harvard International Journal of Press/Politics, 9*(2), 60–75. doi:10.1177/1091191X04263461.

Jones, S. (2013). Ask.fm pledges cyberbullying reform after Hannah Smith death. *The Guardian*, August 19. Retrieved from www.theguardian.com/society/2013/aug/19/ask-fm-cyberbully-hannah-smith-death

Jowett, G., Jarvie, I., & Fuller, K. H. (1996). *Children and the movies: media influence and the Payne Fund controversy*. Cambridge: Cambridge University Press.

Kalyango, J. Y. (2014). East Africans find radio more credible than newspapers. *Newspaper Research Journal*, *35*(2), 56–69.

Katz, E. (1983). The return of the humanities and sociology. *Journal of Communication*, *33*(3), 51–52.

Katz, E., & Lazarsfeld, P. (1955). *Personal influence: the part played by people in the flow of mass communication*. Glencoe, IL: Free Press.

Katz, J. (Writer). (1999). *Tough Guise*. Northampton, MA: Media Education Foundation.

Kellner, D. (1987). TV, ideology and emancipatory popular culture. In H. Newcomb (Ed.), *Television, the critical view* (pp. 471–504). New York: Oxford University Press.

Kellner, D. (2004). 9/11, spectacles of terror, and media manipulation. *Critical Discourse Studies*, *1*(1), 41–64.

Kellner, D., & Share, J. (2005). Toward critical media literacy: core concepts, debates, organizations, and policy. *Discourse: studies in the cultural politics of education*, *26*(3), 369–386.

Keogh, B. (2012). *Killing is harmless*. Marden, Australia: Stolen Projects.

Kim, H. S. (2010). Forces of gatekeeping and journalists' perceptions of physical danger in post-Saddam Hussein's Iraq. *Journalism and Mass Communication Quarterly*, *87*(3/4), 484–500.

Kimmel, R. (Writer). (2015). *Guyland*. Northampton, MA: Media Education Foundation.

Kingsepp, E. (2007). Fighting hyperreality with hyperreality history and death in World War II digital games. *Games and Culture*, *2*(4), 366–375.

Kingston, P. (2007). Confronting risk. *Guardian Online*. Retrieved from https://www.theguardian.com/education/2007/jul/03/academicexperts.highereducation

Kinnebrock, S. (2009). Revisiting journalism as a profession in the 19th century: empirical findings on women journalists in Central Europe. *Communications*, *34*, 107–124. doi:10.1515/COMM.2009.009.

Kitch, C. (2003). 'Mourning in America': ritual, redemption, and recovery in news narrative after September 11. *Journalism Studies*, *4*(2), 213.

Kitzinger, J. (2004). *Framing abuse: media influence and public understanding of sexual violence against children*. London: Pluto Press.

Klin, A., & Lemish, D. (2008). Mental disorders stigma in the media: review of studies on production, content, and influences. *Journal of Health Communication*, *13*(5), 434–449.

Knightly, P. (1976) *The first casualty*. Baltimore, MD: Johns Hopkins Press.

Kolakowski, L. (1993). An overall view of positivism. In M. Hammersley (Ed.), *Social research: philosophy, politics and practice* (pp. 1–8). London: Sage.

Krippendorff, K. (1995). Undoing power. *Critical Studies in Media Communication*, *12*(2), 101–132.

Kuensel Online. (2010). Horsemen from Damchena. *Kuensel Online*. Retrieved from www.kuenselonline.com/2010/

Lafayette, J. (2011). UFC deal is all about FX sub fees for News Corp. *Broadcasting & Cable*, *141*(32), 8–8.

Lafayette, J. (2012a). Fuel rebrands as UFC climbs on board. *Broadcasting and Cable*, *141*(46), 4.

Lafayette, J. (2012b). Fox draws beers as UFC sponsors. *Broadcasting and Cable*, *142*(4), 12.

Lasswell, H. (1971). *Propaganda technique in World War I*. Cambridge, MA: MIT Press.

Lazarsfeld, P. (1941). Remarks on administrative and critical communications research. *Studies in Philosophy and Social Science*, *9*, 2–16.

Lee, S. (Writer). (2016). *Two Fists Up*. YouTube: ESPN.

Leiss, W., Kline, S., & Jhally, S. (2002). *Social communication in advertising*. London: Routledge.

Lent, J. (1995). *A different road taken: profiles in critical communication*. Boulder, CO: Westview Press.

Lewis, J. (1990). *Art, culture and enterprise*. London: Routledge.

Lewis, J. (1991). *The ideological octopus*. London: Routledge.

Lewis, J. (2013). *Beyond consumer capitalism: media and the limits to imagination*. Cambridge: Polity.

Lewis, S., Zamith, R., & Hermida, A. (2013). Content analysis in an era of Big Data: a hybrid approach to computational and manual methods. *Journal of Broadcasting & Electronic Media*, *57*(1), 34–52.

Limbaugh, R. (Producer). (2015). Melissa Click is not who you think she is. Retrieved from http://dailyrushbo.com/rush-melissa-click-is-not-who-you-think-she-is/

Linnell, S. (1996). Bulldogs' eyes on Docklands stadium as a future home. *The Age*, October 19, p. 1.

Linnell, S. (1997). Docklands stadium lease bonus for AFL. *The Age*, August 26, p. 1.

Lipinski, T. (2008). Emerging legal issues in the collection and dissemination of internet-sourced research data: Part I, basic tort law issues and negligence. *International Journal of Internet Research*, *1*(1), 92–114.

Livingstone, S. (2013). Online risk, harm and vulnerability: reflections on the evidence base for child Internet safety policy. *ZER: Journal of Communication Studies*, *18*(35), 13–28.

Livingstone, S., Allen, J., & Reiner, R. (2001). Audiences for crime media 1946–91: a historical approach to reception studies. *Communication Review*, *4*(2), 165.

Livingstone, S., & Helsper, E. (2013). Children, internet and risk in comparative perspective. *Journal of Children and Media*, *7*(1), 1–8.

Livingstone, S., Kirwil, L., Ponte, C., & Staksrud, E. (2013). In their own words: what bothers children online? With the EU Kids Online Network. *LSE Research Online*. Retrieved from http://eprints.lse.ac.uk

Livingstone, S., & Lunt, P. (2007). Representing citizens and consumers in media and communications regulation. *Annals of the American Academy of Political and Social Science*, *611*(1), 51–65. doi:10.1177/0002716206298710.

Lo, V.-H., Wei, R., & Wu, H. (2010). Examining the first, second and third-person effects of internet pornography on Taiwanese adolescents: implications for the restriction of pornography. *Asian Journal of Communication*, *20*(1), 90–103.

Lunt, P., & Livingstone, S. (2009). The regulator, the public and the media: imagining a role for the public in communication regulation. *Intermedia*, *37*(1), 26–29.

MacDonald, D. (1953). A theory of mass culture. *Diogenes*, *1*(3): 1–17.

Macias, W., Stavchansky-Lewis, L., & Smith, T. (2005). Health-related message boards/chat rooms on the web: discussion content and implications for pharmaceutical sponsorships. *Journal of Health Communication*, *10*(3), 209–233.

Maher, B. (2010). Understanding and regulating the sport of mixed martial arts. *Hastings Communications & Entertainment Law Journal*, *32*(2), 209–246.

Maras, S. (2014). Media accountability: double binds and responsibility gaps. *Global Media Journal: Australian Edition*, *8*(2), 1–13.

Markham, A., & Buchanan, E. (2012). Ethical decision-making and internet research. *Recommendations from the AoIR Ethics Working Committee*. Retrieved from https://aoir.org/reports/ethics2.pdf

Markham, T. (2011a). The political phenomenology of war reporting. *Journalism*, *12*(5), 567–585.

Markham, T. (2011b). *The politics of war reporting: authority, authenticity and morality*. Manchester: Manchester University Press.

Markham, T. (2012a). The uses and functions of ageing celebrity war reporters. *Celebrity Studies*, *3*(2), 127–137.

Markham, T. (2012b). The correspondent's experience of war. In A. Plaw (Ed.), *The metamorphosis of war* (pp. 167–190). Amsterdam: Rodopi.

Marriott, S. (2007). The BBC, ITN and the funeral of Princess Diana. *Media History*, *13*(1), 93–110. doi:10.1080/13688800701265048.

Marwick, A. (2013). *Status update: celebrity, publicity and branding in the social media age*. New Haven, CT: Yale University Press.

Marwick, A., & Ellison, N. (2012). 'There isn't wifi in heaven!' Negotiating visibility on Facebook memorial pages. *Journal of Broadcasting and Electronic Media*, *56*(3), 378–400.

Masterman, L. (1985). *Teaching the media*. London: Routledge.

Masterman, L. (2010). *Voices of media literacy. International pioneers speak: Len Masterman interview transcript/interviewer: D. Morgenthaler*. Center for Media Literacy.

McDonald, M., Licari, P., & Merivaki, L. (2015). The big cost of using big data in elections. *The Washington Post*, October 18. Retrieved from www.washington post.com/opinions/the-big-cost-of-using-big-data-in-elections/2015/10/18/cb7bdf6c-7443-11e5-8248-98e0f5a2e830_story.html?utm_term=.e53eb72339ab

McDonald, S. (2014). 'Gamergate': feminist video game critic Anita Sarkeesian cancels Utah lecture after threat. *The Washington Post*, October 15. Retrieved from www.washingtonpost.com/news/morning-mix/wp/2014/10/15/

gamergate-feminist-video-game-critic-anita-sarkeesian-cancels-utah-lecture-after-threat-citing-police-inability-to-prevent-concealed-weapons-at-event/

McGinty, E. E., Webster, D. W., Jarlenski, M., & Barry, C. L. (2014). News media framing of serious mental illness and gun violence in the United States, 1997–2012. *American Journal of Public Health*, *104*(3), 406–413.

McHugh, K. (2014). Of agency and embodiment: Angelina Jolie's autographic transformations. *Celebrity Studies*, *5*(1), 5–19.

McKee, A. (2006a). Censorship of sexually explicit materials in Australia: what do consumers of pornography have to say about it? *Media International Australia*, *120*, 35–50.

McKee, A. (2006b). The aesthetics of pornography: the insights of consumers. *Continuum: Journal of Media & Cultural Studies*, *20*(4), 523–539.

McKee, A. (2012). Pornography as entertainment. *Continuum: Journal of Media & Cultural Studies*, *26*(4), 541–552.

McMahon, S. (2009). New Docklands stadium push. *Herald Sun*, April 30, p. 1.

McNair, B. (2006). *Cultural chaos: journalism and power in a globalised world*. London: Verso.

McNair, B. (2012). Wikileaks, journalism and the consequences of chaos. *Media International Australia*, *144*, 77–86.

McNair, B. (2014). Rethinking the effects paradigm in porn studies. *Porn Studies*, *1*(1–2), 161–171.

McRobbie, A., & Garber, J. (1978). Girls and subcultures. In S. Hall & T. Jefferson (Eds.), *Resistance through rituals* (pp. 209–222). London: Hutchinson.

Meikle, G. (2012). Continuity and transformation in convergent news: the case of Wikileaks. *Media International Australia*, *144*, 52–59.

Meikle, G., & Young, S. (2012). *Media convergence: networked digital media and everyday life*. Basingstoke: Palgrave Macmillan.

Meyer, G. (2004). Diffusion methodology: time to innovate? *Journal of Health Communication*, *9*(1), 59–69.

Michelle, C. (2007). Modes of reception: a consolidated analytical framework. *Communication Review*, *10*(3), 181–222. doi:10.1080/10714420701 528057.

Michelle, C., Davis, C. H., & Vladica, F. (2012). Understanding variation in audience engagement and response: an application of the composite model to receptions of *Avatar* (2009). *Communication Review*, *15*(1), 106–143. doi:10. 1080/10714421.2012.674467.

Miladi, N. (2008). Mediating wars and conflicts: North African TV audiences in the UK and the changing security landscape. *Journal of Arab & Muslim Media Research*, *1*(3), 245–257. doi:10.1386/jammr.1.3.245/1.

Miller, S. (2013). UFC: two decades of eventful growth. *Broadcasting and Cable*, *143*(42), 3–9.

Miller-Young, M. (2015). Race and the politics of agency porn: a conversation with black BBW performer Betty Blac. In L. Comella & S. Tarrant (Eds.), *New views on pornography: sexuality, politics, and the law* (pp. 359–370). New York: Praeger.

Millward, P. (2008). Rivalries and racisms: 'closed' and 'open' Islamophobic dispositions amongst football supporters. *Sociological Research Online*, *13*(6). Retrieved from www.socresonline.org.uk/13/6/5.html

Mondin, A. (2014). Fair-trade porn + niche markets + feminist audience. *Porn Studies*, *1*(1–2), 189–192.

Monson, M. (2012). Race-based fantasy realm. *Games and Culture*, *7*(1), 48–71. doi:10.1177/1555412012440308.

Montgomery, M. (1999). Speaking sincerely: public reactions to the death of Diana. *Language & Literature*, *8*(1), 5.

Moores, S. (1996). *Satellite television in everyday life*. Bedford: University of Luton Press.

Morgan, M. (2012). *George Gerbner: a critical introduction to media and communication theory*. New York: Peter Lang.

Morgan, M., Lewis, J., & Jhally, S. (1991). *The Gulf War: A study of the media, public opinion, and public knowledge*. Amherst, MA: Center for the Study of Communication.

Morley, D. (1980). *The nationwide audience*. London: BFI.

Morley, D. (1989). *Family television*. London: BFI.

Morley, D. (1992). *Television audiences*. London: Routledge.

Morley, D. (2006). Unanswered questions in audience research. *Communication Review*, *9*(2), 101–121. doi:10.1080/10714420600663286.

Morozov, E. (2011). *The Net Delusion: how not to liberate the world*. London: Penguin.

Moss, R. (2016). Alcohol adverts 'Shown once every 72 seconds' during Euro 2016 Games. Huffpost UK. Retrieved from http://www.huffingtonpost.co.uk/entry/alcohol-adverts-during-euros_uk_5770de29e4b08d2c56397688

Murnane, M. (2014). Seven wants Docklands stadium roof closed permanently. *The Age*, August 15, p. 44.

Musa, A. O., & Ferguson, N. (2013). Enemy framing and the politics of reporting religious conflicts in the Nigerian press. *Media, War and Conflict*, *6*(1), 7–20. doi:10.1177/1750635212469909.

Muschert, G. (2007). The Columbine victims and the myth of the juvenile superpredator. *Youth Violence & Juvenile Justice*, *5*(4), 351–366.

N403. (1981). Mass Observations correspondents PDfs 1981 Royal Wedding. Retrieved from https://drive.google.com/drive/folders/0Bz-9hs_TdzGPUkYzYlFMMG9Hak0

National Health and Medical Research Council. (2014). *National statement on ethical conduct in human research*. Retrieved from file:///Users/andyruddock/Downloads/National%20Statement%20on%20Ethical%20Conduct%20in%20Human%20Research%20(2007)%20(Updated%20May%202015)%20-%2015-May-2015.pdf

Nawková, L., Nawka, A., Adámková, T., Rukavina, T. V., Holcnerová, P., Kuzman, M. R., ... & Raboch, J. (2012). The picture of mental health/illness in the printed media in three Central European countries. *Journal of Health Communication*, *17*(1), 22–40.

Neuhaus, F., & Webmoor, T. (2011). Agile ethics for massified research and visualization. *Information, Communication & Society*, *15*(1), 43–65.

Newcomb, H. (1978). Assessing the violence profile studies of Gerbner and Gross: a humanistic critique and suggestion. *Communication Research, 5*(3), 264–282.

Newcomb, H. (1987). Television and the climate of criticism. In H. Newcomb (Ed.), *Television, the critical view* (4th ed., pp. 3–12). New York: Oxford University Press.

Newell, J., Blevins, J. L., & Bugeja, M. (2009). Tragedies of the broadcast commons: consumer perspectives on the ethics of product placement and video news releases. *Journal of Mass Media Ethics, 24*(4), 201–219. doi:10.1080/08900520903321025.

NHMRC (National Health and Medical Research Council, Australia) (2014). *National Statement on Ethical Conduct in Human Research.* Canberra: NHMRC.

Nicholls, J. (2006). Liberties and licences: alcohol in liberal thought. *International Journal of Cultural Studies, 9*(2), 131–151.

Nicholls, J. (2012). Everyday, everywhere: alcohol marketing and social media – current trends. *Alcohol and Alcoholism, 47*(4), 486–493.

Nickel, P. M. (2012). Philanthromentality: celebrity parables as technologies of transfer. *Celebrity Studies, 3*(2), 163–182.

Niederdeppe, J. (2008). Beyond knowledge gaps: examining socioeconomic differences in response to cancer news. *Human Communication Research, 34*(3), 423–447.

Noar, S. M., Willoughby, J. F., Myrick, J. G., & Brown, J. (2014). Public figure announcements about cancer and opportunities for cancer communication: a review and research agenda. *Health Communication, 29*(5), 445–461. doi:10.1080/10410236.2013.764781.

Norris, B. (2002). Media ethics at the sharp end. In D. Berry (Ed.), *Ethics and media culture: Practices and representation* (pp. 325–38). Burlington, MA: Focal Press.

Oakley, K., & O'Connor, J. (2015). The cultural industries. In K. Oakley & J. O'Connor (Eds.), *The Routledge companion to the cultural industries.* London: Routledge.

Oates, A. (2015). UFC 193: drawcard Ronda Rousey works magic as women take centre stage in Melbourne. *Herald Sun.* Retrieved from www.heraldsun.com.au/sport/more-sports/ufc-193-drawcard-ronda-rousey-works-magic-as-women-take-centre-stage-in-melbourne/news-story/f078b8d919c02b8ec3926502c43062de

O'Brien, K.S., Carr, S., Ferris, J., Room, R., Miller, P., Livingston, M. et al. (2015) Alcohol advertising in sport and non-sport tv in Australia, during children's viewing times. *PLoS ONE, 10*(8): e0134889. doi:10.1371/journal.pone.0134889.

OFCOM. (n.d.). The Designation of the ASA. Retrieved from https://www.ofcom.org.uk/tv-radio-and-on-demand/information-for-industry/on-demand/designation-asa

O'Regan, V. R. (2014). The celebrity influence: do people really care what they think? *Celebrity Studies, 5*(4), 469–483.

Paasonen, S. (2010). Labors of love: netporn, Web 2.0 and the meanings of amateurism. *New Media & Society, 12*(8), 1297–1312.

Palmer, C. (2009). The 'grog squad': an ethnography of beer consumption at Australian rules football. In L. Wenner & S. Jackson (Eds.), *Sport, beer and gender: promotional culture and contemporary social life*. New York: Peter Lang.

Pantti, M. (2005). Masculine tears, feminine tears – and crocodile tears: mourning Olof Palme and Anna Lindh in Finnish newspapers. *Journalism*, *6*(3), 357–377.

Parker, A. (2016). Donald Trump's 'Taco Bowl' message: 'I love Hispanics'. *New York Times*, May 5. Retrieved from www.nytimes.com/politics/first-draft/2016/05/05/donald-trump-taco-bowl/?_r=0

Parrott, R. (2009). *Talking about health: why communication matters*. Chichester: Wiley-Blackwell.

Payne, G., & Williams, M. (2005). Generalization in qualitative research. *Sociology*, *39*(2), 295–314.

Pearce, B. (2007). *Making social worlds*. Cambridge, MA: Blackwell.

Pearce, B., & Foss, K. (1990). The historical context of communication as a science. In G. Dahnke & G. Clatterbuck (Eds.), *Human communication: theory and research* (pp. 1–19). San Francisco, CA: Wadsworth.

Peters, J. D. (1999). *Speaking into the air: a history of the idea of communication*. Chicago, IL: University of Chicago Press.

Petit, C. (2015). Gender breakdown of games shown at E3. *Feminist Frequency*. Retrieved from https://feministfrequency.com/2016/06/17/gender-breakdown-of-games-showcased-at-e3-2016/

Phillips, A. (2013). Journalism, ethics and the impact of competition. In N. Couldry, M. Madianou, & A. Pinchevski (Eds.), *Ethics of media* (pp. 255–270). Basingstoke: Palgrave Macmillan.

Pickard, V. (2014). The great evasion: confronting market failure in American media policy. *Critical Studies in Media Communication*, *31*(2), 153–159. doi:10.1080/15295036.2014.919404.

Pieslak, J. (2009). *Sound targets*. Bloomington, IN: Indiana University Press.

Pirkis, J., Blood, R. W., Francis, C., & McCallum, K. (2006). On-screen portrayals of mental illness: extent, nature, and impacts. *Journal of Health Communication*, *11*(5), 523–541.

Portovedo, S. F. F., Tomás, D. R. G., & Carvalheiro, J. R. P. (2015). Ritual television. *Media History*, *21*(2), 150–161. doi:10.1080/13688804.2014.977239.

Powdermaker, H. (1951). *Hollywood, the dream factory: An anthropologist looks at the movie-makers*. London: Secker and Warburg.

Press, A. (1991). *Women watching television: gender, class, and generation in the American television experience*. Philadelphia, PA: University of Pennsylvania Press.

QSR International (Producer). (2015). Easily collect and analyze social media content from Twitter using NVivo. Retrieved from https://youtu.be/02x4uLWBT5I

R470. (1981). Mass Observations Correspondents PDFs 1981 Royal Wedding. Retrieved from https://drive.google.com/drive/folders/0Bz-9hs_TdzGPUkYzYlFMMG9Hak0

Ranney, A. (1976). Thirty years of 'psephology'. *British Journal of Political Science*, *6*(2), 217–230. doi:10.1017/S0007123400000636.

Reading, A. (2005). Professing porn or obscene browsing? On proper distance in the university classroom. *Media, Culture & Society, 27*, 123–130.

Reaves, S. (1984). How radical were the muckrakers? Socialist press views, 1902–1906. *Journalism Quarterly, 61*(4), 763–770.

Reuters. (2016). Heineken's F1 deal leads to further call for ban on alcohol sponsorship. *The Guardian.* Retrieved from https://www.theguardian.com/sport/2016/jun/14/heineken-f1-alchohol-sponsorship-eurocare

Roccor, B. (2000). Heavy metal: forces of unification and fragmentation within a musical subculture. *The World of Music, 42*(1), 83–94.

Rojek, C. (2012). *Fame attack: the inflation of celebrity and its consequences.* London: Bloomsbury.

Rosner, J. (2011). Can WikiLeaks save journalism and democracy? *Global Media Journal: Australian Edition, 5*(1), 1–6.

Rousey, R. (2015). *My fight, your fight.* New York: Regan Arts.

Rowe, D. (2004a). *Sport, culture and the media: the unruly trinity* (2nd ed.). Maidenhead: Open University Press.

Rowe, D. (2004b). Mapping the media sports cultural complex. In D. Rowe (Ed.), *Critical readings: sport, culture and the media* (pp. 1–23). Maidenhead: Open University Press.

Rowe, D. (2015). Assessing the sociology of sport: on media and power. *International Review for the Sociology of Sport, 50*(4–5), 575–579.

Rowe, D., Ruddock, A., & Hutchins, B. (2010). Contradictions in media sport culture: the reinscription of football supporter traditions through online media. *European Journal of Cultural Studies, 13*, 323–336. doi:10.1177/136 7549410363200.

Ruddock, A. (2001). *Understanding audiences.* London: Sage.

Ruddock, A. (2005). Let's kick racism out of football – and the lefties too! *Journal of Sport and Social Issues, 29*(4), 369–385.

Ruddock, A. (2007). *Investigating audiences.* London: Sage.

Ruddock, A. (2012). Cultivation analysis and cultural studies. In J. Shanahan, M. Morgan, & N. Signorelli (Eds.), *Living with television now: advances in cultivation theory and research* (pp. 367–385). New York: Peter Lang.

Ruddock, A. (2013a). *Youth and media.* London: Sage.

Ruddock, A. (2013b). 'Born on Swan Street, next to the Yarra': social media and inventing commitment. In B. Hutchins & D. Rowe (Eds.), *Digital media sport: technology and power in the network society.* New York: Routledge.

Ruddock, A. (2015). Reconciling subculture and effects studies: what do students in Australia want to know about media culture? In S. Baker & B. Robards (Eds.), *Youth cultures and subcultures: Australian perspectives.* Aldershot: Ashgate.

Ruddock, A. (2016). Transgression: what do elite footballers represent. In K. Dixon & E. Cashmore (Eds.), *Studying football* (pp. 187–196). London: Routledge.

Ruddock, A. (2017, in press). Regulating social media: reasons not to ask the audience. In A. Lyons, T. McCreanor, I. Goodwin, & H. Barnes (Eds.), *Youth drinking cultures in a digital world: alcohol, social media and cultures of intoxication.* London: Routledge.

Rüsen, J. R. (2003). Mourning by history's ideas of a new element in historical thinking. *Historiography East & West*, *1*(1), 13–38.

S496. (1981). Mass Observations Correspondents PDfs 1981 Royal Wedding. Retrieved from https://drive.google.com/drive/folders/0Bz-9hs_TdzGPU kYzYlFMMG9Hak0

Saarkesian, A. (2014). Women as background decoration (Part 2). *Feminist Frequency*, August. Retrieved from www.feministfrequency.com/2014/08/women-as-background-decoration-part-2/

Saarkesian, A. (2015). Gender breakdown of games shown at E3. *Feminist Frequency*. Retrieved from www.feministfrequency.com

Satran, J. (2015). Trump Posts #AskTrump Twitter callout and it totally backfires. *The Huffington Post*. Retrieved from www.huffingtonpost.com.au/entry/asktrump-trump-twitter_56005dd5e4b00310edf814ef?section=australia

Scharrer, E. (2004). Virtual violence: gender and aggression in video game advertisements. *Mass Communication & Society*, *7*(4), 393–412.

Scharrer, E., Weidman, L., & Bissell, K. (2003). Pointing the finger of blame: news media coverage of popular-culture culpability. *Journalism and Communication Monographs*, *5*(2), 277–294.

Schatzman, L., & Strauss, A. (1973). *Field research: strategies for a natural sociology*. Englewood Cliffs, NJ: Prentice-Hall.

Schimmel, K. (2015). Assessing the sociology of sport: on sport and the city. *International Review for the Sociology of Sport*, *50*(4–5), 591–595.

Schrager, P. (2012). UFC blazing a social media trail. Foxsports.com. Retrieved from www.foxsports.com/ufc/story/ufc-social-media-twitter-facebook-communicating-with-fans-dana-white-080212

Schrøder, K. (2013). From dogmatism to open-mindedness? Historical reflections on methods in audience reception research. *The Communication Review*, *16*, 40–50. doi:10.1080/10714421.2013.757485.

Schulzke, M. (2013) Rethinking military gaming: America's army and its critics. *Games and Culture*, *8*(2), 59–76. doi: 10.1177/1555412013478686.

Sefton-Green, J. (2006). Youth, technology, and media cultures. *Review of Research in Education*, *30*, 279–306.

Seiter, E. (1999). *Television and new media audiences*. Oxford: Oxford University Press.

Sepehri, M. B. (2010). Local radio audiences in Iran: an analysis of Ardebilian people's trust in and satisfaction with 'Sabalan' radio. *Journal of Radio & Audio Media*, *17*(2), 236–250. doi:10.1080/19376529.2010.519656.

Shanahan, J., Morgan, M., & Signorielli, N. (Eds.) (2012). *Living with television now: advances in cultivation theory and research*. New York: Peter Lang.

Shaw, A. (2010). What is video game culture? Cultural studies and game studies. *Games and Culture*, *5*(4), 403–424. doi:10.1177/1555412009360414.

Shaw, R. (2015). Big Data and reality. *Big Data and Society*, *1*(4), 1–4.

Shen, F., & Guo, Z. S. (2013). The last refuge of media persuasion: news use, national pride and political trust in China. *Asian Journal of Communication*, *23*(2), 135–151. doi:10.1080/01292986.2012.725173.

Sherman, D. J. (1998). Bodies and names: the emergence of commemoration in interwar France. *The American Historical Review, 103*(2), 443–466.

Shneer, D. (2011). *Through Jewish eyes: photography, war and the Holocaust.* New Brunswick, NJ: Rutgers University Press.

Shome, R. (2001). White femininity and the discourse of the nation: re/membering Princess Diana. *Feminist Media Studies, 1*(3), 323–342. doi:10.1080/14680770120088927.

Signorielli, N. (1989). The stigma of mental illness on television. *Journal of Broadcasting & Electronic Media, 33*(3), 325–331.

Silver, N. (2012). *The signal and the noise: why so many predictions fail – but some don't.* New York: Penguin.

Silver, N. (2016a). Three theories of Donald Trump's rise. *FiveThirtyEight.* Retrieved from http://fivethirtyeight.com/features/three-theories-of-donald-trumps-rise/

Silver, N. (2016b). How I acted like a pundit and screwed up on Donald Trump. *FiveThirtyEight.* Retrieved from http://fivethirtyeight.com/features/how-i-acted-like-a-pundit-and-screwed-up-on-donald-trump/

Silverman, R. (2013). Ask.fm: 'bullied girl sent hate messages to herself'. *The Telegraph.* Retrieved from www.telegraph.co.uk/technology/10236272/Ask.fm-Bullied-girl-sent-hate-messages-to-herself.html

Silverstone, R. (1994). *Television and everyday life.* London: Routledge.

Silverstone, R. (2004). Editorial: 9/11 and new media. *New Media & Society, 6,* 587–590.

Sisjord, M. K. (2015). Assessing the sociology of sport: on lifestyle sport and gender. *International Review for the Sociology of Sport, 50*(4–5), 596–600.

Sjøvaag, H. (2014). The principles of regulation and the assumption of media effects. *Journal of Media Business Studies, 11*(1), 5–20.

Skuse, A. (2002). Radio, politics and trust in Afghanistan: a social history of broadcasting. *Gazette: International Journal for Communication Studies, 64*(3), 267–270.

Sky News (2013). Hannah Smith: charge site over death says dad. *Sky News.* Retrieved from http://news.sky.com/story/1125847/hannah-smith-charge-site-over-death-says-dad

Sky News (2015). Edison's lost plan to record voices of dead. *Sky News.* Retrieved from http://news.sky.com/story/1439374/edisons-lost-plan-to-record-voices-of-dead

Smardon, R. (2008). 'I'd rather not take Prozac': stigma and commodification in antidepressant consumer narratives. *Health: An Interdisciplinary Journal for the Social Study of Health, Illness & Medicine, 12*(1), 67–86.

Smith, A., & Higgins, M. (2012). Introduction: reporting war – history, professionalism and technology. *Journal of War and Culture Studies, 5*(2), 131–136.

Smith, C., Barker, M., & Atwood, F. (2015). Why do people watch porn? In S. Tarrant & L. Comella (Eds.), *New views on pornography: sexuality, politics, and the law* (pp. 277–296). New York: Praegar.

Smith, C. M., & McDonald, K. M. (2010). The Arizona 9/11 Memorial: a case study in public dissent and argumentation through blogs. *Argumentation & Advocacy*, *47*(2), 123–139.

Smith, D. (1999). Prison series seeks to shatter expectations. *The New York Times*, July 12. Retrieved from www.nytimes.com/1999/07/12/arts/prison-series-seeks-to-shatter-expectations.html

Smythe, D. W., & Van Dinh, T. V. (1983). On critical and administrative research: a new critical analysis. *Journal of Communication*, *33*(3), 117–127.

Soldatova, G., & Zotova, E. (2013). Coping with online risks: the experience of Russian schoolchildren. *Journal of Children & Media*, *7*(1), 44–59.

Stanyer, J. (2012). *Intimate politics: the rise of celebrity politicians and the decline of privacy*. Cambridge: Polity Press.

Stermer, P., & Burkley, M. (2012). Xbox or SeXbox? An examination of sexualized content in video games. *Social and Personality Psychology Compass*, *6*(7). doi:10.1111/j.1751-9004.2012.00442.x.

Stokes, J. C. (2013). *How to do media and cultural studies* (2nd ed.). Los Angeles, CA: Sage.

Street, J. (2002). Bob, Bono and Tony B: the popular artist as politician. *Media, Culture & Society*, *24*, 433–441.

Stuart, H. (2006). Media portrayal of mental illness and its treatments: what effect does it have on people with mental illness? *CNS Drugs*, *20*(2), 99–106.

Sumiala, J. (2012). *Media and ritual: death, community and everyday life*. London: Routledge.

Tager, M., & Matthee, H. (2014). *Dexter*: gratuitous violence or the vicarious experience of justice? Perceptions of selected South African viewers. *Communication: South African Journal for Communication Theory & Research*, *40*(1), 20–33. doi:10.1080/02500167.2014.868366.

The Gleaner (2016). Appleton Estate, Digicel Takes Party To CPL. *The Gleaner*. Retrieved from http://jamaica-gleaner.com/article/entertainment/2016 0714/appleton-estate-digicel-takes-party-cpl

Thomas, J. (2002). *Diana's mourning: a people's history*. Cardiff: University of Wales Press.

Thomas, J. (2008). From people power to mass hysteria: media and popular reactions to the death of Princess Diana. *International Journal of Cultural Studies*, *11*(3), 362–376. doi:10.1177/1367877908092590.

Thompson, E. P. (1963). *The making of the English working class*. London: Gollancz.

Thornton, B. (1995). Muckraking journalists and their readers: perceptions of professionalism. *Journalism History*, *21*(1), 29.

Thornton, D. J. (2010). Race, risk, and pathology in psychiatric culture: disease awareness campaigns as governmental rhetoric. *Critical Studies in Media Communication*, *27*(4), 311–335.

Tonkiss, F. (1998). Analysing discourse. In C. Seale (Ed.), *Researching society and culture* (pp. 245–260). London: Sage.

Trouble, C. (2014). Finding gender through porn performance. *Porn Studies*, *1*(1–2), 197–200.

Tsfati, Y., & Ariely, G. (2014). Individual and contextual correlates of trust in media across 44 countries. *Communication Research, 41*(6), 760–782. doi:10.1177/0093650213485972.

Tuchman, G. (1978). *Making news: a study in the construction of reality*. New York: Free Press.

Tulloch, J. (1999). *Performing culture: stories of expertise and the everyday*. London: Sage.

Tulloch, J. (2000). *Television audiences: cultural theories and methods*. London: Arnold.

Tulloch, J. (2006). *One day in July: experiencing 7/7*. London: Little Brown Book Group.

Tulloch, J., & Blood, W. (2012). *Icons of war and terror: Media images in an age of international risk*. London: Routledge.

Tulloch, J., & Alvarado, M. (1984). *Dr Who: the unfolding text*. London: Macmillan.

Tungate, A. (2014). Bare necessities: the argument for a 'revenge porn' exception in Section 230 immunity. *Information & Communications Technology Law, 23*(2), 172–188. doi:10.1080/13600834.2014.916936.

Turkle, S. (2011). *Alone together: why we expect more from technology and less from each other*. New York: Basic Books.

Turner, G. (2010). Approaching celebrity studies. *Celebrity Studies, 1*(1), 11–20.

Turner, G. (2015). *Reinventing the media*. London: Sage.

Turner, V. (1978). *Image and pilgrimage in Christian culture*. New York: Columbia University Press.

Turner, V. (1985). Liminality, kabbalah, and the media. *Religion, 15*, 205–217.

Uzunoğlu, E., & Öksüz, B. (2014). New opportunities in social media for ad-restricted alcohol products: the case of 'Yeni Rakı'. *Journal of Marketing Communications, 20*(4), 270–290. doi:10.1080/13527266.2012.684067.

Vaidyanathan, R. (2015). Sandy Hook family seeks to trademark victim's name. *BBC News Online*. Retrieved from https://www.infowars.com/sandy-hook-family-seeks-to-trademark-victims-name/

Van den Bulck, J. (2006). Television news avoidance: exploratory results from a one-year follow-up study. *Journal of Broadcasting & Electronic Media, 50*(2), 231–252.

Van den Bulck, J., & Vandebosch, H. (2003). When the viewer goes to prison: learning fact from watching fiction. A qualitative cultivation study. *Poetics, 31*, 103–116.

Van Maanen, J. (1988). *Tales of the field on writing ethnography*. Chicago, IL: University of Chicago Press.

VandeBerg, L., & Wenner, L. (1991). The nature of television criticism. In L. VandeBerg & L. Wenner (Eds.), *Television criticism: approaches and applications* (pp. 3–17). White Plains, NY: Longman.

W632. (1981). Mass Observations Correspondents PDfs 1981 Royal Wedding. Retrieved from https://drive.google.com/drive/folders/0Bz-9hs_TdzGPU kYzYlFMMG9Hak0

W633. (1981). Mass Observations Correspondents PDfs 1981 Royal Wedding. Retrieved from https://drive.google.com/drive/folders/0Bz-9hs_TdzGPU kYzYlFMMG9Hak0

Wagner-Pacific, R., Mohr, J., & Breiger, R. (2015). Ontologies, methodologies, and new uses of Big Data in the social and cultural sciences. *Big Data & Society*, *1*(2), 1–11.

Wahl-Jorgensen, K. (2012). The strategic ritual of emotionality: a case study of Pulitzer Prize-winning articles. *Journalism*, *14*(1), 129–145. doi:10.1177/1464884912448918.

Wahl-Jorgensen, K. (2013). Subjectivity and story-telling in journalism. *Journalism Studies*, *14*(3), 305–320. doi:10.1080/1461670X.2012.713738.

Wahl-Jorgensen, K. (2014). Changing technologies, changing journalistic episte-mologies: public participation, emotionality and the challenge to objectivity. In M. Schreiber & C. Zimmermann (Eds.), *Journalism and technology change: historical perspectives, contemporary trends*. Chicago, IL: University of Chicago Press.

Wahl-Jorgensen, K., & Pantti, M. (2013). The ethics of global disaster reporting: journalistic witnessing and the challenge to objectivity. In S. J. A. Ward (Ed.), *Global media ethics: problems and perspectives*. Chichester: Wiley-Blackwell.

Wallop, H. (2015). Meet the man who invented the Swingometer. *The Telegraph*. Retrieved from www.telegraph.co.uk/news/general-election-2015/115 11608/Meet-the-man-who-invented-the-Swingometer.html

Walt Disney Corporation. (2014). Citizenship performance summary. Retrieved from https://ditm-twdc-us.storage.googleapis.com/FY14-Performance-Summary.pdf

Watkins, S. (1998). The story so far … – #15 The Docklands stadium. *The Age*, June 22, p. 1.

Watson, A. (2008). Introduction to the second edition. In H. Innis (Ed.), *The bias of communication* (2nd ed.). Toronto: University of Toronto Press.

Weitzer, R. (2015). Interpreting the data: assessing competing claims in pornog-raphy research. In L. Comella & S. Tarrant (Eds.), *New views on pornography: sexuality, politics, and the law* (pp. 257–276). New York: Praeger.

Wenner, L. (2015). Assessing the sociology of sport: on the mediasport interpel-lation and commodity narratives. *International Review for the Sociology of Sport*, *50*(4–5), 628–633.

Wheaton, B. (2015). Assessing the sociology of sport: on action sport and the politics of identity. *International Review for the Sociology of Sport*, *50*(4–5), 634–639.

Wheeler, M. (2011). Celebrity diplomacy: United Nations' Goodwill Ambassadors and messengers of peace. *Celebrity Studies*, *2*(1), 6–18.

White, D. (2015). Donald Trump invited Twitter to #AskTrump anything and here's what happened. *Time*. Retrieved from http://time.com/4043356/donald-trump-twitter-asktrump/

Williams, R. (1974). *Television, technology and cultural form*. London: Fontana.

Wilson, C., Nairn, R., Coverdale, J., & Panapa, A. (1998). Mental illness depictions in prime-time drama: identifying the discursive resources. *Australian and New Zealand Journal of Psychiatry*, *32*, 232–239.

Windschuttle, K. (2000). The poverty of cultural studies. *Journalism Studies*, *1*(1), 145–159.

Winter, J. (1999). Producing the television series 'The Great War and the Shaping of the Twentieth Century'. *Profession*, 15–26.

Winter, J. (2001). The memory boom in contemporary historical studies. *Raritan*, *21*(1), 52–66.

Winter, J. (2014). *Sites of memory, sites of mourning* (Canto Classics ed.). Cambridge: Cambridge University Press.

World Health Organization (WHO) (2013). *Mental Health Action Plan 2013–2020*. Geneva: WHO. Retrieved from http://apps.who.int/iris/bitstream/10665/89966/1/9789241506021_eng.pdf

Wright, P. J. (2014). Pornography and the sexual socialization of children: current knowledge and a theoretical future. *Journal of Children & Media*, *8*(3), 305–312.

Wright, P. J., & Randall, A. K. (2014). Pornography consumption, education, and support for same-sex marriage among adult U.S. males. *Communication Research*, *41*(5), 665–689. doi:10.1177/0093650212471558.

Wright, P. J., Tokunaga, R. S., & Bae, S. (2014). Pornography consumption and US adults' attitudes toward gay individuals' civil liberties, moral judgments of homosexuality, and support for same-sex marriage: mediating and moderating factors. *Communication Monographs, 81*, 79–107.

Xu, J. (2013). Trust in Chinese state media: the influence of education, internet, and government. *Journal of International Communication*, *19*(1), 69–84. doi: 10.1080/13216597.2012.737816.

Yoon, S. (2015). Forbidden audience: media reception and social change in North Korea. *Global Media & Communication*, *11*(2), 167–184. doi:10.1177/1742766515588418.

Young, K. (2015). Assessing the sociology of sport: on sports violence and ways of seeing. *International Review for the Sociology of Sport*, *50*(4–5), 640–644.

Zayani, M. (2013). Al Jazeera's Palestine Papers: Middle East media politics in the post-WikiLeaks era. *Media, War and Conflict*, *6*(1), 21–35.

Zelizer, B. (2013). When practice is undercut by ethics. In N. Couldry, M. Madianou, & A. Pinchevski (Eds.), *Ethics of media* (pp. 271–285). Basingstoke: Palgrave Macmillan.

INDEX